CW01558910

LIBRARY
COPY
DO NOT
REMOVE

CONSTRUCTING UNEMPLOYMENT

Constructing Unemployment

The Politics of Joblessness in East and West

PHINEAS BAXANDALL
Harvard University, USA

ASHGATE

© Phineas Baxandall 2004

All rights reserved. No part of this publication may be reproduced, stored in a retrieval system or transmitted in any form or by any means, electronic, mechanical, photocopying, recording or otherwise without the prior permission of the publisher.

Phineas Baxandall has asserted his right under the Copyright, Designs and Patents Act, 1988, to be identified as the author of this work.

Published by
Ashgate Publishing Limited
Gower House
Croft Road
Aldershot
Hants GU11 3HR
England

Ashgate Publishing Company
Suite 420
101 Cherry Street
Burlington, VT 05401-4405
USA

Ashgate website: http://www.ashgate.com

British Library Cataloguing in Publication Data
Baxandall, Phineas
Constructing unemployment : the politics of joblessness in
East and West
1.Unemployment - Social aspects - Hungary 2.Unemployment -
Social aspects 3.Unemployment - Political aspects - Hungary
4.Unemployment - Political aspects 5.Post-communism -
Hungary 6.Hungary - Economic policy 7.Hungary - Social
conditions - 1989- 8.Hungary - Economic conditions - 1989-
I.Title
306.3'61

Library of Congress Cataloging-in-Publication Data
Baxandall, Phineas, 1967-
Constructing unemployment : the politics of joblessness in East and West / Phineas Baxandall.
    p. cm.
Includes bibliographical references and index.
ISBN 0-7546-3930-4
    1. Unemployment. 2. Unemployment--Political aspects. I. Title: Politics of joblessness in East and West. II. Title.

HD5707.5.B39 2004
331.13'7--dc22
                                                        2004041106
ISBN 0 7546 3930 4

Printed in Great Britain by Antony Rowe Ltd, Chippenham, Wiltshire

Contents

List of Figures

List of Tables

PART I
INTRODUCTION

Chapter 1

Changing Meanings of Unemployment

Most citizens in Hungary had not heard the word "unemployment" associated with their own country for decades, if ever. The unemployment line seemed a distant icon evoked by the government to tout its past accomplishments. The right to work stood as a pillar of legitimacy, an unshakable commitment enshrined in the Hungarian constitution. People therefore took notice in 1987 when the government introduced social programs for the newly "unemployed". The national newspapers carried long articles about the unprecedented changes, and the international press buzzed with dumbfounded incomprehension.

The foreign newspapers failed to understand how the earlier taboo against unemployment had already transformed. Yes, the word "unemployment" was new in the Hungarian mass media. But elite policy circles had long advocated lay-offs. The traditional commitment to full employment had been publicly redefined to include job loss. The meaning of "unemployment" had shifted many times over the previous decades and would change yet again under post-communism.

The Big Picture

Reconstruction of the meaning of unemployment is not unique to former-communist countries. On the contrary, unemployment has been reinvented numerous times in the West, and its meaning continues to change. Scholars, journalists, and policy-makers have struggled to ascertain what unemployment rate is politically sustainable, or why unemployment seems more politically acceptable in some places or times than others.

The concept of unemployment is in flux. We knew when the post-war steelworker was unemployed, and that this was politically destabilizing; but it is not at all clear how we should apply these categories to today's Internet consultant, temp-worker, or independent sub-contractor. The future political economy of unemployment will depend very much on the changing world of work and how it is regulated.

This book is an attempt to understand how and why the meaning of unemployment changes. It examines how governments reshape the meaning of unemployment through policies and public declarations and how it is often in their interest to do so. Unemployment may become more or less dangerous to those in power. And certain kinds of joblessness are more politically dangerous than others.

This research treats the category of unemployment as a social and institutional *construction*. The aim is to understand the causes and consequences of differences in how people understand unemployment. Focusing on how people actually understand unemployment might seem like an obvious place to start; but it is a break with the general tendency to take unemployment as an unchanging and universal category.

Scholars and other analysts typically ignore differences in how people "on the ground" view unemployment. Instead they begin with a universal definition that can be applied to different places or time periods. A fixed yardstick makes it possible to ascertain, for instance, whether or not the unemployment rate in contemporary South Africa is higher than the United States during the Depression. But the presumed equivalence in the concept of unemployment limits the ability of comparative analysis to explain political changes that transform its meaning.

Unemployment tends to be seen through an economistic lens. Politics is not seen as playing a constructive or constitutive role. Instead politics is portrayed as interfering with the market processes that would otherwise drive joblessness down to a natural frictional minimum.[1] According to this view, governments wish to appear as if they are combating unemployment; but they often eschew painful flexibility-enhancing reforms because of interest-group pressures and the logic of electoral posturing.[2] This view interprets political arrangements as hindering the market dictates of deregulation, liberalization and welfare-state retrenchment. Thus, no consideration is given to whether or not the political threat of unemployment changes in different contexts. Much historical research has historicized our understanding of the category of unemployment by showing how it was an invented category that arose alongside industrialization. But there has been no attempt to extend such insights to ongoing reconstructions of unemployment in already-industrialized countries.

The following pages are both an in-depth study of the reinvention of unemployment, as well as a broader inquiry into the politics of joblessness and the social construction of constraints on policy-making. The American and West European cases provide the original inspiration and insight for this analysis. Meanwhile, the bulk of original empirical research is presented in the Hungarian case.

The Argument

Unemployment is a socially-constructed benchmark used for evaluating the competency of economic rule. In different places and in different times the category of "unemployment" has included different kinds of joblessness and excluded others. It has implied different kinds of commitments or accountability by the state.

New meanings of unemployment are more than a byproduct of economic change. They are the result of changing politics and changing policy. Governments make commitments and build institutions that reconstruct the political meaning of unemployment. When governments change the policies regulating employment and unemployment, they also redefine their own accountability by reshaping the lens through which the public evaluates their stewardship of the economy.

Particularly important are policies that distinguish employment from other forms of less-officially recognized work. Gardening, child care, volunteering, black-marketeering and many other forms of paid work are not fully recognized as employment in governmental policies and statistics. In other words, *not all work is recognized as employment. Likewise, not all lack of work counts as unemployment.*

The concept of unemployment is defined against prototypical notions of who is employed and what kinds of work they do. As new policies and other public commitments change the way that certain forms of work are privileged above others, unemployment is redefined. Unemployment tends to be most politically salient when two conditions are met: there are clear institutional boundaries between the employed and unemployed; and the unemployed are more prototypical or "core" workers such as middle-aged, male breadwinners.

Governments also redefine the problem of unemployment when they emphasize new kinds of solutions. New institutional approaches redefine the benchmarks of success and recast which kinds of joblessness are most problematic. Because new policy initiatives create new kinds of commitments for those in power, governments are careful to redefine unemployment only in ways where they can anticipate success.

The research combines a variety of research methods. It uses the empirical record of policies, programs and political pronouncements to link micro-level incentives to larger macro-social political change. The analysis does not explain social change from shifts in the strength of political agents with pre-assigned preferences, or from shifts in the institutionalized rules on which political preferences compete. Instead this research examines the political production of ideas about what is socially beneficial and what counts as success regarding unemployment. Interpretations and discourse are treated as constitutive rather than merely indicative of social change. Institutional and ideational factors are regarded as mutually reinforcing rather than competing forms of explanation. Ideas are understood to be most important when they take the concrete form of institutional constraints and commitments, while rules and norms are only taken as "institutionalized" insofar as they are commonly understood and taken for granted.[3]

Unanswered Questions about Unemployment

Governments fear the political fallout from bad and worsening socio-economic conditions. In the extreme case, governments that lose wars or oversee famines are more likely to suffer political collapse. Lean times make incumbents easier to unseat and even dictators more vulnerable.

An extensive literature shows that economic suffering erodes political support and encourages government instability.[4] Numerous studies link falling popular support to national economic distress.[5] Cross-national data further suggest that deterioration of a variety of macro-economic indicators corresponds to rejection of incumbents (Remmer, 1991; Pacek, 1994). "The government is assumed to possess the tools and abilities to solve social problems" and therefore perceived failure to improve such conditions erodes faith in those who are in power (Weatherford, 1984: 189). In the American context, we need only think of the jobless thousands who angrily marched on Washington under the Hoover administration. More recently, we might recall Ronald Reagan closing his 1984 re-election debate by asking the American viewers to vote according to whether they were better off than four years before. Or recall candidate Bill Clinton's campaign mantra: "it's the economy, stupid". Yet as Rose reminds us, "The Washington catch phrase—'It's the economy, stupid!'—begs the question: Which particular economic conditions are most influential?" (Rose, 1997: 15).

A number of reasons help to explain why unemployment can pose an especially potent political threat to governments.[6] As Piven and Cloward argue, unemployment dilutes social control at the same time that it gives the jobless cause for grievance. Unemployment destabilizes regular work routines that maintain social order. For the employed, political horizons are ordinarily constrained by private interests within the rewards and punishments of their jobs, "but mass unemployment severs that bond, loosening people from the main institution by which they are regulated and controlled" (Piven and Cloward, 1993: 6-7).[7] Heclo similarly points to, "the state's concern with poor relief as a tool of social order; it was not the sick or infirm who burned hayricks and broke shop windows" (Heclo, 1974: 65). Upsurges in unemployment have also historically come after wars when many of the unemployed were volatile and rootless demobilized troops.

Even if unemployment afflicts only a relatively small portion of the population, it nonetheless threatens the average citizens and the swing voters who most concern politicians. The decisive voters in elections are typically employed, but they expect government to do something about the *threat* of unemployment (St. Paul, 1996b). And unlike many social problems like poverty that are often isolated within certain sub-populations and therefore easier for others to ignore, unemployment is typically distributed widely throughout the population at large (Morris, 1985).

Unemployment holds special political importance because it serves as a popular benchmark for the competency of economic rule. Citizens may not fully understand the details or causality of economic policy; but they hold their leaders politically accountable based on their perception of the material situation. Individuals evaluating the effectiveness of their leaders' economic management can only process limited amounts of information and can exercise at best "bounded rationality" (Simon, 1947; March, 1988). They simplify complex information into more tractable "morsels" to evaluate (Lane, 1962; Graziano, 1989). As one sociologist notes, "the monthly unemployment rate may be the most widely known statistic issued by the government" (Morris, 1985: 405). Politicians and citizens focus on social indicators such as unemployment, inflation, and growth as short-hands for gauging economic conditions. This focus is continually reinforced by institutional attention to these same targets.[8] Even in the context of low-unemployment rates in the mid-1990s, Americans expressed deep concern over the prospects of job loss.[9]

There is ample evidence that the political threat posed by unemployment varies greatly between different time periods or between different countries. Government accountability for unemployment is différent in 2004 than it was in 1964 – or for that matter, 1864. The threat of unemployment appears to constrain governments in some countries far more than others;[10] and the same unemployment rate can arouse wildly different degrees of concern among the citizens of different countries. Even among citizens who consistently identify unemployment as one of the political issues most important to them, their concerns about unemployment in different countries do not even roughly correspond to differences in national unemployment rates or trends in these rates over time.[11]

The tendency to treat "unemployment" as a black box with the same conceptual and political meaning across all contexts stymies the examination of these kinds of puzzles. It is this presumption that the present volume seeks to question.

Why Look at Hungary?

The chapters that focus on eastern Europe examine the world's richest history of change in the politics of unemployment. Eastern European governments staked their legitimacy for decades on the eradication of certain kinds of joblessness, only to be followed by the unsettling onset of mass unemployment in the 1990s. Eastern Europe provides an example of a strong claim to legitimacy that was later violated. The Communist Party exerted control over expert and mass portrayals of unemployment. This provides a simplified model of governmental framing and accountability, presenting theoretical building blocks for subsequent analysis of more pluralistic politics.[12] In other policy areas it might seem odd to examine a country whose recent history is dominated by bureaucratic authoritarianism; but the definition and dissemination of information about unemployment everywhere remains an elite and bureaucratic affair.

The Hungarian Communist Party was by no means the only communist regime to alter its commitments against unemployment; but it offers a particularly rich history of continual change in the concept of unemployment.[13] The introduction of mass unemployment in the mid-1980s would have seemed unlikely because the memory of mass uprising in 1956 made the regime wary of undermining social stability and it staked its legitimacy largely on the basis of post-war job security.

As we shall see, each change in the meaning of unemployment has corresponded with new political limits and popular expectations regarding who should work and what kinds of work they should do. By examining the changes in the meaning of unemployment over time we explain otherwise–puzzling features of Hungarian politics.

First of all, and contrary to the portrait of communism painted on both sides of the Iron Curtain, unemployment in Hungary was prevalent and widely acknowledged during the hard-core Stalinist period following World War II. Although the eradication of unemployment is often considered a defining feature of state-socialism, the taboo against lay-offs emerged with the later softening of the communist regime and the reconception of unemployment as defined against state-run industrial work.

Secondly, when communism fell many predicted that fledgling democracies would be gravely threatened by the unexpectedly rapid loss of jobs.[14] In Hungary, all six parties that entered Parliament after the first democratic elections pledged their dedication to full employment. The unemployment rate stood at less than a quarter of a percent at the fall of communism and many feared that it might reach one or even two percent, a figure that was almost universally declared unacceptable. None were prepared for the precipitous pace of dismissals which followed the unexpected fall of the Soviet Union. Yet when unemployment skyrocketed to double-digits, the issue seemed to fall off the political map. We shall see that the political economy of transition eroded the prevailing notion of employment on which the unemployment taboo had been based. Changing norms and commitments toward employment altered the meaning and political salience of unemployment.

Hungarian unemployment also presents a striking case for theoretical debates about "path dependence", or the influence of political legacies on subsequent policy-making. The legacy of communism would seem to present a paradigmatic example of "path dependence", yet the earlier taboo melts away with little trace. The present study shows how micro-level political mechanisms can operate to either reinforce previous political patterns or to undermine them. The Communist Party's commitments to eradicate unemployment first provided definite mechanisms that reinforced the inherited disapproval of unemployment.[15] In economic terms, the political commitments created their own micro-level "barriers to exit" because the eradication of unemployment became an established benchmark for the competency of economic rule, thereby increasing the potential political costs of introducing unemployment. When the Party staked legitimacy on eradicating unemployment, they also created political "returns to scale" for individuals who subsequently sought to claim credit for future accomplishments. Petty officials, supreme leaders, and even aggrieved workers could justify their own ends in terms pursuant to the established goal of eradicating unemployment. In doing so, individuals both benefited from the norm against unemployment and simultaneously reinforced its perceived priority. The presumption of full employment was further embedded in new social policies that delivered benefits through employers. Employment was typically an administrative precondition for receiving most social benefits. The prospect of job loss thus became an even harsher form of social exile. As we shall see, the post-communist period reversed these kinds of micro-incentives by systematically encouraging individuals to perform economic activities and claim political credit in ways that eroded the importance of unemployment.

Organization of the Book

Following this introduction, the chapters that follow are organized in three parts, starting with a close examination of the Hungarian case before moving to more generalizable conclusions about the West and the future of unemployment.

In the book's second part, Chapter Two shows how the early Hungarian Communist Party focused intensely on eliminating unemployment before World War II, but accepted unemployment upon seizing state power after the war. Chapter Three shows how the state-socialist taboo against unemployment was a product of the politics of de-Stalinization, not hard-line Stalinism. It argues that the taboo resulted from the particular emphasis placed on state employment in the implicit compromise between regime and governed that followed the failed 1956 revolution. Subsequent efforts to avoid unemployment during the deep economic reforms of 1968 then reinforced the unemployment taboo by accentuating the distinctions between core and peripheral employment. Chapter Four recounts how during the 1970s and early 1980s lay-offs of core workers were strenuously avoided; but changes in the ways employment was categorized and counted led to a reframing of the importance of core employment that prefigured the subsequent erosion of the unemployment taboo. Chapter Five describes the embrace of "planned reallocations" as a virtuous form of involuntary joblessness. It shows how the Party's embrace of socialist entrepreneurship as a contending prototype of employment further eroded the unemployment taboo. Chapter Six explains how lingering political norms against unemployment were further eroded by a post-communist transition process that systematically diluted what remained of the previous prototype of employment and replaced it with a new conception of employment that was less distinct from unemployment. On the basis of this analysis, we can then explain why unemployment remained a highly important political issue in certain regions within Hungary and certain countries within the larger region. In places where employment still resembled its old prototype, unemployment maintained its old political salience.

The third part of the book presents additional country cases. They illustrate the larger applicability of insights from the Hungarian case, and allow for controlled comparisons between cases. Chapter Seven examines parallel transformations in the meaning of unemployment that took place in Britain, the United States, the Soviet Union, and municipalities near Geneva. In each case government measures to redefine the difference between exemplary employment and other forms of work transform the political meaning of unemployment. Chapter Eight uses polling data in the European Union to test hypotheses about the relationship between the regulation of employment and the political salience of unemployment.

The final part of the book puts forward a general theory and speculates about possible futures in the political economy of employment. Chapter Nine outlines what is called an "institutional-constructivist" theory of how the political meaning of unemployment is determined, and why unemployment presents a greater political threat to some governments than others. Chapter Ten concludes by briefly discussing how future changes in unemployment politics depend on different scenarios of post-industrial employment or new approaches to labor and social policy.

Notes

1   Rigidity explanations can give a credible account for the lower unemployment rates in "liberal" countries, such as the United States and Britain, compared to unemployment in Continental Europe, although there are complementary explanations that may be more important (Modigliani, et al., 1998). From a political point of view the virtue of this analysis is that it shows that there are clear motivations why employed "insiders" wish to exclude unemployed "outsiders" from competition in the labor market. It also helps explain the popularity of training and other active labor policies as solutions to unemployment, despite their questionable effectiveness, because these programs can lower unemployment statistics without exerting downward pressure on wages (Saint-Paul, 1996).

2   In the welfare state literature, see Pierson, 1994, 1996. In the literature on the political economy of economic liberalization, see Diamond, 1992; Duch, 1993; Evans, 1995; Haggard and Kaufman, 1995; Hellman, 1998; Przeworski, 1993.

3   The literature on institutionalism is notoriously vague about what counts as an institution. On one extreme, only formal written rules are included, and no attempt is made to exclude or de-emphasize codes which may be "on the books" but routinely ignored in actual behavior (Carey, 200). In practice, not all rules can be considered and such an approach indirectly becomes tautological because it concludes that institutions shape behavior, but only examines institutions that are behaviorally relevant.

4   In the specific literature on the political effects of macroeconomic trends, there are differing conclusions that follow from different methodological designs. Macroeconomic performance seems to have some relationship to government support, but the results depend on whether opinion polls or votes are counted, whether votes are for prime minister or for president, how long a time lag used in the model, what period is looked at, and so on (Lewis-Beck, 1988; Schneider and Frey, 1988; Rattinger, 1991). For example, in Lewis-Beck's reviews of the literature on six advanced industrial nations, for most questions the findings contradict one another.

5   Finkel, Muller, et al., 1989; Diamond, 1992; Maravall, Pereira et al., 1993; Haggard and Kaufman, 1995; Anderson and Guillory, 1997.

6   While these effects are treated separately below, the rest of the discussion does not attempt to disaggregate them and instead refers more generally to the political costliness, importance, or *political salience* of unemployment.

7   "The regulation of civil behavior in all societies is intimately dependent on stable occupational arrangements. So long as people are fixed in their work roles, their activities and outlooks are also fixed; they do what they must and think what they must. Each behavior and attitude is shaped by the reward of a good harvest or the penalty of a bad one, by the factory paycheck or the danger of losing it" (Piven and Cloward, 1993: 6).

8   "[U]nemployment and inflation ... are by far the most widely used and most consistently significant indicators of economic performance. Moreover, unemployment and inflation are the variables that constitute the chief targets of post-war economic management in Western Europe. Not only did policymakers seek to control these variables as part of their efforts to steer the economy, but public discourse over successful economic

performance has also consistently focused on unemployment and inflation. Public opinion polls show time and again that inflation and unemployment are the economic issues of most concern to most people. Given that citizens can devote only limited resources to gathering and digesting information about the economy and politics, unemployment and inflation are the variables that are easiest to understand and about which information is easily and most publicly available throughout the mass media" (Anderson, 1995: 88).

9 See for instance, the special series in the *New York Times*, March 3-9, 1996 titled "The Downsizing of America", including responses to a Nov.-Dec. 1995 *New York Times* poll.

10 For instance, in the United States, even at unemployment rates below five percent, the threat of increased unemployment prevented legislated wage minimums from rising even to their 1973 levels. By contrast, in the face of unemployment rates more than twice as high, French presidential candidates could credibly propose to further *increase* the minimum wage (Saint-Paul, 1996b).

11 See Chapter Eight.

12 Due to the nature of "democratic centralism", little evidence exists of the inter-party battles over unemployment. Shifting politics tend to take the form of evolution of the forced consensus rather than open partisanship of conflicting interests.

13 Hungary should be situated in a broader context that contains Yugoslavia at one extreme of open unemployment, and Czechoslovakia or perhaps the Soviet Union at the other extreme of full employment. Yugoslavia is arguably the most dramatic example of socialist unemployment, having the highest unemployment rate in Europe for much of the 1980s. But a number of other factors make the Yugoslav case aberrant as a communist economy. The breaking of taboos against unemployment in Yugoslavia was eased by the political rupture with the Soviet Union and encouraged by a system of worker managed profit-sharing that made employees reluctant to hire new workers because their own shares would be diminished. See (Bonin, et al., 1993, Woodward, 1995).

14 For stylistic variation I use the terms socialist, state-socialist, communist, and Soviet-style interchangeably. Occasionally "former East Bloc" is used, but only so as to exclude the former Yugoslavia.

15 Following Pierson (2000), we can think of ongoing political legacies as partly anchored in micro-level mechanisms analogous to the kinds of mechanisms that prevent equilibrium in markets.

PART II
FROM MULTIPLE CHANGES IN A
SINGLE CASE TO INTERNATIONAL
COMPARISONS

Chapter 2

Communism Without an Unemployment Taboo

Unemployment became an unthinkable political taboo under communism. But how did this happen? The eradication of unemployment became a central pillar of legitimacy for state-socialist regimes. But if the Communist Party wanted to demonstrate the superiority of socialist planning, would it not have been enough to handle unemployment more humanely or efficiently than capitalist nations?

The absolute elimination of unemployment was not, we shall see, a constant feature of state socialist regimes. During the inter-war period before the Communists assumed power in Hungary, the Communist Party mobilized against the ills of unemployment and pressed for traditional remedies such as public works, retraining, and relief aid. Although after the Communists seized power in 1947 pockets of involuntary joblessness persisted and were openly admitted, the problem nevertheless received little attention from the government.

This history is a puzzle for the standard view that the elimination of unemployment is a systemic feature of state-socialist economies. In Eastern Europe, and Hungary in particular, the immediate post-war period was the "classical" era of hard-line Stalinism. But this era also was also the time when the regime was *least* concerned and dogmatic about unemployment. The "classical" period of Communism was not the most opposed to unemployment in policy or rhetoric.

The present chapter demonstrates how policies increasingly encouraged continuous full-time wage-earning in large, state-owned industrial enterprises. The first section reviews the pre-war political experience with unemployment, with particular attention to the Communist Party's positions and activities regarding unemployment. The second section examines how the Party's thinking about unemployment after the War was deeply influenced by Soviet concepts and pressures to imitate the USSR. Unlike the earlier Communist leaders, those installed after the War had little experience fighting unemployment *per se*, but were trained in Soviet views which framed unemployment as a secondary problem that would disappear with the general superiority of socialist planning. The third section shows how the lack of concern for unemployment was reinforced by the tasks of post-war reconstruction, the ideology of state socialism, and the strategy for rapid industrialization. Economic and social policy was oriented towards rapid state-led modernization that subsumed the category of unemployment under a broader drive to increase industrial and socialist work.

Pre-War Hungary and the Party's Early Focus on Unemployment

Before the Soviet Army entered Budapest in 1945, two decades of fascist rule in Hungary had forced union organizing about unemployment underground. During the pre-war period, tactical considerations led the Communist Party to focus intensely on the issue of unemployment, though it was also a concern of organized labor more generally. In 1913 an extraordinary congress of the various Hungarian trade unions had been convened to discuss the tasks of the struggle against unemployment. Five years later the democratic government introduced a state system of unemployment relief under the administration of the unions. When the Communists took power for 133 days in 1919, it was they who first organized unemployment insurance and directed the jobless into the army. When the far right seized power later in 1919, state unemployment relief was ended and the Communist party was banned. The Communists were forced to organize clandestinely within the Social Democratic Party which had secured legality by agreeing to refrain from organizing civil servants or organizing in the countryside.[1] The Communists were left to organize the urban proletariat, something that fitted well with their ideology.

The largely undercover Communists used their more militant stance against unemployment as a way to differentiate themselves from their more compromising compatriots, even though they advocated similar policies for relief and training. Their strong stance for workers without jobs supported their claim to represent all workers as a universal class, as opposed to the Social Democrats or the Smallholders Party who merely represented trade unionists or farmers as particular interest groups. The issue of unemployment was also championed by the Communists because it represented an endemic feature of capitalism that could only be abolished with the end of private property.

The pre-war Communists were encouraged to see unemployment as a primary problem in its own right by the Depression and aggressive campaigns against unemployment by the Social Democrats. The Depression struck hard at both agriculture and industry in Hungary. As the price of wheat fell in 1932 to a quarter of its pre-Depression price, larger farms were forced to dismiss hired hands and smaller farmers often simply left the land in search of better paid work. The number of industrial workers fell almost by half, from 654,000 employed in 1928 to 371,000 in 1932. Union-administered unemployment schemes saw their rolls jump from 75,000 industrial workers up to 238,000 unemployed from 1929 to 1932 (Borsányi, 1977).[2] A third of industrial workers were estimated to be unemployed at the height of the Depression. As one Hungarian historian described, "Unemployment was by far the greatest problem of the workers, all the more so since even during the boom period wages were too low to permit any sort of adequate savings" (Borsányi, 1977: 154). In the absence of any national relief program to soften the hardship, the jobless were left to the haphazard care of overburdened municipalities and townships.[3] The government and unions differed in their advocacy of temporary relief but urged and promoted emigration.[4]

The stance of the Communists during the Depression was well demonstrated in their work within the National Committee of the Unemployed, a body established at the end of 1929, reportedly by Communists, within the construction workers union. Organizing the unemployed was an area of particular cooperation between the Communists and the Social Democratic unions, with the unions providing office space for the unemployment committees (Borsányi, 1977: 160). The National Committee of the Unemployed organized several demonstrations in Budapest in 1929-1930. Pressure had been building over time for the government to act against unemployment and the Social Democrats had called for jobs-programs and unemployment relief. After many rallies and foot-dragging by parliament, the Trade Union Council in 1931 set 1 September as a deadline for a general strike if the government did not act against unemployment. The Social Democrats had sometimes wavered in their past support of the unemployed in cases like the raiding of foodstores which involved illegality. In this case they risked alienating moderates and the state in order to produce a major show of strength to the government, the populace, and even to the Socialist Internationale who had been questioning their militancy. When the police refused a permit for a rally, the Social Democrats planned instead for a "silent walk through the streets". But the Communists saw the police intransigence as an opportunity to intensify the class war and they distributed numerous leaflets calling for "bread and work" (Esti, et al., 1984). While the Social Democrats tried to avoid violence and remove troublemakers, the Communists provided piles of stones for throwing and urged greater militance. The police and army were ordered on alert and over 400 were wounded before the army eventually scattered the crowd (Borsányi, 1977: 162).

Four months later in February 1931 an extraordinary trade union congress was convened to discuss the struggle against unemployment. The main speaker, Social Democratic trade union leader Károly Peyer, claimed that at the beginning of the year there had been 150 thousand industrial unemployed and twice that many unemployed in agriculture, a total that came to a million when the families were included. The gathering repeated the unions' earlier demands: a public works program, reduction of the work-week to 48-hours, national unemployment insurance and a one-time emergency allowance for the jobless. That autumn the unions started negotiations with the new Prime Minister, Count Gyula Károlyi on unemployment aid. The result was that unemployed union members would no longer have to go to the municipal relief kitchens but could receive their portion in a cash amount (the amount was the equivalent of about 12 kilos of bread per month). After uproar from Parliament, the Prime Minister reneged on the deal, saying that it would discourage employment. The Social Democrats organized a far more tepid protest on December 17th, 1931. The Communists by this time had become focused on joblessness as a defining issue and their National Committee of the United Unemployed in 1932 distributed *Munkanélküliek Lapja* (Newspaper of the Unemployed) whose masthead proclaimed it to be, "The Class Warfare Newspaper of the Opposition Unemployed" (Esti, et al., 1984: 199). Communist leaflets called for state unemployment relief with payment adjusted by family size (Esti, et al., 1984). But in the face of anti-labor repression from the new, less tolerant Gömbös government, the Social Democrats avoided further militancy and the Communists were forced further underground. Over time, with Nazi fascist rule, the Social Democrats even more strenuously avoided confrontation (Borsányi, 1977), and the war effort absorbed excess labor, de-emphasizing the issue of unemployment until 1946.[5]

After the War the Communist solution to unemployment shifted from relief aid to the more general task of building a socialist economy. The Communists in their 1944 and 1946 programs supported the view that in the last instance the unemployed should be paid aid if the government does not provide work opportunities (Baksay, 1983). The Hungarian government also sent four thousand guest workers to Tito's Yugoslavia in 1947 (Róna-Tas, 1997: 53). But the Communists increasingly declared that relief measures were insufficient palliatives that failed to address the larger problems. Péter Lázár, the secretary of the Hungarian Engineers and Technical Union wrote in September 1946 that "the first and most important task against unemployment is the most complete utilization of industrial capacity and a further focus on strengthening production" (Baksay, 1983: 157-58). Regarding the unemployment relief administered by unions, Communist MP László Piros similarly stated,

> Already up to the present much has been done in the interest of the solution to unemployment. ...Today also there exists unemployment aid, but what I must say is that this aid does not solve the enormous problem. The government is not able to take the view that the tremendous question of the country, that this is the question of the health of our economic life... (Baksay, 1983: 156).

This view is mirrored in a letter from a Communist regional agricultural official to the government in March 10, 1947, "The working class of the country are really in a hard situation such that it is not unemployment aid that is desired but the work which will reconstruct the country" (Baksay, 1983: 156). Speaking on unemployment aid in a September 18, 1946 meeting of Parliament, MP Piros went even further, "Unemployment aid is also found repugnant by the working class. We do not want unemployment aid and not working for a wage. What we do want is that the government brings about the opportunity to work..." (Baksay, 1983: 156).

This diminished emphasis of the Communists on unemployment *per se* was not merely the result of their own success at creating jobs. Before unemployment got better, it got worse. In 1946 the return of demobilized soldiers and prisoners of war swelled the ranks of unemployed. The statistical office in November of that year estimated 360,000 unemployed, including non-union members. Thirteen months later the Construction and Public Works Ministry estimated 412,000 unemployed in December 1947 (Baksay, 1983: 68).

Under the pretext of national emergency, and backed up by the presence of Soviet troops, the Communists successively banned the political parties furthest on the right while making a series of temporary alliances with more moderate parties. At the Ministerial level, the Communists took effective control of the economy in

1947; but they did not declare the end of unemployment until the end of 1949, the year that political control was consolidated with staged elections and a new constitution. If the pre-war focus on unemployment had been partly a strategic way for the Communists to define themselves apart from other opposition groups and as hostile to capitalism, these motivations disappeared once the Communists themselves seized power. Less and less political attention was paid to unemployment, despite the fact the by 1947 the Communists controlled the Economic Directorate and as late as 1948 approximately nine percent of the workforce (five percent of the total population) was still unemployed (Róna-Tas, 1997: 53).

In the Party's new stance unemployment stood as evidence of the desirable inflow of women and peasants from household and village backwardness into more "productive" industrial and wage labor. Unemployment was viewed as an unfortunate side effect of all-important industrialization and modernization. In the National Planning Office's five-year work plan to be initiated in 1950, the single most important task was assigned to employing women and youth, especially in industrial production (Baksay, 1983: 123).

Unemployment problems were dealt with by declaring them solved. The upcoming five-year plan proclaimed the liquidation of unemployment would be a goal of the plan with the hope that growth in the early 1950s would be rapid enough to provide jobs for all. But as late as April 1949 the Planning Office had reported that unemployment still stood at 95,000 industrial workers and more in agriculture (Baksay, 1983: 117). Many of the administering authorities were therefore surprised when unemployment was declared to have been *already* eradicated at the end of 1949.[6] In the short term, declaring the eradication of unemployment made the issue less urgent in the policy-making agenda. It is instructive in this respect to compare the 1948 program of the Hungarian Worker's Party, which unified the Communists and Social Democrats, with later programs. The 1948 agreement included a host of social policy aims, including prominently the abolition of unemployment (Ferge, 1979: 62). By contrast the 1949 Party program, which was created once power had been consolidated and there was less need to gesture towards Social Democratic aims, did not even mention unemployment, much less initiate programs against joblessness.[7]

Soviet Influences on Hungarian Concepts of Unemployment

Any internal struggles within the Hungarian Communist Party as to how closely to take the lead from the Soviet Union were decided when the Soviet army occupied Budapest in 1945. Hungarian Communists who had been in exile in Moscow moved quickly up the ranks and touted their training in the Soviet Union as a proof of their superior grasp of the laws of scientific socialism. We can not understand how the Party approached unemployment without reference to the profound influence of Soviet thought. Even though Soviet employment ideals were not always embodied in Soviet practice, they were nonetheless formative in defining the Hungarian Communist Party goals directly after the war.

The Hungarian Communist Party in the early 1950s emulated the Soviet Union in everything from art to economic planning. Hungarian Party cadre knew that disputes among Party leadership were settled in Moscow and that it was politically dangerous to deviate or even question Soviet ways. Flexibility in imitating Soviet methods was curtailed by Stalin's tendency to "theorize" the past pragmatic strategies of the Soviet Union into his own "scientific principles of socialist development" (Berend and György, 1985: 205-6). The USSR sent ideological materials and instructors and the framework for "building socialism" was chiefly to apply the Soviet model to distinctive Hungarian conditions (Szamuely, 1996). For instance, a pamphlet at the time showed the superiority of the Soviet system by comparing the nine-fold increase in GDP in the Soviet Union from 1913 to 1938 with the mere twenty percent increase in the United States over the same period (McDonald, 1992: 72). The Hungarian economics profession was dominated by the *Hungarian-Soviet Economics Review* which largely ran translations of articles from Russian.[8] The welcoming letter to new professors at the economics university in Budapest proclaimed that the new professors, "are not going to praise capitalism in economics ...they will instruct students in the Soviet Union's true character so that they will love and respect the vanguard country of human progress, the guardian of peace, our big friend".[9] Although the Planning Office consistently grumbled for better statistics, there was little attempt at independent empirical research or professional space for questioning Soviet doctrine in economics.[10]

The Hungarian leaders who assumed power from the late 1940s to the mid-1950s were already well familiar with Soviet economic thought and, unlike post-1956 leaders, lacked political experiences that were focused on unemployment as a distinct social problem. The pre-1956 leadership cut their political teeth during World War I when the war effort absorbed labor and unemployment was not a pressing issue. They despised the Social Democrats and were never active in trade unions. During the high-unemployment inter-war years in Hungary they were away in prison, Moscow, Spain, or elsewhere in Western Europe. The head of the post-war Communist Party and Hungary's self-proclaimed "little Stalin", Mátyás Rákosi had become a professional revolutionary at a young age after having worked in a London bank before the First World War. He was imprisoned between 1925 and 1940 and thereby missed out on the entire Depression. Other important leaders were also professional revolutionaries who similarly did not have first-hand experience of political organizing or job-seeking amidst high unemployment. This includes József Révai, the hard-line ideologue who was a founding member of the Communist Party in 1918 and responsible for ideology and culture after the War. He emigrated, was imprisoned upon return to Hungary and then went into exile in the Soviet Union in 1934, returning only after Soviet victory. Mihály Farkas, later responsible for the armed forces, became a professional revolutionary at a very early age; as did Ernő Gerő who took part in the Spanish Civil War, and became an economist in the Comintern. Hungary's most important economic theorist at the time was Jenö Varga who left Hungary after the defeat of the

Republic of Councils in 1919 and died shortly after the War. As head of the World Political Institute in Moscow, Varga would have had great influence on the others, including his views of unemployment as a pathology specific to late-capitalism.

An interesting example of the development of these Soviet influences can be found in Zolton Vas, responsible for economic reconstruction in the first planning office (Gazdasági Főtanács). Vas, who like so many other important figures had also been a professional revolutionary and temporarily exiled in Moscow, wrote in 1949 a book and accompanying article in the Party theoretical journal, *Tarsadalmi Szemle* entitled "Completing the Three year Plan is Our People's Victory" where he outlined the three necessary steps to emulate the Soviet model. The first step was to consolidate socialist political power, a task he saw as completed. Second, pre-war standards of living had to be restored, a path he viewed as well on the way to completion, based on the tenuous logic that industrial investment targets were being overfulfilled. Thirdly, he stated that unemployment should be ended as proof that socialism was living up to its promise as a workers state (McDonald, 1992). The end of unemployment was viewed as something that could be accomplished by edict and which would support the claim that Soviet-style socialism could better claim to represent a workers' paradise. Freedom from unemployment was not yet regarded as an established right or an established popular expectation of the regime.

Thus, Soviet influence operated in a variety of ways. Soviet ideology provided the template for the ideas of Hungarian Communist leaders. All methods Soviet were championed and directly imported; and Hungarians who were socialized and trained with Soviet views of unemployment were installed in leadership after 1946. To these we should add that in the mid-Twentieth Century there were few other examples of poor countries catching up with the industrialized world. The Soviets, as victors in the war and rapid modernizers, provided an attractive model. Such a model was compelling given the devastated state of the Hungarian economy after the War.

Reconstruction, Industrial Mobilization, and Leninist-Fordism

The devastation of World War II left millions of Hungarians without jobs. Hungary had been a site of intense fighting between the Germans and the Allies. Most of the pre-war industrial capacity was taken by the retreating Germans, bombed by the Allies, or removed as reparations by the Soviet army. The economy was hamstrung by production bottlenecks and a dismantled transportation network. National income in 1946 was only about sixty-two percent of its pre-war 1938 levels, and industrial production was only thirty-six percent of its previous level (Kaser and Radice, 1986: 626). The economic chaos was compounded by hyper-inflation in 1946 that effectively de-monetized the economy and left week-to-week industrial wages to be calculated in calorie equivalents (Berend and György, 1985: 189). Communist policies for land reform, nationalizing industry, and infrastructure reconstruction were, in this context, subsumed within the more general effort to get people (and the country) working again.

In the initial years of Communist rule, from 1949 up until 1956, the issue of unemployment was little more than another form of underutilization, not unlike empty manors, backward peasant agriculture or "anti-social" private speculation. Almost all Hungarians were economically active in some form and the entire population was viewed as the potentially active labor supply to be steered into state enterprises. If not performing industrial piece work then people moved back and forth between farming and other tasks that did not merit state recognition as employment. Under state-socialism such non-employed or "inactive" labor of all kinds was to be mobilized in the push for rapid industrialization.

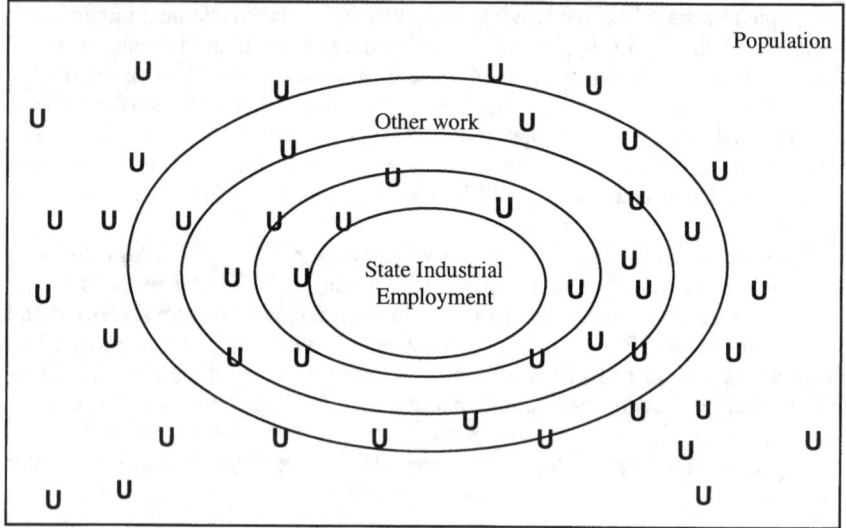

Figure 2.1 The Stalinist concept of unemployment

Thus, the Stalinist-era concept of unemployment is represented schematically in Figure 2.1 above. The central circle represents prototypically "socialist" employment in large, state-run industry. The outer circles represent more marginal forms of work, such as cooperative agriculture, private farming, and work as a private artisan or in a private shop. The "excess" amounts of labor in these activities is unemployed in the sense that it is not fully utilized as it would be under socialist planning and production. Outside the circles are the population who are not involved in remunerative work. An excessive number of these people—such as housewives or wealthy landowners—are also not fully utilized. In this sense, they too are "unemployed". The unemployed are conceptually represented in the schematic figure below by the symbol: **U**.

The superior dynamism of central planning and the skillful adjustment of the active labor pool were themselves regarded as capable of eliminating unemployment. Unemployment in this view was seen purely as a form of production problem, a bottleneck of unutilized workers that could be prevented through proper economic planning and the adjustments in the labor supply. As Article 45 of the 1949 Communist constitution proclaimed,

> The Hungarian People's Republic secures for its citizens the right to work... This right is being realized by the Hungarian People's Republic through the planned development of the productive forces of the national economy and through the economic utilization of manpower reserves according to plan.

Unemployment, like poverty, was treated as a second order problem that would be indirectly solved by a rising tide of increased employment. This view is embodied in the First Three-Year Reconstruction Plan (1947-49), which did not state any commitment to full employment, but only to an ever-increasing number of workers and an end to excess employment in agriculture (Kaser and Radice, 1986: 626).

The Communist strategy of forced mobilization and rapid industrial investment was enormously successful in reviving the moribund economy. Bridges were rebuilt, railroad beds repaired, bombed out factories restored, electrical lines laid down, and agricultural harvests able to reach urban centers. Whereas only 3.7 percent of national income had been invested in 1945-6, investment reached 22 percent of GDP in 1947-8.[11] According to Ivan Berend's calculations, "One unit of investment generated a 2.5 unit growth in GNP" (Berend and György, 1985: 195). National output growth in 1947 and 1948 achieved astonishing rates of 76 percent and 30 percent respectively (Berend and György, 1985: 195). Initial successes ratcheted up expectations and led to still-greater concentration of resources into heavy industrial investment. Two-thirds of industrial investment in the five-year plan went to mining and metallurgy (Berend and György, 1985: 204).

A number of factors supported this strategy of rapid industrial mobilization. Rapid industrialization was wrapped up in the building of a war economy for the impending world war predicted by Stalin. Military spending accounted for half of Hungarian investment in the first year of the first five-year plan and averaged over a third in the following four years (Berend, 1990). Ernő Gerő, head of economic reconstruction during this time, recounted in a 1960 interview that, "We had the information, that we had to count on a forthcoming war in three to four years" (Berend and György, 1985: 205). Many have also traced the Communist obsession with centralization and heavy industry back to Marx's fascination with the efficiency and social coordination of the factory.[12] Others stress continuity with feudal relations in Hungary between landless peasants and their paternalistic landlords.[13] Still others would stress how, regardless of political stripe, authoritarian states embark on modernist projects of social engineering by seeking to establish a standardization and regimentation of social forms for more rational and systematic ordering of society (Scott, 1998).

Whatever the ultimate ideological sources, we can discern a very definite view of idealized employment. We see this view in the words of Lenin as well as the Hungarian policies of the early 1950s. The importance of work was made clear in Article 9 of the Hungarian constitution of 1949, which states:

1] The basis of the social order of the Hungarian People's Democracy is labor.
2] It is a right, duty, and affair of honor of all able-bodied citizens to work according to their abilities.
3] The workers serve the cause of building socialism by their labors, their participation in work-competition, the improvement of work discipline, and the perfecting of work methods.[14]

Work was viewed not only as a redemptive social virtue; but also as establishing a hierarchy of differential virtues calibrated according to the type of employment. Work was more worthwhile if it was industrial, if it was large-scale, and if it took place in the state sector.

Theoretically, capitalist production was acknowledged as having spawned large-scale factory production, but the inherently chaotic and crisis-prone nature of markets made them unable to sufficiently coordinate the emerging mode of production (Marx, 1978 [1848]). Only socialist planning could harness the productive forces of industrialization. The task, as Lenin further explained, was "To organize the whole economy on the lines of the postal service" (Nove, 1982: 32).[15] Not only should all people work. They should ideally work in historically "advanced" employment, that is, in large-scale, centrally planned, industrial enterprises.

In light of the rapid growth that ensued, one might conclude that in the 1950s the lack of emphasis on unemployment resulted from employment increases and labor shortages. In later decades we shall see, however, that the most intense concerns about unemployment were also contemporaneous with labor shortages. And even in the 1950s there continued to be some groups who were very difficult to employ. Their joblessness continued to be viewed by the Party as a problem to be struggled against, but the solution was equated with the more general advance of socialist planning.

Basic categories for conceptualizing the labor force of the 1950s would persist until the 1990s. We should evaluate Communist views about unemployment in their own terms because the economic categories through which the Party framed policy goals subsequently became benchmarks by which the public could judge the competency of Communist rule. For instance, the proclivity to see only large enterprises as economically relevant was reflected in the regular "manpower estimates" reported by firms. This survey, which was the chief mechanism for tabulating macro-data, excluded entities with less than fifty workers.[16] Census and other manpower data were treated as state secrets from the second half of 1949 until secrecy relaxed in July 1953, and was finally reversed in the summer of 1956. During the time of secrecy the main sources of labor force data were reports on the five-year plan in articles, propaganda journals and speeches. Definitions were lacking, numbers were typically given only in percentages, and often restricted to industry and construction data (U.S. Bureau of the Census, 1962: 2).

Despite the seemingly arbitrary manipulation of statistics during this period, the views and strategies of the Party were formally codified in formal conceptual categories by the 1952 decisions of the COMECON statistical committee. Formalization was deemed necessary because of informal practices that undermined the attainment of the prototypical vision of Communist employment. The Party chose to narrow the officially recognized status of valid employment. At issue was the question of whether workers who earned a pension from new or pre-Communist schemes could also draw incomes as active workers. Some workers were choosing to become pensioners in order to increase their income, and this created a group of workers who were less dependent on their jobs. This situation was viewed as slippage that eroded both the meaning of the pension and of work discipline. The COMECON committee decided that either a worker could have a pension *or* they could be employed, but not both.[17]

A three-fold conceptual distinction codified the protection of Communist employment through distinguishing between *active earners, inactive workers, and dependents.* As Gaspar Fajth points out, in the ideally planned economic system these categories would have corresponded to the population who were respectively: in, over, and under the working age (Fajth, 1993: 87-99). Planners viewed the population as a production input whose participation was ultimately limited only by their life cycle or physiology. *Active earners* were persons in legal, paid activity actually working at the time of classification. It included members of co-operatives farms, the self-employed, apprentices, family workers and others having worked at least 90 days during the year (including the armed forces). By contrast, "*Inactive workers* perform no earning activity but receive earnings or income" (Nesporová, 1993: 43). This category encompassed old-age or disabled pensioners, as well as women on maternity leave or receiving child-care benefits. As its name implies, this category described those who had been mobilized into the productive economy but had reasons for being excused from employment that the state recognized as entitling them to supplementary income. Only those who had previously been working consistently or were severely disabled would have been eligible for benefits. The final category, *dependents*, were mostly children, students, housewives and others with no income who did not support themselves.

In the context of this cognitive framework, unemployment was not viewed as the relevant indicator for the utilization of labor capacity. Labor, like other productive inputs, was not-uncommonly unemployed in the sense that it had not yet been fully utilized through socialist planning. But the relevant benchmark was a comparison between actual activity rates of the working-age population compared juxtaposed with the "theoretical labor capacity". Success was defined in terms of closing this gap.[18] After 1956 the unemployed were not reported as part of manpower data. The official estimate for 1956 reported only 30,000 to 40,000 unemployed which is much lower than even published accounts in Party newspapers. The low number suggests that only those jobless receiving temporary aid were counted. A steady work-history would have undoubtedly been a requirement for eligibility; thus individuals who qualified statistically as unemployed would more importantly have also been categorized as "active earners".

Party officials claimed credit for expanding state industrial employment, not reducing unemployment. By the criteria of expanding employment, the Communists could claim great success. Whereas in 1949 two-thirds of the working-age population was economically active, this portion had risen to three-quarters by 1960 (U.S. Bureau of the Census, 1962: 8). From 1949 to 1961 the number of employed workers increased from 3.9 million to 4.6 million, with industrial and construction employment increasing from 750,000 to 1.35 million (p. 31). The post-war push for rapid industrialization quickly brought employment back to pre-war levels, driven mainly by increased employment of women. In 1948 there had been severe unemployment in construction as a result of slow economic times. In other industries such as leather, fur, rubber, textiles, and clothing, unemployment resulted from short supply of raw materials (Róna-Tas, 1997: 54). With the increase of new investment in 1949, activity in these industries was restored and unemployment was greatly reduced.

When the first labor shortages began in priority (heavy manufacturing) industries that spring, unemployment had already been replaced by "labor discipline" at the top of the Party's agenda. As in the USSR discipline was considered a particularly severe problem among displaced peasants who were unaccustomed to the rhythms and routines of factory production.[19] Party chairman Matyás Rákosi on August 31, 1949 bemoaned the ways that skilled workers were manipulating the tightness of the labor market,

> Recently there have been hundreds of cases of one state factory enticing workers away from other state factories. It is even more common that workers leave to work with small artisans, in their workshops. Many times they are able to get their four-weekly pay on Saturday, and by Monday they continue to work in another factory or with an artisan. They just laugh at those who do not understand these manipulations. This problem should be treated more strictly.[20]

The task of increasing labor discipline was viewed as both restricting excess wages and increasing the productivity of existing labor.

Again, we can discern the important repercussions of the lens through which the Party approached economic problems. Their economic categories were at the same time an expression of established strategies and a cognitive commitment toward future action. Confronted by the kind of excess wage increases described above, contemporary Western economics interprets the situation against an idealized view of perfect competition and the problem is thereby defined as one in which too *little* unemployment spurs excessive wage inflation.[21] Although socialists did not regard socialist labor as a commodity, they similarly acknowledged that the relative scarcity of workers with artisan skills clearly gave these workers greater ability to seek higher wages. The critical difference is that they viewed this situation against the idealized vision of scientifically coordinated industrial labor under communism. The Party therefore interpreted excess wage gains as inadequate adherence to the proper organization of work, that is, inadequate discipline. More than semantics is at stake here since the real consequence was that, instead of lifting rules against dismissals, the Party's solutions were instead framed in terms of increasing discipline by making workers more dependent on their workplace and creating new obstacles to job-switching.

In contrast to the immediate post-war period, excess labor was no longer available and new labor had to be actively mobilized to expand industry. General labor shortage, however, was not incompatible with the continuation of particular kinds of situations in which workers were unable to find work. On the contrary, the campaign to channel labor surplus out of agriculture sent many job-seekers into the cities looking for employment. Women and youth were especially difficult to employ because they were unskilled and faced discrimination. Worker dismissals were far from uncommon and a well-integrated (and regulated) feature of labor contracts. Enterprise managers were officially required to consult with the trade union committee and, if the worker had been employed for over a year or if it was their first job then the decision had to be justified in terms of reorganization or staffing problems. Enterprises could not dismiss workers just called up for military service, the disabled, pregnant, or nursing mothers.[22] Workers whose employment was interrupted by forces of nature outside their control (such as flood or fire) would be paid 80 percent of their average wages.[23] It was not until the mid-1960s that the Communist Party explicitly resolved to extend the guarantee of employment to the Gypsy (Roma) minority. As late as 1965 it was considered "progress" and not inconsistent with having eradicated unemployment to note that almost half of gypsies had permanent jobs and thirty percent had seasonal employment for eight to ten months of the year.[24]

In 1950, following the closure of union labor placement offices that had reportedly fallen into disuse, unemployment was announced to be officially eradicated. As one Communist union periodical celebrated,

> "Employment Bureau Discontinued" – announces the poster now on the closed door of the employment office of the Iron Works Union. The Union's Employment Bureau had to be discontinued because weeks passed without anyone registering for this service. On the other hand, the phone of the office rang practically all day long: the factories of the iron industry were asking for turners, welders and other skilled workers. But there is a similar situation at the employment offices of the other large unions as well like building and mine workers. Hungarian planned economy has succeeded. It abolished the terrifying fear of working people – unemployment. The new task, eliminating of the shortage of skilled workers, is already the task of a new organization, the National Manpower Office (*Szakszervezeti Tanács*, Nov. 1949: 12).

Two observations should be made about the above passage. First, the constant phone calls from factories were not asking for unskilled workers, such as those who were pouring in from the countryside. Secondly, the timing of the declaration suggests that it was motivated at least partly by the Party's strategy of eliminating independent functions of the trade unions and centralizing labor allocation.

Centralized labor allocation may have been instrumental in "ending" unemployment but announcing the "end" of unemployment was itself an instrument for centralizing labor allocation.

In the initial years of post-war reconstruction the government used compulsion and coercion to get people working with greater discipline in officially recognized economic activities. In June 1945 obligatory "public work" (*közmunka*) 4 days a month was instituted to help complete reconstruction projects. All women from 18 to 42 and all men 18 to 60 were required to register with the state (Róna-Tas, 1997: 52). The government pressured the Catholic Bench of Bishops in 1950 to sign a seven-point agreement which obliged the Church to have believers assume their share of the work of fulfilling the five-year plan.[25] Labor shortages in the 1950s were often filled by "organized recruitment", which meant the compulsory assignment of work, especially to persons who quit their jobs without legal approval or were fired for labor discipline. Under-fulfillment of the plan without pressing need in the beginning of the 1950s could be punished by up to two years in prison. Some shortages, such as mining and construction were sometimes filled with the prison labor of "class enemies". "Educative-correctional labor" was used against those who had been members of rightist organizations or who had changed their family name to be more German during the War. After January 1, 1945 economic criminals such as tax evaders, price gougers, black marketeers and shirkers were also subject to compulsory work (Róna-Tas, 1997: 54).

Reviving the previous laws from 1945, leaving a job without permission without employer consent was made a civil offense in 1950, and soon after made a criminal offense (Róna-Tas, 1997: 57). It was proclaimed that, "A person commits sabotage when he hinders or stops production ...wastes material or manpower, or leaves capital unused". This is punishable by up to 5 years in prison or, in serious cases, death.[26] The legal logic against work-shirking was that since Article 9 of the 1949 Constitution declared that the social order was based on work, those without a workplace were criminals. A decree by the Council of Ministers in February 1950 made any act harmful to the plan punishable by up to two years in prison. The Supreme Court in 1951 ruled that, "absence from work without harmful intent or leave without proper excuse is covered by this law, and normally should be punished by corrective-educational labor".[27]

In an attempt to control the allocation of labor all hiring was required to go through state-run employment offices which channeled workers into high-priority areas such as construction and heavy industry. Industrial recruitment began in 1950, a practice in which workers signed a contract and were given a small signing bonus that, in addition to providing a positive incentive, could also be the basis for charges of embezzling state property if workers failed to show up. In 1952, seven thousand cases of "refusing to continue employment" came to trial. Many more cases were brought on charges of embezzlement, "crime against the plan", or "endangering the public by shirking" (Róna-Tas, 1997: 59). Few people were actually jailed, but fines and corrective labor were used. Punishments were difficult to enforce because enterprise managers and local Party committees faced serious labor shortages and the last thing they wanted was to send their workers to prison.

When, after Stalin's death in 1953 penalties were softened, industrial turnover rates shot up and over a third of agricultural collective members quit (Róna-Tas, 1997: 61). The most extreme measures were only enforceable so long as they were backed by harsh coercion.

Although imprisonment and other coercive measures provided a dramatic backdrop, the Communist notions of what constituted legitimate employment and non-employment were enforced more effectively through the incentives laid out in social and labor policies. The prototypical ideal of communist employment was long-term, continuous employment in state-run large-plant manufacturing. Incentive structures that kept Hungarians continuously working to achieve living standard norms were regarded as effective, taut planning. Long-term, continuous work histories in the state sector were fostered by institutions which provided strong incentives against leaving state jobs. Sharp wage reductions made it increasingly difficult not to have multiple income earners in a household, especially since health care, family benefits, pensions, and sickness benefits were distributed on the basis of state employment until the mid-1970s.[28] Family benefits, for instance, were not paid to a parent who did not work at least twenty-one days that month.[29] In the case of sickness benefits the official trade union organized home visits by "social security councils [to] guard against the giving of these services to lingerers and swindlers... ."[30] The amount of sickness benefits depended strongly on how many years a worker had been employed in one place. A special category was created for workers who had been employed at one place for five years or more, the "standing staff" or *törzsgárda*. Badges of loyalty and bonuses were presented for five, ten, and twenty or twenty-five years at a single plant. These workers received preferential treatment in the dispensation of future profit sharing plans, an advantage when they applied to colleges or universities, in receiving scholarships, for factory paid vacations, in the distribution of apartments, government loans for building homes, and in their pensions.[31]

The ways that different kinds of employment were encouraged, tolerated, or forbidden depended on the place of these activities within an established hierarchy of social virtue.[32] State policies mobilized casual, agricultural and home workers into more "socially productive" employment, especially into large state-owned manufacturing. Private production was severely curtailed and industrial employment increased nearly fifty percent from 1949 to 1955 (Adam, 1984: 97). The Council of Ministers nationalized all industrial firms with more than 100 employees on March 25, 1948 (Róna-Tas, 1997: 33). Certain kinds of activity such as capital speculation, renting out land, or independent agriculture were regarded as absolutely illegitimate and criminalized. At the end of 1949 firms with at least 10, or in some cases five, workers or more were expropriated. Private wholesale activity was outlawed in February 1950. A special committee within the Communist Party devised ways of eliminating private trades people, including: new license requirements, sourcing intermediate goods only from state factories, eliminating credit, increasing taxes, banning private purchase of machinery (Róna-Tas, 1997: 43). The number of registered independent craftworkers in Hungary fell from almost 170,000 in 1948 to a mere 50,000 in 1953 (Hankiss, 1990: 29). The number of private sector employees fell from about 121,000 in 1948 to less than 3,000 in 1953 (Róna-Tas, 1997: 45). The perceived illegitimacy of the independent peasantry was apparent in the way the Party refuted their right to "strike" against the Party's orders for mandatory food requisition,

> The "peasant strike" is either simply nonsense or something much worse. The peasant is a small-scale producer, an owner of land—the "peasant strike" is just as meaningless as would be that of the other social strata that possess the means of production. Today peasant strike, tomorrow artisan or tradesman strike and the day after tomorrow a strike of the factor owners and corporation presidents? ...[C]ontrary to a strike by industrial workers, a peasant strike... is not aimed at a particular capitalist, but is perforce directed against all of society.[33]

The proportion of independent economic actors of any type (farmers, craftsmen, merchants, clergymen, professionals, etc.) and their families in the population would fall from 51.3 percent in 1949 to 17.0 percent in 1960 to 2.6 percent by 1970.[34]

Social insurance was also reorganized to promote the prototypical forms of socialist employment and to discourage alternatives. The old National Social Institute (OTI) had administrated social security and coordinated the thirty-odd insurance institutes for different occupations. These were amalgamated into four, and then two, and finally one institute in 1950. A Communist union publication at the time makes clear how the shift to enterprise-based benefits discriminated against those in smaller enterprises.

> The center of social insurance activity was shifted to the factories and offices. In factories and offices employing over 100 workers, social insurance work is performed by an elected "Social Insurance Council", functioning under the works committee. Its responsibilities include social insurance services, paid vacations at health resorts and health protection. ...Establishments employing less than 100 workers have no social insurance pay-offices of their own. Employees of such factories and offices get their benefits at the social insurance office in the town of each county. (*Szakszervezeti Tanács*, 1948-51, September 1951 supplement, p. 4)

The average size of state companies increased from 96 employees in 1948 to 483 in 1955, and to 641 in 1960. State companies were reorganized in 1948-49 into industrial centers that were grouped into industry directorates overseen directly by a Ministry. In 1963-63 state companies were merged into even larger conglomerates and in certain industries only a single company was left (Róna-Tas, 1997: 67).

Some kinds of activities were not recognized as fully expressing the socialist ideals of work but were nonetheless tolerated as transitional forms that would gradually give way to more advanced socialist employment. The state's relationship to small-scale production, artisanship and collective farming was one of uneasy and grudging support. Over time these activities came to be conditionally accepted but they held no bargaining leverage or moral clout in internal Party disputes over the planned allocation of resources. As one decree spelled out,

> As our society develops the interest of the population will require for quite a while that we provide opportunities within the limits of the law for the private small-scale industry engaging in honest work. ...The party wants the private artisans and tradesmen to participate actively in the common socialist effort of the working people, and to gradually—and voluntarily—find their way to socialism.[35]

The grudging recognition of artisan activity was similarly expressed in social policies. Private artisans, whose numbers peaked in 1958, were not eligible for any form of pension until 1962, after which they could pay higher-than-normal social security taxes for ten years to qualify for a retirement pension (Róna-Tas, 1997: 64). The Party chose the collectivization of agricultural land as an intermediary step toward fully socializing agriculture. Nove (1982: 42) points to a secret document issued within the Department of State Economy in March, 1949 as an outline of future policy toward private sector and cooperatives which stated, "The cooperative movement is the organizational form through which we can bring small artisans into the socialist sector of production". Cooperatives received allocations for machinery and fertilizer and their members gradually came to be integrated into state health care and retirement pension programs. Between cooperatization and outright nationalization the proportion of cultivated land that was privately owned fell from 96.6 percent in 1949 to 56.2 percent in 1953. A second collectivization drive from 1959 to 1961 would bring almost all agricultural workers (94 percent) into the socialist sector and bring success to the goal of making most Hungarians wage workers (Róna-Tas, 1997: 52).

The compulsion for wage earning was extended to women, with allowances for the productive benefits of motherhood. State propaganda urged women to serve Communism by bearing more children and entering the labor force when they could.[36] For a few years in the mid-1950s abortion was prohibited with explicit pro-natalist aims and up until 1957 there was a tax placed on families without children.[37] According to the chief of the manpower planning department in the national planning office summing up the views of the early 1960s "...Women abandoning household work in effect exchange working in this 'small-scale plant' of minimum productivity for the higher productivity connected with socially organized labor" (Timár, 1966: 1). Campaigns to encourage women into joining the workforce included production of electrical household appliances starting in 1956, production of canned goods, laundry services and stores with semi-prepared meals kept open for extended hours (1966: 35). Women received higher maternity pay if they had worked more during the pregnancy, and they were encouraged to continue working even with small children, by providing on-site childcare, paid nursing breaks, and extra days off (Haney, 2000: 109).

An important feature in the Communist conception of employment was that the wages from one's job were *not* supposed to be a sufficient source of livelihood. Although fewer positions were available for them, and young girls in particular were difficult to employ, women were nonetheless compelled into the labor market by the low wages of their husbands and fathers. Minimum wage levels were calculated in household terms and extensive studies were made to exactly specify how children affected family income flows (Haney, 2000: 106). The female employment rate increased from one-third to one-half over eleven years following 1949, eventually peaking at over 75 percent in the 1980s.[38] During the period from 1949 to 1960 about three quarters of the increase in the total number of economically active persons were women (Barta, 1985: 24). Families made ends meet by having multiple wage-earners and by supplementing wages with extensive non-wage benefits. The first years of the five-year plan forced farmers to deliver produce at prices below cost and forced urban workers to buy state bonds whose value diminished with large price increases. Berend estimates that per capita real wages over this time decreased by 22 percent (Berend and György, 1985: 207). Wages and consumption were held below the pace of growth in national income in order to maximize productive investment. Wage supplements to state workers in 1955 totaled almost twenty-seven percent of wages, including work clothes, subsidized canteen meals,[39] home-building loans, housing discounts and hostels, transportation discounts and subsidized holidays, child care, and emergency funds for births or deaths in the family.[40]

Over time the increases in consumption came largely from the rising value of social benefits (and later secondary income) rather than wages.[41] "Social consumption" was promoted by central planners at the cost of individual consumption.[42] Any worker's income in excess of the necessary minimum which went to household consumption would have better been directed towards the goal of rapid industrialization. This was an important legacy of the Communist era that is reflected in the unusually low portion of wage income in the GDP of post-communism as well (Kovács, 1994). Social policies facilitated lower wages than would otherwise be possible because they compensated for variation in needs or earning abilities which resulted from child rearing, illness or aging. It was possible, for instance, to set wages at levels that were too low to support children because complementary family benefits were targeted to parents. Higher wages would have only diverted resources for state industrialization into needless personal discretionary income for childless workers.

Conclusion

Thus, policy aims and policy-benchmarks were defined to promote a prototype of socialist employment. Long-term, full-time employment in state-owned industry grew while other forms of work became increasingly scarce. Unemployment was treated as a temporary concomitant of industrialization, but was not itself a focus of political or policy-making concern. This attitude was politically expeditious for those in power. Similarly, the accommodation to Soviet ways of viewing unemployment was a political necessity. Soviet influences were very strong after the War, both as a direct pressure on Hungarian policy and indirectly through the socialization of those individuals who came power after the Second World War. The post-war stance stood in marked contrast to the Communist Party's strong emphasis against unemployment before the War. This earlier opposition also had largely political origins as a strategy for appealing to urban workers and differentiating themselves from the Social Democrats.

Notes

1   The Bethlen-Peyer pact was signed on December 22, 1921.
2   In 1930 the industrial unemployed tallied 136,000; in 1931 there were 178,000, and in 1933 there were 234,000 (Borsányi, 1977).
3   In 1924 the Social Democrats had put a bill for relief before Parliament that was rejected.
4   In the summer of 1929 the Minister of the Interior sent a circular to all county sub-prefects informing them of job openings in France and Belgium and that getting the unemployed to work abroad was in the interest of state security. Emigration was organized to France for 169 former silk workers from a factory in Sárvár (Borsányi, 1977).
5   The Third Reich also absorbed Hungary's surplus manpower in seasonal labor (Rothschild, 1989: 40).
6   The first conception of the five-year plan, that was sketched out in the Hungarian Workers Party (MDP) economic and financial committee June 16, 1948 proposal, aimed to accomplish the effective eradication of unemployment, the unaccomplished transformation of the economic structure, heightened emphasis of industrial production. The five-year plan was also concerned with the eradication of unemployment, but like the nominal over-fulfilment of so many Stalin-era plans, by the end of 1949 unemployment was declared to have already been accomplished (Baksay, 1983).
7   The Communist Party initially allied with the Social Democrats against more right-wing parties but turned on them once other opposition had been eliminated in 1949.
8   For a numerical analysis of the number of Russian articles over time see (McDonald, 1992: 89).
9   Laszló Rudas, "Az új Magyar Közgazdaságtudományi Egyetem feladatai" (tasks of the New Hungarian University of Economics) *Közgazdasági Szemle*, 3, 10-11 (Oct.-Nov.): 658-60 (McDonald, 1992: 659-60).
10 Timár claims that in general there were constant disagreements between the Planning Office and the Statistical Office, with the former always trying to get more accurate data for their forecasts and plans (J. Timár interview, Budapest, May 28, 1998). A Marxist-Leninist Institute of Economics was established in 1949 but was abolished in 1952 after having conducted little research. One anecdote holds that the economics minister, Gerö held a discussion with the institute's researchers to inquire on their progress, and "they replied that they were doing fine except that they could not get their hands on any data. Just read the party daily, *Szabad Nép*", said Gerö, "it contains all the data anyone needs" (McDonald, 1992: 94). See also (Treml, 1969) on how after Stalin purged technical economists in 1930s; econometrics was virtually banned.
11 "Between 1948 and 1950, while national income increased about 20 percent, capital accumulation achieved an increase of 54 percent. In 1951 accumulation increased by 70 percent. In general, between 1949 and 1953, the volume of accumulation developed more than twice as fast as the growth of national income. As a result, during the first

five-year plan period instead of the pre-war 5-6 percent level, capital accumulation achieved about 35 percent [within] the national income (Berend and György, 1985: 202).

12 "The common core of the socialist experience can be traced to Marxism-Leninism and its underlying vision of development as an unceasing march toward increasing concentration and a modern economy organized as a single factory" (Róna-Tas, 1997: 15). Unlike Proudhon and other craft socialists, Marx saw the factory and centralization of production as an inevitable feature of modernity. Capitalism would be increasingly crisis-prone in its inability to properly coordinate these new methods of production and socialism's world-historical task would to harness these emerging productive powers through scientific socialist planning.

13 The peasant lived in the landlords huts and depended on their employer for all aspects of their lives. Peasant mobility was similarly restricted, and as under Communism, they were required to carry a little book which they would turn over to new employers (Lampland, 1995).

14 (Juhász, 1965) from Magyar Közlöny, Aug. 20, 1949. Hungarian Constitution—Statute 20, 1949.

15 Rigby (1980: 19) coins the term "mono-organizational society" to describe this organizational vision.

16 Throughout the 1980s labor statistics came only from the "manpower" estimates reported by firms. Although day laborers were not included, these statistics most likely over-estimated the number of employed persons because enterprise managers wanted to seem larger for power and status (Timar interview May 28, 1998).

17 Statisticians kept the old 1952 COMECON accounting system (even though they had effectively neutralized its premise by allowing pensioners to work) and counted the population in terms of active and inactive earners. Initially it was strictly prohibited to hire pensioners in Hungary as well, and exceptions could only be personally granted from the ministerial level and were only for "exceptional persons" such as the Party leaders. As labor shortages grew there became more exceptions to the 1952 COMECON rule. First deputy ministers could grant them; then the maximum earnings levels changed, with an employed person by the mid-1950s able to collect a pension up to five thousand forints without special permission.) By the mid-1960s this grew to sixty thousand; and by the 1980s there was no limit (J. Timár interview, Budapest, May 28, 1998).

18 The Hungarian government official 1961 *Monthly Statistical Report* (no. 2) similarly presents a chart for the "Development of Rates of Employment" in which the chief comparison is between the number of "wage earners" and the "potential labor force". This chart demonstrates how communism has increasingly achieved its productive potential. Further progress is shown by dividing wage earners into two categories: state and cooperative sectors, and the private sector. The former group shows growth while the latter has virtually disappeared.

19 The Bolsheviks, faced with a mostly peasant economy, had to implement wage labor and Taylorism (in Lenin's words) "to teach the people how to work". On the difference between agricultural and industrial norms of work see Thompson, 1967.

20 *Magyar Nemzet*, September 2, 1949. Quoted in Róna-Tas, 1997: 56-7.

21 In neoclassical economics this relationship has been expressed in the theory of the Phillips Curve, the natural rate of unemployment, and the non-inflation accelerating rate of unemployment.

22 *Free Hungarian Trade Unions*, March 1965: 2A.

23 *Free Hungarian Trade Unions*, January 1966: 19.

24 *Free Hungarian Trade Unions*, June 1965: 20.
25 This agreement (cited in Gsovski, 1973: 139-40) was pointed out to me by Jason Wittenberg.
26 *Szabad Nép*, Feb. 17, 1950 as quoted in Juhász, 1965: 141.
27 Quoted in Róna-Tas, 1997: 236.
28 In 1951 Hungary had a currency reform that increased the prices of consumer goods by 50-100 percent while lifting wages a mere 20 percent. Real wages fell 19 percent from 1950 to 1952.
29 Z. Ferge, 1991b: 162.
30 *Szakszervezeti Tanács*, Sep-Oct. 1950: 18.
31 *Free Hungarian Trade Union News*, June, 1961: 5-6.
32 In cultural policy the censors conducted a parallel process of calibrated punishment and support known as the "three Ts": support (*támogatás*), toleration (*türés*), and prohibition (*tiltás*). The Party tolerated the selective publication of literature that did not strongly support Party aims if it was of great literary merit and was not openly hostile to the regime. Hungarian writers, who after 1956 had steadfastly resisted any association that might legitimate the Communists, eventually published their work and the general readership eventually accepted the public art as more than mere propaganda, despite the constrained range of topics. State-managed culture only assumed some semblance of legitimacy and acceptance because exceptionally skilled and well-known artists were treated as exceptions. It was through observing the censors' treatment of politically sensitive topics that the public came to understand the limits of public discourse. Similarly the limits of what individual writers could get away with came to be a measure of their literary stature. As with employment, the contours of the general norms of political acceptability were defined by the regulation of exceptions. For a review of this policy in the life history of long-time Culture Minister György Aczél see Révész, 1997.
33 Juhász, 1965: 16, quoted from *Szabad Nép*, Sept. 2, 1945.
34 Hankiss, 1990: 28, citing Iván Petö and Sándor Szakács, *A Hazai Gazdaság Négy Évtizedének Története, 1945-1985* (Budapest: Közgazdasági, 1985): 144-45, 713.
35 Decree of the Eighth Congress of the MSZMP, November, 1962 (Róna-Tas, 1997: 64). Similar sentiments were expressed by Party chairman János Kádár, "Small industry, small tradesmen, and other petty bourgeois elements do have their particular tasks, and they can attend to them surely for many, many years. We believe the time will come when they will have to step from the small capitalist platform down to where tradesmen in cooperatives stand, where the rest of the people stand, where only work is the foundation of life" (Róna-Tas, 1997: 63).
36 As one testimonial chimed in a Communist women's publication, "The State gives a happy home and bountiful care to my child—I must prove with my work that I am worthy of this solicitude". MNDSz, *Mindent a családért!* (Everything for the family) (BP, 1953), quoted in Goven, 1993: 40-41.
37 *Free Hungarian Trade Unions*, June-July, 1957: 8.
38 Hungarian Statistical Office (KSH) yearly report. These numbers are for women aged 15-54.
39 "The Work Code concerns itself with the fact that the working people shall receive in their places of work, one meal—if necessary, three—a day at reduced prices" ((*Szakszervezeti Tanács*, 1948-51), Jan-Feb, 1951: 7).
40 *Free Hungarian Trade Unions*, Jul-Aug, 1958: 26. Author's own calculations. The official calculation of 39.5 percent included paid vacations and lunch breaks, calculated at 12.8 percent of wages.

41 See Pryor, 1985; Kornai, 1980 on consumption and investment shares of GDP over time.

42 This position was eloquently defended during the conservative backlash to reform in the mid-1970s where a union periodical mused, "We consider it more important, for example, to develop social benefits than wages. It is more important for us to provide rapid and comfortable public transport than to increase the number of private cars. ...We consider it more desirable for an enterprise to build a holiday home where all of its workers can spend their holidays, than to increase wages so that a few workers can build their own holiday homes" (*Free Hungarian Trade Unions*, April, 1975: 17).

Chapter 3

Birth of the Unemployment Taboo and Its Defense in Early Reforms

The Hungarian revolution of 1956 was brutally suppressed, but its aftershocks transformed Hungarian politics and society. Armed citizens tore down statues of Stalin and fought pitched street battles with security forces and Soviet troops.[1] Radical reform-minded Communists briefly took control of the government and declared neutrality and independence from the Warsaw Bloc. Among the momentous changes was a fundamental alteration in the political meaning of unemployment.

A central argument of this book is that states reverse-engineer the policy formulations that frame the social problem of unemployment according to the particular kind of employment they intend to advance. This chapter shows that the Hungarian Communist Party's taboo against unemployment, far from being an inalienable system-feature of communism, instead derived from the politics of de-Stalinization. The concept of unemployment was reconstructed in the context of a new social contract between the Party and the governed, an implicit agreement which made state employment the chief nexus of citizenship and social control.

Three well-established insights about state-socialism support this argument. First, a common process of de-Stalinization took place across Eastern Europe that instituted some form of reciprocal and implicit social compromise between regime and populace. Secondly, in the Communist social contract "work"—and especially work in state-run industry—was accorded a special symbolic and strategic importance as both a redemptive virtue and a mechanism for distributing state largess. Thirdly, and especially in reformist economies such as post-1956 Hungary, the state's attitude toward different kinds of work arrangements changed significantly over time.

This chapter is organized in two parts. The first half integrates the established insights discussed above with archival research and secondary source materials in order to understand the changing politics of unemployment in Hungary immediately after 1956. The second part shows how the taboo against unemployment was maintained in the face of economic reforms of the 1960s known as the New Economic Mechanism. It is shown that many measures to avoid unemployment reinforced the prevailing model of employment, but others set the stage for subsequent erosion of this employment model.

Birth of the Unemployment Taboo

This section outlines how the taboo against unemployment arose, what it meant, and how it was defended. The uprising of 1956 led to widespread unemployment that the regime then abruptly declared to have eradicated. This chapter shows how the political commitment against unemployment arose from the new political compromise that arose after 1956. The "eradication of unemployment" did not mean that jobs were readily available to all. Instead it guaranteed privileged stability for a particular kind of prototypical employment.

Prologue: Unemployment and the Uprising of 1956

After the uprising of 1956 Soviet tanks restored order and installed new political leadership that used harsh political repression to consolidate power. Unemployment was a significant problem after 1956 because production was disrupted and a long general strike against the Soviet occupation paralyzed many areas of the economy and left many thousands jobless. In dealing with the widespread work stoppages, production halts and materials shortages, many workers were placed on part-time work while others were put on compulsory vacation. Exact figures on the total number of jobless at the height of 1956 are unclear, but the largest Party newspaper reported that their numbers had "fallen to less than 100 thousand" at the beginning of 1957, and quickly declined thereafter.[2] In a statement that exhibits the dominant view at the time, the official trade union proclaimed that, "As soon as coal output rises, there will be more power; and more power means more jobs, and, consequently, the sooner there are more jobs, the sooner the temporary drop in the living standard will end".[3] Unemployment was viewed as a politically acceptable production bottleneck.

   The problem of unemployment was defined in terms of the need to improve planning and thus many jobs were actually cut in state administrative ranks which in recent years had swelled to one administrator for every four manual workers in Hungarian industry.[4] The state administrative workforce was cut by 20,000 in 1957 and 4,555 offices were converted into residential living quarters. According to the official trade union,

> The long overdue cutting of a redundant bureaucratic apparatus and the economic effects of the counterrevolutionary rising are now producing, temporarily, comparatively high unemployment figures in this country. However, Hungary is a socialist country, and, consequently, should be able, through the planned development of her industry and agriculture, to put an end to unemployment within a short space of time. Meanwhile, the workers who lose their jobs have to be provided for, and the government is determined to the necessary steps to do so.[5]

The other motive for dismissing these governmental workers was that many civil servants had actively supported the uprising and were therefore regarded as politically compromised. In similar fashion the Communists had been willing to dismiss disloyal public servants who had been on their infamous "B-list" during the middle to late 1940s when they first gained control of the Interior Ministry (Baksay, 1983). In neither case did the Party view the creation of additional unemployment as too high a political price or an absolute violation of Communist ideals.

Unemployment in 1956-57 resulted from production bottlenecks that the Party attributed to "counter-revolutionaries" and "imperialist agitators" who supposedly caused the uprising. According to András Hegedüs, the former prime minister of the early 1950s, in the chaotic aftermath of 1956 the regime evoked the specter of mass unemployment in an attempt to scare people into line.[6] As the Party was clearly not the cause, this joblessness could readily be recognized as unemployment. This interpretation fit well with the Party's notion of unemployment-as-production-problem that, as the previous chapter showed, had portrayed unemployment in the early 1950s as a temporary byproduct of industrial progress. The socialist economy had been temporarily set back by its enemies and would have to be rebuilt. Work patterns had similarly come less to resemble the socialist prototype of employment. Total levels of employment in the economy had lost 69,000 people that fled retribution through temporarily open borders (Berend, 1985). In the few months of revolutionary upheaval the number of private peasants had jumped back to their 1949 levels. About forty percent of agricultural collectives had disbanded and half of agricultural workers simply left their cooperatives (Róna-Tas, 1997: 61).

Some extraordinary social benefits were created to address the pain of economic turmoil. Severance packages were increased from two weeks pay to six weeks of average earnings, plus five percent per year of service up to average earnings. Many dismissed as the result of government decrees and their dependents were deemed as deserving of social insurance services and benefits such as health care and family support for up to a year—which they would not of otherwise been eligible for without state employment. Local labor exchanges were once again established to place job-seekers, 63,200 of whom were registered in February 1957.[7] In addition to the severance pay and social coverage, cash benefits to discharged workers were instituted amounting to thirty percent of earnings paid for up to six months. The low level of payments and administrative difficulty of showing that work could not be found dissuaded all but about 100 people from actually drawing from this program over the next twenty-seven years.[8] Separate provision was made for enterprises to temporarily lay-off workers for at most three months at half wages, and a new category of four-to-six hour daily jobs were introduced to help those having trouble finding work. This addressed an ongoing source of previously unrecognized unemployment. Children under sixteen years old were forbidden to work but many did not enter vocational or secondary school and were left in legal limbo.[9] Provision was even made for some unemployed to set up independent businesses.[10]

An important legacy of the consolidation period after 1956 was that in the face of mounting unemployment, the state diverted active earners into forms of inactive earning. In the face of intense political pressures the boundaries defining employment were relaxed. A wider range of activities were regarded as legitimate employment, and the range of protected exemptions for legitimately not working was extended. Western governments have also been known to ease employment pressures through policies such as disability pensions that reduce effective labor supply. But whereas in market economies the supply of labor is conceptually viewed as a prior constraint, the Hungarian Communists instead saw the distribution between active earners and inactive workers as a normal instrument of planning. During the mass joblessness that followed 1956 in Hungary the pension age was reduced from 55 to 53 for women and from 60 to 58 for men. Many pensioners who were still working because of the inadequacies of their pre-1954 pension law were permitted to retire on the more favorable new terms. Women made up about half of the unemployed and were most difficult to re-employ. "On the other hand", it was reported that, "there [wa]s almost an unlimited number of jobs for skilled workers and unskilled male laborers".[11] By the time of the Nineteenth Party Congress in 1958 unemployment was no longer viewed as a pressing problem.

The resolution passed at this congress to increase labor participation is telling in the way it defines full employment.

> In the interest of ensuring full employment for the population, more opportunities should be given to young people, especially girls. ...We should also make an effort to secure shorter working hours for youth, pensioners still wishing to work, etc.[12]

Recall that girls, pensioners and youth are groups that are more likely to be out of the labor force and harder to employ. Under Western conceptualizations these groups would be described as having less "labor force attachment" and policies that brought these groups into the active labor pool would be viewed as *increasing* unemployment pressures because many of these workers would have trouble finding jobs. But in Hungary the idea of full employment explicitly did not presume a fixed labor pool and was instead synonymous with greater *total* employment. Until the politics of employment changed, unemployment still meant not enough people working in state priority industries.

The Meaning of "Unemployment": What about Automation and Seasonal Work?

What was meant when the Party claimed to have eradicated unemployment? What kinds of situations were included and which kinds of people were excluded? We can best understand what was distinct about the concept of unemployment after 1956 by examining how the regime purported to eradicate forms of unemployment that we are accustomed to considering unavoidable: that is, the displacement and disruptions from automation, seasonal work stoppages, and "frictional" unemployment caused by job-switching. It is not the case simply that communism eradicated unemployment by restricting its definition since, as in the case of seasonal workers who were temporarily out of work, sometimes the communist definition included as unemployed situations that contemporary Western categories would not.

Until 1968 technological change was not viewed as a cause for unemployment because production levels could always be increased to employ more workers. Workers replaced by automation could, at least conceivably, always be utilized to further increase output. One example in the Party trade union literature is an article titled "The Machine is our Friend" which chronicles the story of a food packaging plant where mechanization made many workers redundant. Even though there were labor shortages elsewhere, there was a commitment to avoid dismissals. "The redundant workers would soon find new jobs as plenty are to be had in Hungary. But a new job and the loss of the old one always causes much inconvenience and a feeling of insecurity".[13] Eventually new orders were found and the staff was increased with reduced hours and the same pay. Another article titled, "Automation—A Boon to the Workers" tells of a rubber manufacturing plant where many workers' jobs were replaced by machines.

> The mechanization of the factory will be carried on along the principles laid down by socialism. When factories in the capitalist countries are geared for automation, thousand of workers lose their jobs and find themselves out on the streets swelling the number of the unemployed. For this reason automation is an enemy of the working people in capitalist countries. ...We in the Rubber Manufacturing Works are mechanizing according to the rules of socialism. Automation has a direct effect on the lives of the workers under socialism too, but in the opposite way to that of capitalism. Here the workers are happy about each new machine or any new equipment. They look on these as new 'friends' because they know that with the installation of these new machines their work will become lighter and easier, and raise their standard of living.[14]

Instead of laying workers off, their working hours were reduced and the added productivity was distributed through profit-sharing and for new amenities at the workplace.

The eradication of seasonal unemployment was similarly predicated upon a belief in ever-increasing growth and productivity through planning. Seasonal work was common throughout Hungary because the economy remained largely agricultural and construction traditionally paused during the harsh winter. As late as 1965 over forty-two percent of state farm workers during harvest times were either seasonal or on temporary contracts.[15] These workers migrated back to urban industrial work or to their rural cooperatives during the slack season. The average manpower requirements in May or September were almost twice as high as in January. Even within a given month the requirements could greatly fluctuate with the natural production process and weather. At peak times the working day was sometimes extended to 12 hours while in the winter work might be far less than 8 hours. In the early 1960s, 200,000 to 300,000 workers were required to round out seasonal fluctuations for higher demand. Planners were confident that mechanization would lessen these levels of fluctuation (Timár, 1966).

One Communist trade union article titled, "We Work All Year Round" described how proper planning overcame seasonal employment bottlenecks in construction as a victory over unemployment.

> [U]nemployment has ceased in our country once and for all, and the majority of building workers work at their trade all winter, ...The leaders of the building trades this year, and in the past years as well, made sure that the buildings that were far enough advanced had roofs put on them, windows put in, the heating system completed and steam engines installed to enable the workers—the plasterers, electricians and other workers—to stay at their jobs all winter. Hence with proper foresight and organization there need be no stoppage of work for the majority of building workers.[16]

Reportedly only ten percent of building trade workers were forced to stop for even a short period in 1960. New regulations required state and cooperative construction projects to complete roof, window and heating work by mid-November. All building workers, as well as gravel and rock extraction workers, received a seasonal allowance of an additional fifteen percent of yearly wages regardless of work stoppage.

Unemployment was viewed as wasteful and unnecessary in the context of seasonal and technological changes because, in explicit contrast to the irrationality of capitalism, market demands did not have to constrain socialist production decisions. Unemployment was conceived against an inherited vision of the boundless possibilities social socialist production that were famously laid down in Chairman Rákosi famous 1950 quip, "[W]here is the maximum to building construction? To this I replied: the sky is the limit. There are no such limits of the planned building of Socialism, no such boundaries exist as did under capitalism. In this also lies the difference between Socialism and capitalism".[17] Unemployment—viewed as largely synonymous with unutilized labor resources—was seen to exist only to the extent that scientific planning had not yet made use of the slack. But this does not explain how antagonism against unemployment emerged as a priority in its own right.

The New Social Contract of Kádárism: Unemployment as Political Taboo

How did the politics and policies following 1956 congeal to make the eradication of unemployment a priority and precondition for political stability? After 1956 a new political compromise arose between the Party and the populace. János Kádár, an official loyal to the Soviets but less associated with Moscow, was appointed the new Chairman of the Hungarian Communist Party. For the next thirty years in which Kádár remained at the Party helm the memory of the revolution hung over the regime. Denunciations of the previous leadership, revelations about Stalin's abuses, and the suppression of popular uprising by a foreign army had demoralized Party membership and by the end of 1956 had reduced its numbers to 416,000—less than half the numbers before the revolt two months earlier (Róna-Tas, 1997: 91). If the events of 1956 had shown anything it was that political stability required more than coercion and the secret police; some degree of public satisfaction and legitimacy were necessary. The Party thus sought to expand and reinvigorate its popular base.

The major policy resolution after the uprising in December of 1956 denounced the pre-1956 "ruling clique's disregard for the rise of working people's living standards" (Berend, 1990: 31). In a 1958 speech to the Ironworkers' Congress, Kádár explained, "We have learned that socialism cannot be built without the support of the masses. And raising the living standards is part and parcel of socialist construction".[18] Party documents from this time began to refer to the state's "provisioning responsibility" (*ellátási kötelezettség*).[19] This was a distinct break from the previous ideas of the Party that had portrayed consumption as something to be nobly deferred. State wages were increased 11.4 percent in 1956 and a further 17.9 percent in 1957, even though the existing five-year plan had originally sought average gains of less than five percent for those years (Adam, 1984: 234). Economic policies turned decidedly more pro-consumption, including a renewed emphasis on the production of consumer durables and a steady growth in pensions and other, mostly employment-based, social benefits. The Party still preferred "social consumption", like railroads, but boosting living standards became an end in itself.

Kádárism, as it came to be known, was an implicit social compromise. The party-state ensured rising living standards in exchange for political quiescence. The class war was officially declared to be over and the state increasingly came to tolerate informal initiatives that fell outside the law so long as they did not threaten Communist rule. Stalin's stated principle that "those who are not with us are against us" was replaced by Kádár's, "those who are not against us are with us". Citizens could retreat to their domestic life but this placed increased importance on the employment relationship as the nexus of political life: an ongoing connection where Hungarians received propaganda, participated in works councils, and were provided with basic benefits. Worker involvement in the factory was intended to boost, not only productivity and work effort, but also to foster cooperative political attitudes and an attachment to socialism (Bielasiak, 1981: 97, Hethy and Mako, 1979: 300-302). *Un*employment took on the new symbolic meaning as state failure to keep up with its side of the social contract.[20]

By "social contract" what is meant in a reciprocal set of expectations between the regime and the broader populace.[21] As an explanatory metaphor, the notion of a social contract is limited by the fact that the regime was not governed by the principles of rule by law or democratic consent. The notion of "contract" also typically evokes a formal agreement, whereas in Hungarian legitimacy was secured by informal social norms (Baxandall, 1994). But social contracts are purely historical fictions even in cases where there is a strong rule of law and democratic governance. It may be clearer to describe the politics of state socialist unemployment in terms of the state's *conceded conventions* or what Kornai refers to as the state's reaction to "grumbling" and other signals that result from "the transgression of social tolerance levels" (Kornai, 1980: 278). A prominent formulation of these state-society relations has also been posed in terms of a "moral economy".[22] Regardless of our choice of wording, the absence of democratic procedures under communism increased the importance of material provision to secure stability and quiescence.[23]

The importance of normalized employment within this new basis for social stability is apparent in Kádár's speech to the National Council of the Patriotic People's Front at the end of 1961 and the subsequent speech at the 1962 Eighth Congress of the Communist Party that initiated what came to be known as the "Alliance policy". Compared to previous militancy the language is strikingly conciliatory in its gestures toward "normalization". Citizen normalcy is primarily anchored in employment status.

> It is normal to figure that ninety-five or ninety-six out of a hundred people are working toward something good and gladly progressing in that direction, rather than the opposite, that we can trust only two out of one hundred. ...[W]hoever is not against the Communist Party is with us. Of course, some of those who share our opinions are more conscientious and also share our long-range aims, another group is with us *in the simple everyday things.*[24]
>
> In the Hungarian People's Republic all people who earn their living by work—and do not spend their days and nights plotting and making bombs—go to their jobs in the morning and work; they are actually with us even if perhaps this is not a conscious attitude on their part. If in the country the general policy is sound, then socialist society is being built in industry, in agriculture, in intellectual life; everyone who works is building a socialist society (Gyurkó, 1985: 121).

The timing of the "Alliance Policy" is also telling with regard to employment. The new social contract was premised upon the workforce's transformation into if not the most advanced forms of socialist work, then at least transitional stages more closely bound to the state. The Alliance policy was initiated only after agriculture had been successfully collectivized, that is, only after independent farmers had been tied to state-organized collective farms. Only then was the phase of "class war" declared to be over.[25]

The new priority accorded to avoiding unemployment can be seen in the Party's changing attitudes toward internal migration. The decision in 1959 to accelerate collectivization of agriculture created an exodus of rural workers into the cities and increased the number of job-seekers (Berend, 1979: 134-36). There were severe shortages for many kinds of workers in urban areas but wide-scale migration from the countryside also fueled joblessness among harder-to-employ unskilled workers. This is exactly the kind of unemployment that was rampant in the earlier post-war era, and restrictions had been avoided because industrialization was celebrated and the Party feared that restriction would intensify labor shortages. But after 1962 restricting this migration became a priority (Fazekas and Köllő, 1990). The Alliance Policy's new endorsement of agricultural cooperatives increased the political sway of Party bosses in the rural cooperatives who were protective of their labor, but the restrictions were made in the name of preventing unemployment.

The category of unemployment was defined as against the condition of labor shortages and growing wage-labor. This conceptual opposition is apparent in the way the triumph over unemployment was trumpeted in this 1960 declaration below. Note that from a contemporary Western perspective, neither an increase in total employment nor labor shortages in some trades are logically inconsistent with the presence of unemployment, even rising unemployment.[26]

> Permanent and seasonal unemployment has ceased which formerly caused so much suffering and a feeling of uncertainty to the workers. The number of employees living on wages and salaries [in 1959] was more than two-and-a-half times higher than before the Liberation [of the Soviets from the Nazis]. In 1938, the number of unemployed was over 200 thousand, that is, one fifth of all employed workers. Nowadays, in the course of single year, in 1959 the increase in the number of wage-earners was almost 120,000. There is a labor shortage in several trades.[27]

It is doubtful that the regime was motivated by concern about income insecurity. This is the same period during which factories were increasingly paying through piecework. But in-house piece workers as well as cooperative members depended on the state for a base salary and for sustenance more generally. Unlike independent peasants, private employees or artisans, they were closely tied to the state.

The strategic redefinition of unemployment was not only a political instrument for managing relations between regime and populace. It was also used to secure power against factions *within* the regime. Once power had been consolidated Kádár purged the administration and police of the most hard-line elements and formally expelled Rákosi, the previous chairman, from the Party in August 1962 (Lomax, 1984: 86). Up until 1962 the power balance between Rákosi and more reformist elements had swung back and forth depending on Moscow's favor and the ability to claim economic victories and political compliance. Specific promises regarding unemployment therefore represented a political liability that could be pointed to as "failures" by competing factions within the Party. Directly after 1956 Kádár did not define success in terms of fighting unemployment because the economy was still struggling against joblessness caused by sabotage and work stoppages. It was only once Kádár had consolidated his own power within the Party that new commitments were clearly defined to conform with the accomplishments of recent past.[28] The proceedings quoted earlier from the Eighth Party Congress were finally published and made public. They went on to formally declare that, "the party invites those sectors of society which previously did not sympathize with and even opposed its objectives, to join in helping to build socialism" (Lomax, 1984: 87). Personnel for technical and managerial positions came to be chosen less and less on Party loyalty and increasingly on expertise and qualifications.

The nature of the new political compromise is eloquently voiced in one Party member's published response to the changed mood. Here the requirement of employment was explicitly connected with state withdrawal from private lives.

At one time... the following tenet was hammered home constantly; he who is not with us is against us. He who does not say yes, says no... . What they say today is that eight hours of work a day is one's duty as a citizen. Design machines, build bridges, drive the tram, heal the sick, plough the land, work more and work better for yourself and the Community so that everyone can have a better life, and then weed your strawberry seedlings, go to the cinema, paint your friend's flat if that's what you want to do. Don't claim a faith if you haven't got it; if you are middle class don't profess to be the proponent of the *Manifesto*, no harm can come to anyone if they don't (Gyurkó, 1985: 119).

The state had become overwhelmingly the employer of its citizens and the new regime came to view the employment relationship as the primary means for exercising power. The advantage of the new strategy was that constant political mobilization and terror were no longer necessary. Róna-Tas helps make clear why the new social arrangement elevated the importance of state employment: "The social order in the last three decades of state socialism was maintained primarily by the institution of universal state employment. Universal state employment was designed to organize society in harmony with the requirements of large-scale production and allow the Party-state to exercise power through its ownership rights rather than through coercion" (Róna-Tas, 1997: 4).[29] By promoting greater participation and labor force attachment among citizens, the state promoted a system of mutual accountability that served the aims of both economic expansion and political stability.

State employment gave the regime the ability, with minimal use of force, to punish and reward, as well as to divide groups through internal status hierarchies. If the gulag was the symbol of state discipline under Rákosi; it was replaced by Kádár with the workbook: the document which workers deposited with their employer when they changed jobs. Their employer entered into the workbook a detailed account of each employee's work history, punishments, and achievements.[30] "People were dependent on their bosses, who acted as representatives of the state. Many actions, from travels abroad to adult education classes, could not be undertaken without written recommendation from workplace supervisors" (Róna-Tas, 1997: 84). Moreover, individuals depended on their status within state employment for employment-based benefits and employment-based social benefits such as pensions, sick pay and maternity leave. All of these kinds of non-wage benefits grew in importance under Kádárism. Employment regulations and social policies thus, institutionalized the Kádárist social contract and gave a heightened political meaning to "unemployment". It is in this context that we can understand how the political importance of guaranteed employment was a product of *de-Stalinization* not Stalinism.[31]

As we shall see, this concept of unemployment would change after the late 1960s once the population had already been largely mobilized into state-run employment. During the reforms of the 1960s planners recognized that future growth would require increasing the productively of labor that was already in use, and that this process might entail dismissals. But these "economic realities" of efficiency did not themselves prompt unemployment, and in many cases dismissed workers were moved to less efficient jobs. On the other hand, the fear of unemployment led the regime to accommodate the new economic circumstances in ways that would indirectly erode the reigning industrial prototype of employment in the future.

Defense of the Unemployment Taboo in Early Economic Reforms

If unemployment supposedly results when inefficiencies become impossible to ignore, then Hungarian unemployment would have appeared in the 1960s. During the preparation of economic reforms objective economic and demographic facts exerted powerful influence on the regime to change its labor policies. The government faced slowing growth, overwhelming evidence of mounting production inefficiencies, and hard currency crises from external trade deficits and foreign indebtedness. Planners clearly warned that the previous growth strategy of mobilizing unutilized resources was exhausted and future gains would only come by reallocating already utilized resources more productively.[32]

From a purely economic point of view, unemployment might have been a logical instrument for the government's perennial campaigns to increase labor productivity, tighten labor discipline, and slow wage growth. Communist economists had even been pioneers in theorizing these effects of unemployment under capitalism.[33] But policy changes were constrained by previous governmental commitments and popular expectations against unemployment. Political compromises embodied in the reform policies averted mass lay-offs of core socialist workers. The compromises in some ways reinforced previous distinctions between the core and periphery in the definition of employment but, as we shall see, also opened the door to future changes in the boundaries of employment that would later erode the taboo against unemployment.

Economic, Demographic and Modernization Pressures

Pressure for economic change built up slowly throughout the 1960s. Economic performance over 1961-65 fell significantly behind the goals of the ambitious Five Year Plan. National income increased by 25 percent instead of the planned 36 percent; agricultural output increased 10 percent instead of 22 percent; real wages increased 9 percent instead of the targeted 16 percent; labor productivity actually declined compared to the previous three-year plan; and trade balances were in deficit over the entire period. Even in industry where central planners gave the highest priority for scarce resources, output targets failed to meet their targeted growth (47 percent against 50 percent) (Berend, 1979: 122). Poor economic performance was often blamed on inadequate labor discipline. For example, the Minister of Labor complained in the major daily newspaper, *Népszabaság* (4 Nov. 1960) about low labor productivity, "In many enterprises slack discipline has led to a loss of eight to ten percent of working time. Owing to the inadequate preparation of labor processes, a further five to ten percent of time is spent on waiting for materials, tools, blueprints and other things" (Radio Free Europe, 1961: 213). According to former Prime Minister András Hegedüs, as early as 1962, there was disconcerted realization among higher Party circles that growth was slowing. It was hard to ignore the growing stockpiles of unusable production goods that were tabulated as growing "unplanned stocks" in the national income accounts. [34] The Public Finance Committee of the Party's Central Committee issued an alarm at a 1962 inquiry on growth of unusable inventories, which they reported had grown from 2.3 percent of the national income in 1959 to 8.5 percent in 1961. [35] First Secretary of the Party, János Kádár in 1962 publicly made the connection between superfluous production and the need to reorganize the workforce, "The manufacture of uneconomical, obsolete products must stop, and the productive capacity thus saved be put to sensible use. This will also require a certain planned regrouping of the work force" (Gyurkó, 1985: 131).

The Party's central leadership was also deeply concerned about the inability to sell these inferior goods on world markets and the unsustainable foreign debts that accumulated as a result. [36] By 1962, Hungary's economy was falling rapidly into debt to non-COMECON countries. Such debts more than doubled from 1.6 million forints in 1959, to 3 million in 1961, and 4.1 million in 1961—despite improvements in global terms of trade for Hungary's export products. In 1962 Hungary spent more on servicing its debt than the total value of its exports. Most of these debts were short-term and some credits had to be rescheduled (Berend, 1990: 114). Berend quotes an internal April 1965 memo of the Party's Political Committee that "the deficit in the balance of trade will impose decisive limitations on economic development not only in 1965 but in the years that follow" (Berend, 1990: 115). The growth of debt to non-communist countries was recognized as a fundamental problem with the highest priority. Berend quotes the Party Public Finances Committee discussion of basic guidelines for the Third Five Year Plan (1965-70) that had been prepared by the National Planning Office. The Committee instructed the Planning Office to draw up new guidelines that would better reflect the urgency of the debt situation. The revised plan should, "take as its basis a halt in the growth of the capitalist foreign exchange debt. ...The decisive criterion of the plan variant should be the requirement of the foreign exchange situation" (Berend, 1990: 138). [37]

Internal reports showed that higher growth could not be realized by the same strategies that had worked in the past. Already as early as the summer of 1958 the Soviet-led international Council for Mutual Economic Assistance had developed and initiated efforts for a shift away from older heavy industries such as steel and coal towards the long-term development of East Europe's backward chemical industries, electronics, telecommunications and precision engineering (Berend and György, 1985: 238). With the exception of bus production these endeavors in new industries met with little success in Hungary.

Up until the mid-1960s industrial growth had been largely achieved by mobilizing new sectors of society into the workforce such as housewives and rural peasants. The participation rate of women of all ages was forecast to reach 51.2 percent up from 47.1 percent in 1970, but that was viewed as a "tight maximum" that could only fall in the future. The birthrate, falling since the beginning of the 1950s, had become the world's lowest by the early 1960s (Iván and Mausecz, 1972, Kiss and Timár, 1971). Although the Party sought to mitigate these demographics through pro-fertility policies, the fact remained that reserves of labor supply had been largely exhausted for the foreseeable future. Growth of industrial employment had increased 5-6 percent annually over the previous 15 years, but slowed to one percent increases in the mid-Sixties. The National Manpower Office had ascertained that by the early 1970s the national workforce would actually be declining due to demographic trends (Frey, 1994). The Party's Central Committee regarded it as a basic fact that the level of employment among men could not go up further and among non-working women the greater part did no want to be in organized employment or were not able (KB Gazdaságpolitikai Osztály, 1976: 2).[38]

In the absence of new manpower reserves, great emphasis was placed on technical development, labor mobility and increased productivity. The Ninth Party Congress of 1966 directed the managers of state enterprises to shed redundant workers. In the so-called yellow-brown book that laid out official directives for enterprise managers, the National Planning Board stated that,

> The enterprises will endeavor to get rid of the appropriate surplus manpower, and moreover, as a consequence of more differentiated earning opportunities, the employees will strive for better paying opportunities to occupy secure workplaces (Fazekas and Köllő, 1990: 31).[39]

Given the gravity of these economic problems and the fact that many of the crises existed in foreign export or debt that represented "hard" budget constraints, unemployment might seem like only a short matter of time. The consensus among elites that past economic strategies were no longer effective and the official embrace of "redundancy" could make the introduction of unemployment seem imminent.

Political Commitments and Resistance

But unemployment was not considered an option. The commitment against unemployment had become a central pillar of post-1956 legitimacy and rested upon the critical place of the employment relationship as a nexus of citizenship between the regime and governed. Therefore, "full employment belonged among the unalienable principles of socialism. It was unthinkable to entertain an idea which might lead to unemployment" (Adam, 1993: 21).[40] Unemployment was first on the list of the social ills of capitalism. The eradication of unemployment was the trophy of the socialist "workers state".[41] Nowhere was the conceptual equation of Communist Party rule with the eradication of unemployment more clear than in the 1962 encyclopedia entry for unemployment (*munkanélküliség*).

> *Unemployment*: The inevitable consequence of capitalist production; deprivation of workers from the means of production so that one section is unable to obtain the opportunity to labor. ... After the overthrow of capitalism, in the course of

building socialism unemployment completely comes to an end. The socialist economy grants every worker the right and the opportunity for those who are able to work" (*Új Magyar Lexicon*, 1962).

Ordinary Hungarians also placed great stake in employment security. When Hungarian workers were asked in 1968 to enumerate the benefits of socialism, they placed full employment atop their lists (Molnar, et al., 1970: 130).[42]

To confront the persistent economic problems the central leadership of the Communist Party established working panels after the December 1964 meeting of the Central Committee for the creation of what was to be called the New Economic Mechanism (NEM).[43] In the initial guidelines for the NEM there was agreement to reduce the number of planning indicators that had to be followed by ministries and enterprises, and that planning should be a more indirect system of material incentives rather than rigid edicts. But there was disagreement over whether the mechanism for coordinating the economy should be conceived of as a regulated socialist market or central planning. The broad contours of what emerged was that the NEM was intended to give state enterprise managers greater autonomy in production decisions and incentives to perform more efficiently. The central planning agency would no longer decide particular wage rates or the number of workers hired by individual enterprises. Wage guidelines were set according to skill classifications and each enterprise was allocated a total wage fund out of which it could pay bonuses and hire workers of different skills as the managerial directors saw fit. Planners hoped that productivity would increase, enterprises would discard unneeded labor reserves, and the displaced workers would be promptly reabsorbed into the newly invigorated economy.

After many years of preparation the NEM was finally introduced at the outset of 1968. One article summing up the debates and anxieties during the preparation of the NEM reflected in a leading Party journal that, "Understandably, the general public is concerned above all with the impact of the reform on working and living conditions. People often ask... whether an incentive to increase profitability will not lead to unemployment" (Szatmári, 1967: 99). Party chairman János Kádár, in a speech before the Central Committee that was later published in the leading Party journal *Társadalmi Szemle*, made clear that the policies of the NEM expressed what was perceived as the boundaries of political acceptability: "I think that sufficient guarantees have been attached to the reform as far as our commitments and capabilities are concerned" (Berend, 1990: 160). Policy outcomes had to take heed of the inherited expectations and social pressures about unemployment.

During the preparation of the NEM the Party leadership took note of anxieties and attempted to reassure people that the new policies would not lead to unemployment. Central Committee secretary Rezső Nyers expounded at a lecture at the Party Academy before the introduction of the reforms how proper planning and gradualism could avert social shocks,

What we envisage, in fact, is a slow, gradual, but systematic redirection of the labor force, and so we shall arrange matters through these measures, and not by allowing the regrouping of the labour force to happen all of a sudden... By this economic policy we can and will make the process free of jolts.[44]

The Party attempted to educate its cadre through special courses at its political academies and then combed through reports about the objections and concerns raised in these sessions (Berend, 1990: 152-53). According to T. Nagy, head of the three man secretariat which steered the work of the reform committees entrusted with preparing the NEM, the first of three basic guidelines for what to avoid in drawing up the reforms was to refrain from unemployment (the other taboos were creating major roles for work councils or antagonizing the bureaucracy).[45] On the three years spent planning the NEM, Kádár would later reflect that, "The maintenance of stability was more important than anything else at the time; the shock of 1956 was still too near" (Gyurkó, 1985: 131).

A chief theme of the NEM was that decentralized decision-making was supposed to improve economic performance. In addition to the anticipated economic benefits, decentralization was also politically attractive in case living standards fell because decentralizing economic decision-making could diminish political backlash. In a November, 1965 Politburo meeting chairman Kádár mused,

> There is something that is related to the economic reform, that responsibility will be better distributed among the government, the local authorities, and the workers than it is now, and I think that will be correct and good. Now, if things are available [people say]: long live the government; if things are not [people say]: down with it! (Róna-Tas, 1997: 96).

These were prescient comments because the decentralization initiated by the NEM would enable the Party to claim in the 1980s that the firm was not responsible for full-employment; only the government was.[46]

Protecting Core Workers

The politics of unemployment were enmeshed in the politics surrounding decentralization. One reason that decentralization was on the reform agenda was that a centralization campaign in 1963-1964 was regarded as having been "excessive". But by amalgamating enterprises the centralization campaign had solidified a powerful coalition, what the Hungarian economist Iván Schweitzer has called the "industrial block":

> That is, the circle of large firms and branch ministries, which jointly elaborate development programs and are in a permanent bargaining relation with the government concerning the financing of the programs. The "industrial block" is able to support the suitability or, moreover, the indispensability of its plans by professional arguments, against which the argument of the government can only be the shortage of financial resources or the deterioration of [international debt] equilibrium (1988: 112).

Because these large firms were effectively given national monopolies over their product lines, they wielded inordinate power. Anyone who wanted a photocopy machine or a bus engine, for instance, could obtain it more or less easily depending on the cooperation or passive resistance of the national monopoly enterprise.[47] In resisting threats to their privileges the industrial lobby found an easy ally and poster-child in the workers at large industrial plants. When the industrial block was threatened by proposals for restructuring or decentralization they waved a potent banner: the evils of throwing exemplary socialist workers out on the street. Preexisting commitments against unemployment were thereby magnified and otherwise unrelated policy issues that might be seen as leading to unemployment indirectly became a threat to the power of the industrial lobby.

Perhaps encouraged by its alliance with the industrial lobby, the politically powerful unions were uncharacteristically active in their resistance to lay-offs for core workers. The official trade union federation, normally a quiescent transmission belt for Party policies and propaganda, complained about being excluded from any role of consultation in the NEM. Some reformist politicians such as Imré Pozsgay called in vain for consultations with the unions. As Berend recounts,

> The leading committee of the trade unions raised fundamental objections from the point of employment. In the debate in the Central Council of Hungarian Trade Unions, it was emphasized, in opposition to the fundamental aim of the reform, that 'institutions for ensuring workers' security of employment must be established. Companies should also have an interest in the stability of manpower (Berend, 1990: 153).

Grumbling among unions over the threat of lay-offs even prompted the Central Committee secretary Rezső Nyers to heretically question whether trade unions' views were genuinely representative of the working class. In an article in spring 1968 commenting on the "likely social and political impact" of the NEM, Nyers reflected that, "the trade unions are above all bodies representing the interests of workers in various occupations. I cannot say that they are bodies representing the interests of the 'workers'." Nyers went so far as to suggest that as representatives of particular occupational interests they could not sufficiently represent the interests of the working class as a whole. The prompt union reply in the leading Party journal *Társadalmi Szemle* reminded Nyers of the Political Committee's resolution of May 10, 1966 that "The trade unions are the class organizations of the working class in power. ...The protection of rightful class interests has remained to this day the prime objective. ...Under the circumstances of [working class] power, the statutes of the Hungarian trade unions also define more general political goals."[48] That the mere threat of unemployment stirred up such fundamental infighting over the basis of working class rule must have made the Party worry about political instability.

During the preparation of the NEM publicly expressed anxieties about unemployment focused on the likely fate of workers in large industrial plants. At the time the workers with the greatest employment problems were unskilled women, young workers leaving school, and gypsies. Ongoing measures to collectivize small independent farmers into larger state-managed farms and cooperatives had also sent droves of workers into the cities and raised the fear of restless urban job-seekers. Nevertheless, political objections about the possibility of unemployment invariably worried about the plight of core factory workers.

The following article appeared months before the introduction of the NEM in the major daily newspaper *Népszabaság* entitled, "What will be their fate?" reflecting on the weight of popular trepidation,

> In previous debates on the possible effects of the new economic mechanism the problem of reorganizing the ...ministries and trusts cropped up recently with growing frequency, but inevitably the problems of reorganizing the factories, *particularly the large works*, were mentioned. Above all, the debates focused on the employment of workers made redundant during the reorganization. There were some who considered the task insoluble in the first place, who judged the situation to be one in which the reorganizations would inevitably cause hundreds of human tragedies and mass-produce bitterness and resentment. Most [people] forecast *the worst problems in manufacturing*. Even well-prepared and highly qualified professionals with managerial experience drew the conclusion that the changes at the higher levels of direction would, by their very nature, filter *down to the factories, where people in their thousands would become redundant.*[49]

The emphasis reflected both the ideological commitment to state industry and the archetypal "socialist" worker,[50] as well as the power of industrial unions and heavy industry within internal Party politics. The loss of political support by these workers would have been especially damaging to the Party's claims to represent the emerging proletariat. These workers were also extraordinarily organized and politically engaged. As Hungarian sociologists working through surveys in the 1970s would later conclude, "Highly skilled men in their thirties and forties are by far the most politically aware and, thus, exercise considerable influence over the vague and uninformed views of their less qualified and younger colleagues" (Pravda, 1981: 45).

In practice there was little danger to the most skilled workers because there were great shortages of skilled labor, even while there were surpluses of unskilled manual laborers. A series of new incentives for managers sought to buttress employment of marginal workers while simultaneously reinforcing their difference with more core workers. Managers were given bonuses to hold down their *total* wage bill and restrictions were placed on each enterprise's *average* wages. The genius of such an arrangement was that enterprises were encouraged to both hold down their total wages and simultaneously to hire more workers, particularly low-wage, unskilled workers who otherwise would have had trouble finding employment. Hiring low-wage unskilled workers brought down the average wage bill for an enterprise and thereby gave managers greater slack in offering high wages to recruit and retain scarce skilled workers (Adam, 1984: 152; Berend and György, 1985). The government favored such a policy because it depressed the growth of total wages and forced managers who wished to recruit and retain skilled labor with high wages to also hire less-skilled workers at lower wages. This was consistent with the broader strategy that one economist would later refer to as, "the guarantee of workers' job security coupled with their wage insecurity" (Lukács, 1986: 16). In some respects, the employment incentives worked too well. The number of economically active persons in the population grew in 1966-71 by 7.4 percent, almost double the planned 3.8 percent. In response to the excessive (unplanned) increases in employment, the government in 1970 even created a temporary tax against enterprises on employment increases (Adam, 1984: 155).

Both before and after the NEM the Party often actively intervened against the lay-off of core workers. Köllő and Fazekas' study of the Győr-Sopron region, for instance, tells of the Party's resistance to lay-offs at a heavy industrial plant during a 1964-65 campaign for enterprise restructuring. The local Party council during the course of the campaign actively helped to ensure that there would be "internal rearranging" of many workers to increase efficiency. The local council, however, was greatly alarmed about political perils arising from lay-offs. The director of a wheel and carriage factory recounted the attempt at internal reorganization in the following manner.

> In 1964 we wanted a significant reduction of personnel, we tried to get people back into productive work. We met with great difficulty. As soon as the word got out of the factory that there will be an administrative reduction in workforce, such a traffic shot up for the doctors offices that the doctors were forced to work double shifts. Everybody procured a special medical certification that as a result of their health condition they could not accommodate their present job... Then an assessment was undertaken of the factory's development *with the help of the county party committee*. We were held back by these medical certifications. In the assessment it stated that there were over a hundred such certified conditions (Fazekas and Köllő, 1990: fn 97).

The regional party committee's assistance demonstrates how they regarded the lay-offs of these core workers as politically dangerous. Despite official recognition that lay-offs were necessary to increase efficiency, large-scale lay-offs were nonetheless avoided. The county-level Party committee's draft position statement made clear how mass lay-offs were viewed as "inappropriate":

> They had to proclaim that it would not have been a good thing if the December 1964 resolution from those who had become redundant without work were put out on the street between one day and the next, and that we would provide for placement. All the more so this would have been inappropriate because of the hostile propaganda and above all the labor regulations directed against it. We are only able to approve of these measures in one or two enterprises that are able to provide for the placement of these downsized workers. They could only and can only support putting workers out onto the street who are work-shirkers and the slipshod workers. They thought it good that enterprises pay attention to the social viewpoint, not dismissing our working capacity from one day to the next. (County party draft document position statement, 1966, in Fazekas and Köllő, 1990: fn 123.)

A similar series of events occurred a day after the NEM was launched (January 2, 1968). One of the economic executives at the May 1st Garment Factory faced no orders and the conveyor belts were idled. Because "efficiency was endangered" he proposed to dismiss five hundred workers at once.   The proposal, which considerably panicked the workers, was categorically turned down by the regional Central Committee. The general manager, in agreement with the Party and trade union committees of the factory then arranged an order for 40,000 coats which were later purchased by the trade enterprises (*Népszabaság*, 1 July 1970, cited in Soós, 1987: fn 438).

One area where the state took great care with redundancy was in mining. Miners had been one of the staunchest pockets of armed resistance during the 1956 rebellion (Lomax, 1989: 149) and they epitomized the ideal of "socialist man" whose labor powered industrialization. Autarkic development strategies in the 1950s had rapidly expanded coal mining, despite the generally poor quality of Hungarian ore. To improve efficiency in the later part of the 1960s oil deliveries from the USSR were increased and greater use was made of natural gas. In 1967 the number of active mines was reduced from five to two. By 1968 there were generalized plans to diminish the use of coal in favor of cheaper and more efficient burning oil and natural gas. A thousand jobs had to be provided for displaced miners between 1965 and 1975. It was still hoped that miners would be able to continue in their occupation, but arrangements were made to relocate miners in other mines without reducing their incomes and some miners would have to perform other work. According to the general secretary of the Mineworkers union discussing a resolution passed by the government in official consultation with the union,

> The aim was [still] to enable the majority of the employees of the mining industry to continue their activity in mining. Therefore, the mines which have a surplus of labor arranged the transfer of men to mines which had a lack of labor (Hungarian Trade Union News, June, 1968: 8).
>
> New industries and plants were established even before the mining was scaled down. Under these well-planned schemes, new jobs, especially in the iron industry plants, were waiting for the miners by the time the different shafts were closed. Not a single miner was left without a job (Hungarian Trade Union News, June, 1968, p. 5).

According to the newspapers, miners were able to choose from three or four jobs. In one case new production of gas stoves and glass blowing was created in a town where miners had been laid off. The local councils, the Party and the social organs in the various plants were supposed to work together on each individual case.

> They interviewed each miner separately. They had to be reassured that they would suffer no disadvantages, the reasons for the changes had to be explained to them and the precise occupation and job which was needed to suit individual abilities, interests and physical condition, preferably near the place of residence, etc. had to be established... The most delicate problem was that of balancing earnings, was also solved, although not without difficulties. For the period of

one year the state spent millions of forints in support to bring their wages in the
new workplaces up to the level of their earnings in the mines (Hungarian Trade
Union News, June 1968: 5).

It was difficult to relocate the miners in non-mining jobs because their wages were
thirty to fifty percent higher than the average for industrial workers. Resettled
miners were therefore given relocation funds, priority for newly build state
apartments or loans for building their own house. Long-time miners were given
supplementary financial aid or paid supplementary aid for up to a year while they
trained for other work. Miners who took up new occupations maintained the old
favorable conditions for miners' pensions.

Core labor continued to enjoy a privileged position throughout the 1970s.
Whereas from 1968 to 1970 wages increased faster in small enterprises than large
enterprises, the opposite was true in 1971 and 1972. Even these wage increases
were below planned levels, so in March 1973 a wage hike was introduced
specifically for workers and foremen in large scale industry and construction
enterprises (Timár, 1975: 155). As one planner at the time expressed, "The
measure had not only an economic but also a political importance, expressing the
distinguished attention paid to the leading class of society" (J. Timár, 1975: 155).
Despite problems exporting manufactured goods to world markets the principle
persisted that, as then-Deputy Prime Minister Mátyás Timár succinctly
summarized, "The path of development is industrialization: labor is most efficient
in industry" (Timár, 1975: 121).

In the mid-1970s, partly in reaction to the fact that peasant incomes were rising
rapidly on the cooperatives, there was a trend toward reasserting the priority of
"workers" as opposed to peasants. In 1973 a practice from the 1950s was
reintroduced to give preference to the children of manual workers in university
admissions (Berend, 1990: 223). In the leading Party journal, Béla Biszku (second
in rank behind Kádár) emphasized, "One must mention first and foremost as a
deciding characteristic feature that the policy of the party is a *worker policy*"
(Berend, 1990: 222). It was not until the early 1980s that the absolute priority of
core industry would be challenged. According to interviews by Ellen Comisso with
government officials, the turning point was the austerity measures in 1981-1982
which sought to down scale ambitious expansion plans for steel and metallurgy.[51]

Reducing Employment to Avoid Unemployment

Policies were also instituted to mitigate the employment problems of less-core
workers, even though they were not central to debates about unemployment.
Women after the war were concentrated in the kinds of industries that were
downsized to make room for socialist industrialization: activities such as textile,
apparel, wine, retail and education that fell outside the prototype of socialist
employment and commensurately suffered when it came to allocating investment
and wage funds. The kinds of industries that sought to add workers were industries
that discouraged women such as heavy industry (Zimmermann, 1995). Although

the official policy had been to maximize women's participation in the labor force, in practice many of these women had great difficulty finding jobs.

The chief of the Manpower Planning Department in the National Planning Office, János Timár, attested in 1963 that finding a job for highly trained school-leavers was not a problem, but it was for those girls who left their studies early. "The employment of these young unskilled girls is not an easy task, particularly in the countryside where jobs in any event are available only in limited numbers" (Timár, 1966: 50). The employment difficulties of women are confirmed by the statistics on vacancies, job-seekers and placements compiled on the basis of employment offices of the capital and nineteen county towns.[52] Taking women separately, there were far more job-seekers than placements before 1968 and even more job-seekers than vacancies (Timár, 1985: 263).[53] In the male labor market there was a far more favorable ratio between vacancies and job seekers (though always a gap of 10,000 to 40,000 between the number of job seekers and the number of placements).

Fazekas and Köllő's in-depth study of the Győr-Sopron region confirms how the structure of labor demand and labor supply strongly diverged from one another in the early 1960s. They show that while the greater part of unsatisfied demand was aimed at male professional and semi-skilled workers, on the supply side unskilled young women comprised the greatest part (Fazekas and Köllő, 1990: 94). In the Győr-Sopron region in 1962 60 percent of applications for work in the placement offices were women, compared to 34 percent of the registered vacancies that sought women. There was a 23 percent shortage of men, and a 61 percent excess supply of women. Forty percent of the women seeking work (other Party sources said 50 to 60 percent) did not find work, compared to thirty percent of men (other Party sources say twenty to thirty percent). There was a shortage of industrial students in metalworking and construction while positions in weaving and spinning were so multiply oversubscribed that the hiring enterprises could afford the luxury of proclaiming that girls shorter than 160-cm were not accepted at all as weavers. While there was an excess of people wanting to be schooled for weaving and spinning, many were redirected into construction and metalworking (Fazekas and Köllő, 1990: 95).

Thus the Party was faced with a dilemma. Women were not the prototypical socialist workers, especially relatively unskilled women; but the established official doctrine was that participation of women in the labor force should be maximized. As the planning chief Timár laid out in 1963,

> From the standpoint of employment policy, women, the young, the old and persons partially incapacitated belong to the peripheral area of manpower available to society. [Yet]...Our employment policy is based on the fundamental principle that a precondition for the full emancipation of women is the wide participation of women in socially organized labor. [i.e. outside household] (Timár, 1966: 1).

In light of the problems women had finding employment, policies encouraging women to join the labor force had the unintended consequence of creating a growing pool of job seekers. Even if their marginal position in the labor market meant that women did not constitute "unemployment", their employment difficulties were nonetheless indicative of imperfect planning.

From a political perspective new programs for child-care and maternity leave were a double policy success. They effectively promoted female participation in the paid economy while simultaneously mitigating involuntary joblessness among hard-to-employ young women.   Plans for child leave programs were first elaborated in 1962 in anticipation of the great number of expected school leavers in 1967, the year that child-leave was finally introduced (Timár, 1998: 36n).[54] Maternity leave, which had been extended to five months in 1963, was stretched out as far as three years in 1968.[55] Mothers who stayed at home more than a few months had previously been considered less socially valorous but now enjoyed the stamp of state legitimacy, subsidies, and a guarantee that the same job would be there for them upon return. Seventy to 80 percent of the positions vacated by mothers with small children were filled by female job-seekers who would have otherwise been difficult to employ.[56] According to Erika Horvath, the government considered lowering the retirement age for women but instead paid women to stay home with their children. "It was chiefly the employment of girls that appeared problematic."   The government was, "looking for those conditions that would facilitate the employment of the young workforce as well as increase the inclination of those of child-bearing age to have children" (Horvath, 1986: 15-16, quoted in Goven, 1993: 179).

The government faced a similar dilemma concerning other policies that removed citizens from employment. On the one hand it was politically expedient to ease eligibility and increase generosity in disability, retirement, and sickness benefits.[57] By moving workers out of the workforce these programs reduced the number of citizens for whom the state was obligated to provide employment and freed up job positions for other hard-to-employ job-seekers.[58] But removing citizens from economic activity could also reduce production and compound shortages for scarce categories of workers. The solution was to take advantage of the differences between "work" and "employment": policies were constructed to encourage citizens to exit from employment yet still work.

Policies were introduced to simultaneously expand the workforce and relieve joblessness among the hard-to-employ. Hungarians who had suffered some sickness or accident which partly reduced their ability to work would have been considered a work-shirker in the 1950s, but, due to expanded sickness leave programs in the 1960s, increasingly became legitimate pensioners. In terms of the effect on labor supply, these policies were not fundamentally different from the kind of emergency measures that were taken after 1956; the difference was that these new programs were *entitlements* that were conceived as permanent and productive measures rather than temporary exigencies. As Timár claimed in 1963, able elders should still have the choice to be active, but they should also have the right to leave the active labor force after a certain number of years at work. The extension of life expectancy and active health does not necessarily mean that the retirement age should be extended. "The retirement age should not be confused with the upper age-limit of working capacity" (Timár, 1966: 58).

Conclusion

The creation of a politically-important employment prototype is critical to explaining the birth of the employment taboo, as well as the kinds of workers who received protection, and the kinds of social policies aimed at less core workers. In the aftermath of the 1956 uprising, state employment became crucial to the new social order because it was the mechanism through which security and rising living standards were exchanged for political quiescence. Employment in industry and mining were particularly important for a number of reasons: these workers embodied the ideal of "socialist man"; heavy industrial interests were politically powerful because they were concentrated and central to the regime's task of rapid industrialization; and industrial workers in large enterprises had to be appeased because they had a history of organized resistance. When core workers were threatened by job loss, generous resources were provided to cushion their transition to other jobs or localities. Other social policies sought to ease job loss among less-core workers while encouraging them to remain in the active labor supply.

Notes

1   The greatest armed resistance in 1956 came from iron, steel and mining centers (Lomax, 1989: 149). This helps explain why after 1956 the Party was wary of abandoning the privileges of heavy industrial workers.
2   *Népszabadság*, Mar. 14, 1957, as reported in Adam, 1984: 120.
3   *Hungarian Trade Union News*, March, 1957: 8
4   In 1941 the ratio had been one-to-nine (Berend, 1990: 11).
5   *Hungarian Trade Union News*, March, 1957: 23.
6   Personal interview at his home in Budapest, January 1997.
7   *Free Hungarian Trade Unions*, April, 1957: 25.
8   Ferge, 1979. See also BBC, Internal affairs, Budapest home office, Feb. 18, 1984. Unemployment compensation was available for those who could not find jobs appropriate to their qualifications and physical and mental abilities. Recipients had to report twice monthly to the placement agencies for job offers (Adam, 1984: 131).
9   *Free Hungarian Trade Unions*, July-Aug 1958: 26.
10 *Free Hungarian Trade Unions*, April 1957.
11 *Free Hungarian Trade Unions*, April 1957.
12 Reported in *Free Hungarian Trade Unions*, Mar-Apr, 1958: 12.
13 *Free Hungarian Trade Unions*, Jan. 1959: 17.
14 *Free Hungarian Trade Unions*, Feb. 1961.
15 *Free Hungarian Trade Unions*, Mar. 1966: 17-18.
16 *Free Hungarian Trade Unions*, Feb. 1961: 4.
17 *Szakszervezeti Tanács* (Information Bulletin), Apr., 1950: 16.

18 *Hungarian Trade Union News*, Jan., 1958: 6. In a speech in January, 1957 Sándor
    Gáspár, Secretary of Hungarian Trade Unions explained clearly, "The fundamental error
    of our economic policy of recent years has been our failure to consider the improvement
    of the working people's living and working conditions as the starting-point when
    drawing up our plans: instead, this main objective was subordinated to the development
    of the productive forces of national economy, and, especially, to an extravagant
    industrialization program. As a result, the working class was made to shoulder a greater
    burden than was necessary, and the improvement of its living conditions did not keep
    pace with the rise in the national income" (ibid., Mar. 1957:2).
19 This point is also observed by (Róna-Tas, 1997).
20 There is an extensive literature on legitimacy and social contracts in Soviet-style
    regimes. Feher concurs that, "even in cases where the system of rule is so assured of
    dominance that its claim to legitimacy plays little or no part in the relationship between
    rulers and subjects, the mode of legitimation retains its significance as the basis for the
    relation of authority between rules and administrative staff and for the structure of rule"
    (Rigby and Feher, 1982: 15). The notion of a social contract does not imply normative
    legitimacy and alternative formulations portray the shift from state terror to grudging
    compliance as one of conceded conventions or moral economy. These are distinct
    theoretical differences but they are not significant for the present inquiry.
21 The notion social contracts between government and governed is in all cases a historical
    fiction, a presumption perhaps rooted in Judeo-Christian traditions of a covenant with
    God. Under state-socialism the implicit social contract may be thought of as "conceded
    conventions" which develop over time, and may be seen in what Kornai refers as the
    state's reaction to 'grumbling' and other signals that result from "the transgression of
    social tolerance levels" (1980: 278). For an overview of social contract literature under
    communism see (Cook, 1993). Other statements of thesis that political compliance and
    quiescence rested on provision of social security do not necessarily do some in terms of
    "social contract". These include: (Breslauer, 1984; Connor, 1988; Hewett, 1988; Rigby
    and Feher, 1982; White, 1986).
22 See also Scott, 1976; Thompson, 1971; Booth, 1993, 1994; Sabel, 1982; Posusney,
    1993. A moral economy perspective differs from a social contract view in that whereas
    East European scholars generally see the social contract as emerging after Stalinist
    terror subsided, moral economy views the restriction on regimes' room to maneuver as
    confronted much earlier (Kopstein, 1996: 421).
23 "Under communist systems consumption and the material satisfaction of the population
    replace free voting, political opposition, and other indices of the degree of political
    support of the government" (Mieczkowski, 1978: 263). Feher and Heller describe this
    more general phenomenon disparagingly as "collective bribery of a nation" through
    "group and individual corruption" (Feher and Heller, 1983: 147-48, 154). Lafay
    indirectly shows that government popularity was sensitive to economic conditions in
    Yugoslavia, the Soviet Union, and even ultra hard-line Albania. While government
    popularity polls are not available, Lafay finds that personnel within the government
    change more frequently when real wages decelerates (Lafay, 1981). Perhaps most
    generalizably, Levi (1998) and Rothstein (1996) have shown in democratic contexts
    how compliance that may not be strictly principled is nonetheless premised on perceived
    feelings of reciprocal justice, what they call "contingent consent".
24 *Magyar Nemzet*, Dec 10, 1961. Quoted in Juhász, 1965: 275-79, emphasis added.
25 The concern for split economic loyalties prompted one Party official to admonish in
    1958, "It is necessary to speak about double lives. During the past years, as a
    consequence of the broad expansion of industry—when the number of persons

subsisting from wages and salaries increased by more than a million—many people came from the countryside, from agriculture, to work in industry who are still unable to break completely from farming. For instance, in the Kecskemét foundry about 60 percent of the workers of the factory own land. ...The situation is similar in the socialist plants of agriculture. Among the 71 workers of the Iregszemcse Agricultural Machine Station 40 have land, from two to ten dacastral holds. Among the working people owning land, only a few are members of co-operative farms. Among the workers of the Varsád Agricultural Machine Station only 10 are members of the co-operative farms. These and similar examples, naturally, do not help the socialist reorganization of agriculture" (*Free Hungarian Trade Unions*, July-Aug. 1958: 6-7).

26 This might be because of demographic trends or because the rise in employment may be overcompensated by new entrants into the labor force. Because labor markets are segmented by skill, gender and geography, labor shortages for some kinds of workers can occur simultaneously with unemployment for others.

27 *Free Hungarian Trade Unions*, Mar-Apr. 1960: 11-12.

28 The greater political importance attached to unemployment also made sense from the experiences and perspective of the new post-1956 leadership in ways that differed from the pre-1956 leadership. The conditions following 1956 not only encouraged collective institutions and group strategies toward a vision of unemployment, but also selected for particular kinds of individual political and career histories. The notion that unemployment sets off political disorder and revolutionary agitation is largely the product of the 1930s and the Depression. The leaders who seized power at the end of World War II missed out on this experience. The pre-1956 leadership came of age during the intense labor shortages of World War I and became professional revolutionaries under the pay of Moscow. During the Depression years they were typically in the Soviet Union or prison. By contrast, the post-1956 leadership had typically been semi-skilled workers who came of age during the Depression and whose illegal Communist Party activities operated under the cover of double membership within the legalized Social Democratic Party. Political organizing within the Social Democratic Party must have encouraged them to see the eradication of unemployment as an independent issue in its own right and a major factor for regime legitimacy.

29 "...It was neither the almighty state nor the power of the dominant class that kept society constantly in line. It was an institution, universal state employment, which was created by the state and maintained inequalities of power and privilege among social groups. Universal state employment was a real institution with hard boundaries. It was not purely a heuristic conceptual device invented by social scientists to comprehend a set of seemingly disparate patterns of social behavior. It was real, in the sense that it was the object of people's aspirations, fears, and rational calculations and the subject of state plans, decrees, and policies. State employment was measured, classified, and policed. It was the central fact of life for almost all adults living under communist rule. It was also unique to communism. No other authoritarian or totalitarian state sought to hire an entire populace" (Róna-Tas, 1997: 4-5).

30 The Soviet Union instituted the practice of a work book for all employees.

31 Distinct but similar processes of de-Stalinization took place throughout Eastern Europe, and in each the employment relationship was critical to the new means of social contract. Other have pointed this out, but without extending the argument to examine how the post-Stalinist meaning of *un*employment differed from the Stalinist era; and how it would be altered by subsequent changes in the political role and definition of employment. Róna-Tas (quoted extensively above) has argued that state employment played a direct role in enforcing post-Stalinist political stability. Heynes, has made a

similar case from studying Poland: "Except for independent farmers, which was something of a Polish anomaly, belonging to the labor force was the very meaning of citizenship under socialism, as both a responsibility and a source of rewards" (Heynes, 1997: 2). The most eloquent statement of employment's role as the nexus of citizenship in the USSR is that of Piirainen, who states, "Work was, self-evidently, the central link through which this communion of the working people and their state was to be achieved. Work was therefore also a central ideological category. The status of the concept of work and the image of the worker as cornerstones of this state cult makes also comprehensible the widely displayed mythology around work and the worker in the Soviet Union, familiar to us from the propagandistic literature and the monumental works of art of socialist realism. Besides a central ideological category, work was also the main social institution through which the people were integrated to the Soviet state. Therefore, every able-bodied member of the Soviet society was obliged to have employment and to participate in the labour process. It was first and foremost through the workplace and the work collective; that the Soviet state exerted control on its subordinates. Employment ...[was] the main locus of social integration in the Soviet Union, and the terms of the tacit social contract were realized through the institution of employment. The other contract party, the working people, was obliged to submit itself to the control and discipline required by the social order and to abstain from open dissent" (Piirainen, 1997: 89-90).

32   These means of growth are respectively known as extensive and intensive growth. On the passage from extensive growth see (Bergson, 1983; Pryor, 1985).

33   See especially Marx, 1978 [1873] and later Kalecki, 1972 [1943]. See also Pollin, 1998 on the basic similarities of these theories with that of Wall Street analysts and Milton Friedman's natural rate of unemployment hypothesis.

34   Personal interview, Budapest, January 1997.

35   (Berend, 1990: 122). These stocks, which were not all superfluous, further increased by an additional 33 percent from 1961-63.

36   The historian Iván Berend has well documented the growing consternation within the Party over export performance. He cites, for instance, a report by István Friss to the Political Committee of the central Party leadership in the spring of 1961, "The number of complaints about quality made against industrial products and particularly products for export has grown... The 500 AR-321-type radio sets offered by Orion in April were not accepted because of quality shortcomings ...15.6 percent of the export deliveries of the Duna Shoe Factory, as much as 54.5 percent from the Fashion Shoe Factory, 16.3 percent of cotton fabrics and 60.3 percent of silk fabrics were declared unfit for export" (Berend, 1990: 125).

37   Similarly Berend and György, 1985 quote from a 1966 report of The National Planning Office that, "the key problem of the industrialization policy [is that] ... ever-increasing industrial exports are needed... Industrial export, however, has to be based on a better structure of production" (cited as from Party archives IPH 288 f.15. April 1966).

38   This demographic fact was, of course, also politically conditioned. Were the government willing to force citizens with enough coercion and deprivation they surely could have induced more men and women into organized employment.

39   Government resolution 2012/1966, excepted from Az MSZMP IX. Kongresszusának határozata a gazdasági mechanizmus reformjáról. MSZMP (1966).

40   "The idea of even temporary unemployment had been sharply rejected in the debates before the reform. Full employment was to remain a basic ideological principle. In other words, the government wanted to solve the problem [of structurally inefficient labor allocation] by keeping full employment but gradually absorbing the superfluous

industrial labour in other fields, particularly the services. The obvious economic disadvantages were outweighed by the social considerations" (Berend, 1990: 180-81). And, "Due to long-lasting propaganda the working classes identify socialism *inter alia* with full employment and see the incorporation of the right to a job in the constitution as something natural and to be taken for granted. Unemployment belongs to a short list of phenomena... which, if present even in mild form, might destabilise the regime" (Adam, 1984: 12-13).

41 "The fear of unemployment... has been fanned as an ill imaginable only in capitalist societies" (Völgyes, 1981: 231).

42 The priority was most strongly expressed by skilled workers. Surveys in Poland taken in 1979 show similar results (Pravda, 1981: 46).

43 The basic guidelines were approved in November 1965 and detailed guidelines were approved in May 1966.

44 Berend, 1990: 181 quoting a lecture at the Party Central Committee's Political Academy, Dec 12, 1966.

45 Kádár was against self-management as a result of the workers' councils' active role in the 1956 uprising. The trade unions were also opposed to self-management because it threatened their position. [According to interview with T. Nagy in Ferber, K. and G. Rejtő, 1988 *Reform (ev)fordulón* (BP: KJK) in (Adam, 1993).]

46 A.O. Hirschman argues that centralization makes the legitimation of new inequalities more difficult because winners and losers are more clearly chosen by the state (Hirschman, 1981).

47 See also Szalai, 1981.

48 This debate, which appeared in *Társadalmi Szemle*, in 1968 is recounted in Berend, 1990: 154.

49 Quoted in Berend, 1990: 155, emphasis added.

50 On the general attitude toward prototypical work under Soviet-type regimes, see Piirainen, 1997, chapter 4.2.

51 Intense bargaining took place over how much—but not whether—to scale back investment (Comisso and Marer, 1986: 259).

52 Such statistics do not express the most dire employment situations in some poorer agricultural regions.

53 In 1964-1966 there were about 330,000 female job-seekers and almost 100 thousand fewer vacancies. There were only about 170,000 female job placements during this time. Female vacancies fell sharply after 1967.

54 The demographic boom was the result of the temporary banning of abortion in the early 1950s.

55 According to Timár the desire to increase female participation was chiefly behind the increase of paid maternity leave in 1963 from three months to five (Timár, 1966).

56 A. Vida Horváth in *Munkaügyi Szemle*, 9 (1971), as cited in (Adam, 1984: 52).

57 In anticipation of possible lay-offs from the NEM, doctors at state firms could as of 1967 categorize workers as being up to 40 percent disabled without any oversight of a review board.

58 See on the principle of "disemployment" as a functional alternative to unemployment through reduction of participation, (Kolberg, 1992).

Chapter 4

Eroding Employment to Avoid Unemployment

For decades socialism had pursued the romance of coal and steel without calculating the opportunities forgone in other activities. By the end of the 1980s they awoke to find their old loves aging, demanding, wasteful, and slovenly (Maier, 1997: 99).

The passage above paints an evocative image of the Communist Party opening their eyes to discover that the kind of socialist employment they once saw as so vital and progressive had become awkward liabilities. This chapter argues, on the contrary, that the changing view of employment resulted largely from new policies, many of which were initiated to avoid unemployment.[1] The cognitive apparatus for benchmarking policy success originally privileged employment in large state industrial enterprises such as coal and steel. But the Party's inherited commitments against unemployment led to political compromises that altered the boundaries of the category of employment. These policies changed the ways that Hungarians worked; and employment came to be conceived and counted in ways that no longer favored the old forms of socialist work. Innovations in the categorization of work became their own independent cause for reconceptualizing the economy.

At the outset of the post-Stalinist period, employment in state industry was regarded as the most productive and most virtuous. It enjoyed great privileges in official ideology, as well in bargaining over allocation of central planning resources, and in the formulation of official statistics. The privileged way state-industrial activity was conceived reinforced the rapid growth of this sector, and visa versa. The "socialist sector" was envisioned as the emerging universal norm of the future.[2] Celebrating the 25th anniversary of the Soviets liberation of Hungary from fascism, Central Party secretary Reszö Nyers could trumpet how industry had increased from a fifth to a third of total employment and how it accounted for two thirds of national income and 80 percent of Hungarian exports (Nyers, 1970: 10). Favorable treatment for workers and enterprises in this part of the economy yielded self-fulfilling evidence of its central importance.

By the early 1980s "core" employment in state industry was still a large portion of the economy, but important compromises eroded and transformed this model of employment and eliminated the self-reinforcing sources of power and privilege. Cooperative and household production came to be embraced as more than a transitory stage toward state-owned enterprise. The importance of work outside the state sector was highlighted by new categories for measuring work and counting workers, as well as by studies of workers "leisure" time in response to reductions in the official working week. Perhaps most importantly, entrepreneurship and independent subcontracting through quasi-independent workshops was embraced in new policies that radically altered the norms of work and the place of the "main job" in citizens' experience and ideology.

Collective Farms and the Household Economy

One of the most important policy changes to be initiated during this period was a series of laws that expanded the boundaries of legitimate and fully recognized work to cooperatives and family-plot agriculture. Before 1956 the Party's stated goal was to collectivize all peasant farms and workshops, to nationalize farmland and merge it into large state-run enterprises as had been accomplished with banking and manufacturing. In the early 1950s all non-farm enterprises employing more than ten workers were nationalized and forced to join state cooperatives as a transitional step toward full-state management. The Party similarly viewed collectivization of agriculture as a first step toward full-scale nationalization into state farms (Berend, 1990: 97; Róna-Tas, 1997). Propaganda campaigns encouraged peasants to collectivize and state distribution agencies gave favorable prices when buying collective produce. Another incentive for peasants was the promise of economies of scale from tilling larger acreage and the shared benefits of modern equipment such as tractors and fertilizers. Governance of the collectives, it was promised, would remain under the democratic control of the peasants and their elected managers.

The "Alliance Policy" of 1963, which set down the terms of the post-1956 social contract, was explicitly made with all "working people" (*dolgozo nep*) (Völgyes, 1981: 225). This was a change from previous practice in which the "working class" referred only to industrial workers. With the advent of the Alliance Policy, "the working people" now included cooperative workers and intellectuals. In 1963 the Trade Union Congress called for an expansion of social insurance services for cooperative workers. A campaign was waged to eliminate the gap in living standards between cooperative members and industrial wage workers. As of 1963 cooperative members were entitled to the same use of hospitals as industrial workers. They also came to enjoy other benefits that had been limited to industrial workers such as: false teeth, treatment in medicinal baths and funeral benefits. The system of maternity aid for cooperative members was unified with that of industrial workers and the differences in family allowances were narrowed (*Hungarian Trade Union News*, May 1967: 16). In 1966 the reforms in preparation for the New Economic Mechanism (NEM) reinterpreted the official status of cooperative property and cooperative production. Lampland describes this shift as follows,

> Formerly, cooperative property had been distinguished from other forms of collective ownership, such as state-owned enterprises or state farms. As group

property owned by a limited number of individuals, it was considered less socialist than enterprises owned by the state, and so by extension, by all citizens of the country. With the reform, cooperatives were accorded full socialist status, and as "legitimate" enterprises, expected to play a greater role in the national economy (1995: 207).

At the Party Congress at the end of 1966 it was recommended that by 1970 the level of social insurance for coop members should be the same as industrial wage-workers. As of 1967 a new pension law for coop workers came into effect which was for the first time adjusted to past income. Pensions were credited for the time cooperative members had spent on the community farm and were adjusted downward for the income that pensioners were receiving from use of their household plot. Living standards of cooperative members were still less than for industrial workers but the gap was smaller than in previous years. Cooperative members for the first time enjoyed benefits that industrial workers had for dependent spouses and pensions for surviving spouses of pensioners (*Hungarian Trade Union News*, May 1967: 17). One way in which agriculture was made more ideologically palatable was by merging cooperatives into much larger cooperative farms. From 1960 to 1975 the agricultural cooperatives were consolidated into about a third of their previous numbers (from 4,507 to 1,598) in order to introduce new technologies and enjoy economies of scale as what was referred to as the "industrialization of cooperatives" (Szőke, 1988).

The NEM also expanded the realm of acceptable work by encouraging complementary non-agricultural production out of the cooperatives and even state farms. Cooperatives sought a way to keep their members busy in the off-season, to supplement incomes, and have insurance against bad harvests. Non-agricultural side businesses run as part of cooperatives and state farms improved cash-flow and provided work during the slow winter months. Traditionally, auxiliary activities on farms had included food and wood processing and home crafts, though over time these side activities sometimes moved into light industry and occasionally became the main source of income for cooperative members.[3] After 1968 non-agricultural production increased about three times as fast as agricultural production on the farms. By 1983 non-agricultural activity accounted for 35 percent of gross output at agricultural cooperatives (Szabó-Medgyesi, 1985: 362).[4]

Household (*háztáji* or literally in the vicinity of the house) production was also elevated to a new status. "Household production was now considered a supplementary or complementary realm to large-scale farming" (Lampland, 1995: 215). Produce raised in household plots could be contracted to state purchasing agencies, in contrast to before when it could only be contracted to the collective. Campaigns encouraged women to increase their household production of eggs and poultry. Families were urged to promise specific quantities of household-based production to contracting farm agencies. Although household production was tolerated and endorsed, its official status remained a topic of controversy. A newspaper interview in 1967 captured the official attitude of simultaneous embrace and intended decline for the household plot,

The household plot—the small-scale production—is based on the fact that the older peasants are gladly occupied with it, partly because it means a supplementary income and partly because they are used to it. But as a new generation replaces the old one, the social conditions of such small-scale household production gradually decrease (Fekete and Varga, 1967: 357-58).[5]

But the portion of household plots in agricultural cooperatives that were producing goods for sale instead increased from 18.5 percent in 1967 to 29.9 percent in 1972, and then 56.9 percent in 1976 (Gábor, 1985: 146).[6] Household agricultural production soared. Families active in small-scale production consumed about half the produce themselves, and sold most of the rest through state and cooperative purchasing organizations. Small-scale producers concentrated their efforts mainly on labor intensive cultivation such as fruits, vegetable, pigs, rabbits and poultry, rather than capital-intensive harvests such as grain (Gábor, 1985: 143). Depending on the product, from 30-80 percent of pigs, chickens or vegetables were *háztáji* (Lampland, 1995: 215). By 1972 small-plot production accounted for nearly thirty percent of all agricultural production and a half or more of all vegetables, fruits, pigs and poultry.[7] Time-budget studies at the time revealed that workers on state collective farms were spending two hours or more a day on this personal supplementary activity (Andorka, 1990).

Although these changes were a significant enlargement of the realm of acceptable work, they did not endorse all work activity done in the home. For one thing the state was wary of the effect of the private economy on the state labor supply (Goven, 1993: 227). It also protected against exploitation in the private sector by requiring that private economic activity could utilize only family labor.[8] Employer-employee relationships were unacceptable while those with family bonds were endorsed (Berend, 1990: 189; Gábor, 1985: 125). Such limits were in keeping with the nature of the post-Stalinist social contract. "The essence of this compromise was a tacit acceptance, even a gradual expansion, of the space for individual autonomy, based on the 'rehabilitation' of the one and only institution which was legitimately independent of direct political control, the family" (Szalai, 1996: 71). So long as businesses were strictly composed of family members they were an acceptable domestic escape from the state rather than a capitalist alternative to it.

In September 1971 the Politburo cracked down on auxiliary businesses, restricting them only to businesses closely related to the main agricultural activities. Subcontracting to larger firms was restricted, including wage limits (Róna-Tas, 1997: 104). There was a further backlash in 1972 against non-agricultural activities in cooperatives. Large industrial firms resented that they poached labor and acted as competitors. A government resolution issued in 1972 prohibited subsidiary workshops from engaging in engineering, chemical, or light industrial activities from independently entering the market for finished products. They could continue such activities only in cooperation with state enterprises and wages could not exceed those performing similar work in state enterprises by more than 10 percent. New ventures were forbidden in Budapest and prohibitive taxes were levied (Soós, 1987: 449 from MSZMP 1048/1972/XII.4).

Many within the party and ministries saw the growth of the agricultural second economy as a vestigial capitalist threat to socialist modernization and the leading role of the (industrial) working class. The balance of power swung toward these factions within the Party leadership in 1974 and supports and incentives for household agricultural production were promptly reduced. A precipitating controversy was set off by a small point in a lecture given at the Institute of Economics of the Hungarian Academy of Sciences in 1974. The controversy surrounded whether household plots deserved the official designation as "socialist" labor.

> The lecturer—probably reflecting the comparatively balanced agricultural policies of the preceding years—suggested the term "socialist small-scale production" for small-scale agricultural production as a whole in order to distinguish it from small-scale production under capitalist conditions. On its publication, the suggested terminology elicited within a few days, a sharply disapproving reaction in *Népszabadság*, the newspaper of the Hungarian Socialist Workers Party. According to the writer, the ownership relations, the organization and the distribution relations in small farms mentioned by the lecturer "are not based on socialist ownership constitution the basis for small-scale production". It is hardly a coincidence that this year was the year of restraint imposed on small-scale agricultural producers in Hungarian agrarian policy (Gábor, 1985: 142).

Shortly thereafter extra restraints and taxation followed on small-scale farming.

These restrictions had the unintended effect of highlighting the vital importance of household production. The new prohibitions and rumors about further measures led to an unsettling decrease in agricultural production, a "food fiasco" that ultimately had to be reversed. The vegetable production of small farms, which had increased 24 percent between 1970 and 1974, declined by 3 percent in 1975. Rumors in 1975 that peasant incomes would be taxed more heavily caused farm output to immediately fall so significantly that fruits and vegetables had to be imported in 1976. New restrictions also caused a fall in the number of new homes and the disappearance of many personal services after 1975. In pig raising, which had also been increasing rapidly, the decrease between 1974 and 1976 was 14 percent (Gábor, 1985: 142). A large and retroactive tax on keeping pigs on household plots was instituted in 1976 inducing peasants to slaughter a large part of their pig stock overnight (Berend, 1990: 237).[9] Villagers across the country butchered thousand of sows and otherwise deprived the city of shipments in protest.[10] Lampland discusses the political significance of this episode,

> For the first time in recent memory, basic staples like potatoes had to be purchased on the international market. Party and state agencies had sown disfavor not only among urban dwellers, who were outraged at the scarcity of food-stuffs and the prices demanded for produce actually available. The 'food fiasco' marked a turning point in the support of the the agricultural second

economy, which for the rest of the socialist period was perceived and portrayed in official forums as an integral component of the socialist sector (Lampland, 1995: 217).

Shortages of foodstuff stuck at the Party's core claim to legitimacy: ensuring rising standards of living. They put to rest escalating rumors by appointing a new minister of agricultural and subsequently calling for help for small farmers at the 1977 meeting of the Central Committee (Comisso and Marer, 1986: 262).

In terms of what activity deserved the designation of "socialist" production, the compromise was suggested to apply the term "socialist" only to household plots of cooperatives or specialized cooperative members but not to other small-scale production institutions. The ensuing compromise in practice was that among small-scale agriculture only the very few remaining peasant-owned farms were not deemed "socialist". The future of household plots had been firmly secured. By the early 1980s small scale agriculture was carried out by 1.7 million families, or about half the population. The total labor input was about 10 percent greater than the total labor input that went into large-scale agriculture (despite the fact that small farms constituted only 13 percent of the area of cultivated land).

Re-Regulating Work Time and Leisure

Another way in which the understanding of employment changed was in the official requirements and regulation of working time and attempts to make leisure more politically edifying. In May 1959 Kruschev had famously predicted that under Communism the work day would be 3-4 hours or shorter than under capitalism, an act which set expectations for the entire Soviet Bloc (White, 1990: 20). The Hungarian Party originally intended that reduced time at work would be spent at organized cultural events that would achieve "political enlightenment", that is, extended political influence through the arts and adult education. This policy stood in a long tradition of attempts to politicize the time outside work. In 1949 a cultural-enlightenment Ministry (*Népmüvészeti Minisztérium*) was established and placed in charge of both culture and education. Cultural aims always took a residual, secondary position to planners' aims for greater supplementary work and overtime but, nonetheless, significant resources were spent on culture houses. The government commissioned major studies of leisure time, including what they claimed to be the world's first studies of how women and pensioners spend their free time. With the NEM reforms attendance at culture houses fell off, as people could more easily work in their spare time (White, 1990: 641). The Party worried over the fact that increased leisure was not spent on cultural activities. In 1976 extensive legislation trumpeted the guaranteed right of every citizen to cultural enlightenment and the *duty* to participate, but over the years the enlightenment activities became increasingly devoid of political content.[11] In 1971 Budapest played host to the Second "International Conference on Profitable Leisure Activities" organized by the Hungarian Society for the Dissemination of Scientific

Knowledge (TIT) under the auspices of UNESCO with cooperation of the European Center for Leisure and Education (ECLE).[12] Hungarian delegates stressed the importance of workers' education for shaping leisure habits.

Of more lasting significance, in the lead-up to the introduction of the NEM plans were made for a steady reduction in the work-week as a way to spread the demand for labor and avoid involuntary joblessness. Up until 1968 the general forty-eight hour week had remained basically unchanged since its establishment in 1945 by the Soviet Military Council. Work time in state employment had initially *increased* under communism. Overtime was rampant as were campaigns to "contribute" additional time such as for "Communist Sunday". The work-week was then reduced four times from 1968 to 1984 to forty or forty-two (depending on the kind of work). Work-week reductions were introduced first in industry and construction, where there was perceived to be a great threat of redundancy. Special measures were introduced early for miners and chemical workers and later on for other workers.[13] Slogans proclaimed that as a result of work-week reductions "greater time will go toward rest, self-education social and family life" (Magyar, 1969).

The results of the government's time studies, however, showed that people did otherwise. The reduced official work week in state enterprises was instead used to increase income-supplementing activities. For men the daily extra half hour of time away from their main jobs was used entirely for extra time spent in income supplementing activities such as auxiliary jobs and tending household plots (Andorka, 1990: 106).[14] It was also no secret why this was the case. As one pair of economists explained in 1972 on why people work in their free time, "It is a fact, that certain objects which are considered part of elementary living conditions (e.g. a flat, and some other durable consumer goods) cannot be procured from today's average basic wages" (Márkus and Hegedüs, 1972: 239). In 1972 the Agricultural Ministry decided for the first time to compile data on household and auxiliary plots as well as state farms and cooperatives.[15] The government was surprised to find 1.7 million such plots and that half of Hungarian households participated in cultivation (Andorka, 1990: 99).

The results of these studies were well known as they were widely cited in the early 1970s by those who were opposed to liberalization of the economy. The statistics were oft-cited as evidence of creeping petite bourgeois materialism.[16] The statistics also fueled debates about growing "rural capitalism" and the enrichment of the peasantry that inspired the backlash on household production precipitating the "food fiasco". Others made a number of points in defense of household production: more workers than peasants were involved in this activity, household production was not especially lucrative compared to the number of hours of work performed, and because these activities were "auxiliaries" performed outside regular hours they were unlike capitalist farming and did not compete with socialist enterprises for labor (Andorka, 1979). The attention to growing forms of work outside of the main job encouraged Hungarians to think of employment as only part of a larger set of income sources.

New Categories for Counting Workers and Work

Three important innovations in the categorization of work became their own independent cause for reconceptualizing the economy. The first was a shift in the census classification of households from class-based statuses to a more varied description of the work performed. The new categories thereby revealed how the prototypical "workers" were a shrinking portion of the population rather than emerging as the inevitable majority. Secondly, the perspectives of planners and officials changed as national income accounts, which initially had only recognized material production, began gradually to count services as adding value to the national economy. Thirdly, a change in the categories for manpower planning highlighted the importance of secondary and supplementary incomes in the national economy and encouraged politicians to consider this income as a source of growth in future planning.

From 1949 to 1969 the Hungarian census grouped households according to social strata on the basis of class relationships. At the time of its creation this system of measurement had been well-suited to show the speedy eradication of landlords and capitalists, and the relative prospering of workers over the backward peasantry. The system became increasingly cumbersome as the final two classifications became increasingly heterogeneous and overlapping. The peasantry mostly became cooperative members and employees on state farms, often with one part of the family working in industrial enterprises while the other member farmed. In 1969 the Central Statistical Office reclassified the population into six groups on the basis of the nature of the work performed. In *worker* households, the head of household was a non-agricultural manual worker and no other member was engaged in agriculture. In *peasant* households the head of household was a manual worker in agriculture and no member was engaged in non-agricultural branch of the economy. In *mixed or double* income households the household head was a manual worker and there were active manual workers in both agriculture and some other branch of the economy. *Intellectual* households had a professional household head. *Self-employed* households had among the members some non-agriculturally engaged self-employed persons such as a private artisan. In *retired* households there was no active earner.

Had the old statistical categories been unaltered they would have only demonstrated that the peasantry and capitalists had not risen from the grave. Instead the new categories showed a troubling trend: that the rise of the "working class" under socialism peaked in the early 1980s. Intellectuals and planners speculated about the implication of the rise of the intellectual class and the eventual emergence of a service-economy. To understand the significance of this reorientation of thinking we might draw parallels to revolutionary workers' movements in Western Europe. Przeworski's study of the rise of social democracy in Western Europe has stressed that the realization that the industrial proletariat were not destined to become a numerical majority indicated not only that they could never count on out-voting the other classes, but also that the industrial working class was not the emergent universal representative of an imminent future.

Although the electoral logic is missing in the Hungarian situation we can nonetheless speculate that those who observed statistics such as those below would no longer see the industrial larger-scale producer as the prototype for conceiving of all employment.

Table 4.1 Distribution of Hungarian households by work performed, 1949-85[17]

Class	1949	1960	1970	1980	1984	1985
Working class	38.0	49.0	54.0	57.0	55.7	55.4
Cooperative farmers	0.0	12.0	18.0	12.0	14.0	13.4
Intellectual workers	8.0	17.0	23.0	28.0	26.3	26.8
Small-scale producers and retailers	51.0	21.0	3.0	3.0	4.0	4.4
Capitalists, landlords	2.0	0.0	---	---	---	---
TOTAL	100.0	100.0	100.0	100.0	100.0	100.0

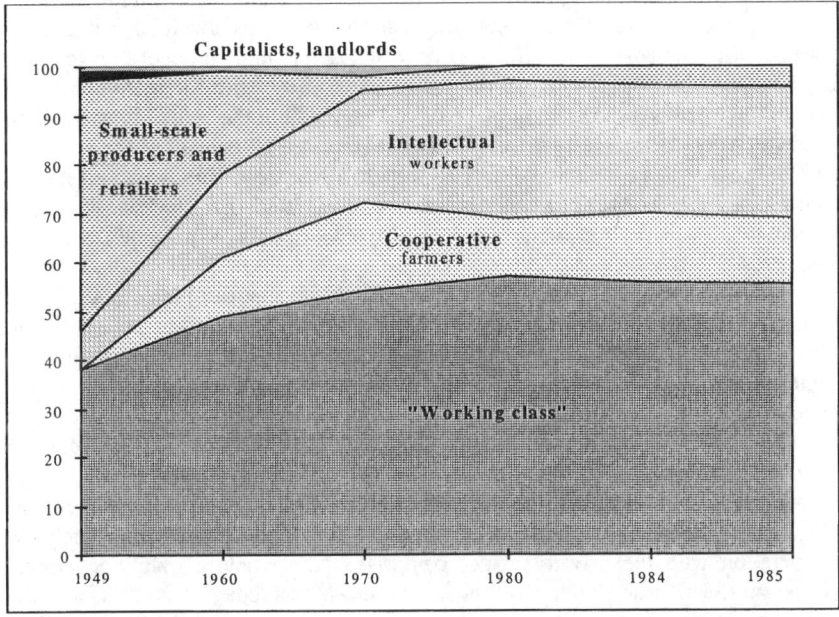

Figure 4.1 Composition of Hungarian working population, 1949-85 (percent)

The second change was in how national income and planning statistics counted the value produced by different kinds of workers. Following Marxist theory and Soviet methods, Hungarian planners and statisticians initially defined national income as consisting only as net value created in *material production*.[18] In conversations about whether to include income from services the issue that inevitably arose was where to draw the line. Some advocated that certain activities such as administration and defense clearly meet human needs and should therefore be recognized in planning statistics. Some argued that all services should be recognized so long as they were commodities. Others argued that services such as domestic labor and sports satisfied crucial human needs and therefore should not be excluded. Still others advocated including whatever services increased living standards or foreign trade. The issue of adding services to national income accounts was first officially discussed as part of the Party's Theoretical Working Group which decided in 1966 not to change the system of national accounts but to conduct trial calculations. The first practical broadening of the concept included productive services such as laundry and passenger transport. Time series of national accounts including services were calculated by the Central Statistical Office and distributed among experts in 1967. The inclusion of services in national accounts more generally did not begin until later. The relative importance of industry to the economy compared to agriculture was also exaggerated as a combined result of holding down consumer food prices and then using final prices as the methodological basis of counting national accounts. As food was a basic means of sustenance, the final prices of agricultural products were kept deliberately low. As economists began to experiment with alternative national accounting methods the leading place of industry within the economy was not so evident. When measured by prices, industry comprised 63 percent of the economy in 1963, whereas agriculture comprised a mere 19 percent. But as one economist noted, "at input-proportionate prices on the other hand, industry's contribution would fall to 38 percent while agriculture would rise to 35 percent" (Schmidt, 1968: 224).

A similar story is to be told in the more detailed manpower planning statistical categories that took individuals rather than families as their unit of measurement. Only starting in 1978 did the official statistics of the central planners include members of agricultural cooperatives as employed (*foglalkoztatottak*) in the socialist sector. In the beginning of the year the Purchasing Power and Employment Group of the Finance Committee (*Pénzügyi Főostály Vásarlóerő és Foglalkoztatási Osztálya*) made a correction in the labor law category of "active earner" to include supplementary private activities in the agricultural cooperatives. Together these groups were to be regarded as the "socialist sector", which "in cooperation with the private sector" comprised "the whole people's economy" (Káposztás, 1979: appendix 1). The Economic Measurement Committee of the Economic Committee (*Közgazdasági Főostály Népgazdasági Mérlgoszálya*) established that this supplemental agricultural employment would be included as part of general data on employment.

The methodological improvement was framed by a June 1978 document from the Central Planning Agency's Regional Social Research Committee titled, "Guiding Principles and Principles for Guiding the Modernization of Manpower Planning" (Káposztás, 1979: 3).[19] Considering the blind spots of the previous categories, one planner Ferenc Káposztás stated, "From the perspective of long-term labor planning policies the active earner concept is the main methodological instrument for working out the balance of labor" (Káposztás, 1979: 12). Included as active earners were those: with an ongoing search for regularly paid work, or who in the given period of time held a labor contract or were official members of a cooperative. Active earners included those in enterprises, institutes, offices, productive cooperatives, self-employed worker, a non-agricultural self-supporting person helping with a family member, an inductee who withdrew from previous active earning, a criminal inmate who had previously been working. In practice the active earner measure was little more than a statistical measure of those considered personnel under labor law.[20]

Káposztás argued that even the amended active earner measure was not fully sufficient because, while recognizing the cooperative sector, it still failed to measure supplementary work and household production outside of the cooperatives. "For long term labor planning the well known category of 'active earners' can be recommended. [But] this by itself is not sufficient" (Káposztás, 1979: 14). He noted that both the old and new methods were unsuitable for observing certain important economic relationships. "This question arises most pronouncedly in agriculture and in the building industry where a large part of capacity is in [workers'] free time (during weekends, holidays)". He noted that great amounts of national income were still unrecognized and escaped the purview of planners.

> In the household and supplementary economy, production has reached an estimated 50 billion forints. Household services of home residences has reached some 15 billion forints. The income in agriculture of some 500 thousand people do not count as playing a role in [official] agricultural employment. In the building industry in construction of dwellings in 1977 the work accomplished was equivalent to that of 70 thousand people working the entire year (Káposztás, 1979: 14).

Finally, the document suggested how a wider vision of work might be of use in social policies aimed at laid-off workers. He writes,

> The relationship must be improved between employment policy and social policy. Labor demand exerts influences on the working out of social-economic arrangements and we must work out arrangements for labor provision, regarding the effect on workplaces and the decisions that must be asserted in the labor plan and predictions. For these, special attention must be placed in particular areas. …The social-economic question of structural transformation of work groups must be examined (Káposztás, 1979: 18-19).

Although these thoughts were buried in an obscure working paper and were not popularly discussed, they are notable both for their prescience and as an indication of subtle but important shifts in the categories of expert opinion. Combined with the innovations in the counting of families and workers evidence of such debates constitute an additional influence on the re-conceptualization of employment.

Entrepreneurship and "Socialist Workshops"

The final and perhaps most important change in the concept of employment was the embrace of entrepreneurship and endorsement of "the second economy" of work activities such as those whose lack of recognition Káposztás bemoaned in 1979.

The previously discussed compromises over auxiliary activities in agriculture paved the way for the toleration and encouragement of other supplementary activities such as home-building and moonlighting on secondary jobs, especially in the under-developed service sector. While estimates and definitions of this informal "second" economy vary, it clearly grew over time and compensated for stagnating wages.[21] By 1982-83 about two-thirds of the population combined wage labor with at least one form of partial self-employment.[22]

The further recognition of legitimate work activity outside of state or cooperative sector (and cooperative household plots) began gradually with the preparation of the NEM. The shift in tone was evident in contrasting proclamations about private artisans from one Party Congress to the next. The official statement endorsed by the Eighth Congress in 1962 proclaimed,

> In the development of our society, the interests of the populations will continue for quite some time to demand that we provide opportunities for private artisans to operate within the framework of our laws. Small private industry… will continue to exist until state and cooperative industry… can supply the increasing demands of the population better than the individually working artisans in all respects. The artisans'… honest labor is an aid to the development of our society. However, the capitalist tendencies appearing within their sphere must be limited. The Party's aim is that private artisans… take an active role in the socialist cooperation of the working people and gradually—of their own free will—take the road to socialism (MSZMP, 1963: 530).

Like work in cooperatives previously, the official stance toward artisans shifted from one of escorting-tolerantly-toward-extinction to one of grudging acceptance of its lasting place in the economy. At the Ninth Party Congress in 1966 artisans were endorsed as serving a necessary role for meeting ongoing social demands,

> Everyone must understand that in the period of building socialism, we are in need of the socially useful work of a certain number of independent artisans and small tradesmen, and since they meet a social demand, they will be necessary in the future as well (MSZMP, 1967: 519).

This place of artisans was explicitly residual. It was not economical for the state to provide many kinds of services. In services the possibility of mechanization and division of labor are limited, so small-scale production may be useful, especially in personal and retail services. From 1968 onwards state-sector workers and pensioners could legally work part time in private small-scale industry and some of the more onerous taxes on this activity were eased. Although the number of formal private workers did not appreciably increase, the semi-legal, informal workers did. Vigorous media campaigns against legal small scale private activities took place periodically during times of conservative backlash, especially in 1972. But the expansion of the category of employment into cooperatives and their non-agricultural business helped create the theoretical and legal space for legitimate entrepreneurial work activity.

The ground work was also laid for recognition of private activity by a political reorganization of the quasi-governmental organs representing non-industrial and non-state enterprises. These ostensible "representative organizations" had previously functioned to oversee and actively discourage such activities. During the late 1960s some of the governmental tasks were taken away from these organs and their powers to issue direct orders to those they purportedly represented instead became "suggesting" directives. They began to actually advocate for the interests they were charged with representing. This is evident in the powers of the representative organizations for agricultural cooperatives, small-scale enterprises and independent craft workers. OKISZ (The National Association of Small Scale Industrial Cooperatives) as of the late 1960s issued mere "suggestions" and the industrial cooperatives could reject these suggestions (although if once they accepted them compliance became mandatory). By 1980 OKISZ had become influential enough within its policy-sphere that it formulated a series of suggestions for encouraging small-cooperatives that was taken up in government decrees (Kónya, 1981). The National organization of Craftsmen (KIOSZ), which in the 1950s had been a governmental organization for eradicating self-employed craft working, assumed more genuine representative functions, although its old-cadre were not replaced until 1976. The national Council on Agricultural Cooperatives (TOT), a new body, was created without powers to impose commands on its constituents. Although these interest representation bodies had little formal power they nonetheless participated in the preparation of decrees, which is the level at which policy decisions were typically most important (Pokol, 1986: 272-273).[23]

Despite the generally conservative politics in the 1970s a number of legal changes further encouraged supplementary work. While the studies of work time revealed the alarming amount of work outside of main employment, this picture disarmed the opposition of the powerful industrial lobby because it was clear that private work activities were done outside and alongside of primary jobs and therefore would not intensify shortages of scarce skilled labor. In 1978 despite official denunciations and prosecutions of unlicensed second-economy activities, the Party's Central Committee concluded that the most likely source of improved living standards in the immediate future was "the utilization of leisure time", a euphemism for time spent working in the second economy (Seleny, 1991). That year restrictions on overtime limits were lifted and workers were permitted a second job at the enterprise where they held their main job. Second jobs could now be equivalent to 50 percent of one's first job's work-time from the previous 30 percent. In September 1979 the Party's Political Committee resolved to amend the labor law, urging that "Within justifiable limits certain restrictions on the employment of manual workers outside their main jobs must be eased".[24]

Ákos Róna-Tas has traced the decision process that led to the official recognition and encouragement of the second economy. He cites a confidential 1980 memo prepared for the Politburo by the Economic Policy Commission. The process of proposing a rejuvenation of the private sector was secretive and circumvented the more normal process of circulating proposals through the ministries. The Politburo discussed and approved a rejuvenation of the private sector in February 1980 and the Twelfth Party Congress endorsed the Politburo decision in March. The eventual new laws were adopted in October 1981 and took effect in January 1982.[25] The 1980 memo noted that three quarters of the workforce already participated in the private sector (an expansive estimate) and laid out a number of goals. The Party leadership hoped that the private sector could fulfill unmet needs for consumer goods and services as well as housing, and that it would be better suited than large centralized enterprises because consumer needs in these areas were more differentiated. The Party hoped that the private sector would tap new sources of capital and labor. By officially recognizing private activities the Party hoped that they could be better planned and regulated compared to when such activities were illegal and invisible.[26] Moreover, the Party hoped that the private sector would absorb workers displaced by restructuring, at least until workers could be reabsorbed into state jobs (Kónya, 1981; Róna-Tas, 1997).[27] According to former Prime Minister András Hegedüs, Party circles during this time often mentioned how the black market had helped the Italian government out of crises in the 1960s.[28] Seleny similarly concludes that, "anticipation of wholesale reduction of subsidies to state firms and the possibility of bankruptcies led reformers to think of private firms in terms of potential job creation in the event of state-firm lay-offs" (Seleny, 1991: 17).

The embrace of supplementary work led to new political expectations and norms around employment, and with them new definitions of unemployment. Interviews conducted by Anna Seleny show that by the early 1980s Party officials conceived of the complementary effects of the second economy as a "helper economy" and "completer economy"; and they were explicitly aware of its benefits for political stability (Seleny, 1994: esp. 458). Seleny reports that,

> The State Wage and Labor Office began to emphasize that employment was not properly only the business of the state-firm and state-cooperative sectors, but of the entire economy—which was already understood as including the small formal private sector in existence before 1982—and that *it was the job of the government to create the conditions which would allow the economy as a whole to supply employment opportunities* (1994: 444, italics added).

By the beginning of the 1980s the official understanding had further evolved to be, "all those employed in 'socially useful' activities, including [those] in the second economy, in households, etc." (Seleny, 1994: 446). "As for ideological consistency, it seemed enough to emphasize that although some of the newly-permissible forms were wholly private, they were all compatible with socialism because they were *partnerships* of individuals" (Seleny, 1991: 18). Encouragement and selective toleration of the second economy became a part of socialist planning.[29]

The second economy expanded the role of market supply and demand, but it would be inaccurate to claim that pressure was created for unemployment by introducing market forces.[30] Because participation in the second economy was parallel to what Hungarians called their "main" job, it did not diminish the supply of labor for state enterprises. On the contrary, the rise of the second economy made it easier for planners to avoid lay-offs. Informal and secondary incomes supplemented the otherwise insufficient social payments, such as pensions and maternity benefits that planners used to move hard-to-employ workers out of the labor force.[31] There was even an official system of labor placement for pensioners and they were exempted from general restrictions on part-time or temporary employment. The growth of secondary incomes was important for unemployment because the normal conception of employment became one in which the "main job" was typically only a piece of one's income earning activities. The proliferation of secondary economic activity marked a shift in what was understood as sufficient employment. Those who were unable to find secondary activities turned increasingly to overtime as their supplement (Galasi, 1985). Consumption and aspirations for consumer durables increased even while wages stagnated. Such aspirations were fed by rising wage inequality, which was itself pushed by the way secondary incomes diluted the incentive effects of primary job wage differentials (Gábor, 1994). A single job came increasingly to be viewed as a form of under-employment to be further supplemented.[32] Thus the state's side of the social contract was no longer simply to provide jobs for all; it was to ensure job opportunities as part of a larger incomes mix for different kinds of work and subsidized non-employment.

Conclusion

The state's commitments against unemployment led the government to compromise its earlier positions on collective farms, household agriculture, entrepreneurship, the distribution of work time, and even the categories for counting the population. Employment in state industry still constituted some kind of an exemplary core, but its centrality had been deeply eroded. Official rhetoric, public policy, and statistics no longer regarded working in large state factories as the strict focus of considerations about work or the creation of value. "Core" employment was no longer the path of the radiant future, nor even the surest means of growth for the next planning cycle. Core jobs were now conceived of as typically situated within a range of governmental social programs and alternative work incomes, including "socialist entrepreneurship". As the next chapter shows, the reconceptualization of employment had profound consequences for the boundaries of politically-feasible unemployment.

Notes

1   "Western countries had to close down their foundries or stabilize production with fewer workers. It made more sense for Western societies with their increasingly high-cost labor to switch to services, to products that required less labor per unit (chemicals), or to the manufacture of value-added items in which the costs of highly qualified labor were more easily recouped, such as specialized steels, machine tools, or electronic assembly" (Maier, 1997: 98). One version of the economic-logic argument holds that the Hungarian Party only gave into the imperatives of economic efficiency once they had joined the World Bank at the beginning of the 1980s and were thereafter hostage to their creditors. No one I spoke to who was close to the actual decision-making could support this view. According to György Noteny who was present at the meetings at the Ministry of Industry, the Bank had recommended massive downsizing at car and bus-making plants but the government rejected this. Instead the first industrial restructuring loans were for programs in plastics that were technologically advanced, already had foreign markets, and where lay-offs were not initiated. The second industrial restructuring loan also was for plastics and the strong agricultural machinery industry. Again the Ministry rejected downsizing at the car and bus plants. According to him, governments have sometimes sought to implicate the Bank for political cover, but Bank policy was never to push aggressively for restructuring flagship firms (Interview at Budapest World Bank office, January 1997).

2   One additional reason that large enterprises were privileged in Hungary was that they simplify the task of central planners (Révész, 1979). For a more general similar argument see also Scott, 1998.

3   Priority industrial enterprises were greatly irritated and cried afoul at industrial production on cooperatives because it broke their monopoly powers (Schweitzer, 1981: 295).

4   It accounted for 47 percent of profit at state farms and 44 percent in agricultural cooperatives (Szabó-Medgyesi, 1985).

5   The interview was with professor Ferenc Erdei in *Népszabaság* on April 7.

6   The other plots included those producing for self-support or not producing significantly.

7   By the early 1980s small scale agriculture constituted nearly 49 percent of total vegetable production, and over half of poultry (52.5 percent), fruit (53.6), and pigs (58.3) (Gábor, 1985: 144).

8   Although as early as 1964 concerns about poor quality and availability of labor prompted the state to begin granting part-time licenses to retirees and state workers. Credential requirements were relaxed, especially in the country-side (Róna-Tas, 1997: 64).

9   The national pig stock fell by 20 percent in 1976.

10 This is a classic example of what James C. Scott calls "everyday resistance".

11 One Hungarian journal in 1984, compiling a survey of press articles on the effects of introducing the 5-day week, criticized the non-intelligentsia for being 'home-centered' and simply watching more television (Gyorgyné, 1984: 48).

12 A similar conference was hosted again in 1977.

13 In 1974 the 44-hour work-week was introduced for about 400,000 workers in commerce and catering without shortening shop hours. About 60 percent of the commercial workers and 80 percent of the sales staff were women (*Hungarian Trade Union News*, April 1974).

14 For women the conversion of leisure into supplementary work was still the trend, though less dramatic.

15 The definition of a household and auxiliary plot was at least 0.14 hectare or land or at least one large animal or at least 50 poultry (Andorka, 1990: 99).

16 The Party mistakenly thought that rising living standards would saturate consumer needs. Berend cites a confidential memo of the National Planning Office in the late 1960s which envisaged that growth of production up to 1980 would "not merely exempt our people wholly from problems of livelihood but allow the attainment of consumption targets... sufficient to satisfy the harmonious physical and intellectual needs of man" (Berend, 1990: 147). Similarly, the Public Finances Committee of the Party Central Committee opined, "According to out present knowledge, the proposed levels of consumption will arrive at a standard of *saturation* on a society-wide scale" (Berend, 1990: 147). For a review of the debate about petite bourgeois values and the materialist tendency of Hungarians to forego children in order to save for consumer items such as automobiles see Goven, 1993: 292-94.

17 Hungarian Central Statistical Office (KSH) Statistical Yearbook (various years).

18 This paragraph draws heavily from Schmidt, 1968.

19 Unfortunately I have been unable to locate this document and the only other information offered by Káposztas is that it concentrated on medium term planning and that its Hungarian title was "Iranyelvek és elvi módszertani útmutató a munkaerőtervezéhez" (OT Pénzügyi és Területi Szoc. Kutató Főost).

20 This is not strictly the case. Labor law considered women on child care leave and pensioners continuing employment after retirement age as employees while they were not counted as "active earners".

21 One well-executed study measures the "illegal economy" not observed by state-centered statistical authorities is (Lackó, 1992). It estimates that as a portion of GDP the illegal economy constituted an additional 13 percent in 1973, 18 percent in 1987, 26 percent in 1988, 31 percent in 1989, 34 percent in 1990. This study is an exceptionally long time-series and its numbers are consistent with other approaches (Árvay and Vértes, 1995), but hidden income is only a rough approximation of the second economy, which was sometimes regulated by the state. See Gábor, 1985; Galasi, 1985; Hankiss, 1990; Sík, 1996.

22 Nineteen percent had only agricultural supplementary income, 27 percent only non-agricultural income; and 21 percent had both (Manchin, 1988: 88-89).

23 Private craftsmen were obliged to be members of the National Organization of Artisans and were supervised by the Ministry of Industry, the Ministry of Finance and the local councils. The number of legal persons pursuing private service and production activities (excluding family helpers) was 116,000 in 1980—99,000 of which were self-employed, and 17,000 their employees. Sixty-two percent of self-employed did so as a primary occupation, 28 percent as a secondary occupation, and 10 percent as pensioners. Part-timers were the only permitted employees. The net value of their production (minus material inputs) constituted an estimated 2.2 percent of GDP (Gábor, 1985: 161).

24 Political Committee Resolutions on Amendment of Labor Law Regulation, September 18, 1979, in *A Magyar Szocialista Makáspárt határozatai és dokumentumai 1975-1980* (Resolutions and Documents of the Hungarian Workers Party, 1975-1980) p. 1069, in (Berend, 1990: 283).

25 While legitimated, the second economy still was greatly restricted. Partnerships could not themselves become legal entities and they were thereby forbidden from healthcare,

child care, most educational or legal services, wholesale trade and advertising (Róna-Tas, 1997: 144). Full-time participation did not increase much by 1986 but there was a large increase in part-time licenses. New business partnership were the fastest growing part of the private sector, and by 1986 they produced one-tenth of GDP according to party documents. They constituted perhaps nine percent of the work force (Róna-Tas, 1997: 146). Only with the 1989 Law on Associations was the private sector formally given equal status. "The 1982 reform changed the basis of entrepreneurship and private business ownership from *privilege*—licenses granted at the discretion of local authorities—to that of a *right* based in government degree and a broad regulatory mechanism" (Seleny, 1991: 6).

26 This view is confirmed by Nyers who describes one surreal slogan for acceptance of the second economy as "with small ventures against the second economy" (Nyers, 1982: 11). Kóvacs also confirms Rona Tas' conjecture that the marketized state economy was expected to bring into regulation the shadow economy: "The survival of the shadow economy also surprised reformers, who had expected that the marketized state economy would make both the 'old mechanisms' and the illegal/informal private entrepreneurship superfluous" (Kovács, 1992: 314).

27 Róna-Tas clearly shows the transformation in the meaning of employment but fails to see the effect this had on the meaning of unemployment. He treats the effects on unemployment only in terms of individual incentives. Róna-Tas says that in terms of lay-offs this "turned out to be medicine for an illness never contracted. The economy was not restructured, and no unemployment occurred" (Róna-Tas, 1997: 151). "If anything, the reform impeded a restructuring of the work force. Internal subcontracting made it possible for state firms to keep their workers, even if these companies were piling up losses. What attracted workers to a firm was not that it was profitable, and therefore able to pay its employees better, but that it was able to provide subcontracting jobs and thus higher pay" (Róna-Tas, 1997: 151-152).

28 Personal interview, Budapest, January 1997.

29 The Party leadership had concrete evidence that the expansion of the second economy bolstered their popularity. In surveys during 1982-83 the lowest level of trust in politics, 25 percent, was found among workers who had no private income of any sort. In general secondary income was associated with higher levels of trust in the system, even if controlled for education and age (Manchin, 1988).

30 For statements of these kind of elective affinities see, for example, Porket and Bornstein, 1978; Bornstein, 1978.

31 The minimum pension has typically been set at or near the minimum wage. The minimum wage has in recent years fallen below the official minimum for sub-poverty subsistence.

32 It is a telling fact that official Party language eschewed the word "poverty" and instead used the phrase "multiply disadvantaged position" (Örkeny, 1994: 174).

Chapter 5

Migrating Birds, Work-Shirkers and the Redefinition of Unemployment

Contrary to notions that unemployment was impossible under Soviet-type regimes, the Hungarian Communist Party introduced policies that explicitly encouraged "unemployment" in the mid-1980s. This was no secret act. Newspapers and television touted the benefits of "socialist unemployment" and the new social programs to aid unemployed workers. The international press buzzed with curious articles about the heresy of unemployment within the Eastern Bloc.[1]

As we've seen from the earlier chapters, there *was* a taboo against unemployment. What had happened to it? How was unemployment introduced when the political order had been virtually premised on job-security? And why did these changes take place in the mid-1980s rather than earlier or later?

Up until this point, it was possible to claim both that there was no unemployment in Hungary; and at the same time, that there had always been unemployment in Hungary. On the one hand, all Hungarians in the active pool of laborers were able to find paid work. But for many Hungarians—who lacked proper skills, failed to conform to stipulated work norms, or had worked in obsolete factories—finding adequate new employment could be a very protracted process with no promise of success. We learn nothing about the unemployment politics of the time by imposing an arbitrary definition of "unemployment" that was not reflected in Hungary's own institutionalized conventions.[2] Instead, we examine the construction of Hungarians' own conception of unemployment and why it changed over time.

At first glance, the government's changing stances on unemployment might seem utterly incoherent. At any given time, some kinds of joblessness were treated as politically unproblematic; while other kinds were treated with the greatest care and regarded as politically dangerous or even intolerable. Some kinds of joblessness were touted as necessary, efficient, and even virtuous; while other forms were criminalized. The Communist Party repeatedly altered its basic principles about what constituted unemployment and why it was unacceptable. And at the very moment when the government advocated mass lay-offs, it simultaneously pursued a campaign to imprison "social parasites" without jobs. Given such apparent incoherence, it is no wonder that scholarship has described the political constraint posed by unemployment in extremely simple and static terms that are themselves inconsistent regarding whether unemployment existed,[3] and how it differed from the West.[4]

This chapter makes sense of changing political expectations about unemployment by showing how they were redefined over time through associated changes in the kinds of work that constituted employment. The government held close to received expectations and commitments, while it embraced new concepts of unemployment as a way to resolve the tensions arising from economic pressures. Changes in the economy created political pressure to redefine employment, but not as simple reflections of new economic "realities". Successive definitions of unemployment in Hungary reflected shifts in the government's dominant views about what employment should be and what strategies would best promote that prototype of employment.

Redefining Unemployment

The crux of the regime's commitment against unemployment was never that everyone could readily find work. Employment problems persisted for groups such as unskilled women and gypsies. Also excluded from the category of unemployment (and job security protections in labor law) were those whose negligence or lack of discipline on the job categorized them as "work-shirkers". But state employees, especially in core industries, enjoyed almost complete job security. Even when the economy was in dire straits and leading officials were determined to profoundly restructure the economy, unemployment was nonetheless regarded as a taboo that could not be violated. As we shall see, the commitment against unemployment only changed with redefinitions of employment.

Politicians, ideologues and planners adjusted to economic and political pressures while attempting to remain consistent with past political commitments. As events changed, the ideology of unemployment could not remain completely static. The redundancy of coal miners, for instance, was a deviation from the old maxim of chairman Rakosi's adage from 1953 that technological unemployment was impossible since in production "the sky is the limit". During parliamentary debate of the new labor code accompanying the New Economic Mechanism (NEM) reforms of the mid-1960s, there were reportedly questions over whether the reforms would violate the constitutional guarantees of the right to work. After some debate the apparently satisfactory answer was that all people had the right to work, but not necessarily to keep the same job (Radnay, 1985: 22).[5] Another principle with continuity to previous modes of justification was that with proper planning jobs could be eliminated without the social shock that characterized unemployment. As János Timár, an economist closely involved with the planning process of the NEM reflected,

> The detailed ideas about the reform emerged in the framework of the *political requirements* ...justified principally by employment policy considerations, that is, to forestall massive dismissals in some industries or enterprises. The viewpoint emerged that—even at the cost of sacrifices—the structural

transformation should be carried out gradually, not suddenly, so as to avoid shocks (Timár, 1975: 54).

The new policy commitments were also consistent with the past in the way that they sharply distinguished between rules that applied, on the one hand, to the core workers that exemplified socialist employment, and, on the other hand, to politically marginalized workers. "The most 'socialist' type of work was employment in the state sector. Work in cooperatives was less positively evaluated, and work in other sectors, be it in self-employment or the household, as strongly depreciated" (Ferge, 1992: 158-59).

Newcomers to the labor market or more marginal workers who lost their jobs did not count as unemployed. A 1988 discussion paper from the State Wage and Labor Office reports that during the 1970s several thousand school leavers were unable to find employment and more than ten thousand casual workers at any time were unable to find work (Állami Bér- és Munkaügyi Hivatal (ABMH), 1988: 6). When an artisan or cooperative farmer had no work to complete, or an unskilled worker was dismissed—especially if she was a girl or a gypsy—their joblessness was also not regarded as unemployment. It was politically unproblematic to dismiss workers who had only been employed for a short duration or who did not keep up work norms. These "migratory bird" job-switchers and "work-shirkers" were not considered unemployed.

The policies toward core workers shifted over time with changing definitions of unemployment. In general it was unacceptable to lay-off workers employed by the state in core employment. Core workers could only be removed without becoming "unemployed" if there were other core-employment positions waiting for them. But, as the previous chapter demonstrated, the importance of core employment was eroded over time as a symbolic indicator of the government's success and as a unique source of dependable livelihood. As the commitment to ensuring employment was redefined to be one of merely ensuring "income opportunities", unemployment also became politically redefined as a situation in which a core worker had been dismissed and lacked a portfolio of alternative sources such as informal work and state social benefits.

Figure 5.1 below illustrates how the political taboo of unemployment came to be defined as against the prevailing model of employment and other recognized sources of income. The symbol **U** demarcates the recognized situation of unemployment; the circles overlapping with state industry indicate other sources of income: non-core work and social programs for inactive workers. Whereas dismissing a core worker for non-disciplinary reasons previously counted as unemployment; in the new understanding of employment, eventually only those core workers who did not have alternative income sources counted as unemployed.

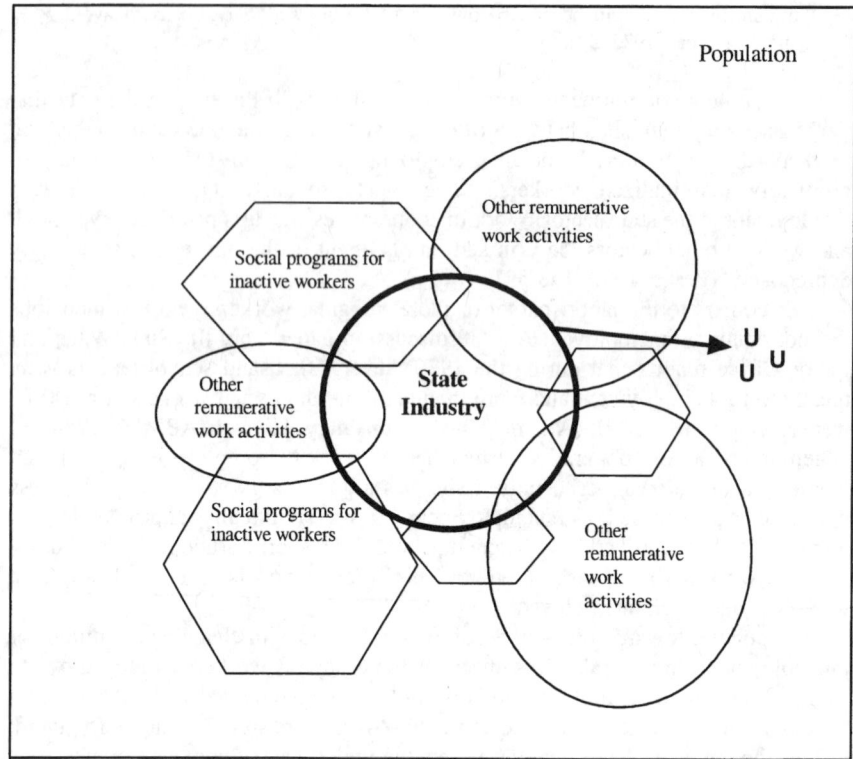

Figure 5.1 The Reform-Communist concept of unemployment

The remainder of this chapter examines various reconceptions of unemployment during the post-Stalinist reform era. It shows first how unemployment was redefined in terms of social policies to regulate the inflow or outflow of marginal workers into the labor force, a desirable two-way flow between households and employment. Next, we see that lay-offs for more core workers were redefined as part of a policy of "planned reallocations of labor". Control of the flow of labor in this context motivated more dismissals and other harsh policies for so-called job switchers and work-shirkers. Finally we see how the acceptance of entrepreneurship as a legitimate form of employment paved the way for the embrace of "socialist unemployment", which was distinguished from its evil capitalist twin by its supposed humane efficiency.

The "Two-Way Flow" between Households and Employment

The view of unemployment during the preparation of the reforms of the "New Economic Mechanism (NEM) can be seen in a prominent article by a leading Hungarian economist, János Timár, entitled "The Level of Employment and its Equilibrium in Socialism".[6] As is typical of the pre-1980s period, the discussion in the paper centers around the meaning of socialist full employment rather than its shadow side—that of socialist *un*employment. "Unemployment" is described as a purely capitalist phenomena, and bourgeois Western economists are berated for considering full employment as consistent with a reserve army of job seekers. Timár distinguishes between two meanings of full employment under socialism. The first equates full employment with total utilization of the labor force and uses policy to achieve the "maximum enlisting of the available labour resources in socially organized activities" (Timár, 1969: 169). This roughly describes the post-war view up to the mid-1960s.[7] He contrasts this view to his own,

> Others—to whom also the present author belongs—interpret full employment as a *particular* state of equilibrium, in which all persons wanting to work can be employed, in other words, the demand for labor is sufficient to absorb the supply on a social scale. To bring about this equilibrium is *one* of the principle objectives of socialist employment policy (Timár, 1969: 169).

Rather than treat labor purely as a factor of production to be mobilized, the latter understanding of full-employment was "social" in the sense of the post-1956 social contract. Socialist full-employment addressed social needs and popular expectations "to offer a job for everybody wanting to work".

Thus, Timár continues, proper socialist employment policy *should* create temporary joblessness as workers change rapidly into new jobs in sectors of the economy where they are most needed. Far from intentionally hiding idle labor behind the factory gates, planners intended to devise an ever-shifting array of incentives for managers to eliminate slack labor (Falus-Szikra, 1979). Yet temporary joblessness, Timár is quick to point out, should not entail even limited unemployment.

How can temporary joblessness *not* entail unemployment? It would be tempting to conclude that Hungarians simply did not count frictional unemployment as part of the category of unemployment.[8] But the answer is more complicated and more political. According to the Hungarian view at the time, under capitalism even purely frictional unemployment still acts to discipline labor and this function is implicit even in the so-called natural unemployment rate. By contrast, it was claimed that socialist workers never needed to fear of finding work when they were jobless. Capitalist economies utilize a labor reserve for the dual functions of adaptability and labor discipline. Socialism, on the other hand, accomplishes the first function through effective planning and rejects the second as "socially irrational".

The state adjusted the labor supply with a wide array of new social programs that provided a more fine-tuned group- and skill-specific approach that could reduce or increase targeted types of labor supply. As János Timár put it in the late 1960s, "a reserve of a different character [from capitalism] is supplied by the continuous, *two-way flow* of labor between the household and the national economy" (Timár, 1969: 173, italics added). This flow was both between state jobs and back and forth to the household economy. Central Committee secretary Rezső Nyers argued that the changed employment flows extended naturally from the exhaustion of reservoirs of unutilized labor.

> Now, with labor reserves nearing exhaustion, ...Raising productivity of labor and efficiency throughout the economy requires a flow of manpower different in character from that of the past years. The importance of migration from agriculture into industry will diminish and the flow of labor within industry and into the service branches will gain in importance. There is no interest in tying labor too much to their jobs, either from the point of view of the technical progress or from that of their own welfare. It is, of course, of decisive importance to secure that the direction of the flow of labor should be in harmony with the interests of the economy as a whole (Nyers, 1970: 12).

As the Deputy Prime Minister Matyás Timár attested in 1975, economists and policy makers discussed the flows between active earners and "the labor reserve (in households, etc.)" (Timár, 1975: 72). The potential labor supply was still envisioned as virtually the entire population, but those for whom it was politically necessary to provide jobs could be accommodated through alternative income sources such as the maternity, retirement, disability, and sickness programs described earlier. These policies redefined who was expected to have employment. For the more marginal members of the labor force—such as gypsies, young unskilled women, or those who work outside the state sector—their joblessness was not unexpected and did not therefore constitute a problem, a shortcoming, or a broken promise. So long as social programs existed to subsidize the joblessness of non-core workers, their lack of employment did not constitute unemployment.

Positive incentives	Negative incentives
• Equalization of rights for women • Equal wages between men and women • Increases in female education • Childcare and arrangements for easing work at home	• Increases in women's incomes • Family benefits nearing minima for maintaining a family • Child welfare system helping those staying at home • Agricultural work binding women to home • Relative reductions in women's wages

Figure 5.2 Policy incentives for regulating the flow of female employment

Central to the state's role in adjusting the two-way flow was the encouragement or discouragement of women's employment. As a 1979 document of the State

Wage and Labor Office argued, male activity was stable over time and the chief source of variability in the labor supply was female participation. Women's employment could be increased or decreased through positive or negative incentives and aids. They were listed as indicated in Figure 5.2 (Káposztás, 1979: 8-9):

When labor shortages appeared in jobs where women were considered appropriate, then incentives could increase the flow of women out of households into employment. In the face of unemployment fears, women could be induced to return to the household, thus freeing up positions for male job-seekers. As István Markó, the Party's regional department head proclaimed at a January 1983 roundtable discussion in the major daily newspaper *Népszabadság*, manipulation of social policies could alleviate strains on full employment.

[F]ull employment in the future is going to be maintained surely with all possibility. The strains on full employment can be diminished in countless ways. The government has many means for which to deploy—successfully I believe— the growing supply or to channel labor to demand, perhaps by encouraging, or not encouraging, pensions or women's employment (*Népszabadság*, 1983).

The state did not have to provide jobs for pensioners, the disabled and maternity recipients; but these groups could still be encouraged to work outside of "core" employment. In September 1971 the Party's Central Committee passed resolutions to promote old-age pensioner employment, called the "rational employment" of pensioners. In January 1972 part-time employment for retirees was encouraged (Fazekas, 1985: 57).[9] The resulting increase in working pensioners is shown in the table below.

Table 5.1 The number of working pensioners in Hungary, 1970-81

Year	Employed pensioners (000s)
1970	262
1972	285
1973	295
1974	320
1975	321
1976	409
1977	383
1978	378
1979	406
1980	408
1981	432

SZOT Társadalombiztositási Főigazgatóság, 1981

Workers with skills that were in high demand were less likely to leave full time employment. They could use their leverage as a scarce commodity to increase wages, reduce work norms, and—after 1982—even find supplementary work opportunities through partnerships that subcontracted to the state enterprise where they were employed.[10] Other more marginal and less scarce kinds of workers were more likely to combine a pension with various forms of supplementary work.[11] Disability pensions were also an active instrument for regulating labor flows. Special workshops were established for disabled workers to gain supplementary incomes and firms were required to set aside a quota of positions for disabled workers.[12] After the 1960s much of the increase in the absolute disability numbers was simply that more people were insured with the inclusion of coops into the larger social security system. When there was special concern about job-losses, access to disability could be eased. In the mine closures in the 1970s, for instance, miners were allowed to receive disability if they had only fifty percent physical incapacity, instead of the ordinary sixty-seven percent threshold.[13] The degree to which disability pensions were functional substitutes for lay-offs was apparent also when the mix of claims tended toward conditions that were more difficult to prove or disprove, such as back pains, depression or rheumatism that involved more of a judgment call on the doctor's part.[14]

Disability claims could increase suddenly with shifts in the labor situation. When workers first caught wind of the possibility of lay-offs they would avoid any claims so that they would not be laid off, reassigned or given poor jobs. But once they knew that mass lay-offs were likely they had a better chance getting their claims accepted if they applied while still employed.[15] Naiser Alajos, the director of the Nation Medical Examination Institute, recalled that during the 1980s he could predict the onset of large-scale lay-offs in an area by the sharp rises in disability claims a month before.[16] On the other hand, during times when labor shortages became particularly severe, such as in 1974-75 efforts were made to restrict the outflow to disability.[17] In 1976 "By restricting health standards an attempt was made to limit the extraordinarily rapid increase in disablement pensions, and measures were passed in order to improve labor rehabilitation [to leave disability]" (Fazekas, 1985: 60). As Figure 5.3 shows, disability claims then slowed until high unemployment in the 1980s. At that point disability was again used as an instrument for minimizing unemployment.

The government deftly used social policy to simultaneously pursue economic goals and help maintain commitments against unemployment. These strategies would not have been politically attractive during the earlier Stalinist era because policy "success" had been too closely linked to increasing the core labor force. Under post-Stalinism such strategies of dis-employment flourished. The creation of new categories of disabled and elderly jobs nonetheless further eroded the prototype of employment by further loosening the association between the employed and those who work.

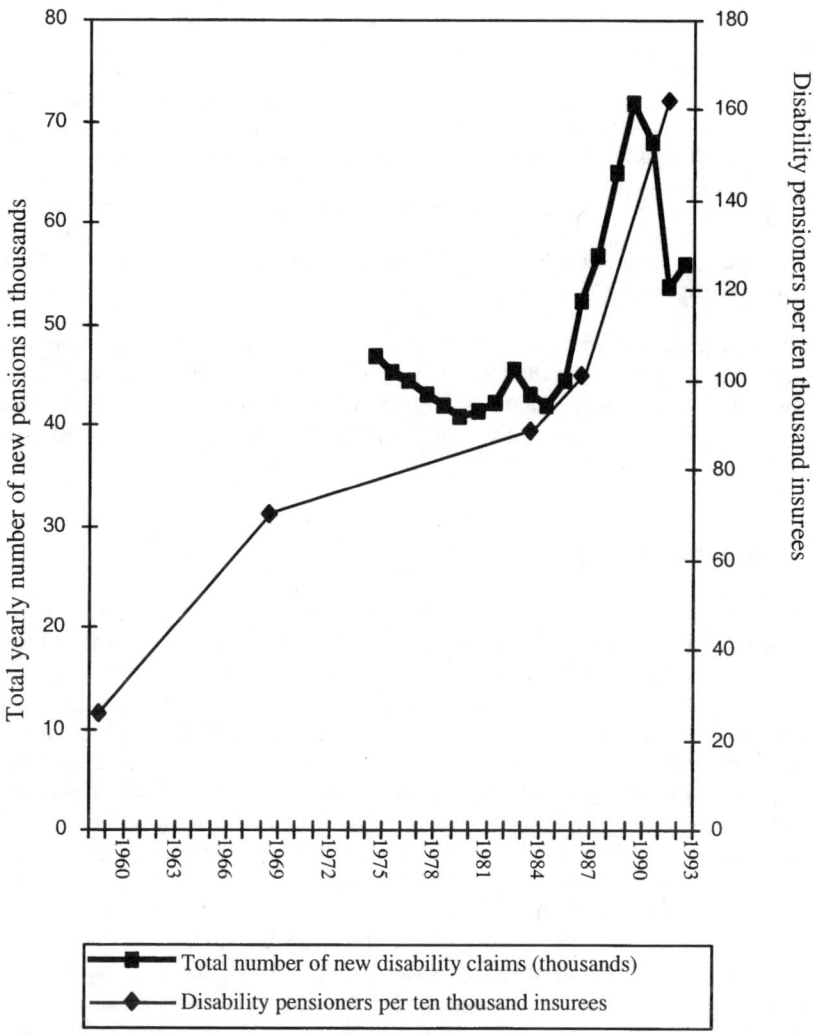

Figure 5.3 Disability claims in Hungary, 1960-94

The two-way-flow concept was a redrawing of the boundaries of state responsibility for joblessness. This logical conclusion was articulated clearly at the end of 1971 after the National Planning Office and an advisory committee completed a major review of manpower planning and living standards policy. A summary of the framework jointly written by many of the experts proclaimed,

> ...*[F]ull employment must be maintained and further developed in a more
> rational way in the future than in the past.* Ensuring full employment is
> primarily the task of the state and council bodies representing social interests,
> while the major task of enterprises and other employing organizations is to
> increase the efficiency and productivity of labor. ...Employers should reassign
> unneeded or unsatisfactory manpower *to other productive places or else dismiss
> the workers.*
> ...The central bodies responsible for full employment – and not the enterprises –
> must see to it that there be satisfactory job opportunities and that everyone be
> able to obtain work suitable to his qualifications and talent (Huszár, et al., 1972:
> 140, emphasis in original).

These principles were eventually condensed into the slogan that full employment
was the responsibility of the state while productivity was the responsibility of the
enterprise. It was acceptable to direct more marginal workers out to the household
economy and its social policy auxiliaries. But the government had greater
obligations to more core workers.

Planned Reallocations

Displacement of state industrial workers took the form of "planned reallocations"
which was distinguished from unemployment because other firms were willing to
take the displaced workers and the workers were protected by special programs
which ensured they did not suffer loss of income or benefits. The planned
reallocations were not merely putting a good spin on surrenders to the dictates of
economic efficiency over politics. On the contrary these lay-offs were the result of
successful lobbying pressure from relatively *less* efficient but politically powerful
larger firms who sought scarce skilled labor from the liquidation of smaller,
generally more efficient enterprises with less political clout. Lay-offs throughout
the 1970s were thus due to the political power of large inefficient enterprises, not
due to their economic failings.

One of the original stated goals of the NEM was to decentralize economic
planning. Direct central planning was supposed to be replaced with planning
indicators, in which enterprises managers were expected to meet certain production
goals but were given greater discretion and responsibility for ensuring productivity
gains. In theory this might have decreased the political power of large enterprises
because they were expected more to manage their business without direct
governmental oversight and assistance. But in the NEM's wake the bargaining
power of the largest, most exemplary socialist enterprises instead increased.
Politics dictated that the largest industrial enterprises did not get liquidated, partly
because of the ideologically privileged position they held, partly because of the
political influence of their leaders, and partly because they simply contained too
many workers to displace. As the managing director at Csepel Iron Works, Vilmos
Garai quipped about the threat of liquidation of his enterprise in 1981, "Everybody
knows that not only parameters, product prices and exchange rates are in question

but also the fate of twenty two thousand employees" (Fazekas and Köllő, 1990: 202, from *Népszabaság*, Aug.7, 1981). Berend quotes the central Party periodical in 1972 as urging that the largest industrial firms be given special status as "priority" enterprises,

> Economic management organs should examine separately, and watch the activities of, the biggest 50 state-owned enterprises which produce the greater part of Hungary's industrial output and, where it is necessary, special measures must be taken to guarantee for them the necessary working conditions (Berend, 1989: 115).

The next year the Council of Ministers took direct central control of some of the largest fifty industrial enterprises, which meant that the enterprises had direct access to governmental dictates and subsidies—even while other enterprises were asked to manage from their own resources. Selection of how many and which enterprises to choose as priority enterprises was not solely based on economics. As one anonymous participant interviewed by Erzébet Szalai explained: the number fifty was chosen mostly because it was a round number, enterprises were chosen to be representative of the various regional interests, and those enterprises which were led by Central Committee members enjoyed a distinct advantage (1982: 33).

Although planning indicators suggested that these priority enterprises were generally less efficient and profitable than average, they had inordinate political importance because they produced approximately half of industrial output and accounted for over 60 percent of exports (Berend, 1989: 115).[18]   Within the National Planning Office the industrial block could rely on political support from the industrial ministries against the encroachments of the Finance or Foreign Trade Ministries.[19] They were also able to protect their interests because they could rely on the ideological positions their enterprises represented as bastions of exemplary workers. This is apparent, for instance, in one press account of a heated district Party meeting about changes at a shipyard and machine factory,

> Referring to the long tradition of these factories as strongholds of the industrial workers, the contributors challenged the efforts which had been directed at the structural transformation of production. ...In their judgment the decisions had brought "difficult times" to their enterprises and had caused uncertainty of existence (Berend, 1989: 117).

One reflection of the exemplary status was that wages of workers in the preferred enterprises had climbed to twenty percent higher than the average wages of non-preferred enterprises by 1975. The National Planning Office and Ministry of Finance offered this justification of that premium, "the wages of the large industrial enterprises' workers not only reflect their individual performance and skill, but the national economic importance of their field of employment as well" (Antal, 1989: 142n). Similarly, at the Eleventh Party Congress in 1975 secretary Béla Biszku admonished, "Development of the large state factories is not simply an economic issue, it is an important constituent of our party policy ...Thereby we are also doing good service in strengthening the class basis of the society building socialism" (Berend, 1990: 212).[20] Through this special designation the conceptual and ideological centrality of these large industrial enterprises was institutionally enshrined and reinforced in public policy.[21]

Politically powerful enterprises created pressure for lay-offs because they were otherwise unable to obtain labor for increased production. The shift into an *intensive* stage of development meant that unutilized labor was no longer available. As the central Party's Economic Committee made clear in 1976, growth could only come from productivity increases and this would require moving workers out of some firms into others.

> The present economy is at a stage of development where new sources of labor have been exhausted and future growth from the rationalization of employment must be from an increase in productivity. In the current situation—that in practice achieved full employment—the objective success of these policies depend upon branch, county and work-skill structures being better planned and scientifically conducted (KB Gazdaságpolitikai Osztály, 1976: 1).

As a result of unusually severe labor shortages in 1974-75 the Central Committee ruled in November, 1975 that

> There is a labor shortage disturbing uninterrupted production and supply within certain industries and jobs. ...The labor demand of up-to-date, productive, profitably exporting dynamically developing big firms should be promoted with the help of planned restructuring of labor. ...The unnecessary employment of labor and "unjustified" job-leaving should definitely be put a stop to (Fazekas, 1985: 60).

The government encouraged labor flows toward preferred enterprises through a variety of measures: by limiting staff increases at non-priority enterprises, by liquidating other factory units and plants, by consolidating units, by prohibiting the placement of factories where they would draw away priority enterprises' labor, by selectively directing job seekers using employment offices, and by limiting the issue of licenses for small enterprises. In 1977 those enterprises scheduled for labor force reduction or liquidation were subject to compulsory placement while hiring was frozen in administrative jobs (Adam, 1984: 179). According to documents of the State Wage and Employment Office, the Party's Central Planning Committee in October 1977 made a decision to focus on structural transformation of employment by promoting the reallocation of manpower (Állami Bér- és Munkaügyi Hivatal (ABMH), 1988).[22] The resulting dismissals, the Party referred to as "planned reallocations", were understood as mergers rather than unemployment, especially because they were the result of labor shortages as opposed to labor gluts.

As a result of centralization and mergers, the number of state-owned industrial enterprises decreased by 48 percent and the number of industrial cooperatives fell by 44 percent from 1960 to 1977 (Kónya, 1981: 77). Between 1962 and 1964 the number of economic units under the direction of the Ministry of Heavy Industry was consolidated from 103 to 38; 126 enterprises of the Ministry of Metallurgy were reorganized into 28 units (Schweitzer, 1981: 293). Between 1979 and July 1985 there were 175 economic entities liquidated, 149 of which without a legal successor. Only five of these enterprises were of the prototypical state-owned form. The liquidated enterprises were overwhelmingly cooperatives, cooperative trusts, joint enterprises, subcontracting partnerships and economic associations rather than firms supervised by ministries and local councils (Voska, 1986: 60). There is strong evidence to show that these mergers followed primarily a political logic rather than dictates of efficiency. The production histories indicate that more dynamic and growing enterprises did not swallow up stagnant ones.[23] On the contrary, the enterprises which incorporated others tended to have been less profitable, more subsidized, and previously had less dynamic output despite enjoying better than average growth in personnel (Laki, 1982).[24] Small enterprises were merged or liquidated at a disproportionately high rate. Almost always the larger enterprise absorbed the smaller one in mergers. Cooperative enterprises were somewhat over-represented among those enterprises that were merged. Industrial enterprises were more likely to be merged or liquidated if they were controlled only by local councils as opposed to politically more powerful Party bodies such as ministries.

Ideologically, dismissals became more palatable after austerity measures imposed in 1978. After years in which the rate of economic growth had been a primary measure of success, the Central Committee decided on December 6th, 1978 to deliberately cool off the economy by restricting investments, imports and domestic demand. As one contemporary observed, "growth" was abandoned as an indicator because they no longer expected progress by that benchmark. "They forecasted temporary stagnation, and moreover a decrease in production in different subsectors of the light and machinery industries. Under these conditions it was impossible to maintain growth as a success indicator" (Laki, 1985: 196).

The Central Committee's resolution declared the need for enterprise closures,

> Enterprises, plants which are not profitable, the activities of which are not in harmony with the interests of the national economy and which are not among the given investment priorities, i.e.: those which cannot be profitable by the means of rationalization, their losses might not be covered by state subsidies. In such cases, the state organs helped by Party and social organizations—as a last solution—have to be determined to deploy their means towards partial or total liquidation.[25]

Dismissals in these liquidations were, however, sharply distinguished from unemployment, first because alternate jobs were available, but also because measures were taken to protect the workers from hardship. One union publication trumpeted its support for these measures and asserted that they were ultimately in the workers' best interest.

There are quite a few workplaces where fewer workers could carry out the tasks and workers have become redundant with the modernization of production. It is in the interest of society for the workers who have become redundant in some enterprises to be employed for production of greatest value to the national economy, through planned reorganization. The trade unions fully support such manpower movements, while they keep in sight both profitability and individual interests. For this is a case of the planned guidance of manpower and not of the dismissals of workers and employees! (*Hungarian Trade Union News*, Nov. 1979).

Mine closures were a high profile example where extraordinary efforts were taken to protect dismissed workers. As described by the Deputy Prime Minister in 1975,

The rationalization of coal mining implies a reduction of employment in mining. The government has worked out a large-scope economic and social operative plan for the employment of the about 40,000 coal-miners to be released. The most important elements of this policy are: creation of new jobs in the mining region affected, complementary payments (for a definite period) to those redirected, in certain cases the payment of compensations, and the earlier retirement of old or disabled workers (M. Timár, 1975: 123).

A similar story is told in a 1976 article in the *Hungarian Trade Union News* entitled, "What Happened to the Workers?" It paints the picture of politically acceptable redundancies in textile factories in Mosonmagyóvár. "No one needed to fear that they would be unable to earn a living, since unemployment is unknown in Hungary and there is actually a shortage of labor". The government arranged that displaced textile workers received in their new jobs the pensions, bonuses, profit share, annual leave, and other amenities as if they still had their old seniority. In the article one official is quoted as saying, "Dissolving the enterprise was an economic problem, but providing for the workers was a political question! We can say that we have solved the problems of two hundred people and guaranteed their future" (*Hungarian Trade Union News*, April, 1976: 14-15). Other articles in a Hungarian union publication also describe similar criteria for addressing "the political question",

Ever since the factories have been in public ownership in Hungary, no one has ever told a worker to take his employment card and go find a job elsewhere because production has been closed down. It has of course happened that out-dated factories have been closed and years ago we began to close coal mines. But even in these cases the state institutes provided for new jobs and retraining for the workers. And the trade unions take care to ensure that their earnings are not lower in the new workplace. At other times and in other places the closing down of superfluous and unprofitable old factories is put off for months until all the workers have found new jobs (*Hungarian Trade Union News*, Apr. 1975: 8).

Structural change in the national economy and economic development always produces manpower movements. ...This leads to a transitional shortage of manpower in one place and redundancy in another. This is partly solved by spontaneous flow of manpower and partly by organized redeployment of workers as happened in several cases in recent years. Such restructuring is always preceded by thoroughly preparations. It can only be carried out when the new workplace has made all preparations to receive the workers. *A fundamental consideration is that the transferred workers must not find themselves in as less favorable position than in their previous workplaces.* The shortage of labor makes it possible for the workers in those workplaces to be closed down to select the job which most suits them from a number of possibilities (*Hungarian Trade Union News*, December 1975: 7).

A 1977 article describes the 1972 reorganization of the Zalaegerszeg Clothing Factory in Western Hungary which even brought in Swiss consultants for the reorganization. One hundred and twenty-seven workers were placed "in reserve" on minimum wages (but without the all important bonuses which comprised a large part of their pay) and filled in when the remaining workers were absent or on temporary leave. Another 1979 article titled "What happened to the hundred and thirty workers?" describes the closing of a foundry at the Csepel Iron and Metal Works located directly outside Budapest.[26] The 130 workers who made crankcases were dispersed among the other 30,000 workers until the reorganization was completed, at which time the article claimed most would return to the old plant. Their old wages were guaranteed during the interim.

Many of these protections were codified in the long-neglected Labor Code that received new attention in light of the dismissals. An article titled, "Where they are most needed: Reorganization—without disadvantages" describes the protections of the Labor Code and the Labor Ministry regulations as follows: Before beginning a manpower reorganization the enterprise must draw up a plan that must be approved by the local trade union. It must specify those who are to be reorganized. "It must also give details on the measures to be taken to ensure that no one is left without a job." Workers transferred within a single plant must be guaranteed their original wages. Travel expenses are also to be paid by an employer if an employee takes a position at a distant work site. "The worker may only be given notice if he has been offered and has refused an opportunity for a transfer in keeping with his qualifications and previous job" (*Hungarian Trade Union News*, June 1981: 5).

The most controversial series of lay-offs from this period is fortunately also the best documented. Károly Fazekas and János Köllő conducted an in-depth study of the nationally prominent lay-offs at the Rába wheelworks enterprise in Győr. The lay-offs at Rába marked a turning point because the enterprise was an industrial center with 25,000 employees, one of the largest and most prominent in Hungary. It was perhaps the first instance of lay-offs at one of the most "core" enterprises. Fazekas and Köllő describe how in November 1978 after demand for their product had dropped precipitously the wagonworks Party secretary appeared at the county and city Party committee and reported that in more or less two months 500 workers would be laid off. This announcement was unforeseen and stupefied the leaders of the Party committee not only because this was without precedent, but also because for years Rába had been struggling with serious labor shortage, and no small part of the Party apparatuses' efforts the difficult task of keeping the region's largest enterprise supplied with sufficient manpower. The regional plan in 1976 had even planned to increase Rába's staff by 850 individuals. The county council had counted that 330 students leaving from industrial studies and 150 from technical vocational middle school would be directed to work at the plant. In 1976 a manpower redeployment campaign had been launched which specified that in 1979 thirty positions from the auxiliary branches of a nearby cooperative would be reallocated to Rába.

The director for the city's Party Economic Policy Division responded that they were completely dumbfounded, First that, "it was politically unimaginable to simply lay-off the people, that it would be preferable to reduce the high overtime". The Party offices' initial rejection that this was explicable and that layoffs were unfamiliar as an instrument of regional economic management. In Fazekas and Köllő's words, "Lay-offs were not in the dictionary of governance [of an enterprise] which had met with such problems of labor shortage". The local governmental organs were deeply ambivalent. They had been pressing heated campaigns whose principles were that, "enterprises had to reveal their internal reserves, and the redundant but not convenient workers had to be laid off". Yet they were afraid that employment troubles could lead to serious political tensions. They reiterated their great support that Rába had been laying-off work-shirkers and malingerers but that such a mass dismissal was outrageous and unacceptable.

The terms on which the Rába lay-offs were affirmed among the upper levels of the Party display great continuity with past ideological commitments at the same time that the dismissals marked a turn of events. On the December 6th, 1978 meeting of the Győr county Central Committee it was resolved that "full employment was not the mission of enterprises. Their mission was economic efficiency and that the problem of full employment should be left to the Party's regional organs" (Fazekas and Köllő, 1990: 173-74). Further, it was stated that:

> It can happen that longer term surpluses of labor develop. There must be a provision that the liberated labor goes into services and are re-routed to other economic branches. This is the duty that must be prepared for by labor law and planning and not the least of all, social policy.

The lay-offs at Rába created a political storm and were big news throughout the country. The Győr Party archives describe the apparent reaction to the news in Budapest as if to an atrocity[27] but the national reaction was more supportive. The news was first broken publicly in a large article appearing in the magazine *Kisalföld*. It stressed the need for flexibility and efficiency, and the good care of those laid off. It also stressed how the lay-offs would improve work discipline and productivity at the plant, stating that at the plant there should be, "only those people that will work effectively" and that "there is no room here for alcoholics and work-shirkers". It discussed the rational planning process behind the decision and how up till that time the plant had patiently watched a proliferation work-shirkers and causal job switching (Fazekas and Köllő, 1990: 181-82). On May 29th, 1979 the Party Central Policy Committee proclaimed that every enterprise in every region must reduce their unwanted labor capacity. The Győr example was seen as a success to be emulated: "Like in Győr county and in other county experiences we should take into consideration the local peculiarities and make the most of every organ of county and management".

Those laid off were core workers: they averaged 46 years old, were 89 percent male, 49 percent metallurgical workers, 44 percent engineers, technicians and administrators (Fazekas and Köllő, 1990: 215). Of the 800 workers who were laid off, Fazekas and Köllő interviewed 249 and compared their responses to a sample of 200 elite workers from the same branches of the company.[28] The largest group of the dismissed were elderly workers with administrative or blue-collar jobs that were auxiliary to the main workings of the plant. The dismissed were also less skilled and had worked at the enterprises for less time. Compared to the elite, the dismissed group were less integrated into the workplace in terms of tenure, values, and upward movement on the occupational ladder (Köllő and Fazekas, 1990). In follow up studies Fazekas and Köllő found that 95.5 percent of those laid off were able to find another job within eight months and 73 percent found work within the 30-40 day notice period in which the firm paid their full wages. Ten percent of the elderly workers dropped out of the labor force (Köllő and Fazekas, 1990).

If the lay-offs at Rába mark a certain decline in the power and ideological privilege of the core industrial enterprises, the power of the "industrial block" was further shaken by the amalgamation of the Heavy Industrial Ministry, the Light Industrial Ministry and the Metallurgical and Machine Ministry into a single Ministry of Industry in 1981 (Schweitzer, 1988: 113). The new Ministry of Industry was not supposed to allocate government resources, but to act as an advisor and coordinator for the enterprises. This transformation of function was far less radical than the attending rhetoric, but the industrial block nonetheless lost some of its influence in government bargaining.

The ministerial consolidation was arguably brought about indirectly by the government's desperation with increased debt pressures and the threat of international insolvency.[29] But there is no clear relationship between "market pressures" and the political weakening of large inefficient firms. In fact one effect of the heightened international economic pressure was an increased emphasis on exports to service balance-of-payment problems. Because the core firms were already the leaders in export, their bargaining leverage in some ways increased. Thus, we can say that *despite* the effect of market pressures increasing the power of core export enterprises, the ministerial consolidation nonetheless weakened the power of large firms to use the instrument of lay-offs to extract scarce labor.

Distinguishing Individual Pathologies from True Unemployment: Migratory Birds and Work-Shirkers

"Planned reallocations" were meant to increase labor productivity by reassigning workers to higher priority tasks, but—even when the political will could be summoned—other obstacles remained. The government tried to redirect labor to preferred enterprises, but nothing guaranteed that labor would actually go where planners intended, or that workers would stay in existing high-priority jobs. And in high-priority industries workers could abuse their job security to shirk their responsibilities or extort concessions from managers. The attempted solution was much the same as in programs for disciplining the unemployed in Western Europe or North America. The "true" unemployed were conceptually and institutionally distinguished from workers who merely chose to switch jobs or were dismissed for personal failings. Special administrative categories were created for dealing with frequent job-switchers and work-shirkers, and the government relinquished responsibility for ensuring employment for these individuals. Politics would redefine the boundaries of these categories over time.

The government asserted that it was not responsible if people were laid off for their own personal failings. As Ferge would later explain, "As long as the ideology denied the existence of unemployment as a social phenomenon, it could be explained only as a result of individual deviant behavior" (Ferge, 1992: 161). Chief among these pathologies was the charge of being lazy or work-shy. In legal terms this constituted a form of gross negligence, or what was called "public endangerment through work-shirking" (*közveszélyes munkakerülés*).

After 1968 there was a sharp drop in these convictions. In order to pre-empt lay-offs during the NEM, rules were changed which made it easier for a worker to leave their job "without permission" and search for other work. The hope was that workers would spontaneously leave less efficient firms in favor of the bonuses and profit-sharing offered at more successful enterprises. The Council of Ministers and the Presidential Council in December 1964 had previously amended the labor code, allowing workers to terminate their labor contracts but giving incentives not to do so.[30] Although job-switching had not been officially sanctioned it was nonetheless widely practiced. A subsequent measure in 1964, which had given new powers to managers to punish quitting workers, was ineffective at curbing labor turnover because the new firms were responsible for punishment, something they were not inclined to do as they were eager to woo the new workers to their enterprises in the first place (Róna-Tas, 1997: 101). Measures officially permitting workers freedom of choice in employment were thus issued between 1965 and 1968. Proclamations against undesirable and undeserving job-seeking began even before the introduction of the NEM. One prominent writer, Péter Veres worried in the pages of *Népszabaság* in 1967 about whether "some new species of sponging will not be bred by the new mechanism, some new parasitism against which we shall have to struggle anew for the substance of socialism and genuine collectivism".[31]

Skilled workers and other groups for whom there was a shortage could jump from job to job in search of higher wages and lower norms of effort. The new rules made job-switching easier and rapid increased labor turnover, which roughly doubled after the introduction of the NEM.[32] The rate of labor turnover (job change) in Hungary was 23-25 percent before 1968 and rose to approximately 41 percent in 1970 (Porket, 1995: 33).[33] The most widely used method of county administration for placing skilled workers was "forced schooling" which meant that the quotas for certain trades were filled by redirection from other trades. Not everyone who wanted to could receive training in lower-priority industries like textiles, for instance. In other fields with labor shortages it was easier for students to be accepted for training. Young specialists who had been forced into a priority field, however, tended to leave their jobs in much larger numbers.[34]

The increase in job switching was seen as hurting the "old guard" to the benefit of the "migrating birds" (*vándorlás*) who frequently changed jobs. The high-turnover of "migrating birds" was blamed for deteriorating work discipline,[35] since workers compelled into great exertion could instead find other jobs with better terms.[36] Research by Fazekas and Köllő in the Győr-Sopron region found that the surge of job-leavers after the NEM distressed the regional and local authorities, as well as the officials at the large enterprises that were unable to recruit and retain labor. They document how the regional Party committee tried "by force" to discourage what officials termed the "unprincipled labor allurement" of smaller competitors by merging them with a larger enterprise, Magyar Vagon- és Gépgyár (Fazekas and Köllő, 1990: 99-110). Starting in November, 1969 the government began to react to the rapid turnover (Fazekas, 1985: 57). In the Party's sessions of November 26-28, 1969 they resolved to address the "recent unsound labor turnover" (Fazekas, 1985: 57). In mid-1970 the Politburo, with the Statistical Office and the Labor Ministry would create a working committee to prepare a report for the Central Committee on "The Size, Causes and Directions of Labor Turnover". Berend describes a speech by second-in-command Béla Biszku at the national propaganda meeting in 1975 recounting the labor-enticing sins of fourteen agricultural cooperatives near Budapest where only a fifth of income came from agriculture,

> They had drawn thousands of former larger enterprise workers away from the Budapest factories... These subsidiary workshops could pay much higher personal incomes than large enterprises. ...Rules and regulations must be adjusted in order that such phenomena should not spread, but rather be driven back. (Berend, 1989: 123).

In an effort to stem migration local government organs also restricted the excessive outflow of workers to cities, a move that was pushed by the agricultural cooperatives who themselves suffered from a shortage of labor (Fazekas and Köllő, 1990: fn 116).

New policies categorized certain kinds of joblessness as outside of normal government obligations. In 1970 county councils decreed that those who had been summarily dismissed (as well as those who had discontinued their employment contrary to the law, those who changed workplace twice or more within the year, and those of certain trades) were only permitted to find employment with county enterprises through labor exchanges who would place them only in priority enterprises (Adam, 1984: 159; Soós, 1987: 439). Certain kinds of workers were prohibited from directly applying for jobs in Budapest, the most popular location for those exploiting labor shortages. These workers were: "Those who have been dismissed through disciplinary action, those who have left their previous workplace without giving notice and those who live more than 60 kilometers from Budapest" (*Hungarian Trade Union News*, 1975/7, p. 5-6). Officially these categories of jobless people could only accept jobs offered them through the labor offices. Enterprises could then dismiss them without special reason or notice.[37] In the light of the "planned reallocations" of the 1970s, the old Labor Code statutes from 1949 were revived which stipulated that workers with less than a year's continuous employment at one enterprise did not enjoy the same legal protections against lay-offs and could be dismissed at will after consulting with the trade union committee.[38] *Vándor* dismissals therefore did *not* constitute lay-offs, and certainly were not unemployment.

Workers who had been dismissed from their jobs were also not unemployed if they had been shirking, negligent or incompetent. They were viewed as merely being disciplined for their own individual shortcomings and these situations carried little political importance. Public officials, internal Party documents, and popular media almost never bothered to justify the joblessness among marginal or undisciplined workers.

In 1965 for instance, enterprises were pressured to reduce redundant workers and some eight thousand were dismissed in the hope that they would fill jobs in shortage-plagued sectors. This was reported matter-of-factly in the leading newspaper.[39] The Party had little concern about the political consequences of laying-off work-shirkers. For example, Köllő and Fazekas found in the Győr Party archives that in 1965 certain categories of workers could be laid-off with no protections.

> We can just approve one or two enterprises for such measures that provide for placement of a group of laid-off workers. That is all we have been able to subsidize while filtering out the work-shirkers and slip-shod workers from our enterprises, putting them out on the street (Fazekas and Köllő, 1990: 167fn, quoting from Győr-Sopron Communist Party Labor Committee archives T/60/1966).

During this period joblessness that resulted from the mismatch between individuals' skills and the demand for skills in the economy was not considered politically problematic because there was more than sufficient demand for industrial workers overall.

The boundaries of these categories were not static. The definition of unemployment was continually redefined as against the changing definition of work-shirking. At the end of 1971 the National Planning Office and an advisory committee completed a major review of manpower planning and living standards policy. A summary of the framework jointly written by many of the participating experts articulated the tension between state generosity to those without jobs and maintaining discipline on the job. They urged that, on the one hand, the government should, "make it possible for redundant or improperly utilized workers to be transferred to other jobs, in accordance with the qualifications of the individual and the needs of the national economy". But on the other hand, excessive aid would hinder work-incentives,

> Experience with respect to [job] security and full employment shows that we must also increase the social demands on individuals. Security without such demands leads to social injustice and hinders economic development which creates the material basis for social progress with a better formulation and implementation of targets we must see to it that, beyond certain minimal social norms, people share in the fruits of economic security according to the work performed for the benefit of society. Indeed, no one can demand from society that all his needs be unconditionally satisfied (Huszár, et al., 1972: 140).

Fazekas and Köllő find even more direct statements about using lay-offs to calibrate the intensity of work and punish work-shirking,

> Where the work-intensity is low, there is no place for leniency... The regional party and union organs must be circumspect with aiding displaced production workers who have been made redundant. ...There must be stepped up firmness in putting out the work-shirkers, those who come late, the slip-shod workers we confront. And if the warning does not help, there must be recourse to the instruments of lay-offs (1990: 167).

Lay-offs could be justified in terms of the salutary effects for defending the meaning of employment. During the decision about what to do at the Rába plant the first secretary of the Regional Party Committee met with the city Party Committee and stressed how strong material incentives rather than mere propaganda were ultimately needed,

> It is not possible for just the activity of propagandizing to tighten a good labor plan. We are very pleased that in our factories are honest, consistent, individuals who shoulder what is required. Those people who do not keep up a stiff pace of work to the end, can be first disciplined, then punished, and finally laid-off (as a result). In this I say in all sincerity—to support this is within our country's public opinion, which feels responsibility for the fate of the nation and the future we want to build. For this our work truly must have value.
>
> Not always must the money have to be waved in front of individuals' eyes, but that is what is done (Fazekas and Köllő, 1990: 174, from MSZMP GYVB Ach. T/39/1/1978).

The adjustment of policies regulating work-shirking were integral to redefinitions of the state's commitment toward unemployment because work-shirkers (and excessive job-switchers) represented the undeserving jobless who were to be conceptually excluded from other considerations about unemployment.

Since 1913 there had been some kinds of laws against criminal idleness or vagrancy, but the severity and enforcement had varied over time. Criminal prosecution for not working evokes the image of the gulag and we might associate it with hard-line Stalinism. Sure enough the law against work-shirkers was created in the 1950s. It was illegal to be without employment without cause. If an individual could not demonstrate that they had worked in the previous three months or show other sources of income, then their funds were assumed to have been improperly obtained and they could be charged with "public endangerment through work-shirking" (*közveszélyes munkakerülés*).

One might imagine that with further reform and economic liberalization in the early 1980s these prosecutions would have tapered off or ceased. But it is ironic and at first puzzling why government laws against unexcused joblessness were more strictly enforced—and official rhetoric more heated—in exactly those years that the state began initiating mass lay-offs and expanding long-term involuntary joblessness.

In 1979, the very same year that high profile lay-offs were underway at Rába, stipulations were adopted in the criminal code clarifying that anyone who remains without employment for a period longer than three months if they lacked another legitimate source of income was to be considered a "social parasite", punishable by fine, forced corrective labor, or imprisonment (Kis, 1985 [1989]). The penal code spelled out that such lifestyles were under the jurisdiction of criminal law because the person was a potential criminal. The Penal Code brief of the Justice Department stated that, "From the point of view of criminal law, a person who is capable of working, but does not engage in employment, in spite of the fact that he does not posses means to insure his livelihood, is a social parasite" (Kis, 1985 [1989]).[40]

At the beginning of the 1980s there was a move to strengthen enforcement against crimes against work discipline (especially for absenteeism and alcoholism) (Ferge, 1992: 162).[41] By order of the 19th decree of the Presidential Council in 1984, social parasites were henceforth to made accustomed to regular work by the state through assignment of a new institution called "restrictive forced corrective labor". A person was required to work at a designated place, for a specified time, and was not permitted to relocate from their assigned place of residence (Kis, 1985 [1989]).[42] This decree increased the penalties and ended the previous distinction between first-time offenders as a misdemeanor and multiple offenders as felons. Under the new decree even first time offenders were classified as felons. The number serving a prison sentence for penal idleness rose from a little more than a thousand in 1983 to four thousand in 1984 and reached its height at seven thousand in 1985.[43] In January 1985 a new penalty was introduced: "corrective educational labor". This was originally meant for those with a criminal way of life such as pimps, prostitutes or other "parasitic ways of life". But it was often used against those who were newly not employable, especially gypsies (Ferge, 1992: 162).

Gypsies typified the kind of deviant whose joblessness was by definition a problem of their own shortcomings rather than the state's. A formal policy statement on "the gypsy problem" was issued in 1961. It found that about thirty percent of Gypsies were assimilated, enjoyed relatively normal living standards and held regular work. Thirty percent were said to be in the process of assimilation, working only occasionally and living in isolated communities. Forty percent were *vandor*, or "migratory birds": non-assimilated and wandering from day jobs or mostly through periods without work, frequently changing residence and living as parasites on society. Work-shirking charges were used disproportionately against gypsies (Valkó and Sáfrán, 1988). The joblessness of gypsies never counted as unemployment. New sanctions against joblessness could be legitimated by associating them with the criminal pathology of gypsies.

But why did this seemingly anachronistic policy of a sharp criminalization against those without employment occur during a wave of "reform"? More importantly, why did this new criminalization of joblessness take place at the same time that mass lay-offs were underway?

The answer is not that lay-offs had created criminal vagrancy. In 1984 the government claimed that its stiffer penalties against social parasites were made necessary because of an increase in the number of social parasites, but the evidence refutes this claim. As János Kis has shown, the number of social parasites had remained relatively constant from 1970 to 1983 (Kis, 1985 [1989]).

The new criminalization of certain categories of joblessness is instead understandable as part of parallel campaigns for "work discipline" and "in defense of work time". In the early 1980s the central government was disturbed by what was perceived as flagging work-effort in the socialist sector. A 1983 survey of 8,400 clients at service outlets and government offices found that about half of them were on personal errands during time that they were supposed to be at work, half of whom had permission from their bosses (Timár, 1985: 115). Consequently, shop hours and office hours for government services were extended so that employees could shop and do personal administrative business outside their work hours. There was also a push against unwarranted use of sickness leave by those conducting personal business or working in the secondary economy.

More importantly the campaign against social parasites makes sense in the context of generous new social benefits for socialist unemployment. Given these programs which were introduced in 1983 and expanded greatly in 1984 and 1985, the timing of the anti-parasite campaign makes sense. The governmental category of unemployment demarcates between needs-based and work-based distribution. New lay-offs and social benefits for core workers thus threaten the boundary between deserving and undeserving joblessness.[44] New punishments of undesirable joblessness are the other side of the coin of new forms of recognition for legitimate unemployment.

Embracing Entrepreneurship, Instituting "Socialist Unemployment"

The new concept of unemployment was delineated according to the social treatment of redundant workers. The key distinction rested on whether labor lived in fear of joblessness and whether unemployment was used as leverage against workers. In the crudest terms, socialist unemployment was not regarded as "unemployment" in so far as it did not become a social problem. The definition of the problem depended on the kind of solutions that were used against it. This was articulated most clearly in a 1981 article in the leading official journal of economics, "On (Structural) Unemployment".[45]

The practically used concept of full employment does allow for a certain extent of unemployment—just so much as not to cause major social problems, although it can raise soluble "organizational problems" (*szervezési feladok*). We can speak about relative full employment—or simply full employment—so long as society does not have to take care of the unemployed as unemployed (through unemployment benefits, permitting employment abroad, etc).[46]

Periodic modernization of production processes will, in this view, necessitate some occasional structural disequilibria with resulting unemployment. Unemployment was conceived to occur when fuller utilization of labor would have ultimately led to a negative marginal material product for society. Under such conditions it is not inhumane to create unemployment because it is better for the whole community and because the task of unemployment should be recognized for its important function.

Unemployment under socialism can be characterized as humane efficiency. ...[T]he historical achievement of socialism can be the elimination, moderation of the economic and non-economic disadvantages which up to now have always accompanied unemployment. ...Some will contribute to the desired production result by remaining outside production. The division of labor might prescribe for them to stay in the reserve, and take part in retraining programs. To this extent their unemployment is a production task ...Unemployment can be *justified precisely by the main argument for full employment, namely: the achievement of maximum production result.*[47]

Planners still had the task of adjusting the two-way flow between the pool of active earners and inactive workers. Temporarily idle workers served a productive role and under socialism their treatment would also not be inferior. It follows that the unemployed should not be deprived of material subsistence. "The unemployed get their share from the result of production of the basis of their task in production, and not out of charity" (Bihari, 1981: 67).

The author explains the cause of unemployment as the segmentation of the labor market and technological advance. Skill mismatches lead to unemployment because open positions can not be filled by any job-seeker and competition for certain jobs is limited to workers with particular skills. This explains how labor shortage can co-exist with unemployment.

Due to technological development certain skills and areas of expert knowledge become outdated, certain trades gradually cease to exist, and, at the same time new requirements arise in other trades as well. People are forced to change jobs often because, due to technological change, old employees are unable to perform their duties because they were trained for other tasks (Bihari, 1981: 1172).

What is true for skills is also true for the regional distribution of labor. When regional demand for labor changes, there is also a lag before the labor supply can be changed to meet these demands. Bihari argued that these structural imbalances were "transitory" in the sense that the direct forms are transitory but one imbalance will be followed by another so the general phenomenon of these imbalances is continuous.

This article is also noteworthy for recognizing the ambiguity in definitions of employment and the consequences for conceptions of unemployment. Bihari described how actual economies exist between impossible theoretical extremes. On the one hand is what he calls "absolute full employment" (*abszolút teljes foglalkoztatás*), a situation when nobody is without work for any period of time. At the other extreme, are persons completely without work, a situation that is only possible with society's active care through social policy because "it is only a special case of unemployment (if such a case ever comes about) when there is absolutely no work to be had" (Bihari, 1981: 1164). To some extent, the existence of unemployment represents the ability of workers to hold out in wait for jobs that they are better qualified for.

The key features of the new political meaning of unemployment can be seen in this article. It was not an official statement of the Party line; nor did it pre-empt resistance to the new stance on unemployment. It did not even unify the meaning ascribed to the vocabulary of unemployment. But in addition to its theoretical richness, the article's theoretical richness makes it possible to encapsulate how much the concept of unemployment had changed and see how the changes were embodied in policy and public proclamations.

First of all, the particular notion of unemployment was now to be regarded as a desirable outcome. As János Timár stated in a 1998 interview, it became politically possible to count unemployment because the new economic reforms were now *supposed* to lead to lay-offs if they were successful. Statisticians earlier would not count unemployment when politicians claimed that unemployment could not exist under socialism and their translated Soviet textbooks said the same (Timár interview May 28, 1998). A 1982 law reoriented the local labor offices from the task of merely punishing excessive job-switchers to placing workers in vacant positions. An unintended consequence was that the labor office data created new kinds of information about involuntary joblessness. In a 1983 roundtable discussion that appeared prominently in the main newspaper, the Secretary of State and head of State Wage and Labor Board, Albert Rácz would explain, "For unemployment there are two conditions: an individual not be working for reasons apart from their own fault, and also have registered with the state institutions as seeking a workplace". He noted that the data showed about 70,000 people who had left a workplace and remained without job placement for six months or longer (*Népszabadság*, 1983).[48] Statisticians were able to keep a rudimentary database of registered unemployment before unemployment was legally accepted and legal unemployment assistance introduced. Implemented in 1985, this system collected data from regional labor employment offices as well as on the number of vacant jobs.[49] Figures showed 600 unemployed in 1985, 6,000 in 1986, and 10,000 in 1988 (Fajth, 1993: 90).

Secondly, the goal of "full employment" now included some limited amount of involuntary joblessness. Party officials repeated endlessly the notion that full employment was the task of the state, not individual enterprises.[50] Enterprises were thereby freed up to lay-off workers. The government's obligation was to organize and coordinate the most efficient mobility of labor. When accompanied by dynamic training programs unemployment was conceived a form of slack that increased productivity. In the new conception, spelled out in the directives from the 13th Party Congress, the introduction of unemployment was justified because it was defined as a productive utilization of labor than would have occurred without unemployment.

Third, a key element of the state's responsibilities was the proper care for upstanding workers who had lost their jobs through no fault of their own. Berecz quotes one internal Party draft document in the early 1980s as saying that,

> In the interests of the increase of efficiency the staffing levels must be reduced, but …it is not possible to divorce this question from the social nature of socialist work (we must not place into question our socialist character). That is, staffing-level dismissals must not result in uncertainty of existence, not place into doubt the constitutional guarantee to work as a right, not be able to reduce certain stratum of workers' living standard. Thus is ensured by standing by with the appropriate aid (Berecz, 1983).

One instance is when Party secretary Károly Nemeth visited the Csepel Iron Works in 1981when the threat of liquidation hung in the air. According to the major daily newspaper *Népszabaság*, he guaranteed to the workers, "It is clear we have to find a solution which is good for the country and for this politically and economically important big enterprise too. He said: nobody should be afraid of not having a job equal to his skills and knowledge" (Laki, 1985: 205). Similarly, when the Tungsraum Electrical Company in 1984 cut its work force by 3,000 workers and closed down its typewriter division, the National Bank declared that there were at least a hundred other enterprises that were "permanently insolvent". Referring to the lay-offs, officials were quoted as saying that "Every worker in a plant which now will be closed down because of unprofitability will be found another job". In another instance, György Szepesi at the National Planning Office stated, "At IGV [the typewriter plant], 1600 workers were affected. But no one was thrown out on the street". He continued, "We cannot guarantee... the same kind of job in the same industry as before. But other jobs are still available in the labor situation we have in Hungary today".[51]

Unions voiced discomfort with the growing acceptability of unemployment but in practical terms they were in accord with the general policy implications. At the 1980 meeting of the Central Councils of Hungarian Trade Unions and the Twenty-Fourth Congress of the Hungarian Trade Unions endorsed the principle that, "socialist society guarantees the right to work for all, but this cannot be interpreted to mean that everyone can insist on one particular workplace". The unions pledged to ensure that such reorganizations would be done in the least burdensome way possible. In the previously mentioned 1983 roundtable discussion on unemployment which appeared in the national daily, the Central Union department head, László Bukta held to the notion that limited lay-offs would not constitute unemployment,

> In our opinion the chances of unemployment are so remote to our conceptions that many imagine unrealistically that they pertain only to negligent workers, and not to regular workers being put out on the street. Unemployment is not some style, not a disciplining instrument, but a serious social sickness, and neither will the symptoms be chosen restrictively.

On Budapest television the secretary of the unions, Sándor Nagy, defended in 1984 the unions' right to veto certain governmental decisions. He said the union vetoed 165 decisions in 1984 (but did not mention whether any of these vetoes involved lay-offs). In the mid-1980s the unions were still largely transmission belts for the central government, reduced to at most loyal opposition. The objections to unemployment were strong, but also only held insofar as negative social repercussions made unemployment evident.

> We cannot reconcile ourselves to the thought of unemployment. Not because this is some kind of religious precept—let there be no misunderstanding—or because we have said in the framework of some kind of sermon that in socialism there can be no unemployment, but because I believe that, if we think responsibly and calmly, we cannot accept the numerous moral, human, economic, political and million other consequences which would accompany a certain perceptible degree of unemployment.[52]

The various features of the new concept of unemployment led to a tendency to frame governmental defenses about unemployment in terms of the ratio between vacancies and job-seekers. When the chief public spokesman on unemployment, József Rózsa was asked on the Hungarian TV news magazine "168 Óra" about whether there was unemployment within Hungary he responded by discussing the relative availability of jobs and rarity of dismissals,

> Most people do not worry when they go to bed at night about whether they will have a job the next day. This means that social security exists at a maximal level. ...[T]here are some sixty to seventy thousand unfilled jobs, half of them in the capital.[53]

He noted that 650,000 occasions in which workers changed jobs in 1980, but only 20,000 of those cases were dismissals. The official Party line, at least through 1984 continued to be that these were lay-offs—due to exceptional and transitory circumstances—but that there was not and would not be "unemployment".[54] Reference was often made to the great number of job vacancies relative to the few number of job seekers to indicate that the jobs were there but the time between finding a suitable new job was sometimes protracted.

The emphasis on vacancy ratios was theoretically problematic as far as distinguishing Hungarian socialism from capitalism. A striking article confronting the official hypocrisies appeared in 1985 by Károly Fazekas and János Köllő. In the journal *Valóság*, they asserted that full employment and "rational management" of the economy were not completely compatible.[55] They questioned the maxim that, so long as there were more open positions than job seekers, then capitalist-style unemployment need not be feared. In Great Britain, they noted, areas which had significant unemployment rates also had an excess of registered vacancies relative to the number of job-seekers.

The mid-1980s saw dramatic new initiatives in social benefits for joblessness, though these were first applied only a small scale. Already in 1983 the state planning board initiated a program through which laid-off workers could receive training at a new enterprise for six months to a year while the government continued to pay their previous wage. Only one percent of the 200 million forints allocated to this program were ever used, partly because there were so few lay-offs, but more importantly because the wages were too small amounts to be much incentive for enterprises to use the program (József Rózsa, public spokesman on unemployment during the 1980s from the State Wage and Labor Office, interview, January 1997).

In July 1986 "an extended-waiting-period-before-terminating-employment" benefit was enacted decreeing that if ten or more people were dismissed they had the right to six months with full pay and six more months of means-tested assistance.[56] No provision was made for those dismissed in smaller groups. A state enterprise that wanted to dismiss ten or more redundant workers simultaneously had to inform the local labor exchange at least three months in advance. If the exchange considered new placements unlikely within the year they could instruct the enterprise to extend the notification period to six moths. During these six months employees did not work but were paid their monthly salary from the central budgetary fund. After the six-month period re-employment benefits began at 75 percent of former earnings for three months and 60 percent for the next three—thus providing a total of a year's compensation. This kind of unemployment constituted 0.05 percent of the labor force at the beginning of 1984 and would climb to 0.3 percent in 1989.[57]

Policy distinguished between terminations for "economic" and other reasons. The justification was that there was a distinction also between "wasteful" and. Individuals in "structurally non-efficient" employment were viewed as dismissed for purely economic reasons and were deserving of aid; while individuals that were merely "wasteful" or non-efficient were undeserving. The less-than-ten-people rule was a way to distinguish those who were individually at fault from those whose plant unit was simply being reorganized. Wasteful employment occurred wherever there was over-employment: that is, when more people were employed than if everyone worked with full intensity or if only necessary jobs were performed. These additional people were superfluous and not deserving of aid. On the other hand, structurally inefficient employment was productive but took place in technically obsolete branches or activities that had to be subsidized by the state (a fifth of GDP went to subsidize losing firms). These victims had to be compensated (Ferge, 1992).

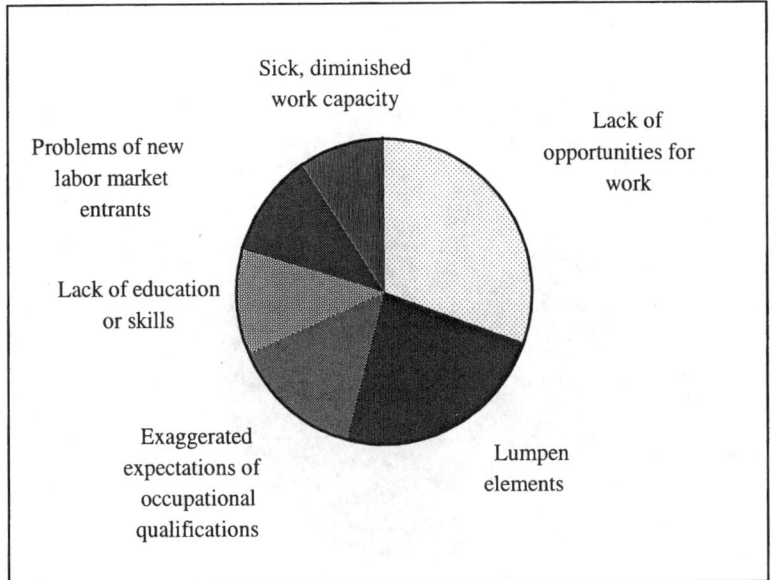

Sick, diminished work capacity

Lack of opportunities for work

Problems of new labor market entrants

Lack of education or skills

Exaggerated expectations of occupational qualifications

Lumpen elements

Figure 5.4 Reasons popularly associated with "employment difficulties"

The Party was concerned with public reaction to the growing threat of job loss and, in the 1980s expanded efforts to track opinion polls. Particularly interesting is a study of public opinions about unemployment that was undertaken in Hungary during the period between 1984 and 1988 (Angelusz, et al., 1989).[58] Already in 1984 "a considerable section of society perceived the existence of *difficulties in finding employment* at the time, and was prepared for their increase, but there were very few who considered this process as emerging *unemployment*".[59] Fifty-four percent anticipated "employment difficulties" in the coming years but only 40 percent predicted any unemployment.

The most detailed surveys from 1984 make it possible to see clearly how these two concepts were split from one another.[60] The chart above compared with the one below illustrates how the concept of "employment difficulties" was disassociated from that of "unemployment". Notice how it is the concept of "employment difficulties" rather than unemployment that is closely associated with the lack of work opportunities. "Employment difficulties" were associated less with personal deviance and more with the situations of less core workers such as the disabled, those new to the labor market, and the unskilled. The notion of "unemployment", on the other hand is attached to personal deviance including convicts and, especially, the "lumpen elements". But it is also interesting that plant closures and lay-offs are associated with unemployment more closely than with "employment difficulties".

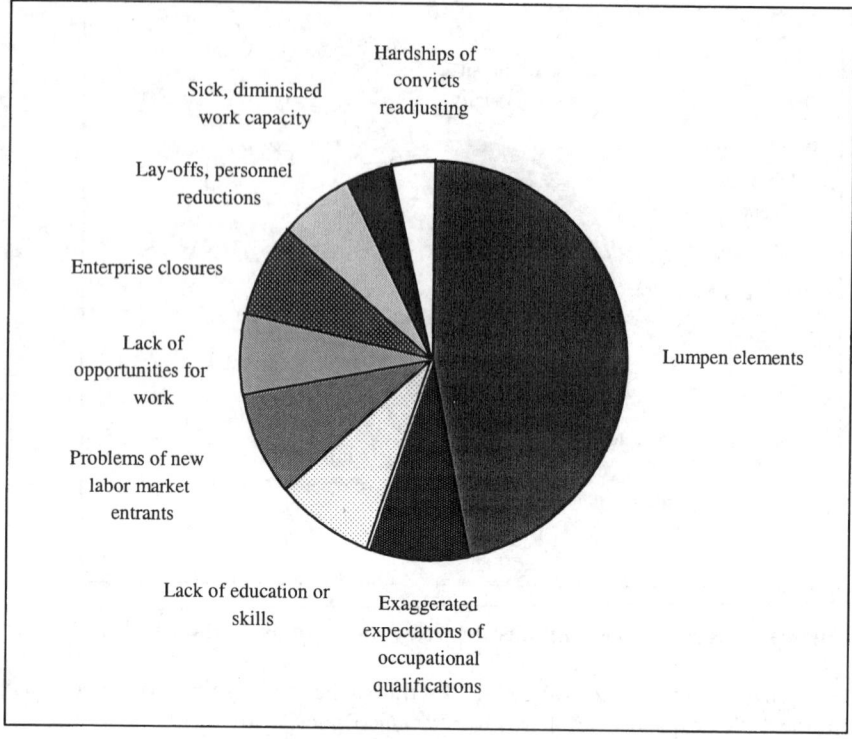

Figure 5.5 Reasons popularly associated with "unemployment"

Table 5.2 Attitudes toward joblessness in Hungary, 1984, 1987, 1988

Percentage of respondents saying that:	1984	1987	1988
• Employment difficulties exist in Hungary	42	66	83
• Employment difficulties will exist in coming years	54	81	88
• In coming years some people will be unemployed for a short or long time	40	73	84
• Consider an unemployed person to be one whose enterprise has been closed and cannot find a job	33	54	--
• Consider an unemployed person to be one who is dismissed and cannot find a new job	38	58	--
• Consider a housewife who seeks a job in vain to be unemployed	23	35	--
• Consider as unemployed the young looking for their first job but are unable to find employment suiting their qualification	33	42	--
• Refer to personal deviancy as the cause of unemployment	43	26	--
• Refer to structural causes as the cause of unemployment	19	46	--

Public opinion perceived deterioration in the Hungarian employment situation but unemployment was not conceived as a problem that threatened average workers. By 1987 four-fifths of Hungarians expected both "employment difficulties" and "unemployment" in their future.[61] But up until 1984 the most popular opinion about unemployment was that "only work-shirkers have to fear unemployment".[62] In 1987 respondents who felt that unemployment was wholly disadvantageous constituted sixty-nine percent against twenty-five percent who cited advantages in work discipline, incentives, or (rarely) structural adjustment.[63]

A key element in the shift in the meaning of unemployment was that given the expansion of the "helping", "completer" or "second" economy from the 1970s to the beginning of the 1980s, full employment no longer had to imply that job seekers were guaranteed a position in the socialist sector. In an internal Party memo the chief public spokesman on unemployment, József Rózsa argued that a redefinition of unemployment to accommodate these changes would be advisable,

> It seems that we currently consider as unemployed, those in a residing area who are not able to be placed in their profession and are not able to be offered traditional opportunity which is similar to his profession, guaranteeing the ongoing career [i.e. not able to meet the definition of the 1970s]. Perhaps those could be [instead] regarded as unemployed who in the residing area we are not able to offer opportunity for work from such that they would be protected from making ends meet (Rózsa, 1983).[64]

Ultimately, Rózsa offered an astute argument that the consequences of redefining unemployment along his proposed terms would define success along already-existing goals of employment policy: "Insofar as the above definition is acceptable, then it can be seen that unemployment can be avoided with a well-functioning training and assistance system, which moreover perhaps also relieves the shortage of labor" (Rózsa, 1983).

István Gábor, a sociologist and governmental expert who collaborated in changing regulation of the second (non-state) economy, argues that from the beginning of the 1980s, "the governmental departments concerned with labor hoped for an increase in the second economy as workers were squeezed out of the socialist sector". He is worth quoting at length on how this altered the official understanding of unemployment.

> For the interpretation of the principle of full employment in our days crossed over to another altered form. In this case full employment was also compatible with open, frictional and structural, long-term unemployment, if there existed a reasonable and fair aid system, training institutions, transitional employment, etc. Moreover, the interpretation of employment expanded for itself (to private employment): such forms of activity can also qualify as employment which up to now would not have been regarded as activities that counted.
>
> With the economic crisis dragging on and the lingering dysfunctions of the economy connected to employment, deliberations were launched over expanding the full employment concept. It was decided for a wider stratum of enterprise staff reductions and that many young school-leavers will face difficulties finding a

job. In the presence of such circumstances the data are undeniable that the broadening of the second economy would be an urgent remedy for satisfying the expectations of the population and supplementing the performance capacity of the large factory sector (Gábor, 1988: 804-805).

The problem of unemployment was redefined once the second economy became central to the solution.

The introduction of "socialist unemployment" was the final step in an accumulated process of change. An elaborate set of social policies relieved labor market pressures by subsidizing exit from the labor supply for vulnerable groups— a process that softened the prospect of job loss and made "staff reductions" conceptually distinct from "putting workers out on the street". For core workers in industrial plants, a generous system of "planned reallocations" helped them continue their occupation elsewhere, retrain for different work, or at least maintain their living standards. Meanwhile layoffs were accepted as harsh but necessary medicine for workers who slacked-off on the job or drifted between jobs in search of higher wages and easier work norms. Combined with a concept of employment that expanded to include the second economy, unemployment could be seen as a solution to other problems rather than an untouchable problem in its own right.

Notes

1   For example, "Hungary's Leaders go to work on unemployment", *Christian Science Monitor*, Oct. 25, 1984; "Hungary Tries to Adjust to Unemployment", *Financial Times*, Jan. 5, 1988: 2; "With Prime Minister Grosz determined to push ahead with the modernization of the Hungarian economy, some social unrest seems inevitable" (*The Washington Post*, August 18, 1988).

2   First of all, it matters little how *we* think people *should* have conceived of the issue. Secondly, even if the Communist Party had administered a standardized ILO/OECD population survey for counting unemployment, they still might not have identified any unemployed. Such a survey might not have found any working-age individuals who simultaneously: lacked an ongoing employment contract, had recently searched employment channels, and had received no pay for any even casual labor. Thirdly, any counter-factual that speculates about the unemployment rate using different categories than those which existed must also correct for political decisions which would have been made differently if unemployment had been understood differently.

3   There are many theories which argue how unemployment *could not* exist under communism, but they provide little insight about the changing ways that unemployment *did* exist or how its meaning might change over time.   Involuntary joblessness did exist under communism. In some industries laborers regularly had to search to find casual labor.   Despite regulations that discouraged the practice, workers often changed between jobs or were dismissed. Job changers in the Soviet Union were legally required to find a job in a specific amount of time, and anti-parasite laws persecuted those jobless without excuse (Porket, 1995: 34). Communist governments continuously struggled to find employment for certain groups of workers and in certain regions.   Yugoslavia institutionalized unemployment relief programs as early as 1964 and had the highest unemployment rate in all of Europe in the 1980s (Porket, 1995; Primorac and Babic,

1989; Woodward, 1995). Unemployment compensation systems existed in the USSR before the end of the New Economic Policies (NEP) in the 1920s and in various East European countries throughout the period of communist rule. Hungarian unemployment and formal unemployment benefits existed in the 1950s and 1980s. East German benefit schemes existed until 1977 and statistics which were kept up until 1958 show an average of 10,000 to 15,000 yearly recipients. Bulgarian unemployment was reportedly very high in the mid-1950s and an entitlement scheme was established in 1958.

Any argument about the political economy of unemployment under communism should account for the exceptions and changes over time in the Party's adamant position against unemployment. It is insufficient to argue merely that the Party lied about unemployment or gave in to economic pressures. Communist governments undoubtedly avoided discussion of some forms of involuntary joblessness and changed their definitions in order to disguise their own shortcomings, but the regime was still constrained by its own commitments. Indeed, Party officials' dissimulation is evidence that they felt the need to uphold their promises. Communist regimes did not simply relent from their commitment to full employment out of sheer economic necessity. Fiscal and productivity pressures to lay-off workers were present throughout the entire Soviet era. The economic costs of "eradicating" unemployment do not explain why it was regarded as politically worth the trouble in the first place. The economic pressures can only explain half the story because they can not tell us why full employment ever came to be a central priority, why its importance changed when it did, and why certain forms of unemployment were regarded as less acceptable than others.

4 Due to the lack of official measures, estimates of Soviet unemployment have varied widely and used widely varying definitions. Adirim argues that Soviet unemployment was much higher than 15 percent, especially in Asian regions (Adirim, 1989). Looking at different sets of scattered data on labor turnover, Wiles and Grannick each concluded that the "frictional" unemployment from changing jobs amounted to between 1.3 and 3 percent unemployment of the labor force (Wiles, 1972; Grannick, 1987). S Wiley used a much smaller set of findings from the 1960s and estimated unemployment at 1.3 percent. Grannick, using a richer set of later data concluded a range of 1.5-3 percent. See also Lane, who extrapolating largely from the turnover data of a single region, estimates 1-3 percent (Lane, 1987: 66). Another study by Gregory, using a large data set of structured émigré interviews from the late 1970s, included only those more "salient" spells of unemployment that lasted a month or more. Soviet economists and planners assumed that such protracted jobless spells did not to exist, or only occurred when people rejected job offers. Quoting from a leading Soviet work on labor markets, "Under conditions of socialism, the condition of being without work (*nezaniatost*) is not a synonym for 'unemployment'. It means only an interruption of work caused by reasons of a private character (family, circumstances, changes of location)" (Gregory and Collier, 1988: 613). The émigré data suggest that 8.2 percent of respondents had suffered an average of 1.6 such prolonged spells over the previous five years, with the average spell lasting 4.8 months. The lower boundary estimate of the Soviet rate of prolonged unemployment was therefore derived at 1.2 percent of the labor force. That rate falls directly in between the contemporary American rate (1.9 percent) and the West German rate (0.5 percent) of spells lasting a month or more for similar years. In this respect it is difficult to see what is distinctive about even the degree of Soviet unemployment.

5 Also cited in Róna-Tas, 1997: 101n.

6   First given as a lecture at a 1967 symposium on socialist employment, this paper is reproduced in Timár, 1969. Similar views can be found, for instance, in Berényi, 1967.

7   Already by 1963 Timár was circumspect about the limits of maximizing the utilization of the labor force, "increasing employment of the able-bodied population does not mean that the objective should be full-employment in any absolute sense. The extent of employment is determined not only by the level of economic development, but also by the demographic characteristics of the population—primarily its distribution by age and sex. It is a prime task of employment policy to secure the possibility of participating in socially organized production for everybody willing to work and able to perform productive work" (Timár, 1966: 1).

8   Frictional unemployment in neoclassical macro-economics refers to the unavoidable jobless search time that results from people normally switching between jobs,

9   The government directive 45/1971 took effect on 1 January 1972 and allowed pensioners to earn 6,000 forints per year and work up to 840 hours yearly (or for some groups 1200 hours). It was determined that with commensurately smaller pension stipends people could work without restriction.

10 On this leverage, see especially Sabel and Stark (1982).

11 On the distribution of these worker strategies, see Kertesi (1985).

12 Nonetheless, disabled pensioners at least officially worked substantially less than old-age pensioners and did so generally at the bottom of the wage ladder (Könczei, 1995).

13 Interview with Pauka Tibor, Budapest May, 1995.

14 Interview with Naiser Alajos, Director of Nation Medical Examination Institute, Budapest, May 1995.

15 Interview with Pauka Tibor, Budapest May, 1995.

16 The rising share of applicants who assigned statuses of less than fifty percent disability, which carries only minimal benefits, is an indication of people's increased desperation.

17 On the particular severity of labor shortages during these years see Fazekas and Köllő, 1990.

18 Antal notes that between 1968 and 1972 the ratio of these enterprises' subsidies to profits was twice that of the industrial average (Antal, 1989).

19 Interview with former Prime Minister András Hegedüs, Budapest, January 1997.

20 Similarly, the Finance Minister had argued in 1965, "The small enterprises are—by their very nature—incapable of recognizing social interest" (Schweitzer, 1981: 294).

21 "The large enterprises were called into existence through administrative measures—to a certain extent independent of whether creating them at the given moment was reasonable or not. They have become organic and indispensable elements of the national economy, and got hold of key economic positions. The could and did make it possible for the managers and experts interested in the existence of these large enterprises to enforce the interests of their enterprise at the expense of other spheres of the economy (Szalai, 1982: 26).

22 János Timár states that in the late 1970s he served on a special subcommittee team of the Central Committee on how to deal with "unemployment" (Munkanélküliség Bizonság). I have been unable to find further information about this committee.

23 Laki also finds considerable variation between sectors. Few mergers or liquidations took place in the politically powerful metallurgy, the electric power industry, the chemical industry, the building industry, and the food industry. Engineering and light industries were merged or liquidated more frequently. Some branches were particularly vulnerable—namely miscellaneous wood-working industries, footwear industry, particular branches of machinery and equipment, or mass metal wares. An extraordinary loss also took place in the canning industry (Laki, 1982: 93).

24 It would have been logical if the economically more dynamic enterprises swallowed up the economically stagnant or troubled ones. Laki's study makes very clear that this was not the case. She looks at mergers which had a changing product pattern in the 1978-79 period, a total of 19 events involving 38 enterprises. There was no relationship between whether an enterprise was swallowed up and if it had stagnant or declining production or employment. In so far as any difference exists the enterprises that got swallowed up (incorporated) were very slightly *less* likely to have declining or stagnant employment or production. Dynamic enterprise growth does not explain which firms were merged. The fact that enterprises which were merged tended to have a decreasing number of employees in prior years indicates that they might be less politically powerful (Laki, 1982). On the question of profitability the author looks at data for 110 enterprises participating in 55 mergers in the engineering industry between 1970 and 1979. Enterprises were examined for their profit per unit of capital, and their subsidy per unit of capital. The only slight difference between merging and merged enterprises was that the enterprises which were swallowed up were somewhat more likely to have been more profitable than the merging enterprise (this was also true of the three year average preceding the merger). The merging companies had worse profits, but they were somewhat more likely to be improving than the merged companies. After the mergers, enterprise profitability tended to get worse and remained persistently so, at least for the subsequent three year period. The same conclusions can be drawn in terms of subsidies. By a variety of measures the enterprises that were swallowed up generally had been less propped up by subsidies than the merging enterprises. "The incorporators are frequently not better but even worse than the incorporated enterprises" (Laki, 1982: 104).

25 Cited from Az MSzMP Központi Bizottságának határozata az 1979 évi népgazdasági terv és költségvetés irányelveiről (6 December 1978) (The resolution of the Central Committee of the Hungarian Socialist Workers Party on the principles of the national plan and budget in 1979) in (Magyar Szocialista Munkáspárt, 19: 914).

26 *Hungarian Trade Union News*, 1979 (June) p. 5-6.

27 (Fazekas and Köllő, 1990) from MSZMP GYSMB Arch. T-22/1979.

28 The elite workers were those who had been decorated as outstanding workers (*Kivalo Dolgozo*).

29 There was a liquidity crisis in 1981-1982 in which Hungary came close to defaulting on its international debt. Western lenders restricted access to credit because Polish and Romanian insolvency in 1981 had eroded lending confidence in East Europe. In 1982 foreign exchange reserves fell from $1.7 billion to half a billion from January to March. A half billion dollars was sufficient merely to cover a month of imports (Comisso and Marer, 1986: 254). Austerity measures curbed internal consumption and investment while prioritizing hard-currency exports.

30 If a worker gave notice without approval from the enterprise they lost their status of continuous employment (when calculating pensions and other social benefits) and they were not permitted to receive a higher salary than their previous rate for six months.

31 "Néhány szó a kollektiv gondolkozásról" (A few words on collective thinking), *Népszabaság*, Oct. 15, 1967.

32 Comparing the monthly average of the period from Jan 1-Sept 30, 1968 to the monthly average over 1964-67 ("Szilard munkafegyelment" [for Work Discipline] *Népszabadság*, 23 Nov. 1969). By another measure Seleny claims that when the 1968

reform abolished laws punishing workers for changing jobs, labor turnover increased 74 percent between 1968-1969 (Seleny, 1991: fn 55).

33 These numbers include separations due to death, retirement, return from conscription, maternity, administrative transfer, etc... . Without these inclusions labor turnover was 9.9 percent in 1976 and 6.3 percent in 1986.

34 Köllő and Fazekas characterize the government's task as like bailing with a leaky bucket (1990).

35 See also E. Soter, "Szilard münkafegyelment" [For Firm Work Discipline], *Népsabaság*, 1 July 1969.

36 "For the interests of society with appropriate firmness and strictness labor discipline must be stepped-up and job-positions changed-over" (quoting from MSZMP GYVB archives T/30/1/1978 in (Fazekas and Köllő, 1990: 167n)). "At the end of the 1970s great tensions were mounting in urban manpower planning. ...There were constant indications of labor shortage and deteriorating work discipline." (Fazekas and Köllő, 1990: 167) (from an interview with a member of the economic policy committee of the MSZMP GYVB at that time). See also (Sabel and Stark, 1982) on how tight labor markets made it possible to bargain for lesser exertion

37 Although other enterprises hired casual labor anyway, only certain priority industries were officially permitted to hire drifters at their gates.

38 "If the enterprise ceases to exist; if the reorganization of the enterprise or of production justifies a depletion of personnel; if cuts are required due to overstaffing; if the worker is not able to perform his work; if the worker has gained the right to a full or partial old-age pension... . After consulting the trade union committee, an enterprise may give notice to a worker without any of the reasons given above, if the workers continuous employment status covers a period of less than one year. This does not, however, apply to a worker who has entered into employment for the first time and whose employment status is continuous" (*Hungarian Trade Union News*, March 1965, 3B).

39 *Népszabaság*, 28 March, 1965, as cited in Adam, 1984: 123.

40 Penal Code paragraph 266.2, brief of the Justice Department. Only in 1991 did police stop fining vagrants under the work-shirking law (József Rózsa, public spokesman on unemployment during the 1980s from the State Wage and Labor Office, interview, January 1997).

41 The disciplinary campaigns were effective in reducing voluntary job leaving. Among job leavers the portion who "quit" fell from 56.7 percent in 1976 to 44 percent in 1985. In 1985, 5.7 percent of leavers were transfers initiated by employers and 1.3 percent from "redundancy", two categories that did not officially exist in 1976. Dismissals for disciplinary reasons more than tripled from 1.1 percent of job leaving in 1976 to 3.6 percent in 1985 (Szirácki, 1990: 715).

42 See also Stewart, 1990: 156n.

43 In 1983 Kis indicates that there were 1,105 cases of convicted social parasitism. Punishment was up to 1 to 3 years of correctional labor for the first and second offences (Kis, 1985 [1989]). According to pp. 98-99fn in Ákos Róna-Tas's dissertation at the University of Michigan in 1990 titled "The Second Economy in Hungary: The Social Origins of the End of State Socialism" (Goven, 1993).

44 Karl Polanyi similarly shows how in pre-modern social policies, work house tests and residency certifications for paupers appeared when relief was institutionalized (Polanyi, 1946).

45 Bihari, 1981 and *Acta Oeconomica*, 28 (1-2): 53-70 (1982).

46 Ibid., p. 5. (pp. 1165-66).

47 Ibid., pp. 53, 68.

48 Rácz, in another interview in September 1984 deployed a somewhat different definition of unemployment but basically the same idea: "Some people honestly think that 'a little unemployment' would be a blessing in the interest of work discipline. I do not share this viewpoint. In the future, with more rational economic organization, manpower will be more unrestricted. But these processes—when they begin—will occur over a long time and the economy will be able to absorb the freeing of the work capacity. Therefore there will not be unemployment. Nevertheless, it must be said about this that the structural economic changes might—temporarily and not in general—give rise to transitional difficulties" (*Népszabadság*, 1984).

49 Up until the mid-1970s information on the number of job-seekers was information used by local party bureaucrats to obtain new investment funds for local factories (Interview with Gyula Nagy, Budapest 1997).

50 Rózsa, in an internal memo dissented somewhat from the view that full-employment was not the responsibility of enterprises. He pointed out that firms must cooperate in the introduction of part-time work and work-sharing. Also, "If somebody is not able to be placed in a position, it is completely all the same, whether it is fundamentally a state decision or fundamentally an enterprise decision that they lost their place of work" (Rózsa, 1983).

51 Christian Science Monitor, "Hungary's Leaders go to work on Unemployment" Oct. 25, 1984.

52 21:45 GMT 19 Nov 1985 (quoted in BBC Summary of World Broadcasts).

53 Quoted in BBC Summary of World Broadcasts, EE/7241/B/1 from Budapest home service 15:00 GMT 22 Jan. 1983.

54 See in the major daily newspaper *Népszabadság*, these examples: Sept. 15, 1981. "Teljes foglalkoztatás és hatékonyság" [Full employment and efficiency]: p.13; Aug. 28, 1982, "Vállalkoznak-e a nagyvállalatok?" [Are the large enterprises prepared?]: 7; Jan. 22, 1983, "A teljes foglalkoztatásról" [About full employment]: 5; Sept. 8, 1984, "A Munkaerő- és Bérhelyzetről" [About Manpower and Wages]: 8.

55 "Elbocsátások, Munkanélküliség, Allami Gondoskodás" [Lay-offs, Unemployment, and State Provision], *Valóság*, 85, 11 (1985): 54-63.

56 The benefits programs were expanded in 1988 and an unemployment-insurance system was established with financing from wage contributions in January, 1989 under the Communist Németh government.

57 Timar, 1991, cited in Adam.

58 Based on a representative survey of 1000 adults in 1984 and 1987.   A follow up examination was made in spring 1988.

59 Ibid. p. 213.

60 On how the "splitting" of concepts can be used to dissociate undesirable properties to another category, see Smith, 1987.

61 When asked in a separate poll whether the right to work was better in Hungary than in the West 93 percent answered "yes" in 1981, 96 percent did so in 1986 and 80 percent in 1988 (Nagy, 1989: 55).

62 That answer received an average score of 4.04 on a scale from one to five with five being the greatest agreement. Signaling the continuing importance of full-employment for legitimacy was the popularity of the view "that unemployment may cause incalculable political tensions" (score 3.72) which was slightly above, "that a slight degree of unemployment may do a lot to improve work discipline" (3.7). Less popular was the statement that "a low level of unemployment is acceptable if it helps to

overcome economic difficulties" (3.39). Other opinion scores were that, "it is better to have a slower pace of economic progress than unemployment" (3.48); and "unemployment should not even be mentioned in this country" (3.32). Ibid. p. 218.

63 Ibid. p. 217. Arguments for unemployment were least accepted by the most threatened groups, especially unskilled manual laborers. Comparing the extremes, ten percent of those with only a primary school education and in the lowest income quintile (at their main firm) saw advantages; 68 percent of those with a secondary education in the top quintile saw advantages (p. 218).

64 When Rózsa gave a lecture on manpower management, social policy and income relations to Western students studying abroad at the University of Economic Sciences they were, as he told the BBC, sceptical about how the claim was defined that no unemployment existed in Hungary (quoted in BBC Summary of World Broadcasts, Aug 17, 1985 "In Brief; Definitions of unemployment and minimum income" 16:30 GMT).

Chapter 6

Rising Unemployment and its Political Disappearance after Communism: Toward Regional and International Comparisons

> [In] Hungary... far from *intensifying* political opposition to economic transition, rising unemployment *diminished* it (Bartlett, 1997: 229).

Just as social scientists failed to predict the fall of communism, they did not predict post-communism's central political issues. Unemployment was supposed to be the great threat to post-communist political stability. It was anticipated that perhaps the greatest danger to political support for the transition to liberal democracy would be the loss of jobs in this region where employment had been virtually guaranteed. Scholars joined journalists and politicians to warn of the political fallout if unemployment were to increase precipitously. Evans and Whitfield, for instance, predicted unemployment to be first among the "formative issues" of post-communist politics (Evans and Whitfield, 1995: 532).[1]

These were not unfounded prognostications. A long literature in political science suggests that even short-term economic hardship can erode political support,[2] and unemployment is considered a basic benchmark for blaming the government.

In Eastern Europe a number of factors were thought to make the political threat of unemployment especially grave. Newly elected governments after the fall of communism inherited social welfare institutions that were not only ill prepared to handle mass unemployment; they also threatened to magnify the pain of job loss because many workplaces delivered social services such as child-care or housing (Rein, Friedman et al., 1996). The Hungarian Constitution continued to proclaim, "the right to work, to freely choose [a] job and occupation" (section 70/B). In Hungary, as in much of the region, there had been no radical legal break with the previous order and old communist commitments were never disavowed.[3] All six parties that entered Parliament after the first democratic elections of 1990 pledged full-employment (Frey, 1994).[4]

The economic downturn was sharper than any had anticipated,[5] and was especially steep in industrial production where most jobs would be lost. The final

Communist-appointed President of the State Office for Labor and Wages reflected in 1989 about the acceptable magnitude of job loss, "The sole question is how far we can go in accepting the risk of unemployment. No further, in my opinion, than a certain degree of transitional or frictional unemployment; to oversimplify, one might say that some workers would be momentarily between jobs" (Halmos, 1990: 45). Hungarian unemployment had been a mere 0.3 percent in 1989.[6] It had been anticipated that the adoption of western-style markets would entail greater unemployment.[7] But the COMECON trading arrangements which had previously guaranteed markets for Warsaw Pact countries were unexpectedly dismantled overnight, leaving firms scrambling to find new customers and suppliers.[8] Many firms that might have been able to navigate these problems failed because of a lack of banking infrastructure to substitute for old sources of state credit (Amsden, et al., 1994; Jacoby 2000: 133). Even firms that remained afloat tended to reduce their staffing levels to cut costs. The fall in GDP across the region was greater than the Great Depression was in the West. The move from almost no unemployment to 10 percent is far more dramatic than a similar increase from 10 percent to 20. With the collapse of COMECON markets, the Hungarian unemployment rate shot up from 2.1 percent in January of 1991 to 13.6 percent only 13 months later. Between 1990 and 1993 Hungarian employment fell almost 24 percent.

Yet through most of the region unemployment virtually disappeared as a political issue at the same time that unemployment rates skyrocketed. The end of a taboo against *some* unemployment that we observed during the final years of communism is one thing, but the post-communist acceptance of high levels of rapidly advancing unemployment is another.[9] General deterioration of economic conditions certainly did contribute to the unpopularity of post-communist governments, but field research on the years since 1990 found little public record of politicians talking about the issue.[10] This is also reflected in electoral outcomes, which seem to lack much independent effect from unemployment between counties.[11] No major new Hungarian initiatives or commissions were established. Benefits were extended for the long-term jobless, but no "War on Unemployment" was declared. The height of public concern was, if anything, the period before unemployment skyrocketed in 1991 to 1992, when intervention funds were created and politicians spoke more about the issue.[12] The state of the economy may have been an important influence on political views but unemployment was not the focus of how people made judgments about the economy and the competency of economic rule.

While any indicator of an issue's political salience is bound to be problematic, it is safe to say that across the post-Communist world unemployment has been a less politically volatile matter than other economic issues such as privatization, pensions, and wage arrears. When the 1992 New Democracies Barometer asked citizens in nine former communist countries whether they were more worried about unemployment or inflation, unemployment lost out by a ratio of almost two to one. Over the following three years inflation generally abated throughout the region (from a median rate of 93 percent to 28 percent) while unemployment increased; yet the follow-up poll in 1995 found that the fear of inflation relative to unemployment had moved in the opposite direction, widening to almost three to one (Rose, 1997).[13] Post-communist survey data even show that support of government responsibility for unemployment assistance is significantly weaker than for other social programs (Lipsmeyer, 2001). One study of press coverage similarly found that of seven hundred protest events mentioned in major newspapers between 1989 and 1994, there were only eight events in which the unemployed are identifiably involved and very few in which unemployment or lay-offs were even mentioned as grievances.[14] Another study found that unemployment was included in the themes of the nightly news less than one percent of the time (Bartók and Terestyéni, 1995).[15]

As we shall see, the same explanation for the general disappearance of unemployment's political importance can also explain why some regions or some countries were more or less an exception to this rule. But first, we review a number of possible explanations.

Alternative Explanations

One possible explanation is that unemployment was accepted as normal in the context of the transition to market democracy and the "return to Europe". Incumbent politicians certainly tried to push the view that unemployment should be an acceptable feature of restructuring. One Czechoslovak Economics Minister famously quipped that if unemployment failed to reach high levels "It would be a sign that the reforms were not working".[16] Western advisors also repeated this message. In Hungary, the 1990 Blue Ribbon Commission which included Western economists recommended that Hungary should copy the West as quickly as possible. They urged that mass unemployment should be seen as a sign of success rather than failure.

> This should be partly temporary if free entrepreneurship can grow fast enough to absorb those resources liberated from the shrinking state sector. Therefore, the fact that there is pain should not be an indication of a failure of the transition program but rather that the program may indeed be effective (Blue Ribbon Commission, 1990: 29).

In the vision of integration with Western Europe many must have noted that European Union unemployment was also rising into double digits.

While this may be an accurate description of how unemployment was normalized, it does not constitute an explanation of why this occurred. A large body of research on post-communist norms indicates persistent continuities in political values from the communist era.[17] The Return to Europe is an important feature of post-communist transformation, but especially given the resurgence of other national particularities,[18] it would just as easily explain why Eastern post-communist polities clung to the job securities that distinguished their societies.[19]

The general trend toward "Europeanization" tells us nothing about *which* norms would be swept away and which would become badges of political distinction.[20]

Generous Unemployment Benefits?

Another possible explanation is that the generosity of unemployment benefits diffused the political threat of the unemployment bomb. Bartlett supports this view, describing a "politically inert population of hard-core unemployed workers who were far more inclined to stay on the public dole than to undertake active opposition to market reforms" (Bartlett, 1997: 230).

This view is however triply flawed. First, as discussed in the first chapter, the political costs of unemployment do not come mostly from the unemployed themselves so much as from others wishing to avoid unemployment. Secondly, political opposition arising from unemployment does not come directly from the effect it has on people's incomes but indirectly through the kind of interpretations about the economy and government responsibility that citizens do or do not make.

Finally, a closer look at the unemployment benefit system shows that benefits were not generous enough to support recipients. Benefits were relatively generous only for the few who qualified for the earliest benefits established under communism. As a result of decades of public denigration of the jobless as social parasites, unemployment moreover carried a strong social stigma.[21] Post-communist unemployment benefits in Hungary and across the region were generally linked to the minimum wage which was not inflation indexed and fell far below the subsistence minimum. In Hungary at the beginning of 1994 most unemployment benefits were indexed to the minimum wage which was only 73 percent of the minimum subsistence level (Standing, 1995: 22). At the end of 1993, 57 percent of unemployment insurance recipients received benefits under the official subsistence level and according to an ILO study the subsistence level covered only 64 percent of the most modest costs of living (Frey, 1994). By contrast Polish benefits were substantially more generous than neighboring countries but rather than diffuse opposition, Poland experienced especially strong militancy against unemployment.

Rapid Job Churning?

Similarly, it was not the case that unemployment could be ignored because people moved quickly into new jobs. The oft-voiced hope was that a booming private sector would create demand for unemployed workers and make unemployment spells short. If this were the case it could account for the low political salience of even high levels of short-lived unemployment spells. But despite political rhetoric suggesting that the unemployed were necessary to provide staffing for new enterprises, the truth was that unemployment tended to be long-term and led to exit from the labor market rather than private employment.

Unemployment rates climbed so high in Eastern Europe largely because of the very long jobless spells people suffered. Even with relatively modest inflow to unemployment the stock of unemployed tended to grow rapidly precisely because there was little outflow from unemployment (Koltay, 1995; Köllő, 1995). As one World Bank study concluded,

> The net flow is *from* private employment *to* unemployment rather than the other way around. ...[T]he dominant source of employment growth in the private sector is hiring directly from the state sector (and/or privatizing existing jobs). Hiring from the pool of the unemployed plays a minor role (Commander, et al., 1995: 24).

The characteristic pattern of unemployment was not of constant job churning but that of stagnant pool, and should if anything increase our expectation that political resistance would arise.

Changing Meaning of Employment

This chapter puts forward an alternative explanation of the disappearing political costs of unemployment in Hungary by carrying forward the relationship between employment and unemployment that we have examined during the communist period to the new context of post-communist transition. Post-communist changes in the political significance of unemployment can be explained largely as a result of changes in the political meaning of *employment*. Under post-communism the wages of core industrial workers fell especially steeply. Informal work and multiple job-holding were encouraged by the new demands of the tax-system coupled with a more general retreat of the state. New social policies encouraged large numbers to officially leave their official "main" employment while working to complement their social benefits. Across the region, employment in state industry, instead of being the model of future growth, was viewed as the millstone around the economy's neck. Citizens became less and less reliant on their main job to be their sole source of livelihood and these main jobs were no longer the measure of government success.

Entrepreneurship was celebrated and institutionally encouraged as the new prototype of successful employment policy. Moreover, those places where employment relationships changed the least since early communism are also the places where unemployment received the most political attention. Only in those exceptional places where old-style employment had been largely maintained did unemployment emerge as an important and volatile political issue. Let us turn now to the processes by which the meaning of employment was transformed.

Changes in the Political Meaning of Employment

Falling Wages and the Declining Importance of Employment for Livelihood

The meaning of employment was eroded by sharp declines in post-communist wages in real terms. Post-communist price levels were pushed upward because suppressed demand and suppressed price rises were unleashed and fed by expensive imports.[22] Government policies deliberately kept annual wage increases below inflation as a way to prevent upwardly spiraling prices. The state also suppressed wages in the sectors they believed needed down-sizing: the state-sector and especially jobs in heavy industry. In other words, wages suffered the most in traditionally socialist prototypical jobs.

As the figures below show, employment, at least in one's main job, became less and less central to the livelihood of Hungarians. The first figure shows the percentage of total family income which came from wages which until statistical changes in the early 1990s counted only main jobs in state employment.[23] Main jobs also lost many kinds of non-wage benefits as profit-conscious large enterprises began selling off their worker housing, health-spas, vacation homes, and child-care crèches.

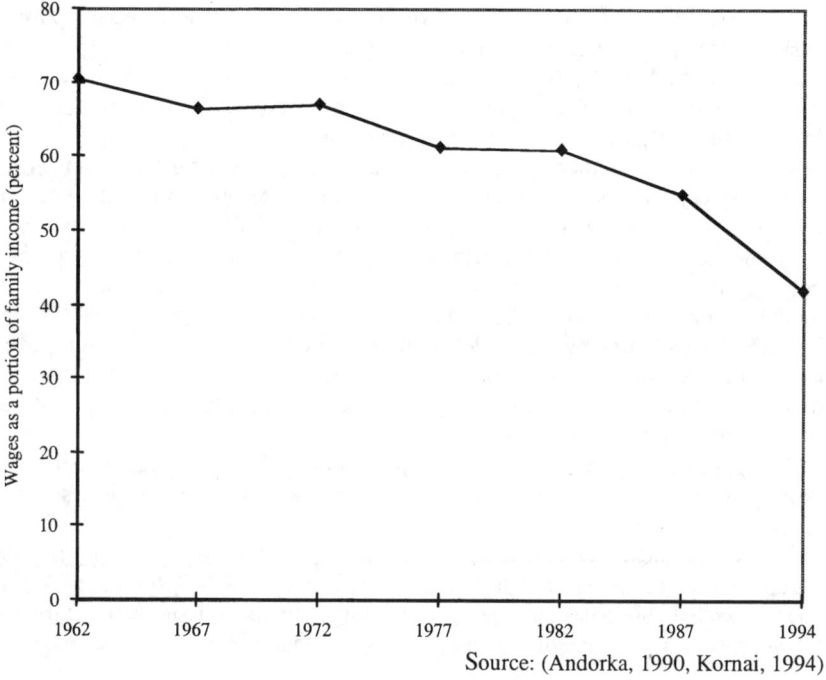

Source: (Andorka, 1990, Kornai, 1994)

Figure 6.1 Wages as a portion of family income

Table 6.1 Wages as a portion of family income (percent)

Year	1962	1967	1972	1977	1982	1987	1994
Percent of income from wages	70.4	66.4	67.0	61.3	60.9	55.0	42.0

Even while wages fell, Hungarians worked longer hours in more jobs and received partial compensation in social benefits. Figure 6.2 below shows how official wages in a main job became increasingly de-linked from income and livelihood.

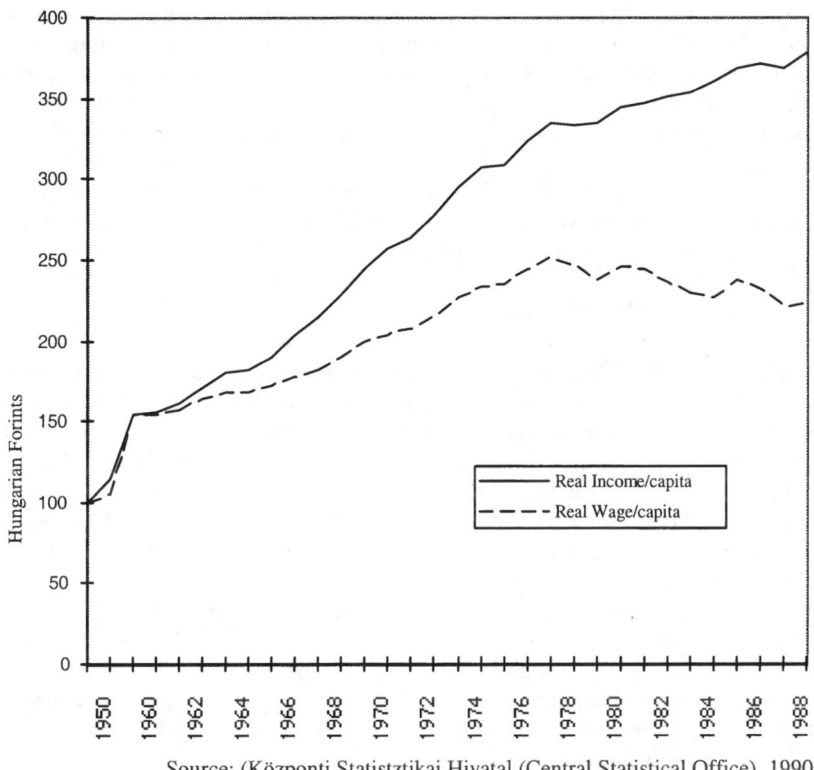

Source: (Központi Statisztikai Hivatal (Central Statistical Office), 1990)

Figure 6.2 Real wages and real incomes in Hungary, 1950-89 (1950=100)

As the status of employment became less and less capable of providing a livelihood, a fundamental divide between employment and unemployment began to disappear. Being employed no longer guaranteed protection against destitution. Statistical analysis of household panel data in the early 1990s found no significant differences existed in the level of consumption of Hungarian households with unemployed members compared to those without (Keszthelyiné, 1995). Galasi shows instead that the best predictors of poverty are whether the head of household is a woman, elderly, or poorly educated (Galasi, 1995). Sík similarly finds that once the statistical incidence of poverty is controlled for age, gypsy origin, education, and rural location, the independent effect of unemployment as a predictor of poverty becomes quite weak. That is, the unemployed are more likely to be impoverished than other Hungarians, but not necessarily more likely than other Hungarians who share the low education, remote location, and other characteristics that typify the unemployed (Sik, 1996). As Julia Szalai argues poverty is not associated with unemployment as strongly as it is with the lack of supplementary economic activities. Post-communist poverty strikes hardest at the kind of exemplary profile of the communist workers, families who might have been former peasants and were mobilized into socialist industry in search of higher living standards. These individuals tend to have been excluded from the "second economy" under state-socialism because they lacked the entrepreneurial skills and had been uprooted from their traditional social networks (Szalai, 1996; Laki, 1998). Secondary and informal economic activity was a lifeline for poorer Hungarians, but as the previous chapter explained, income from these activities increasing flowed to the upper income strata.

Increased Informal Work and Multiple Job-Holding

In the face of the inadequacy of employment in official full-time jobs, Hungarians further accelerated the long trend toward multiple job-holding and informal work was that had begun already with the NEM in the 1960s. When a 1992 poll asked Hungarians, "Do you get enough money from your regular job to buy what you really need?" only a quarter responded that they received even barely enough," compared to almost three times that amount in neighboring Austria. Only twenty-two percent of Hungarians relied solely on activities officially recognized as employment (Rose and Haerpfer, 1993). In a 10-country poll of eastern European countries only 48 percent of families said that a regular job was their main source of income.[24] As main jobs became less and less consequential, Hungarians turned increasingly to multiple jobs and informal work. Measures of the informal economy are speculative by definition but they all seem to indicate a distinct increase during the waning years of communism and further growth under at least the first years of post-communism. The most thorough estimate puts the size of the hidden economy at about a third of GDP in 1990.[25]

There are a number of reasons for an increase in unofficial or unreported economic work outside of main jobs. For one thing, radically uncertain business conditions encourage economic arrangements which are less formalized because people will seek out parallel, personal assurances and prefer short-term arrangements with high profit margins and low sunk costs (Bunce and Csanádi, 1993). Moreover, the retreat of post-communist states from regulation of the economy eliminated many of the potential benefits from formality. In accordance with the "liberalization of the market economy" the government cut back sharply on state-assisted development such as credits and export incentives. In order to harden the budget constraints of firms and promote the dissolution of inefficient firms the government cut back on assistance to businesses in financial distress.

Even when the Hungarian government wanted to provide services and aid for businesses it typically lacked the administrative capacities for doing so. Contrary to the view that central authorities held great power as the result of communism, the important institutional legacy of late-communist plan bargaining is that there was very little capacity to hand over. Toonen suggests, "that the real problem is not only that there are no local authorities, but, even worse, initially there was hardly any effective central power to hand over to them" (Toonen, 1993: 158).[26] Even in terms of sheer numbers of civil servants, the image of the bloated communist state is belied by paltry number of staff in central ministries. According to Rice, there were only eight thousand staff in all Hungary's central ministries in 1992 (Rice, 1992: 121).[27] Toonen points out that by comparison "the Netherlands has over 150,000 *national* civil servants without ever having had the ambition to be a centrally planned economy" (Toonen, 1993: 158).[28]

Post-communist administrative and legislative capacities were typically overwhelmed, under-funded and neglected. At every level of government the administration was overloaded with a flood of new tasks for which it had little experience or resources. Standing has asserted more generally that the region suffered "state desertion": deteriorating public services and salaries of public officials had the consequence that "the capacity of the public administration to regulate the labour market was seriously eroded" (Standing, 1997: 136). In Hungary the problems were compounded because one objective of the political compromises from roundtable talks in 1989 was to ensure an effective separation of powers by preventing any one part of the state from gaining dominant executive power over the others. According to Hungarian political scientists, this led to an over-burdening of legislative competencies of the parliament (Balázs, 1993; Verbélyi, 1993). In the initial flurry of legislation laws were often intentionally vague to help them gain passage in a condensed schedule (Szabó, 1993). The result of all of these overwhelmed and hamstrung administrative capacities is that post-communist public administration worked badly, and therefore the benefits of formal state recognition were less likely to outweigh the bureaucratic hassles and incompetencies.[29]

Formal employment also became increasingly costly as a result of what has been called the "financial crisis of the post-communist state" (Campbell, 1992). Declining GDP and tax receipts led to a vicious cycle of rising tax rates and tax evasion (Kornai, 1992: 13). Governments faced increased demands for funding social benefits and modernization projects but their tax receipts declined. Post-communist governments were typically forced into short-term increases in taxes and contribution rates, which in turn increased the incentive for tax evasion. A 1996 study of the share of unregistered sales in total sales found that hidden sales were lowest in shrinking areas of the Hungarian economy such as industrial products (10 percent) and highest in the fast-growing service industry (69 percent). Tax-revenue was well below the share of reported income that would be expected given the official tax rates (OECD, 1997). One study that cross-checked the tax-receipts of business partners found that the exaggeration and concealment of production for tax purposes was greatest in more private types of firms and in those fast-growing sectors such as business services and foreign trade, in other words, tax evasion was highest in more modern kinds of post-communist businesses that grew at the fastest rate.[30]

Punitive state measures against unregistered economic activity were very rare. The inherited norms of regulatory evasion from the communist era (that "everybody does it") were reinforced by a greater emphasis on profit-seeking. The government explicitly tolerated certain levels of informal work. In 1996 the Socialist-led Parliament passed a package of new labor laws to expand the powers of the Hungarian Labor Inspectorate that may have reversed the trend toward informality of the economy, but at least in the initial years penalties were generally mild.[31] Before the late 1980s the government did not worry at all about major enterprises conducting activity "off the books" because virtually all payments were tallied through a central system of accounts. "When the country was under Communist rule, raising payroll taxes was merely a statistical manipulation because firms were state-owned and both their profits and expenses were part of the total state budget" (Cox, 1993: 356). The marketization of the economy and the economic retreat of the state left little capacity for tracking economic accounts. Governmental bodies typically had little idea of who was really working or how much they were earning. The Hungarian Labor Inspectorate in 1996 had only 200 inspectors, 80 percent of whom were devoted to safety issues.

Social Policies Undermined the Distinction between Employment and Unemployment

As discussed in previous chapters, different kinds of social policies can increase or decrease the salience of unemployment depending on how sharply they distinguish "employment" from others forms of work, and depending on the degree to which social benefits to the non-employed provide enough resources so that recipients are not forced to work. Social policies greatly affect how distinct the status of unemployment is from employment or from other forms of non-employment such as retirement and disability. As this section shows, post-communist social policies intensified a growing trend of Hungarian social policies under communism to blur rather than reinforce the line between the employed, the unemployed, and those who have left the labor force. Post-communist policies have fostered growing ranks of the working non-employed who have been displaced from employment and work alongside their social benefits. These policies diminish the political importance of unemployment by making the status less distinct from other labor force conditions. This is the effect not only of the administration of unemployment benefits, but also of programs for retirement, sickness,[32] and disability.

The Unemployment Insurance and Unemployment Assistance Programs

The unemployment insurance (UI) program was administered in such a way that it encouraged informal work among beneficiaries and depresses wage levels below the nominal minimum wage. Prior to 1996 UI recipients could continue to receive their full benefits while earning up to the full-time equivalent of the minimum wage. For additional earnings up to the maximum benefit level, earnings were to be deducted from the benefit.[33] The incentives of the benefit system promote a set of norms in which the unemployed work and are therefore less distinct from the employed. People receiving unemployment benefits are also required to accept jobs in which they can earn at least the equivalent of their unemployment benefit, even if the benefit may be less than the statutory minimum wage. The UI system thereby undermines the already low minimum wage. The minimum wage, which is the anchor defining the bottom of the UI benefit system, fell from 112 percent of the subsistence minimum in September 1990 to a mere 73 percent in of the minimum three years later (Standing, 1995: 93).

The first post-communist government had believed that unemployment would be small-scale and that people would soon be able to find jobs. Benefits were to be paid originally for a maximum of two years but were shortened to 18 months with lower maximum payment when it became clear how expensive the program was becoming for the government. When the mass of unemployed had still not found jobs, the government in 1992 created a residual assistance system for unemployed to be administered through local governments with financing split between the local and national government.[34] This system was therefore a commitment to help the unemployed until they could find jobs, but at much lower cost to the central budget than if people could collect UI benefits indefinitely. Benefits in this Unemployment Assistance (UA) system are equal to 80 percent of the current minimum old-age pension and paid for an unlimited period of time based on need. In 1993 the local governments were allowed to require that beneficiaries do public work as a condition for receiving benefits and could then pay those beneficiaries up to the minimum old age pension (Frey, 1994). There was no test to ensure that the unemployed were job-seeking and local government officials in various interviews confirmed that they have little idea of who actually works.[35] The UA benefits were means-tested to be available only to those whose UI eligibility had expired and whose total per capita income was less than 80 percent of the minimum old-age pension. Local government officials require applicants to bring tax forms demonstrating that their official income came underneath this bar, but they had no effective way of accounting for income that was not divulged to tax authorities. The local governments operated under the presumption that because UA benefits were so paltry everyone must supplement their benefits somehow, but they did not worry much about screening for those "truly in need" because the time and hassle of obtaining the meager benefits screened out those who did not really need it.[36]

The fact that the unemployed worked was not just an open secret; it was also an active presumption institutionally embedded into (and perpetuated by) social policies. In the 1990 party platform of the newly reformed Socialist Party (MSZMP), they acknowledged that the official unemployment numbers grossly understated the true extent of job losses. Their stated attitude regarding unreported work was that on the one hand it is harmful, but that it also mitigates the resulting social conflict from unemployment and falling wages (Frey, 1994). The unemployed, they concluded, should be encouraged, not prohibited, from taking up extra work. When a journalist asked the Labor Minister in 1995 how unemployment recipients make ends meet , she did not mince words on the matter,

> By working in the black economy, of course. We are pretending we are the nice state giving them at least a little bit of money, But, while this money is too little to starve on, it is clearly not enough to make ends meet. Then we close our eyes, and don't ask the unemployed what they live on. Whether they get a job for a day or two at a construction site, for instance, we don't know. These poor people provide cheap, temporary employees for the black economy.[37]

As Géza Kovács, a Labor Ministry deputy secretary in 1992 describing the conception of new employment policies, characterized the black market work as presumed as "the normal condition" (*Figyelő*, 1993). The Deputy Labor Secretary of Labor confirmed that the authorities did not know who was really working and who was not. If she could rebuild the policy from scratch, she said, she would not even try to distinguish those who were "unemployed" from others in need of social benefits.[38]

The preferences and concerns of the government are reflected in the internal distribution of Labor Ministry personnel. At first there was no special unit within the government devoted to check on unemployment benefit violations. In 1992 the government finally set up an independent control unit for the UI benefit system and the number of disqualifications of benefits for violations increased from about 200-300 to 1100 to 1300 a month (Budget and Social Policy Project, 1990: 56). Tax collection officers conducting a 1992 mass raid on a giant outdoor vegetable market in Budapest, for instance, found that about a quarter of those selling without a license were registered unemployed (*Figyelő*, 1993). In 1995 there were two hundred Ministry of Labor employees assigned to a whole variety of inspection tasks. Eighty percent worked for the National Safety and Labor Control Office devoted to safety checks, child labor, discrimination, and minimum wage violations. The remainder had the residual responsibilities of controlling against benefit violations, but concentrated most of their efforts against illegal work by foreigners.[39] The unemployed were not disqualified if they were working on "special assignments" and only if it could be proved that their income did not exceed half the monthly minimum wage. Employers could easily claim that employees who are working off the books were instead family or friends who were just helping out without working for pay. The authorities had the burden of proof (Interview with Kelmán Laszlo, May 10, 1995).

Old-Age and Disability Pensions

Changes made to the old-age pension system also encouraged a blurring between employment categories by encouraging able-bodied workers to leave the official labor force. This was reinforced even in the official National Labor Market Center brochure titled, "The Laws and Opportunities for those without Jobs in 1990". It opens with a section called "Labor market services" that promises that "everyone can find a solution" and then lists the eligibility requirements for pre-retirement pensions alongside other unemployment benefit programs and benefits (Országos Munkaerőpiaci Központ, 1990). "Pre-retirement" was instituted in 1988 for workers within five years of retirement.[40] Firms could take the option to retire a worker early by paying six months advance pension insurance payments. The government also assumed between 50-100 percent of this cost if firms went bankrupt, were liquidated, conducted large scale lay-offs, or operated without a profit. Workers fearing lay-offs rushed to these programs and pre-retirement was 12 times as numerous in 1991 than it was in 1989 (Szémen, 1994:12). Anticipatory retirement, another program, was introduced in 1991 and gave pensioner status to unemployed workers who met three conditions: they were within three years of retirement age, had been unable to find work for six months, and had worked the minimum service requirements. The program was a kind of subsidized early retirement for the long-term unemployed. Eleven percent of all new pensions awarded in 1993 were for anticipatory retirement (Szémen, 1994). These programs were very effective at redesignating older workers who were likely to become unemployed into official retirement from the labor force. By the end of 1993 less than 2 percent of the unemployed were over 55 years of age (Frey, 1994).

The disability system was also been used as an alternative to unemployment in ways that blurred the boundaries between the categories of employment, unemployment and labor force exit. As mentioned earlier, disability pensions were used as a way to avoid unemployment under communism. The proportion of new disability pensions among the total number of pensioners increased six-fold since 1960 with most of the jump taking place since the mid-1980s.[41] Already as of 1989, registers indicated that 27 percent of pensioners were on a disability pension (Ehrlich and Révész, 1993, 18). These increases were noteworthy because they took place despite a reduction in new accidents reported. Numerous government proclamations under both communism and capitalism condemned inauthentic disability pensions and threatened crack-downs. But the doctors who evaluate the claims have no incentive to reject them. On the contrary, doctors are paid very poorly by the government and receive most of their pay from illegal tips from their patients.[42] In the waning years of communism and the first years of post-communism disability grew especially rapidly, continuing a trend which, as we saw from last chapter, began in the 1960s. By 1995 there was approximately one disabled person for every 10 healthy Hungarians above the age of 15 (International Monetary Fund, 1998, 33). Disability pension recipients were officially supposed to declare any earned income, which would then be subtracted from their pensions, but there is no real system for ensuring compliance. Not surprisingly new disability pensions increased nationally alongside the rise in the unemployment rate and then fell with an easing of unemployment.

Moreover, we can observe the close relationship between disability and unemployment by disaggregating the national data on unemployment and disability into regional data for the years 1990-1993. The closeness of fit between unemployment rates and disability *by region* also increased with the unemployment rate and then decreased with an easing of the unemployment rate.[43] Regional disability claims were most closely correlated to the regional unemployment rates at the end 1992, just before unemployment rates peaked a year later.

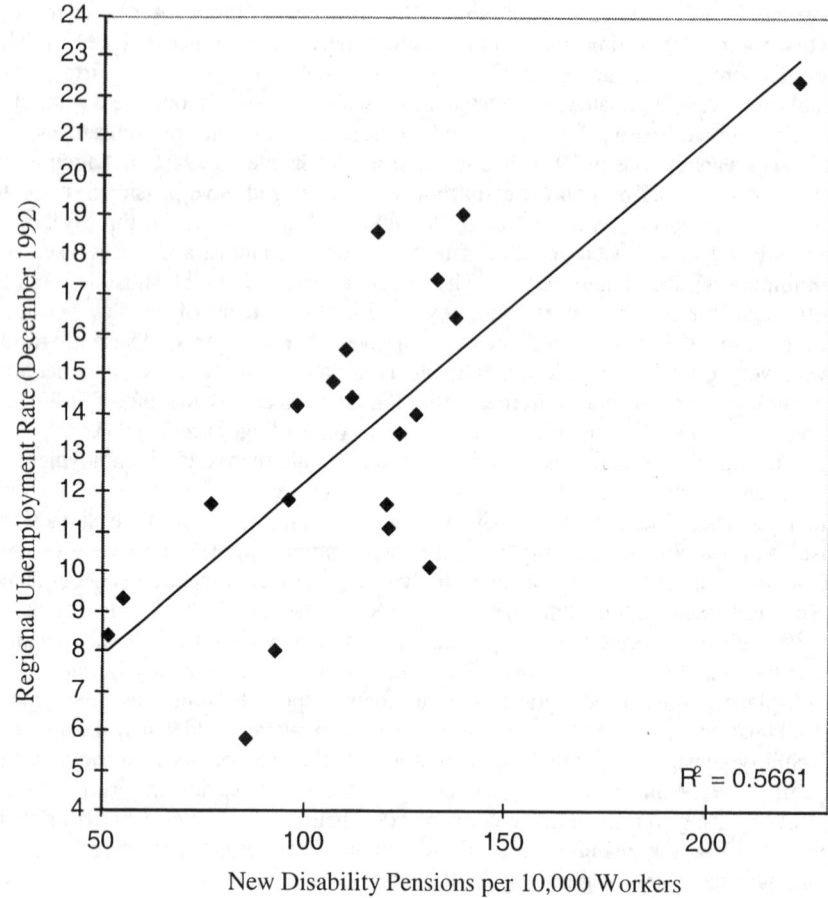

New Disability Pensions per 10,000 Workers

Országos Orvossakértői Intézet, 1995

Figure 6.3 New disability pensions and unemployment rates by region, in Hungary, 1992

In other words, when unemployment most became a threat the incidence of disability pensions was most closely linked to the threat; when unemployment was less of a threat the dispensation of disability pensions was less closely linked to unemployment.

There are two reasons why we would expect disability pensions to have peaked *before* unemployment reached its zenith rather than at the same time. First, unemployment levels grew as a result of inflow. There was never much outflow to employment from unemployment (Koltay, 1995; Köllő, 1995). Thus, we would expect that high unemployment was *preceded* by high incidence of job loss. Second, the doctors who certified that workers have disabilities were often doctors at the enterprise from which they would otherwise be fired. Company doctors might be encouraged (financially or otherwise) to help the enterprise by issuing certifications of disability. The company doctors might also be especially sensitive to the impending plight of workers at plants where lay-offs are imminent. Thus, we would expect that increased disability claims would anticipate lay-offs and be administered before workers are displaced.

The rise in unemployment after the fall of communism was relatively small compared to the fall in employment.[44] Only about a third of those leaving employment became unemployed (Timár, 1998). Those displaced from their jobs typically received some kind of social benefit which they supplemented through informal work. The difference between those entering unemployment and those receiving other forms of social benefits for the non-employed was often quite arbitrary. Together these groups comprised a kind of hybrid between unemployment, employment, and exit from the labor force that blurred the boundaries between each of these categories and made them less politically salient.

Entrepreneurship as the New Employment Prototype

In the post-communist period entrepreneurship was held forth as the chief solution to income and employment difficulties. It was the solution that encouraged a reorientation of political stances about unemployment. Not only were these typically supplementary entrepreneurial activities now recognized as the fastest growing source of national income in the government economic plans, it was also presented as a source of livelihood for the more marginal workers who were eased out of the workforce through expanded social programs. As the preceding pages have made clear, there was a definite economic reality behind entrepreneurship as a new prototype of employment. The income effects of unemployment were indeed less devastating as a result of increasing informal supplementary work, entrepreneurship and multiple job-holding. But it was also significant in its own right that policy commitments and debates came to *presume* that most Hungarians held a diverse portfolio of income sources and a lack of a primary job could therefore be acceptable so long as alternative income sources were made available. Against the backdrop of political expectations for prosperous self-employment, unemployment became less politically salient.

The issue of unemployment did not simply become less salient because the second economy made job-loss less economically consequential. While the second economy was increasingly portrayed as a solution to unemployment, the unemployed did not actually participate disproportionately in the "supplementary" and "helping" economy. The unemployed were concentrated most in depressed industrial towns where there were the fewest entrepreneurial resources and there was little consumer demand to tap (Fazekás, 1993). Far from the second economy being targeted at the unemployed, the unemployed were no more likely to be involved in supplementary incomes than other workers.[45] In the words of, István Gábor, a long-time Hungarian expert on entrepreneurship, "rather than serving to decrease unemployment in regions afflicted by depression, self-employment is itself the victim of local depression" (Gábor, 1997: 163-64). Unemployed individuals tended to be unskilled and were therefore less able to make money in the second economy.[46] The unemployed had relatively less access to second economy income, but it was important that people now generally conceived of employment in terms of multiple sources of income.

The notion that the "second economy" was a bastion of the less fortunate drew from its earlier agricultural roots. In agriculture informal work was more prevalent among the poor and unskilled, groups who came to be over-represented among the unemployed. The pivotal 1980 Party memorandum Róna-Tas cites for expanding the second economy, for instance, justified this course of action partly through the justification that participation in the second economy was more prevalent in the lower rungs of the socio-economic ladder. By the mid-1980s the Party was publicly discussing solutions to employment difficulties in terms of providing greater opportunities for entrepreneurship (*Népszabadság*, 1988). The second economy was viewed as relieving political tensions by compensating the less well off. This helped make the second economy politically acceptable because it was not seen as likely to produce usurious capitalists.

But by 1986, as the second economy had expanded outside of agriculture, it also lost its redistributive compensatory function.[47] The old theory put forward by Szelenyi was that the second economy reduced the inequalities generated by state salaries and social benefits (Szelenyi, 1969). But already by the mid-1980s even Szelenyi agreed this was no longer the case (Szelenyi, 1987). According to one study the Gini coefficient in the mid-1980s for formal income was a relatively egalitarian 0.3; for welfare payments it was a lightly less equal 0.35; and for informal income it was an inegalitarian 0.55 (Elteto and Vita, 1987 in Sík 1992, p. 23). Secondary labor incomes in 1989 were more than twice as important a component of income for the richest 20 percent of the population than such income was for the poorest quartile (Ehrlich and Révész, 1993: 253). As Andorka concludes, "On the whole the incomes originating from the second economy differentiated income levels much more in 1987 than in 1977" (Andorka, 1990: 110-111). By 1987, "the income originating from other [non-agricultural] second economy activities is very strongly differentiated, the share of this income source being much greater in the higher income categories" (Andorka, 1990: 110). Members of new after-hours subcontracting partnerships were most often core workers who were also the best paid in the state sector. It is unclear if earlier informal work really had an equalizing effect on total income. One argument is that Communist Party members had been much less supportive of the second economy until the 1980s when they themselves began to depend upon informal sources of income (Róna-Tas, 1995).[48] Party members became vastly over-represented in these partnerships (160). With the reforms of 1982 "The private sector was now the economy of the strong, the domain of dominant groups. To discontinue the reforms would have required the leadership to turn against its own cadres" (Róna-Tas, 1997: 162).

Regardless of the fact that the unemployed, rarely started their own businesses, entrepreneurship nonetheless became the benchmark of success in employment policy. Gábor describes "the exaggerated and one-sided propaganda campaign advertising entrepreneurship as a wide and preferable alternative path to success in life" (Gábor, 1997: 166). Surveys showed that the proportion of Hungarian adults who saw themselves as prospective entrepreneurs had skyrocketed to over 40 percent, among the world's highest (Lengyel and Tóth, 1993). Stark notes how for post-communist governments eager to show their success in encouraging the private sector, their success was often measured by the number of new private firms. He describes how international pressures encouraged "the ever more excited and breathless tones" of assertions about the percent of GDP that post-communist governments claimed were generated from their budding private sectors.[49] In describing these "political pressures" he makes direct comparison to the pressure of earlier communist prototypes of employment.

> Measurement problems are compounded, moreover, by political pressures to show higher and higher levels of "private sector" activity in order to represent better the government's case to international lending institutions, potential foreign investors, and the domestic electorate. The race among Hungary, Poland, and the Czech Republic to show the highest private sector statistics to the IMF recalls, of course, an earlier race during the period of "building socialism" (especially immediately following the ouster of Tito's Yugoslavia from the Cominterm) when the parties and governments of these countries competed for the right to claim the highest proportion of collectivized or state property in their national statistics. Indeed, it is an open secret in Budapest that high government officials urged the use of different statistical cut-offs and measures upon returning from international conferences where Polish officials proudly displayed figures showing that the Hungarians no longer deserved the yellow jersey as first place in the statistical race to capitalism (Stark, 1995: 7-8).

In the light of such pressures to conform to a particular metric of successful transition, it is not hard to see why post-communist governments embraced the large numbers of new "firms" created by entrepreneurs. It mattered little that these start-ups very often had no employees and little business activity. Some governments, such as in Hungary, passed laws that greatly encouraged citizens to start their own business, if only to write off their taxes on their apartment and telephone (Gábor, 1991). Firms with 50 people or less accounted for 56 percent of employment yet only 26 percent of employee income in 1995 (Kőhegyi, 1998: 399, 404 my calculations based on data). By 1996 there were over one million registered private ventures, three-quarters of which were individuals. Ninety-seven percent of all enterprises employed less than 10 people and an estimated 30 percent of all registered companies were completely dormant (Kőhegyi, 1998: 399).

Even the unemployment insurance system attempted to encourage entrepreneurship by giving those who qualified for unemployment the opportunity for below-market interest rate loans meant explicitly for starting up new companies. This program, a kind of regional development policy folded within active labor market policy, had no equivalent in any other OECD nation (Frey, 1994: 61-62).[50] Spending on these start-up loans for the unemployed increased more dramatically than other active labor market measures in its first years (Láng and Bonifert, 1994: 28).[51] In addition to financial support equal to up to six months of lump-sum unemployment benefit, the program reimbursed or covered up to fifty percent of professional counseling, training, or credit insurance costs (Frey, 1994: 1). Frey reports that only 17 percent of those receiving start-up loans would not otherwise have launched the business (Frey, 1994: 11). The program was discontinued when the government realized that many people were simply recycling these low interest loans into higher-interest bearing bank accounts (Braun, et al., 1993, Munkaügyi Ministérium [Labor Ministry], 1991).[52]

The privileged place of entrepreneurship in Hungarian policy, discourse and statistics accelerated the late-communist trend toward small proprietorships.[53] By the beginning of 1998 more than half of Hungary's economic organizations, a full 54 percent, were self-employed "entrepreneurs". As many as 97 percent of all operating businesses employed less than 10 people (*Népszabaság*, July 29, 1998, p. 5). Small-business and self-employment continues to be the fastest growing forms of employment. As of the beginning of 1997 there were only 3.4 employees per registered enterprise in a Hungarian economy which had inherited an industrial structure heavily biased towards super-large scale units. There were almost 750,000 registered sole proprietor enterprises in an economy with only 3.6 million active workers (OECD, 1997: 97).[54]

There are two additional ways that the new prototype of entrepreneurial employment undermined the political saliency of unemployment. First, entrepreneurship was not well matched for the new statistical standards for unemployment statistics. And second, the presumption of self-employment undermined the power and militancy of unions.

Given the rapidity of the fall of communism and the subsequent uncertainty and lack of civil society, Western models offered a reassuring template and at least some source of authority (Jacoby, 1998: 6). The first regular labor force survey was instituted with a pilot study in 1992. But recall that the ILO/OECD "labor force" method of defining unemployment is particularly poorly suited for situations where self-employment is prevalent because the fact that someone has a (self-employed) job means little in terms of whether they have paid work. Moreover, much of the typical activity of the self-employed involves soliciting clients or publicizing one's services in ways which are often indistinguishable from the "job-seeking" activities that are supposed to distinguish the unemployed.[55] The labor force model suffers even greater conceptual ambiguities when we consider how escalating Hungarian norms of multiple job-holding. The Hungarian survey makes some attempt to acknowledge these problems by asking respondents to designate a category of their "main work". But this in no way addresses the key problematic assumption underlying the logic of standard ILO/OECD concepts is that those who are employed are a separate category from those who are actively seeking work. But in Hungary, even wage earners who have open-ended full-time labor contracts at well-established firms still typically seek other means to supplement their earnings.[56] These sentiments are later echoed by post-communist officials and the media.[57] Labor Minister Magda Kovács quipped in 1994 that, "If you ask me if unemployment will grow in the months ahead, I'll have to answer that, statistically speaking, it will not. But as long as the economy doesn't grow, then the group of inactive workers will continue to grow".[58]

Similarly, the entrepreneurial prototype undermined union militancy. Organized labor is an obvious potential opponent of unemployment because lay-offs harm workers and diminish their bargaining power with management (Golden, 1997). In Hungary the official organization of unions became more independent from the Communist Party during the 1980s and tried to fashion itself as more of a movement defending the interests of those who were threatened by economic reform.[59] Yet, despite high unionization rates[60] and the advent of unprecedented unemployment, unions did not try to mobilize collective action or take strong political stands against rising unemployment.[61] First, union leadership was preoccupied with how the new forms of work organization undermined their bureaucratic power. Secondly, the fact that workers had largely shifted their concerns and aspirations about their livelihood to supplementary work and entrepreneurship made it easier for the state to buy off the unions with additional income-supplementing schemes. In 1984 the umbrella organization of official unions (SZOT) proclaimed that, like the government, they were committed to full employment but conceded that temporary involuntary displacement of workers resulting from the reorganization of manpower would be a feature of the future Hungarian economy. SZOT agreed not to contest dismissals from reorganization, endorsing the principle that enterprises would only employ the manpower they needed (*Magyar Hirlap*, 5 May 1984). Newly appointed Secretary General Lajos Mehes proclaimed in public speeches that obstacles to layoffs for technological development would be a serious mistake (*Nepszava*, 5 Oct 1984). "The question", as Noti notes, "remains however: why did the unions concur so readily?" (Noti, 1987: 70).

During the time when unemployment was first introduced in the mid-1980s the unions were preoccupied with the introduction of new kinds of subcontracting units that bypassed union representation. In 1982 the government had introduced a variety of new quasi-private ways to organize production, the most popular of which was the "enterprise work partnerships" (*vállalati gazdasági munkaközösségek* or VGMKs) in which workers in a state firms could create their own after-hours sub-contracting firms. Generally more skilled workers, typically using the enterprise's tools and materials, could earn higher than normal rates on sub-contracted projects. The work was typically subcontracted from the state enterprise in which they worked during normal hours.[62] VGMKs grew quickly because they were lucrative and legal sources of supplementary income. In 1982 twenty-nine thousand employees earned extra income in VGMKs, while by 1986 this number had jumped to 268,000.[63] VGMKs were also popular with management because their payments to these units were officially accounted as company costs, not wages. Sub-contracting costs therefore circumvented the severe penalties they would otherwise incur for exceeding their allotted wage-fund limits.

The sub-contracting system gave managers a whole new range of tools for meeting production quotas and granting favors they could use to recruit, retain or motivate their workers, especially scarce skilled labor. Unions opposed VGMKs because they undermined their ability to control working hours or conditions as well as their ability to collectively bargain for wages.[64] Workers were increasingly concerned about the opportunities and access to VGMKS and unions were frozen out of the entire process of bargaining and favors. Publicly unions opposed the VGMKs for their fostering of materialist values and the fact that they took away time for family and political or union activities. Unions also accused VGMKs of deliberately under-producing during normal hours or using normal hours to prepare for VGMK work. Union attempts to gain jurisdiction over the VGMK, however, were rebuffed by the central Party leadership. New union leadership appointed in 1984 expressed support of the VGMK.

Unions were not entirely passive about unemployment but they eschewed any militancy and unwisely focused their efforts on boosting redundancy payment laws. In March 23, 1988 the chairman of the trade union council (SZOT), Sandor Nagy in the newspaper *Magyar Hírlap* requested a repeal of the 1986 laws that made it easier to fire small groups of workers, noting that companies had abused the rule by staggering mass dismissals over many days to keep them below the threshold. In November of that year the trade union board opposed the government's motion to introduce unemployment benefits in the coming January. They favored redundancy pay that would be financed solely through the employer and would continue until another job was found. They correctly argued that the projected budgetary provisions would prove insufficient for covering unemployment compensation costs.[65] Their pressure was able to secure stronger redundancy pay but they were mistaken in thinking that these payments would effectively discourage employers from lay-offs.[66]

The stress on entrepreneurship as the solution to employment problems encouraged unions to see severance payments as a palatable compensation for lay-offs.[67] They pushed for amendment to the Labor Code in late 1991 that mandated seniority-based severance payments to workers not dismissed for disciplinary reasons.[68] The unions' public position in the fall of 1991 when the bill was before Parliament was that they would only accepted the rest of the Labor Code if it included generous lump-sum severance payments.[69] By the time one-party rule ended in 1990, it was already well-established that unions would not militantly resist lay-offs the way they had in Poland. But unions in the 1990s would have been more militant against unemployment if they saw themselves as protecting old-style bread winner jobs rather than securing entrepreneurship and sub-contracting ventures.[70]

The Exception Proves the Rule: Ózd

Insofar as the issue of post-communist unemployment has been politically salient in Hungary, it was most so in places where *employment* more closely resembled the patterns of the early post-Stalinist era.[71] The former steel town of Ózd is a telling exception which helps prove the general rule that the changing characteristics of employment diminished the political salience of unemployment.[72] Unemployment rates in Ózd grew to almost forty percent in the early 1990s. But terrible though the situation was in Ózd, unemployment rates were often worse in other more rural towns and former cooperatives. But unemployment rates above 33 percent could be found in 10 of the 176 labor placement districts in 1992 (Koltay, 1995). The Blue Ribbon Commission noted the paradox that the worst hit areas were rural while the most publicized were industrial like Ózd,

> An important outcome of the research on regional differences is that the really hard-hit areas are almost all rural ones with an agricultural rather than an industrial character [such as] the highly publicized cases of run-down industrial centres like Ózd (Budget and Social Policy Project, 1990: 18).[73]

The exceptional political charge attached to unemployment in Ózd makes sense in the context of how Ózd had been a show case for the Stalinist industrialization drive. Shortly after the war the Communist government had nationalized the steel works from its patriarchal entrepreneur, Tivadar Rombauer. It flourished, churning out the basic materials for industrialization such as steel reinforcing bars, wire and rod and structural steel.[74] The steelworks were expanded and Communist propaganda of the period depicted the steelworkers as shock troops in the building of a new society in a "country of iron and steel".[75] At its peak the town's huge foundry, steel mill and mines employed 22,000 workers, producing 1.5 million tons of steel a year, much of it for export.[76] Nearly a third of Hungary's iron ore and over a third of its steel came from Ózd.[77]

The jobs at the Ózd steel mill were also the model of the old communist idea of generous paternalism. The factory had provided workers with culture, housing and child care (Fazekás interview, February 1997). Jobs had been relatively high-paying and workers had less need to rely on supplementary work arrangements than in most places. Wages of workers in the Ózd steel plant averaged in 1987 a monthly 7,311 Ft., compared to 5,889 Ft. in other machine industry and compared to a mere 4,593 Ft. for light industrial workers in the area (Kormos and Munkácsy, 1989: 41). By contrast to Ózd, the character of employment in most of the other high unemployment areas was irregular and non-industrial.[78]

Employment at the Ózd steelworks came to resemble the industrial prototype even more closely in the late-1980s as a result of earlier downsizing initiatives which had eliminated less prototypically "core" workers. After five years of heavy losses the government in mid 1986 instructed the company to reduce its operations and restructure in order to gain profitability. Between September 1986 and

December 1987 the plant reduced production by 15 percent, junking some old furnaces and rolling mills. The work force was reduced by 17.7 percent, or 2,400, the largest personnel reduction under state socialist Hungary (Szirácki, 1990). The shake-up in Ózd was viewed as a laboratory and a model for redundancy policies more generally. "The intention was to develop a model (it became widely known as the 'Ózd model') which could later be applied to other regions if, as anticipated, job losses and unemployment became more common in Hungary" (Szirácki, 1990: 128). In April 1988 the Party's Planned Economy Committee resolved to reduce state subsidies in the steel sector toward the goal of eventually eliminating such subsidies, scaling down production, and changing output to better match world market demand.[79] Management used a number of methods to reduce employment at the steelworks. In addition to a recruitment ban, it reduced the number of working pensioners (who worked on short-term contracts), and workers with less than 6 months until retirement were placed on the re-employment scheme so that they could collect their earnings until retirement. The government eventually allowed them to let go of those close to retirement or with some disability with new anticipatory retirement pensions. Moreover, management began to apply new governmental disciplinary guidelines. A single repetition of unjustified absence, a failed alcohol test, violation of technical or safety rules, refusal to obey orders, or abuse of sick pay could incur instant dismissal. Late arrival or early departure from work was now punished firmly with reductions in pay-scale or elimination of taken-for-granted bonuses (Szirácki, 1990: 129).[80] The discretionary nature of the lay-off criteria gave managers the ability to lay-off the politically less core workers while being easier on (at least the well behaved) Hungarian breadwinners.

> [S]hop floor managers enjoyed a good deal of freedom in bringing their power to bear on those who were prone (or thought to be prone) to lack discipline. The policy of raising disciplinary standards seemed to be aimed deliberately at those groups of workers who were least integrated into industrial work organization— because, for example, of their youth, their low qualifications, or their ethnic minority origins (Szirácki, 1990).

Gypsies were disciplined the most under the new rules while middle-aged Hungarian males were disciplined least (Szirácki, 1990). An official of the Central Metallurgical Union in Budapest succinctly summed the underlying political logic of these ethnic patterns: "When Gypsies are laid off, workers' solidarity is low. If skilled, educated people are laid off, then solidarity will be much greater".[81] Among the registered unemployed 70-75 percent were male unskilled gypsies under thirty years of age (Szirácki, 1990: 135). Ex-steel workers comprised only 24 percent of the registered unemployed in Ózd.[82] When mass lay-offs eventually were ordered at Ózd they disproportionately struck at "core" socialist workers in heavy industry. The later job-losers in Ózd were disproportionately male and typically had been working in the same steelworks for many years (Bajka, et al., 1996).

When it came to government attention to particularly severe pockets of employment, the devastated villages and cooperatives were largely overlooked in the budget while places like Ózd were showered with special initiatives. This was despite the fact that poor rural areas also had little tax base to pay for the unemployment assistance (UA) benefits of workers who exhausted their unemployment insurance. Almost half of spending budgeted to "crisis areas" in the 1992 budget went to Ózd, with about 80 percent of what remained going to the railways and a metal works plant in Diósgyőr (Budget and Social Policy Project, 1990: 27).[83] Politicians feared that the Ózd steelworks might become the Hungarian version of the Gdansk shipyards in Poland.

Unlike other places, the workers in Ózd protested repeatedly and even came to Budapest to stage highly visual demonstrations in front of Parliament.[84] The opposition parties did not prompt these demonstrations. The opposition Socialist party had actively aided organizations of the unemployed in 1990 to 1993 by providing office space and encouragement. But Ózd was not among the approximately sixty places where local chapters were established.[85] The particular political saliency of unemployment in Ózd also can not be ascribed to an unusually militant group of workers, since lay-offs in Ózd had struck a deep chord when they took place years. Even before the lay-offs became larger scale Pál Mátyas, the section manager at the State Wage and Labor Office in 1987 proclaimed that "there has never in the nation been such heinous difficulties with finding employment as in Ózd" (Juhász, 1987). As Kormos and Munkácy observed, the papers referred already at the end of 1987 to the "Ózd syndrome", its "stone cold furnaces" and "slow agony" when 3,000 workers were laid off and mainly reassigned or took up early retirement and a total of twenty workers had to have their period of notice extended (Kormos and Munkácsy, 1989: 7-8).

The plant closures in Ózd also left workers without entrepreneurial skills or opportunities. Despite training centers,[86] long-time factory workers were ill-prepared with the business and personal skills for starting their own businesses, and there relatively little effective demand for the typical kind of small private endeavors in food-service, personal services and taxis.[87] Government programs seemed to recognize the different regional capacities for generating entrepreneurship. The regions hit hardest by unemployment spent proportionally more money on job creation subsidies and especially public works; whereas the regions with less unemployment spent more on start-up loans and training (Köllő, 1995). In an interview with the Labor Minister in 1996, she distinguished between "*real* unemployment like that in Ózd, and other kinds" (Kovács interview, 1997). Minister Kovács states that the government had once even struggled with the statistical office to try and distinguish the "real kind" of unemployment from a variety of other approaches where individuals either: struggled with legally allowable hours of low-paying work but were still eligible for benefits, or unable to work because of disability or problems such as alcohol, those who simply had no skills, or those who preferred to work unofficially. The preponderance of informal work encouraged this kind of thinking and made many in the government (and especially the Finance Ministry) hesitant to pay higher jobless benefits. But the low benefits also made it clear that those who were "really" unemployed could not subsist. Ear-marked funds to the regional labor board of the tripartite Interest

Reconciliation Council (ÉT) therefore presented an attractive solution that seemed to target funds to genuinely unemployed populations.

Post communism led to the proliferation of blurred forms of quasi-unemployment, but not in Ózd because employment in Ózd resembled the old Communist prototype and carried with it the earlier expectations and state commitments. The Ózd case reminds us that *differences* in the types of labor market boundaries can be critical for explaining differences in unemployment politics.

International Comparisons

Just as Ózd was an exception within Hungary, there are exceptions across Eastern Europe more generally. Observers of the region are familiar with scenes of Polish labor militancy against proposed lay-offs or with the great importance attached to unemployment in the former East Germany. Scholars note that the degree of popular anxiety about post-communist unemployment does not seem to reflect the differences in macroeconomic conditions.[88] How might we explain these cross-national differences in the political salience of post-communist unemployment?

In Hungary regional differences in the political salience of unemployment were explained by differences in the prevailing character of employment. In the Hungarian area of Ózd, where employment resembled the old communist prototype, unemployment was likewise still a highly salient political issue. Variation in the political salience of unemployment between post-communist countries can also be explained in this manner. Since the political salience of unemployment depends on the distinctiveness of unemployment from the category of employment, we should predict greater militancy about unemployment in those exceptional places where employment remained a status that was distinct from work more generally. Unemployment will be politically most salient when there have been extensive lay-offs of workers whose employment has been a protected category ensuring minimum livelihood and security and particular institutional supports not accorded to other forms of work. Unemployment has been more politically-salient in places such as Poland or the former-GDR where employment has remained more distinct from other forms of work.

	Employment indistinct from unemployment	Employment distinct from unemployment
Many lay-offs	Hungary	Poland, East Germany
Few lay-offs	Russia	Ø

Figure 6.4 Post-communist political salience in four countries

Differences in the political salience of unemployment match what Sík has found to be the relationship between unemployment and poverty in the three countries in the top row of the table above. Comparing similar data in Hungary, Poland, and former East Germany, he concludes, "Although the factors that cause poverty in [these other countries in] Central Europe and Hungary are more or less the same, the role of unemployment in Hungary seems to be less significant" (Sik, 1996: 367). Let us very briefly consider the three other cases from the table above.

Poland

Poland is the post-communist country where unemployment has been the most contentious issue.[89] When the Polish polling agency CBOS asked Poles what were the most important problems facing Poland, two-thirds mentioned unemployment in 1992, a proportion that rose to 69 percent in 1993 and fell to 65 percent in 1994.[90] In second place was "low wages and high prices" which received 59 percent in 1992, 49 percent in 1993, and 54 percent in 1994.[91] Bell (1997) shows that in Polish elections in 1990, 1991, 1993 and 1995 regional differences in unemployment corresponded to less support for free-market candidates. In high unemployment areas support was generally higher for populist and former communist candidates (Bell, 1997). This effect was independent of the effect of rising or falling incomes for that region. Similarly, Przeworski's study of Polish polling data and elections leads him to conclude that,

> While Poles support pro-market reforms and the institutions that forge them, when incomes decline and prices mount, they are not willing to continue reforms and withdraw confidence from democratic institutions in the face of mounting unemployment. And, in the end, fear of unemployment overwhelms everything else (1993: 180).

Przeworski's analysis concludes that anxiety about unemployment was crucial in eroding popular support for Poland's "shock therapy" program in 1990. Four months into the program 85 percent of respondents deemed unemployment "despicable". "And those threatened with unemployment were willing to resist it: 65 percent of them said... that they were willing to strike in defense of their jobs" (Przeworski, 1993: 181).

Unemployment is a bigger political issue in Poland than places like Hungary or Russia because, due to the exceptional militancy of industrial labor during the late communist period, jobs in heavy industry continued to pay a family wage. Polish wages fell after communism and multiple-job holding surely increased somewhat, but industrial workers (who were hit hardest with the threat of job loss) still regarded their jobs as a solid source of livelihood. In a 1991 New Democracies Barometer, Poles were more than 50 percent more likely than Hungarians to say that their regular job provided them with the money to buy what they needed (Rose, 199). The size of the informal, unreported economy in Poland is estimated at 15.8 percent in 1993-1994. This is sizable, but is about half the estimated extent of informal activity in Hungary (28.1 percent) or Russia (36.8 percent) at that time (Rosser, et al., 2000: 164). Poland also did not have the strong legacy of multiple job-holding that had emerged out of the agricultural cooperatives in Hungary because the Polish peasantry instead kept their independent farms and generally worked solely in farming. Another reason Polish employment maintained exceptional distinctiveness as a labor force category was because Poland was the only post-communist country where post-communist minimum wages rose as a portion of the average wage (Standing, 1995: 21). In other countries sharp declines in the real value of the minimum wage meant that a job no longer guaranteed subsistence.

East Germany

On the face of it East German unemployment should have been less politically contentious than in other post-communist countries. While unemployment reached high levels, there was an initial moratorium period on lay-offs and a tremendous effort and resources were dedicated to making the process of transition humane and efficient.[92] Huge sums of money were spent to cushion the effects of displacement from restructuring the East German economy.[93] Half or more of the unemployed were placed in training or make-work programs without large drops in pay (Jacoby, 2000: 133). There were generous early retirement programs (*vorruhestand*) and "further training programs" (*Fortbildungsmaßnahmen*). The latter program had limited success relocating workers into the private sector because unemployment is chiefly the result of a general oversupply of labor than a mismatch of skills. Thus these workers were placed into job creation programs (*Arbeitsbeschaffungsmaßnahmen*) to perform production for tasks for which no private demand exists (Pohl, 1999: 18-19).

But far from exemplifying quiescence about unemployment, East Germany has seen some of the most contentious unemployment politics in the region. The most publicized examples were the metalworkers strike in spring 1993, or the hunger strike by potassium miners protesting against their mine closing. As case studies by Turner make clear, East German militancy was the norm despite inauspicious circumstances of a weakened bargaining position and an economy that declined in real GDP by 42 percent from 1989 to 1992 (Turner, 1998: 43).[94] In Leipzig the weekly protests that had helped bring down the communist regime were repeated in 1991 with unemployment a central grievance, slogans such as "close down the closer-downers", and participation reaching as high as 80,000. The head of the *Treuhandanstalt* privatization agency was assassinated in 1991. East German voters in 1990 elections voted overwhelmingly for the party most closely affiliated with the center-right CDU but after the Kohl government was perceived as caring more about inflation than unemployment Eastern voters subsequently turned their votes to the Social Democrats and even the reconstituted Communists (Party of Democratic Socialism).[95]

A critical part of explaining the political salience of unemployment must be the nature of East German *employment* and the changes that took place in the employment model during this time. First of all the GDR was the most industrialized country in the former Soviet-Bloc which made lay-offs particularly difficult and dramatic. Post-communist protests were concentrated in industrial centers such as Dresden, Leipzig and Chemitz. But more important is the fact that the changes that took place in employment were the opposite of that in other post-communist countries. Rather than falling wages and a relaxation of the distinction between employment and other forms of work, the distinct status of employment was maintained and even bolstered by the adoption of the West German industrial relations system. There was a wholesale institutional transfer of the West German industrial relations and social policy institutions.[96] These institutions are the quintessential example of a employment-based insurance-style model with strong restrictions on the nature of employment and relatively few opportunities for casual work (Esping-Andersen, 1990). German welfare state institutions have been designed to discourage downward pressures on employment standards. This encourages workers to fight for their jobs. For example, during the 1993 metalworkers strike, "Leaders also reminded eastern workers that if unemployment came, it would be better to be laid off at a higher wage than a lower one, since unemployment benefits were based on the last monthly wage" (Jacoby, 1998: 159). Wages did not fall. In fact in manufacturing and construction wages increased almost 60 percent from April 1990 to April 1991 (Pohl, 1999: figure 4). Nominal wages for East Germany as a whole increased from 47 percent of West German wages in 1991 to 71 percent in 1994 (Pohl, 1999: 7). In the simplest terms, unemployment meant more in post-communist Germany because the job one lost meant more.

Russia

Russia has been almost the diametric opposite of East Germany. "It has often been assumed that the greatest tension would come from rising unemployment, but there are many other social discontents" such as low pensions or late wages that have been the focus of political discontent (Roxburgh and Shapiro, 1996: 19). Outright lay-offs have been relatively rare. Soviet production was so centralized, that the least efficient firms slotted for downsizing were often one-company towns. The geographic concentration of labor in huge enterprises made mass lay-offs and plant closures politically infeasible. Even in smaller enterprises, Russian managers have tried to avoid outright lay-offs because of severe tax penalties and mandated severance payments of two-three months salary. Russian taxes on the average wage encourage firms to retain surplus workers and pay them very little—so as to bring down their wage average and thus their tax liability. The excess wages tax is effectively an indirect subsidy to retain surplus workers (Roxburgh and Shapiro, 1996). Instead of lay-offs managers try to get workers to quit by delaying their wages or placing them on extended leave.[97] Wage arrears are most acute in heavy industries that would otherwise be prone to lay-offs, such as ferrous metals, where

62 percent of companies have wage arrears, or oil production where 86 percent do.[98] There were also 4.6 million workers simply placed on "administrative leave" at the end of 1995.[99]

Enterprise directors can afford to retain surplus workers as a way to avoid taxes or severance payments because the minimum wage in Russia is kept very low, insufficient even to buy a daily loaf of bread and liter of milk. It fell from about a quarter of the average wage in 1990 and 1991 to less than an eighth of the average wage since 1992 (Roxburgh and Shapiro, 1996). Russian wages in 1995 comprised only 40 percent of total money income, down from 46 percent the year before.[100] Only a mere seven percent of workers in state enterprises said they earn enough from their first job to live on. Among all Russian workers only 13 percent earn enough from their regular job to get by; 54 percent do not earn enough from regular job but do with additional incomes; 33 percent do not earn enough and must borrow or sell household goods. People have turned to secondary informal jobs and household work. The typical (mean) Russian participates in 3.7 different forms of activities for income or food (Rose, 1993).

Russian workers often have been kept nominally employed but paid only part of their wages, and permitted to continue to enjoy non-wage amenities such as factory housing, kindergartens, cut rate groceries etc.[101] The diminished meaning of employment is clear from the 1995 New Russia Barometer (Rose, 1996). Fifty-six percent of Russian workers said their wages had been paid late last year (82 percent of whom by 3 months or more), 9 percent said their wages were not paid at all. The Russian statistical agency Gomostat even started keeping track of wages-actually-paid as a separate statistical category from wages-formally-allotted. The use of sham employment to lower taxes is such common knowledge in Russia that the St. Petersberg booklet for new Russian taxpayers, *47 Legal Ways of Lowering your Taxes*, recommends hiring casual workers to "wash windows, sit at telephones, courier duty, etc." (Roxburgh and Shapiro, 1996).

Not surprisingly, Russian unemployment statistics are also viewed with deep suspicion. In 1994 the International Labor Organization estimated that the 1.6 percent unemployment rate was at least five times too low. They noted the difficulty of concluding anything about unemployment when an estimated third of all Russian workers were in "suppressed unemployment", that is, employed Russians without real jobs or real pay. At any moment they estimated that another seven percent of workers were idle because of work stoppages, twelve percent were on short time, and about 15 percent of workers were kept on at lowest pay just to keep the average wage bill below levels where taxes kick in.[102]

Russian deviation from international statistical norms is perhaps encouraged by the knowledge that the standard methods are ill-suited to track the Russian labor force. To the Russians this point was made brutally clear in speech by ILO representative, Guy Standing, who emphasized to new Labor Ministry officials that while the Keynesian frameworks of unemployment the Russians were adopting distinguish between mutually exclusive employed, unemployed and inactive,

[T]he threefold distinctions can only be applied with reasonable validity to an industrialised market economy in which one part of the population is in regular full-time employment while the remainder are firmly outside the labour force and thus not part of the labour reserve. Labour markets in industrialised market economies no longer correspond to anything like that pattern. ...In short, the labour force approach, which remains the basis for labour statistics in market economies, has become unreliable for the purposes that it is supposed to serve (Standing, 1991: 398).

With such skeptical views about the reliability of unemployment indicators it is not surprising that the measure has not been a major bone of contention.

Conclusion

The process by which employment lost its political salience after the fall of communism can be seen as a reversal of the dynamics which created the unemployment taboo in the first place. There was a transformation in societal norms that also took place at the micro-political level, though with different intensities in different countries.

Recall that the Communist Party's commitments to eradicate unemployment had earlier provided definite micro-level mechanisms that reinforced the inherited disapproval of unemployment.[103] The political commitment created its own micro-level "barriers to exit" because once the eradication of unemployment became an established benchmark for the competency of economic rule, it then became more politically costly to reintroduce unemployment. The presumption of full employment was further embedded in new social policies that delivered benefits through employers. Employment was typically an administrative precondition for receiving most social benefits, which made the prospect of job loss represent an even greater social exile. Once legitimacy had been established along particular benchmarks, this also created political "returns to scale" for individuals who subsequently sought to claim credit for their accomplishments. Once "success" has been defined in terms of eradicating unemployment there was an incentive to claim success along the same lines. Petty officials, supreme leaders, and even aggrieved workers could justify their own ends in terms pursuant to the established goal of eradicating unemployment. In doing so, individuals both benefited from the norm against unemployment and simultaneously reinforced its perceived priority.

Such self-reinforcing patterns began to erode the political threat of unemployment when entrepreneurship was officially embraced as an alternative kind of work relationship. Under post-Stalinism the informal economy and multiple job-holding began to proliferate in different countries with different timing, speed, and official recognition. We have seen how in Hungary the indirect effect was to create various mechanisms of self-reinforcing "returns to scale" which undermined the salience of unemployment as a political issue and as a focus of the struggles of organized labor. Once workers received incomes from a variety of sources, job loss no longer seemed so grave a threat. The self-employed might sometimes lack income; but they would not lose their means of livelihood and identity in the way that state employees could. Once workers became increasingly oriented toward the second economy as their means of opportunity and advancement, they also became less inclined toward union militancy in their official main jobs. This in turn made it easier for employers to cut wages and thereby make "main" jobs still less important. As governments had difficulty collecting taxes on secondary and informal work, they were forced to raise taxes on officially registered work, and thereby created even greater incentives for people to avoid official registration. And once "entrepreneurship" was embraced as a public virtue, then individuals could claim credit or justify their own selfish goals in terms of promoting "entrepreneurship" in much the same way that they had earlier claimed to be championing universal employment in state enterprises.

Finally, we have seen how differences in the meaning of employment can be a basis for international comparisons in the meaning of unemployment. The next section shows both that we can observe similar dynamics in *how the meaning of unemployment changes* across a variety of countries, and also as a basis for comparing *how politically important* unemployment is in different countries.

Notes

1   See also Offe, 1992; Przeworski, 1991.
2   See Chapter 10 for sources.
3   The political transition to democracy in Hungary was negotiated over round-table talks and was technically little more than a constitutional amendment ending the Party's leading role. See Elster on the various legitimacy deficits—upstream, process, and downstream—all of which were lacking under post-communism (Elster, 1993). See also Offe, 1992.
4   The definition of "full employment" was rarely specified. Officially in 1988 the State Wage and Labor Office defined full employment "as having meant the abolition of unemployment. In capitalist countries [they clarified], 2-3 percent unemployment can be associated with full employment. But this would be an unacceptable reinterpretation for our society". The union council full agreed with this view (SZOT, 1988: appendix 4).
5   A sign of the unexpected scale of unemployment is evident by comparing planned against actual budget allocation for benefits and labor market programs from the general budget during the initial years of these programs. In 1989 actual expenditures came in almost 13 percent *under* budget (2.1 versus 2.4 billion forints). In 1990 the actual budget was 32 percent *over* budget (7.8 versus 5.9 billion forints). In 1991 budget estimates were almost doubled to 11.6 billion forints, but were still 6.4 billion forints short of actual requirements (35 percent). Aided by large increases in payroll tax requirements to fund the benefits, the government anticipated budgetary outlays of 10.2 billion forints in 1992, but the actually expenditures were almost three and a half times greater (35.3 billion forints) (Budget and Social Policy Project, 1990: 24). Despite its formal insurance-based format a majority of unemployment insurance expenditures came from the general budget.
6   The unemployment rate was a mere 0.1 percent in 1987, 0.2 percent in 1988 and 0.3 percent in 1989 (Frey, 1994).

7   Governments initiated price liberalization, subsidy cutbacks, and the opening of foreign trade with the West. Previously protected state enterprises were exposed to stiff new competitive pressures and the threat of bankruptcy.

8   Sales to the USSR as a portion of exports fell from 33 percent in 1987 to 12 percent in 1991 (Bartlett, 1997: 218).

9   In September 1988 the State Wage and Labor Board defined "large-scale" (*tömeges*) unemployment as when the registered unemployed rose to a full 1-2 percent. The union council's official reaction was to state that they could agree with such a concept "with the proviso that from their perspective and that of society, smaller amounts were also unacceptable" (SZOT, 1988: appendix 4).

10 Congresses of major parties held special sessions on health care and pensions but not unemployment. Parliamentary debates arose about reducing the costs of unemployment benefits but not about the human costs that only recently before would have been regarded as scandalous and intolerable.

11 Tucker's in-depth statistical analysis of the 1990 and 1994 Hungarian national elections show that once controlled for other independent effects (from income change, GDP/capita, urban population, agriculture, and industry) the only party who received statistically higher level votes in high unemployment counties was the unreconstructed hard-line Workers Party. This was the only party who absolutely opposed plant closures and western-style unemployment. This party narrowly failed to gain the minimum threshold of three percent to enter Parliament in 1990 and then fell in popularity in 1994 (Tucker, 2000: Tables AIII.2 and AIII.3). Tucker's results do not deny that the unemployed did disproportionately vote for leftist parties. Opinion polls indicate they did, but only in proportion to what we would otherwise expect due to the fact that these unemployed voters tended disproportionately to live outside Budapest and were more likely to be poor (Simon, 1994).

12 Interview with Károly Fazekás, labor economist, governmental expert advisor, and participant in national tripartite bargaining meetings for the union LIGA, February 1997.

13 Anxiety about the relative threat of unemployment versus inflation was not a simple function of the rates of these measures in a country. In Belarus, for instance, the lowest portion of people felt inflation was the larger threat, despite the fact that unemployment was low and hyperinflation ran at 1,500 percent. Rose found that macroeconomic conditions explain a "trivial" amount of the variations in the perceived relative threat. Individual characteristics explain much more. People over the age of 60 are much more likely to be concerned about inflation, which makes sense because they are less likely to have a job that they could lose and they are typically on fixed incomes. In a separate study using this data to examine four post-communist elections from 1992 to 1994 Harper finds no statistically significant relationship between unemployment and voting against incumbents (Harper 2000).

14 Five major dailies were coded, encompassing the bulk of readership and a spectrum of ideological leanings. The three latest years contained no protest events which cited involvement by the unemployed, despite the fact that these were the years of highest unemployment. Protest by the unemployed *per se* may be a highly imperfect measure because the largest political costs of unemployment on government support result from employed workers' fears of unemployment (Saint-Paul, 1996).

15 Despite the recent surge in unemployment, it was a theme in the in the nightly news 0.09 percent of the total topics from the end of July to mid October 1994.

16 *Financial Times*, 6 February 1991. The minister is Vladimir Dlouhy.

17 As late as the end of 1993, 84 percent of Hungarians agreed that the state should be mainly responsible for employment (Miller, et al., 1998: 114). Almost half (47 percent) of Hungarians held that "unemployment is unacceptable" and only eight percent agreed that "unemployment is necessary" (1998: 117). When asked about societal goals in 1988, "full employment" was regarded as more important than "freedom", "democracy", "national independence", or "efficient economic reform". Other research that traces the strong legacy of communist-era norms on post-communist political evaluations, especially regarding issues of social justice includes (Csepeli, et al., 1994; Csepeli and Örkény, 1994; Miller, et al., 1998; Örkeny, 1994; Rose, 1993).

18 It was not the case that unemployment was lost as a political issue simply because political energies were absorbed in ethnic-nationalist crises. Popular discontent about job loss has fed the flames of ethnic separatism in less cohesive states such as former Soviet republics and has fostered virulent racism and anti-immigrant violence in other places such as East Germany. This might serve as a partial explanation for why surging unemployment was not politically salient in places like Yugoslavia or Soviet Georgia, but not Hungary, where there has been no similar intensity of ethnic conflict.

19 On communities' tendency to magnify small distinctions as a means of affirming solidarity, see Freud's discussion of "the narcissism of minor differences" (Freud, 1961: 72).

20 The "Return to Europe" thesis would also suggest that political parties had no significant differences on their stances toward unemployment because they closely conformed to "European" norms. But, studies of citizen perceptions of the parties on major issues at the end of 1993 shows that voters did not perceive their stances on unemployment as any less dispersed than on other issues (Karajánnisz, 1994).

21 In a comparative study with the Netherlands, 66 percent of Hungarians said that they were ashamed of being unemployed, compared to 20 percent in the Netherlands. Only 6 and 7 percent of Hungarians agreed with the statement that unemployment was respectively a freedom or that it was good because their leisure time increased— compared to 49 percent and 48 percent who agreed with these statements in the Netherlands (Simon, 1997).

22 Time series data indicates that Hungarian inflation in the early 1990s was caused by cost-push factors, not wage-price pressure (Bartlett, 1997: 192n).

23 Wages as portion of income comprised an average of just under sixty percent in East Europe at the end of communism (Poland 53.0, Czechoslovakia 69.5, Hungary 55.0, Yugoslavia 62.2, Bulgaria 56.5). East European wages are those of state-sector workers only. In capitalist countries the average was almost 70 percent (Sweden 64.5, W. Germany 63.1, Australia 71.2, USA 75.8, UK 72.0) (Milanovic, 1992: 5).

24 In Hungary regular jobs were the main income source for 59 percent of families.

25 One well-executed study measures the "illegal economy" not observed by state-centered statistical authorities is M. Lackó (1992). It estimates that as a portion of GDP the illegal economy constituted an additional 13 percent in 1973, 18 percent in 1987, 26 percent in 1988, 31 percent in 1989, 34 percent in 1990. This study is an exceptionally long time-series and its numbers are consistent with other approaches (Árvay and Vertés, 1995), but hidden income is only a rough approximation of the second economy, which was sometimes regulated by the state. When managers were asked what their perception was of the incidence of unregistered sales for the economy as a whole, only 10 percent believed they were rare compared to 90 percent who felt they occurred often (Semjen and Tóth, 1997a). See also Gábor, 1979; Galasi and Sik, 1988; Sík, 1996 and Hankiss, 1990; *Figyelő*, 1993.

26 This is consistent with Ekiert's description of societies in East Central Europe as having a weak state and a weak society (Ekiert, 1991).

27 According to another estimate the number is a still meager 11,257 with an additional 44,000 in sub-national state offices and another 38,700 on local government staff (Balázs, 1993: 78).

28 The Hungarian numbers are particularly small if we consider that western administrations rely heavily on subcontracting and informal delegation to the non-profit sector and that this sector was virtually absent at the outset of post-communism. On subcontracting to non-profit organizations in the American welfare state see Smith and Lipsky, 1993.

29 Stark describes, "When private entrepreneurs look to government policy, they see only burdensome taxation, lack of credits, virtually no programs to encourage regional or local development, and inordinate delays in payments for orders delivered to public sector firms" (Stark, 1996: 999).

30 Evasion is highest among the new limited liability companies, for whom it was found that, "On the average 87 percent of gross production value and 581 percent of labor cost is 'missing' from the balance sheets" (Vertes and Árvay, 1994, 13).

31 In 1997 200 additional inspectors were hired for labor relations inspections and be given powers to enter without special permission or advance notice and to obtain and copy labor related documents. They could now routinely ask for social security numbers or work permits and employers were fined on the spot. In a shift, the new law was aimed more at large, established employers, not small-timers.

32 Programs granting sick leave have also been used to avoid unemployment. Sick leave pays 75 percent of wages and is financed largely through the central government. In 1994 the average worker lost 26.5 days per year due to health problems, over twice the rate of 12 per year back in 1970 (OECD, 1997: 102). By contrast, the 1996 rate for the United States is 5.6 days per year. In 1995, 7.8 percent of Hungarian employees were off sick on any given date. As a quasi-control we might note that in 1994 the incidence of sick-leave by employees was twice that of the self-employed (the average duration was easily twice as long) (OECD, 1997: 102, 104).

33 In 1996 benefit penalties were instituted for amounts less than the minimum wage. Excess earnings beyond the maximum benefit level incurs a complete cut-off of benefits.

34 In January 1993 UI eligibility was then cut to 12 months.

35 Interviews with local government officials.

36 Director of the Kesckemét regional labor office, Pál Feleki similarly estimated that eighty to ninety percent of unemployment-benefit recipients worked informally and that this money exceeded their meager benefits (interview, January 1997).

37 March 17, 1995 Budapest Business Journal: 18 "Labor Minister wants to 'tidy up the mess'".

38 Personal interview with Lilla Garzo, January 29, 1997. Ministry of Labor, Budapest.

39 As legal expert, András Sajó puts it, "All monitoring of employment and aid has essentially been an ethnic policy. This keeps everyone happy. The bureaucrats get to show that they are doing something, and the domestic population is not put out" (Budapest interview May 15, 1995). Until forced to do so as a condition of preparedness for EU entry, the Hungarian unemployment insurance system disqualified foreign workers.

40 Workers could go into pre-retirement they were within 5 years of retirement, had been employed for 25 or 35 years (for women and men, respectively), and had worked at least 5 years in their current firms.

41 The number of disability pensioners per ten thousand insurees has gone from 26 in 1960 to 70 in 1970, 89 in 1985, 101 in 1988, and 162 in 1993. All data from Hungarian Social Security Yearbook 1994 (draft copy) tables 4.2.2. Some part of this increase is undoubtedly due to deteriorating health.

42 Officially there is condemnation of the high-priced tipping that is now necessary to get medical attention. The government is unwilling to pay doctors enough so that they will reject tipping and the state implicitly condones this illegal practice, even including doctors tips as a category in income tax forms.

43 The correlation coefficient between disability and unemployment climbs and then falls steadily from 0.24 in mid-1990, 0.28 at the end of 1990, 0.30 in mid 1991 and the end of 1991, 0.48 in mid 1992, 0.57 at the end of 1992, 0.38 in mid 1993 0.33 at the end of 1993, and 0.30 in mid 1994. Mid or end-year rates apply only to unemployment; all disability data are for that year as a whole. Attempts to lag the relationship between disability and unemployment do not produce higher correlation coefficients.

44 Note that the employment rate is different from the participation rate. It is tabulated by taking the totals for employment of those aged 15-74, excluding parental leave and conscripts, and dividing the sum by the working age population. For men the employment rate fell to 59 percent—below the OECD average of 66 percent, but not far below the OECD Europe average of 60 percent. Women's employment dove below OECD and OECD European averages, to a mere 46 percent. For those 56-74 years old the employment rate was merely 11.2 percent in 1996, among the lowest in the OECD. Employment rates for those 25-50 are still higher than similar age cohorts in most other OECD countries (OECD, 1997: 76). Core employment remained unchanged since 1989: Employment rates for males 25-55, at 75 percent, are relatively unchanged over the 6 years following 1989, despite the massive reduction in employment. It is reductions in the employment of young, old and women that has brought the employment rate down.

45 Similarly Fazekas and Köllő find that at the lay-offs at Rába 28.9 percent of those dismissed reported a secondary income compared to 43.8 percent of the elite workers.

46 On the correlates of entrepreneurship, see Fazekas (1993). On how social connections diminish unemployment duration see Csoba, 1993.

47 Róna-Tas states, "The fact that the private sector was compensatory precisely because of the restrictions that were about to be lifted most certainly occurred to many in the leadership" (Róna-Tas, 1997: 142). The unemployed lack the skills, contacts or equipment and are too often concentrated among depressed areas to have much opportunity for moonlighting income. Tax evasion is more the province of the self-employed than the unemployed (Pahl, 1987). See also (Róna-Tas, 1994, Szalai, 1997).

48 (Manchin, 1988: 88-89) found that in 1982-83 Communist Party membership was already associated with higher levels of non-agricultural second income and multiple income strategies in general (including overtime).

49 Stark points especially to the special section of *The Economist*, March 13, 1993 (Stark, 1995: 7). On international ideological pressures on post-communist governments see (Deacon and Hulse, 1997; Jacoby, 1998; Cox, 1993).

50 On entrepreneurial start-up loans see Munkaügyi Ministérium [Labor Ministry], 1991; Munkaügyi Ministérium [Labor Ministry], 1990a; Braun, et al., 1993; *Népszabadság*, 1988.

51 Spending for start-up loans for the unemployed to become entrepreneurs rose from 1.2 percent of all active labor market spending in 1991 to a peak of 6.2 percent in 1993 (Frey, 1995: appendix).

52 According to József Rózsa, then a prominent government spokesman on unemployment from the State Wage and Labor Office, the loan programs did have some success. He believes that while half the recipients bought things like furniture, the other half did start businesses. Their business ideas were sometimes misguided and prominent press accounts told how these failed entrepreneurs were still saddled with paying back the loans (Interview with author, January 1997).

53 According to Köllő's studies of firm behavior before 1990, paid employment fell 11 percent in the 5 years before 1990 despite the fact that total GDP increased 5.8 percent over this time period. This decrease occurred all within the large enterprise sector where surveyed firms cut employment an average of 20 percent. Self-employment took up the slack (Köllő, 1995).

54 Forty percent of the sole proprietorships were not officially operating. A number of reforms were instituted on 1 January 1997 to address abuses of this system. 1) The rate for employer contributions to health care was reduced but a minimum contribution of 1,800 forints a month was established—increasing the tax on reportedly low income earners. Firms may apply for special subsidizes to offset this hardship. 2) The social security tax base was expanded in early 1997, levying a 39 percent social insurance contribution on entrepreneurial income in addition to the 10 percent pre-existing accident insurance they were already paying. This 49 percent social security payment is roughly in line with that for other employees. 3) As of 1997 individuals with a secondary entrepreneurial activity must pay a minimum social security contribution equal, at minimum, to 39 percent of the one-half monthly minimum wage for each of their first two enterprises. All entrepreneurial income less than 1.2045 million forints per year from additional enterprises, including income in excess of half the monthly minim from each of the first two enterprises is subject to the same 39 percent social security contribution.

55 "In economies in transformation, the very idea of having a job is problematic" (Rose, 1997: 14).

56 The problem was not simply that the first public measures of unemployment were an awkward admixture of communist-era labor categories that seemed to obscure as much as they revealed (Köllő, 1990: 117). Statistical measures of the economy changed much more slowly than the economy itself was changing. It was not until 1991 that Hungary had population surveys for measuring unemployment statistics. Until then the number of "unemployed" was simply the number of people who were registered as unemployed through local labor offices. Those who were not eligible for benefits had no reason to register. As labor economist, János Köllő estimated, in 1988 the official jobless numbers were only one twelfth of the actual number of those who were unable to find official work. "[A]t least 90-95 per cent of the unemployment stock is unregistered and only 10 per cent of the registered workers is supported by one or more of the existing schemes" (Köllő, 1990: 105). The census was especially slow to change its accounting system. Their 1994 data, published in 1995, still used the old 1952 categories of active and inactive earners (Timár interview May 28, 1998). Throughout the 1980s macro-labor statistics came only from the manpower estimates self-reported by firms with over 50 people. Fifteen percent of these firms did not even give their data and day laborers were not included. On statistical problems and conceptual issues in East European unemployment numbers see Chernyshev, 1994. Conclusions about the labor market

often depended on the choice of incompatible data, the choice of measure, or the choice of contradictory interpretation. Even with technically sound data techniques, there were still deep contradictions concerning what the unemployment rate was supposed to be an indicator for. If, for instance, unemployment was supposed to be counting lost labor capacity, then the half million unemployed in the mid-1990s is a serious underestimate of the 1.5 million reduction in employment since 1990. On the other hand, if unemployment is primarily a leading inverse macro-indicator for inflationary pressure, then Hungarian rates may be an overestimate because, as studies suggest, the approximately 50 percent of long-term unemployed exert no pressure on wage inflation (Layard, et al., 1991).

57 A prominent article in the largest newspaper in 1993 titled "Is the measure accurate?" discussed how the official reduction in the unemployment rate did not reflect an improvement in employment but mass exits of the labor force altogether (*Népszabadság*, 1993).

58 *Budapest Business Journal*, July 8, 1994, "Jobless Count: The Real Numbers?": 2. The disparity between statistical and administrative realities is evident in the relative lack of overlap between those who can register as unemployed and those who count in labor force surveys. A 1996 comparison of the 520,000 registered unemployed in the second quarter of 1996 found that barely half counted as unemployed by ILO criteria. Conversely, barely forty percent of those counted as unemployed by ILO the labor force survey were are also registered as unemployed with the labor office (OECD, 1997: 142).

59 Before the 1980s, unions' power derived from their position within the Party. The president of the union council (SZOT) sat on the Politburo and upper level representatives negotiated wage contracts with the Ministry of Industry and the State Offices for Wages and Labor (Noti, 1987).

60 At the fall of communism, Hungary inherited unionization rates that were as high as seventy percent. More recent estimates place the unionization of the workforce at 25-30 percent (Neumann, 1997).

61 Hungarian officials granted greater autonomy to their official unions in the 1980s because they feared the rise of unofficial unions such as Solidarity in Poland. Unions exhibited some militancy around other kinds of economic issues. In 1988 and 1989 SZOT was involved in unprecedentedly confrontational wage negotiations with the government (Bartlett, 1995). In 1989 May Day demonstrations were able to rescind utility price hikes and institute wage increases and during roundtable talks the union also challenged hikes in the price of meat (Bartlett, 1995). After 1989 the communist trade union council (SZOT) reorganized itself into a new body (MSZOSZ) that had no formal links to the government or the Communist Party, they still eschewed confrontation or even sustained attention regarding unemployment.

62 Although less common, VGMK could also conduct projects for other enterprises. There were a variety of limits placed on who and how many people could work in a VGMK, etc. For a detailed discussion of VGMKs see Seleny, 1991; Stark, 1990. For a description of other forms of private partnerships see Seleny, 1991.

63 These numbers are from an untitled mimeographed table from Teréz Laky. They also appear in Seleny, 1991: fn104.

64 Workers trying to supplement their wages with divergent strategies also diminished solidarity, especially because privileged core workers started their own VGMKs and focused on these side businesses rather than the unions (Neumann, 1997).

65 BBC November 19, 1988 from Hungarian Telegraph Agency November 16, 1988.

66 Interview 1997 with László Csaba and separately with Uri Csaba.

67 As Labor Ministry deputy László Hercogh noted in a January 1997 interview, severance payments were especially attractive because they could be collected simultaneously with other income so long as income remained unreported.

68 The 1991 labor law made severance pay up to six months of salary compulsory for dismissals due to economic reasons and obliged negotiations with employee representatives if there were more than 50 redundancies over six months. Enterprises could largely get around these regulations by claiming that the lay-offs were due to individual performance problems rather than "economic reasons". According to Köllő that only about 40 percent of redundancy qualified for severance pay (Köllő, 1995). Maximum compensation paid 6 months salary to workers who had been at a firm for 25 years or more.

69 Author's interview with Labor Ministry deputy László Hercogh, January 1997.

70 The policies of the new post-communist government further fragmented organized labor by encouraging inter-firm battles over "spontaneous privatization" and inter-union battles to re-register members. Just as union members and their leaders were preoccupied with VGMKs in the late 1980s, they were most concerned about "spontaneous privatization" in the early 1990s. Within months of taking office the new post-communist government realized that privatization was a more difficult process than they anticipated and that the State Property Agency was unable to effectively manage the thousands of state enterprises it controlled. Unions were not given a role in this process and they were thereby closed out of the most important opportunities for workers to get rich during the initial post-communist years. Including an inner circle of workers helped cast buyouts in less exploitative terms. These often-complex arrangements represented a parallel system of reward and privilege that undermined union power and froze them out of a process that was informally negotiated around management initiatives. On the spontaneous privatization experience and the effects on organized labor see for instance, Stark, 1991; 1996; Móro, 1991; Voska, 1990; Neumann, 1990; 1997. Unions were also forced into a protracted three-year campaign against each other for representation on new works councils and on social security and health fund boards. The inheritor of the socialist union mantle, MSZOSZ won about half the seats at the social security and pension boards and over seventy percent of the vote for works councils in 1993; but the extended campaign, which began with its announcement in 1990 and involved nine separate unions, absorbed much of organized labor's political energies and sapped its ability to initiate other forms of collective action.

71 The other exception to the rule is the successful stand-off between another group that epitomized the old prototype of socialist work. A group of miners at the Mecsek pits in southern Hungary demonstrated against the new Party General Secretary, Karoly Grosz who was preparing a major restructuring of the mines in 1988. Despite the fact that the loss of production from the miners strike did not in itself create any pressure on the government, Grosz himself came to the mines and negotiated a settlement (Bartlett, 1995). Another instance that might qualify as an exception is that teachers could sometimes be militant in resisting lay-offs by local governments. The teachers union organized by the non-communist union LIGA received training from American teachers unions as a result of American government-funded programs to advise non-communist unions in the Soviet Bloc. The US unions recommended organizing unemployed workers in Szatmár, and the leadership council considered organizing among the unemployed in Ózd, but declined. In the first instance the prospects for success were considered distant; while in the second workers were regarded as already to close to the

former communist union (Interview with former LIGA official, Mihály Csako, Budapest, January 1997).

72 On the particular situation in Ózd see Bajka, et al., 1996; *Figyelő*, 1989; Kormos and Munkácsy, 1989; Szirácki, 1990.

73 Hungarian employment in agriculture was hit harder than industry, losing 41.3 percent of its employment from January 1, 1990 to January 1, 1993 compared to a twenty three percent loss (and a few thousand less total numbers) over the same period (Budget and Social Policy Project, 1990: 2).

74 *The New York Times*, April 8, 1988.

75 *The Washington Post*, August 18, 1988.

76 "Hungarian steel town anxiously seeks rebirth", *The Financial Post* (Toronto), January 11, 1996, p. 50. In the early 1980s the Ózd Steelworks employed 36.2 percent of the region's labor and 46.5 percent of the region's working males (Szirácki, 1990: 127).

77 "Doom and Boom: Tale Of Two Hungarys" AP Worldstream, April 12, 1994.

78 In fact registered unemployment rates would have been far higher in these agricultural areas if the government had not excluded those with temporary lay-offs from the unemployment rolls in February 1992. Agricultural coops in 1991 had used the uniform national unemployment system to subsidize a kind of informal work-sharing arrangement in which individuals were temporary laid off (to work informally in the cities) during seasonal slow downs. Two peculiarities in Hungarian regulations made this possible. First, unemployment benefits were not experience-rated, that is, benefits were not smaller for those with shorter continuous employment histories. Second, the high severance payments were supposed to discourage temporary lay-offs but a loophole in the law allowed employers to forgo these payments if they had "mutually agreed" with workers to cancel and employment contract. "In Feb. 1992 the authorities decided to exclude these workers on temporary layoffs from the UI benefit on the grounds that their employment contract had not been terminated. More than 50 thousand workers were removed from the register at that time" (Köllő, 1995: 191).

79 The plant had been using turn of the century technology and unjustifiably high levels of energy consumption.

80 The disciplinary redundancy was effective immediately, unlike the softer methods which typically required three months notice (sometimes extended to nine), approval from the workers, and the task of selecting which workers to dismiss.

81 *The Washington Post*, August 18, 1988.

82 The others were mostly those who had quit other jobs or who were school-leavers or were coming from maternity, sickness or military leave. The employment exchange arranged opportunities for seasonal and casual work outside of the area. The municipal government also organized some public works brigades (Szirácki, 1990).

83 Rural unemployed are less likely to register as unemployed because they are rarely eligible for benefits, but according to the head of the Ózd social welfare committee, Ózd had the highest total registered unemployment for any single municipality in the country with 4,100 registered in 1993 and 9,700 registered in 1994 (Zsolnay, 1995).

84 The exceptional political activity and attention around Ózd was also confirmed by Mihály Csako, a professor at who was a leader of the alternative union LIGA during the late 1980s and early 1990s (interview, Budapest, January 1997) and by József Rózsa, a prominent government spokesman on unemployment issues in the last communist years from the State Wage and Labor Office (Interview, January 1997). Károly Fazekas also stresses the perceived importance of Ózd for social peace.

85 Interview, Anna Betlen, February 1997. See also (Betlen, 1993). These organizations of the unemployed were comprised mostly of laid-off government administrative workers. They mainly served as mutual support groups but sometimes were able to secure some individuals jobs and to gain representation in local level tripartite bargaining. There had been a failed attempt in December 1988 by SZOT to establish a trade union in Ózd, as well as neighboring Miskolc, as a way to keep these workers loyal to the official union ("Report Unions Established for Unemployed", *The Associated Press*, January 12, 1988).

86 A special German-style training center was set up in Ózd (and nearby Diós-Győr). The Diós-Győr training center was the result of a compromise worked out between representatives of the National Labor Board who were called in by the Ministry of Industry to assuage discontent about pending mass lay-offs (Fazekas interview, February 1997).

87 On the statistical correlates of entrepreneurship and their relative absence in old industrial centers, see Fazekas, 1997.

88 Rose's study of opinion data in post-communist countries finds that macroeconomic conditions explain a "trivial" amount of the variation in people's perceived relative threat between inflation and unemployment. In the nine post-communist countries studied, the relative fear of unemployment was strongest in Belarus, despite low unemployment and 1,500 percent hyper-inflation (Rose, 1997: 14).

89 Another familiar example is the miners in Romania. They were also a relatively privileged group of workers under communism who maintained high wages and lived in economic conditions where there was little other income opportunities for work. For miners, in other words, there was little other work than their employment and their employment meant a good deal in terms of livelihood, security and prestige. The loss of such jobs was particularly politically salient.

90 This is consistent with New Democracy Barometer data on the inflation-unemployment trade-off which also indicates that unemployment concerns peaked in 1993.

91 CBOS, "Poland's Most Pressing Problems", Polish Public opinion, February 1994, p. 1 (n=1226).

92 From 1989 to 1991 the national product of East Germany fell by about a third and industrial production by around two-thirds. About four million East Germans were out of work or in make work positions (Maier, 1997: 290). Employment in industry dropped from 8 million at the fall of communism to 3.7 million in 1992 (Maier, 1997: 300).

93 An estimated 750 billion Deutsche marks were transferred between 1990 and 1995 (Jacoby, 2000: 133).

94 In terms of strikes, their incidence typically decreases during times of loose labor markets. Striking workers have less bargaining leverage because employers need workers less and workers face more competition from others willing to take their jobs with lower pay, lesser benefits and worse conditions. See Kennan, 1986; Soskice, 1978.

95 Through the mid-1990s the PDS had significantly higher party membership than any of the major parties from the West (Eith, 1999: 13). In 1994 in the state of Brandenberg that surrounds Berlin the PDS finished second in regional elections, leaving the CDU in third place.

96 As Jacoby shows, in the process of implementing this transfer many innovations and accommodations of the German model resulted (Jacoby, 2000). For more on industrial restructuring in Eastern Germany see Locke and Jacoby, 1997.

97 Lehmann, et al., 1999 argues that the dominant form of labor-market adjustment in the Russian transition process has been delayed receipt of wages.

98 Cited in Penny Morvant and Peter Rutland, "Russian Workers Face the Market", *Transition*, 2, 13 (June 1996): 7.

99 Interfax, 28 May, 1996. Cited in cited in Penny Morvant and Peter Rutland, "Russian Workers Face the Market", Transition, 2, 13 (June 1996): 7.

100 Gomostat, 1995 cited in Penny Morvant and Peter Rutland, "Russian Workers Face the Market", *Transition*, 2, 13 (June 1996): 7.

101 In state enterprises workers received the following for free or very cheap as part of compensation from the firm: meals (22 percent), medical care (50 percent), housing (11 percent), holiday facilities (43 percent), kindergarten (42 percent), food (12 percent) (Rose, 1996).

102 *Moscow Times*, International Weekend Edition, "ILO Scorns Official Jobless Statistics", Nov. 6, 1994: 41.

103 See Pierson (2000) for a discussion of the micro-foundations of path-dependency in politics.

PART III
COMPARATIVE CASES

Chapter 7

Comparative Cases of Conceptual Change: America, Britain, the USSR, and Municipalities near Geneva

Reinventions of unemployment are not restricted to state-socialist regimes or to Hungary. This chapter examines four other cases where unemployment has been reconstructed. In the municipalities around Ghent officials framed unemployment policies in terms of skilled organized labor because this was the kind of employment that was most politically threatening. In Britain unemployment policies and concepts were framed by the intent to discourage casual work and encourage full-time work. In the Soviet Union the concept of unemployment was reinvented around a new prototype of *orgnabor* employment. In America during the Depression unemployment was loosely defined to indicate the number of needed public works positions; but this definition was changed to match the new policy tools of aggregate demand management and to help sort out those who would not ordinarily have been employed if not for the war effort.

The Definition of Ghent: Union Employment, Union-Defined Unemployment

The first institutionalized definitions of unemployment arose with the first government institutions that specifically compensated the unemployed in ways distinct from other impoverishment. It took place in trades where the criteria of acceptable employment were narrowly prescribed by skilled trade unions and guilds in the municipalities around the city of Ghent. Trade unions had developed mutual benefit funds to sustain members without work earlier in the nineteenth century.[1] When unions started setting up their own unemployment benefit schemes the primary goal was to prevent the underbidding of wages, and only secondarily to relieve social distress (Harris, 1972: 297). Only in the 1890s did some municipal governments begin to subsidize these with public funds, a practice that spread quickly through Germany and the surrounding area.[2] These early efforts reflected a compromise between municipal governments and dangerous revolutionary unions. Union employment was promoted, and unemployment was defined only in terms of unionized labor.

State-funded unemployment insurance was a topic throughout Europe since Bismarkian programs for industrial insurance and old age. It was the Depression of 1890 that finally spurred more serious discussion and eventually action on state programs. Sporadic revolutionary violence had broken out and sympathetic municipalities set up pre-emptive funds for job-losers.[3] The mayor of Schönberg argued in a report to the Imperial Ministry of the Interior that unemployment insurance was needed as a preventative against "dangerous movements" (Steinmetz, 1993: 206). Evidence indicates that organized labor was relatively less effected by job loss than other workers, yet unions were more politically organized around the issue and represented a troubling threat to local governments. "In 1887 the free trade unions began collecting statistics on joblessness among their members" (Steinmetz, 1993: 204). Because of the political organization and threat of organized labor, the only workers eligible for government subsidized unemployment programs were union members.

Representatives of organized labor were encouraged to both articulate workers' interests and to implement public policies that they would then defend to the rank and file (Steinmetz, 1993: 202). Local business elites reconciled themselves to the existence of a permanent organized labor movement and made concessions to municipal socialists as political players.

> Proto-corporatist policies were addressed primarily to the more stable, industrial male, better-paid sector of wage earners—to the group that made up the bulk of the socialist trade unions. Union members were the privileged participants in the Ghent system, for example, and no real effort was made to create a viable form of unemployment insurance for non-unionized workers (Steinmetz, 1993: 203).

Funds were organized like private insurance along actuarial lines, with contributions made by employers and employees and municipalities typically paying a fifty percent subsidy to labor unions who administered payments to members and policed against false claims (Steinmetz, 1993: 204). As for the less skilled and unorganized workers, the argument advanced at the time was that emergency relief would be adequate. Other forms of employment loss were not treated as distinct from poverty more generally.

For organized labor, not only did the Ghent-style funds serve an insurance function for workers who were able to afford it; the cushioning of workers from unemployment also helped circumvent the problems of upholding minimum wage standards.[4] The Ghent system insured that decisions about which workers should be denied a benefit for rejecting suitable jobs would not be implemented in such a way as to undermine wages (Rothstein, 1992: 41). Benefits made job-losers less desperate and therefore less likely to undermine wage norms. Topalov even argues that before state subsidies the out-of-work fund of trade unions was less a form of unemployment insurance than it was a strike fund to be used in the event of industrial dispute or when workers turned down jobs available in shops that would not abide by union scales (Topalov, 1998: 9). The initial state efforts to expand and extend the union funds with subsidies curbed this effect by denying benefits to workers who were on strike or who refused to accept reasonable job offers.

The Ghent system of organizing unemployment relief through unions spread rapidly throughout much of Europe, an outgrowth of the social democratic compromise to strive for workers' interests within the electoral system. The first grants were made in 1901 and favorable results led the program to be adopted through most of Belgium over the following six years. Ghent-type arrangements were initiated in Milan, Amsterdam, Strasbourg and other cities by the end of the decade and it covered a majority of French municipalities by 1907. In 1904 the national government of Norway instituted a Ghent-type program which also included union contributions (Heclo, 1974: 70). Most unemployment insurance programs adopted by German cities before the world war were structured along Ghent-style lines. In Germany Steinmetz reports, "unemployment insurance was directed toward the long-term domestication of the Social Democratic party" (Steinmetz, 1993: 211).

Ghent style arrangements still exist in four countries where unions administer unemployment insurance. Non-unionized members are not outrightly excluded from benefits, but the unionized prototype is nonetheless significant. The four countries using this system (Sweden, Denmark, Finland and Iceland) have the highest unionization rates in the world. Norway, which is otherwise quite similar to Sweden in terms of industrial relations, does not use the Ghent system and its unionization density is a mere 55 percent compared to Sweden's 80 percent. Belgium has a near-Ghent system in that unions administer the insurance programs but they are not voluntary; and Belgium's unionization rate is far higher than neighboring Netherlands (Holmlund and Lundborg, 1999). Rothstein shows that all the industrialized countries with the highest unionization rates in the 1980s had some form of Ghent system; and that these countries did not have relatively high unionization rates in the 1930s but have built them over time (Rothstein, 1992: 41-46). In Ghent-style countries the traditional negative relationship that exists over time between unemployment rates and union density is also reversed: whereas in other countries higher unemployment encourages more people to accept non-unionized jobs, in countries with Ghent-style unemployment programs when unemployment rises more workers join unions (Lange and Scruggs, 1997).

English Unemployment Defined to Discourage Casual Work

In England the creation of unemployment as an institutionalized category was not a compromise between government and trade union. Instead it resulted from the confluence of concern for social distress from periodic industrial downturns, and an attempt to discipline casual laborers into continuous full-time work. Policies and political rhetoric explicitly sought to foster an employment prototype of the full-time male breadwinner, and the resulting concept of unemployment reflected this prototype.

Before the end of the nineteenth century "unemployment" was not a social category that was distinct from pauperism. The *Encyclopedia Britannica* did not include an article on unemployment until the eleventh edition in 1911.[5] Heclo reports that before the Beveridge social-security model was established there had been little attention to unemployment because of "the traditional viewpoint of the Poor Law: worklessness as a basis of need resulted from personal failings and not from any impersonal workings of poorly adjusted economic aggregates" (Heclo, 1974: 67). Charles Booth's seventeen volume study of London poverty, *Life and Labour of the People in London*, conducted from the mid-1880s to its completion in 1913, concluded that the majority of poverty was caused by low wages and insufficient work; but he did not try to distinguish between these causes.[6] Alfred Marshall's *Principles of Economics*, which became the standard textbook in neoclassical theory from the 1890s, similarly did not mention unemployment, only "inconstancy of employment" (Garraty, 1979: 121). Topalov claims that the term "unemployed" as opposed to terms like "idle" or "loafing" or simply "out of work" only became commonly accepted with the prominence of the London "unemployed riots" of February 1886. "'the unemployed' for the middle classes meant a threatening mass of out-of-work men" (Topalov, 1998: 7). Heclo and Schweber also stress the importance of these riots and the fact that the local government board issued a curicular encouraging work projects to give public works relief to the unemployed (Heclo, 1974: 79). In March 1886 Joseph Chamberlain, then head of the local government board, issued a circular encouraging local authorities to administer these public works without stigma but paying less than unskilled workers. "While the Chamberlain circular had little short-term effect, in the long run it contributed to the expectation among workers, radicals and local Poor Law administrators that the national government could and should take responsibility for the problem" (Schweber, 1996: 167). The recognition and even suggestion of action, in other words, created public expectations about the government's commitment and accountability to the problem in the streets. But how would the problem of unemployment be conceived?

The next bouts of public demonstrations by the jobless and subsequent legislation did not resolve the question. The depression of 1903-04 ignited huge street demonstrations and fear of domestic violence. Numerous attempts to aid the jobless with local charity culminated in the 1905 Unemployed Workman Act of 1905. The program created a joint metropolitan committee to separate respectable workmen temporarily unemployed from ordinary paupers without clear criteria for how to do so (Heclo, 1974: 79). It was hoped that the former would receive relief work or rural labor colonies, although the major reliance was placed on private charity and no money was budgeted from the Exchequer. William Beveridge served as a member of the Joint Metropolitan Committee for London on the basis of his work as a sub-warden of a settlement house and with the surge in unemployment in 1903-04 became administrator for the canon's new Mansion House Relief Fund. He reported in the paper he wrote that after two winters, "the attitude of nearly all those engaged in its administration may fairly be described as one of growing hopelessness" (Heclo, 1974: 79). During the depression of 1903-04 Beveridge personally selected, interviewed and organized relief works for the unemployed. He, unlike other social workers, re-interviewed them after they left relief work. The whole experience formed the basis for his, *Unemployment: A*

Problem of Industry.   Beveridge's book was not intellectually innovative but it clearly framed the problem as a *social* problem: "the inquiry must be one into unemployment rather than into the unemployed" (Beveridge, 1909: 3). Beveridge showed statistically that fluctuations in the number of unemployed did not depend on fluctuations in the characteristics of the workforce but in changes in business conditions.

What eventually made Beveridge's work influential was that he attached his concern for the jobless with a program for changing the character of employment and a policy instrument that harnessed these two agendas to each other.[7] As Topalov argues, Beveridge's concerns were profoundly shaped by fact that he was primarily concerned with London dock workers who worked sporadically from one day to the next and were more than happy to accept public aid as a way to delay their next day of work (Topalov, 1998: 13). Sidney Webb, the British social reformer and ally of Beveridge, explained in 1909, "The evil to be grappled with is, in fact, not the loss of permanent situations by the particular men who are found to be out of work, but the vast majority of them have never held such situations. ...It is the chronically intermittent character of the employment of the whole class for which we must find some remedy." He quotes Beveridge as saying that the problem is more accurately not so much unemployment as "under-employment" (Webb, 1909). As Esping-Andersen concurs, "The Beveridge-model for Britain [was] designed to promote maximum labor-market dependence" (Esping-Andersen, 1990: 146-47). Unemployment had to be regulated in such a way as to discourage casual work and the use of relief as a tool for avoiding full-time work.

Thus the vision was not that unemployment should be eliminated or even minimized. It had long been recognized that a reserve of job-seekers served a useful purpose for production. Karl Marx had not invented the idea that capitalist production required a reserve army of available labor. Already in 1807, in response to Malthus' criticisms of the Poor Laws, an English justice of the peace, John Weyland had argued that the excess labor encouraged by the Poor Laws was necessary for the economy to grow (Garraty, 1979: 105).[8] Beveridge saw some unemployment as unavoidable and desirable. It was, "as necessary to the [industrial] system as are capital and labour" (Beveridge, 1909:103). He saw each business as having its own reserve pool of labor slightly larger than its maximum needs. He characterized the problem as, "essentially one of business organization" and believed "in diminishing the extent of the reserves or their interval of idleness and in seeing that men of the reserve are properly maintained both in action and out of it" (Schweber, 1996: 168).

Through a system of labor exchanges Beveridge hoped to replace these separate pools with a single organized pool, "a single mobile reserve" instead of "the enormous stagnant reserve" (Beveridge, 1909: 203). Labor exchanges were to concentrate on the best workers who would then be more fully utilized, while the inefficient and degenerate elements would be "squeezed out" altogether (Garraty, 1979: 140). Labor exchanges, he believed could remedy the problem that afflicted the Unemployed Workmen Act of 1905 in attempting to separate workers who were unemployed due to business downturns from less deserving types. That act had established make-work programs, emigration to the colonies, migration within Britain, and even some forms of employment exchanges.[9] But the programs were regarded as a failure, largely because of their inability to delineate between deserving and undeserving unemployed (Garraty, 1979: 132-33). He argued,

> The state is forced into the costly and degrading harshness of the Poor Law simply because it has no control or supervision of the labor market... It must rely always on the assumption that the applicant for help could find work if he looked for it because it is never in the position to satisfy itself that there is no work for him (Heclo, 1974: 80-81).

The Unemployed Workman's Act of 1905 in England created some mild and ineffective incentives for year-round work, but these were geared toward encouraging employers to use short-time rather than seasonal lay-offs. By 1907 Beveridge saw how labor exchanges could decasualize labor by linking dispensation of unemployment insurance to use of the exchanges (Heclo, 1974: 80). The solution was to make registration at an employment exchange rather than the acceptance of the pauper's disgraceful workhouse the test of willingness to work.

Beveridge became the most forceful British advocate for national employment exchanges and, as a member of the Employment Exchange Committee of the London joint committee, he participated in organizing such exchanges for the London area. He left no doubt about how the regulation of unemployment through labor exchanges would discourage casual labor and encourage the model of the full-time bread-winner.[10]

> For the man who wants to work once a week and lie in bed the rest of the week the labour exchange will make that wish unrealizable. For the man who wants to get a casual job now and again the exchange will gradually make his mode of life impossible. It will take that one day a week he wanted to get and give it to another man who has already four days a week and so will enable that other man to get a decent living (Topalov, 1998: 13).

The anticipated effects on the character of employment were critical in garnering political support for new system of labor exchanges. In 1909 Winston Churchill (then president of the Board of Trade which regulated the few existing local exchanges) was enthusiastic about the 1905 Unemployed Workman Act as a national system of labor exchanges because "the results anticipated by Mr. Churchill from the establishment of labor exchanges were greater mobility and decasualization of labor".[11] In 1909 the National Labour Exchange Act established a network of employment offices which soon filled over a million jobs of year. In December 1911 the National Insurance Act then provided unemployment insurance in certain trades, financed by worker and employer contributions and state subsidies.[12] R.C. Davidson noted approvingly in the September 1912 *Westminster Review* that, "the scheme is less concerned with insurance against Unemployment and the troubles of the unemployed man, than it is with the better organization of the labour market. The latter is the primary aim, the former only a powerful means" (Johnson, 1921: 238).

The Soviet Union Reinvents Unemployment as a Result of the New *Orgnabor* Prototype of Employment

Involuntary joblessness did exist under communism. In some industries laborers regularly had to search to find casual labor. Despite regulations that discouraged the practice, workers often changed between jobs or were dismissed.[13] Communist governments continuously struggled to find employment for certain groups of workers and in certain regions. Yugoslavia institutionalized unemployment relief programs as early as 1964 and had the highest unemployment rate in all of Europe in the 1980s.[14] Unemployment compensation systems existed in the USSR before the end of the New Economic Policies (NEP) in the 1920s and in various East European countries throughout the period of communist rule.[15] As in the West, some forms of involuntary joblessness were considered more acceptable than others. The communist taboo against unemployment was anything but absolute. As Cook, commenting on the Brezhnev era, notes,

> This regime accepted some level of open unemployment in small- and medium-sized towns, where it was scattered and affected predominantly women. Later, in the 1970s, the Brezhnev leadership also failed to take effective measures against rising levels of unemployment among Central Asian youth. Both situations indicate that the leadership was willing to tolerate some joblessness among politically and regionally peripheral strata (1993: 58)

Due to the lack of official measures, estimates of Soviet unemployment have varied widely and used widely varying definitions. Adirim argues that Soviet unemployment was much higher than 15 percent, especially in Asian regions (Adirim, 1989). Looking at different sets of scattered data on labor turnover, Wiles and Grannick each concluded that the "frictional" unemployment from changing jobs amounted to between 1.3 and 3 percent unemployment of the labor force (Wiles, 1972; Grannick, 1987).[16] Another study by Gregory, using a large data set of structured émigré interviews from the late 1970s, included only those more "salient" spells of unemployment that lasted a month or more. Such protracted jobless spells were assumed by Soviet economists and planners not to exist, or only to occur when people rejected job offers. Quoting from a leading Soviet work on labor markets, "Under conditions of socialism, the condition of being without work (*nezaniatost*) is not a synonym for 'unemployment'. It means only an interruption of work caused by reasons of a private character (family, circumstances, changes of location)" (Gregory and Collier, 1988: 613). The émigré data suggest that 8.2 percent of respondents had suffered an average of 1.6 such prolonged spells over the previous five years, with the average spell lasting 4.8 months. The lower boundary estimate of the Soviet rate of prolonged unemployment was therefore derived at 1.2 percent of the labor force. That rate falls directly in between the contemporary American rate (1.9 percent) and the West German rate (0.5 percent) of spells lasting a month or more for similar years. In this respect it is difficult to see what is distinctive about even the degree of Soviet unemployment compared to the West.[17]

To understand the political economy of socialist joblessness, we thus need to get beyond the sweeping dualities of socialism and capitalism. Institutional configurations are important in establishing the background rules for competing interests, but also for the role they play in what gets designated as unemployment. A brief look at the Soviet "eradication" of unemployment makes four points undeniably clear. First, there never ceased to be functioning labor markets in the Soviet Union. Second, the supposed eradication of frictional unemployment was an expression of the Party's aspirations for a new prototype for labor allocation. Even lower Soviet turnover rates (and hence lower "frictional" unemployment) were an artifact of the different boundaries of the firm in a highly centralized economy. Third, the political redefinition of unemployment was a byproduct of the new model of labor allocation: a new solution that redefined the problem of unemployment. And fourth, the changes in Soviet unemployment reflected campaigns for employment discipline that shifted the boundary between needs-based and work-based distribution towards the latter.

The Bolshevik seizure of power and command of the economy in 1917 did not lead to the immediate abolition of unemployment. Sizable unemployment existed after the First World War that abated as demobilized soldiers found jobs but subsequently climbed throughout most of the 1920s. Officially recognized forms of employment—which included workers and salaried employees—grew steadily during the twenties, but so did registered levels of unemployment. The unemployed remained at about 10 percent of the labor force throughout the middle and latter part of the decade.[18] The cause of this unemployment was primarily the affluence and job growth in towns and cities that drew the surplus agricultural population from the villages. As late as 1928, peasants still comprised well over 70 percent of the population (Schwartz, 1951: 10). Between 1928 and 1932 the urban workforce in the Soviet Union doubled from eleven million to twenty-two million (Christian, 1985: 92). Markus, writing in 1936 described the unemployment of the 1920s in terms that are confirmed by the table below.

> ...[U]nemployment in the U.S.S.R. was not due to the shrinkage of production and the displacing of previously employed labour. On the contrary, it developed at a time when economic expansion was in full swing and extra labour was required. It was precisely the increased employment available that helped to attract to the labour market the surplus labour which had hitherto stagnated in the villages (Markus, 1936: 369-70).

Unemployment growth in the towns corresponded to rising output and wages, not the reverse. Such unemployment is far from uniquely communist; it is typical of industrializing countries with large agricultural populations.

Table 7.1 Employment and unemployment in the USSR ('000 persons)[19]

	Registered unemployed	Vacancies per 100 registered job-seekers	Employment in large-scale industry	Total employed workers and salaried employees
1918	800	64		
1919		115		
1920		168		
1921		96		
1922	160	67	1,096	
1923	641	67	1,352	7,300
1924-5	1,240		2,107	8,532
1925-6	1,017		2,678	10,173
1926-7	1,241	98	2,839	10,944
1927-8	1,289	125	3,072	11,350
1928-9	1,242 (Oct. 1929)	171	3,096 (1928)	11,599 (1928)
1930	725 (July) 0 (October)			

Government policies at the end of the 1920s were aimed at industrialization and improving labor discipline and were relatively unconcerned about unemployment. As Davies argues,

> In preparing to industrialize the Soviet Union, Soviet political leaders and officials were at first pessimistic about the prospects for eliminating mass employment... The deliberate aim of eliminating unemployment quickly was not a decisive factor in the switch to rapid industrialisation between 1927 and 1929. Unemployment was not a prominent issue in the speeches of Stalin and his associates justifying accelerated industrialisation; these were primarily couched in terms of such factors as the need to overtake the capitalist countries in the interests of the defense of the USSR and to provides the base for the industrialisation of peasant agriculture (Davies, 1986: 25-27)[20]

Tightened restrictions during these years were aimed at improving job discipline by eliminating workers' exit options, especially for those footloose workers who traveled back and forth between the countryside and the city in search of higher pay. A decree was passed in 1927 that restricted registration for relief to those who had never previously held employment to those whose parents had been "employed" (meaning in enterprises recognized by the Communist state). Other efforts were also made in 1929 and 1930 to eliminate what the authorities saw as inauthentic unemployment registrees from the rolls. "[P]eople were removed for unjustified refusal of jobs offered or because they were 'alien' or 'declassés', or eventually, in September 1930, because they 'registered for trades for which there was no demand' over a long period" (Davies, 1986: 29). The 1930s began a campaign for labor discipline and against job turnover. Rimlinger quotes from a 1933 address to the Soviet Party's official trade union congress, where social insurance was described as a way of fighting low productivity and eliminating turnover, both of which were seen to have been encouraged by the introduction of egalitarian pay scales.

> We must reconstruct the whol social insurance practice in order to give the most privileged treatment to shock workers and to those with long service. The fight against labor turnover must be put into the forefront. We shall handle social insurance as a weapon in the struggle to attach workers to their enterprises and strike hard at loafers, malingerers, and disorganizers of work (Rimlinger, 1971: 279).[21]

Worker absences from their place of employment were to be met with eviction from state housing and confiscation of ration cards. "Quitters" were denounced in newspapers and bulletin boards and unions and Party cells were urged to expel them from their ranks. Workers were urged to sign a pledge stating that they would not leave their job (Christian, 1985: 97).

Severe as these formal measures may sound they did not "abolish" unemployment by replacing the labor market with planned allocation. Unemployment was officially abolished despite the fact that labor continued to move in search of higher wages. It was the restriction of administrative benefits to the new definitions of what constituted "real" unemployment that brought down the unemployment rolls and thereby the number of unemployed. Christian argues that the abolition of unemployment was almost an accident.

> In reality, the elimination of unemployment was as big a surprise to the Soviet government as to anyone else. The decree of October 1930 which announced the liquidation of unemployment was in fact little more than a retrospective justification for a number of other measures designed to tighten labour discipline, one of which was the abolition of unemployment benefits (Christian, 1985).

In late 1929 Soviet officials in the final draft of the first Five Year Plan had still anticipated that unemployment levels of half a million would continue as late as 1933 (Schwartz, 1951: 43-4).

The new regulations of 1930 did not signal the end of the labor market but they did correspond chronologically to the emergence of a new model of labor direction. In 1931, the year after unemployment was said to be officially eliminated, the Soviet *Orgnabor* system was initiated to directly recruit and place individual workers in specific enterprises. *Orgnabor* was primarily a system in which collective farms were meant to supply industrial establishments with labor. Because the individual farmer was to be denied mobility and because the state directly placed the worker within this system, even transitional unemployment was thought to be eliminated. Much as this model fits the ideal vision of socialist planning and the "totalitarian" picture painted by western Cold War scholars, it never came close to being the dominant form of allocating labor. It was the *prototype* of employment placement by which unemployment was conceived to be wholly eradicated. But at most a quarter of new labor entrants were ever placed by *Orgnabor* and most did not remain long in their allocated jobs before seeking higher wages or benefits (Lane, 1987: 44). Opportunistic labor turnover never ceased to be a highly significant feature of Soviet economies.

Policies continued to be oriented toward increasing discipline and decreasing mobility. Rural migration back and forth to the cities was inhibited by the collectivization of agriculture and policies requiring internal passports for travel within the USSR from 1932. Also in that year employers were obliged to dismiss without notice any "truant" worker, defined as someone with a day's unexcused absence. Penalties for lateness were also increased. Those who quit their job lost all health and maternity insurance rights until they held a new job for six months continuously. In 1938 work books were introduced in which employment histories were recorded along with the reasons for any job changes. From 1939 three latenesses to work within a month could also be punishable by forced labor. As of June 1940 workers who left their jobs without permission could be imprisoned for 2-4 months. Some managers were imprisoned for insufficiently enforcing work rules. The official right to leave a job was abolished in 1940, a law whose official status was not formally changed until 1956. Leaving a job without permission became a criminal offense punishable by forced labor.[22]

The revision of labor legislation to increase discipline in 1938-1940 was never fully implemented because it produced discontent in nearly all strata of the Soviet population. Although people were afraid to criticize the regulations openly, managers were willing neither to impose the prescribed penalties for minor offenses against work discipline nor to send the more serious cases for criminal prosecution. "If a case of this kind was brought before a magistrate he was disposed to look for excuses. The new regulations were obviously in conflict with the legal conscience of Soviet society" (Swianiewicz, 1965: 155). Implementation would, as Kornai shows, also have been in conflict with the micro-incentives of state managers to retain labor. By the end of the 1930s about 75 percent of workers were on various piece work systems (Swianiewicz, 1965: 156). In light of the Second World War, a series of further decrees were issued in 1941-1943 for more direct allocation of labor. Workers were not allowed to leave their jobs for the duration of the war, or face penalties of 5-8 years of corrective labor. But here again the regulations were extremely difficult to administer. "The law of December 1941 fixing 8 years of imprisonment for quitting a job without authorization was applied only in some exceptional cases. It is difficult to apply very stern measures if an offense becomes a mass phenomenon" (Swianiewicz, 1965: 172). Swianiewiecz argues that the regulations were more sternly imposed in the war time 1940s but the main change during this time may have been that the authorities resorted to piece work as a way to internalize incentives for labor discipline.

Despite momentary improvements, absenteeism and job turnover continued to rise as workers migrated to the best jobs and enterprises competed for more labor.

> The general picture... is one of an employment policy still in practice based on a free labour market. For the majority of Soviet workers in the 1930s, the existence of a highly authoritarian government, willing to use harsh sanctions against its

population to achieve its ends, nonetheless did not mean the end of freedom to choose their place of work. The factor which eventually inaugurated the era of compulsory labour direction was not Stalinist industrialisation but war (Barber, 1986: 63).[23]

In some ways the *Orgnabor* system became less significant after the Second World War. By 1953 *Orgnabor* agencies were mainly directing urban workers from surplus regions to shortage areas. In the pre-war period urban workers comprised 15 percent of the *Orgnabor* total; by 1971-74 they constituted 73.7 percent (Lane, 1987: 47). *Orgnabor* came to be primarily used for relocating surplus urban workers to less desirable places like Siberia, Kazakhstan, the Urals and the Far East. In the 1951-69 period a third of transferred workers in the Russian part of the USSR went to Siberia and the Far East; by 1974 this had risen to 74 percent. Of the total number of workers taken on in industry by enterprises in 1974 only 4.7 percent came through *Orgnabor*. Most workers coming through *Orgnabor* were unskilled, unmarried, over 25 years of age. They signed on for short contracts for 6 months or 1-3 years (Lane, 1987: 47). Conditions were generally poor and, despite numerous penalties, many workers left before their contracts were fulfilled. By 1980 in the USSR only about 15 percent of labor was placed through any sort of organized or administrative channels.[24] Most workers got their jobs through informal channels or simply showing up outside the factory gates (Lane, 1987: 45).[25]

Managers could and did dismiss employees. Reportedly 800,000 persons were dismissed from organizations of industry, construction, transport and communication for disciplinary reasons in 1981 alone (Lampert, 1986: 260). The Soviet press reported that over a million workers were dismissed from industrial enterprises in 1964 (CIA, 1967: 12). Management could dismiss those who were not keeping up with work plans or for absenteeism. They frequently ignored the requirement to get trade union agreement for dismissals. If workers were dismissed for staff cuts rather than fault of their own then management was required to provide possibility for other suitable work; but they reportedly often ignored this requirement as well.

The contours of Soviet joblessness were the product of specific policies that shaped the behavior of individuals and defined a set of institutionalized administrative categories. To focus on the master logic of communism or the inevitable results of stifling markets is to overlook how unemployment was constructed through particular political choices.

> Some economists claim that full employment in Soviet-type economies resulted directly from the economic system's over demand for labor, but in fact empirical evidence reveals that in the Soviet Union some groups, especially youth, women with young children, older workers, and the disabled, were not readily absorbed into the labor force (Cook, 1993: 54-55).

Cook looks at the particular institutional interventions around youth unemployment in February 1966 policies shortly after Brezhnev's accession to power. Part of the reason that youth were less employable was the additional social protections that required enterprises to exempt 15-18 year olds from night shifts or overtime, to pay them for eight-hour days while they worked six hours, and to give them paid leave for part time study. Moreover, the post-World War II baby boom had produced a large cohort of these youth and a change in the schooling requirements created a one-time doubling of the size of the graduating class (Cook, 1993: 55). The policy response was that quotas for youth hiring were effectively doubled and for any youths under 18 that was dismissed a new job had to be found in cooperation between the dismissing enterprise and local Party authorities. Hiring quotas during the Brezhnev era were similarly established for disabled workers, pregnant women, and women with very small children. "The Soviet economy did not spontaneously generate full employment, ...the Brezhnev leadership did in fact intervene to deliver on this provision of the social contract" (Cook, 1993: 57).

Purely frictional joblessness from labor turnover was less in Soviet economies than in the West, but even this difference is largely an artifact of institutional classification and particular policies, rather than grand ideological or system logics. Turnover averaged 22.1 percent per year in the USSR in 1967, highest in light industries. Lane claims that Soviet industrial turnover was about 20 percent whereas the Western (mostly American) studies of industrial turnover suggest a norm of 50 percent (Lane, 1987: 68). Lower Soviet turnover was largely the product of a less fluid housing market and gargantuan Soviet firms that were so large that many transfers didn't technically count as job switches because workers remained within the same administrative unit. Soviet preoccupations with centralization and economies of scale translated into much larger enterprise units than in the West. Lower Soviet turnover can be chiefly explained by the Soviet firm size, since larger scale units in the West also have lower levels of turnover. Soviet turnover in small (less than 200 people) factories was three times as great as in the largest (greater than 1000 people) firms.[26]

Larger Soviet firms were also more likely to provide day care and housing, which tied workers to their enterprises. Soviet firms were obligated to find alternative work for workers displaced by new technology or reorganization and this encouraged within-enterprise mobility. Soviet policies also maintained uninterrupted nominal job attachment in many situations that for most western workers would count as having left their jobs.[27] Maternity leave recipients officially maintained their positions while at home, workers dismissed for reasons of redundancy were kept on the old firm's books for an extended time until they found a new job. Frictional unemployment was furthermore reduced because workers often preferred to first find a new job before quitting their old one to ensure that they did not lose bonuses that accrued for uninterrupted work. Both employees and managers had a powerful incentive to keep workers nominally on the books, even if they were barely paid and did not work. Employees wanted to enjoy social benefit bonuses that were pegged to continuous employment histories, and employers enjoyed higher pay and greater bargaining leverage based on larger staffing levels.[28]

The American Labor Force Model as a Problem to Match New Keynesian Solutions and a Method to Enforce Employment Prototypes

The "Labor Force Model" of unemployment which was embraced by the United States government after World War II had two kinds of political inspirations. First, the experience of having inadvertently induced sharp down-turns and upturns in the economy through changes in fiscal policy gave the government confidence that if unemployment was constructed as an indicator of labor demand joblessness could be soaked up through spending increases. Secondly, politicians wished to uphold a particular kind of core prototype of employment that had been undermined by war-time policies that had extended core kinds of employment to untraditional groups. In America, as elsewhere, we find that the definition and redefinition of unemployment as a problem followed from the government's embrace of particular kinds of employment solutions and a particular prototype of employment.

A concept of "unemployment", as distinct from poverty or social distress more generally, emerged gradually in the United States from the end of the nineteenth century to the depression of the 1930s. There was no institutionalized national measure of unemployment until after the Great Depression. There had long been large populations of rootless persons known as "backwoodsmen", "vagrants", or "tramps" (Garraty, 1979). The state of Massachusetts created the first bureau of labor statistics in 1869, established by the legislature in the hope that it could explain what at the time was perceived as the incoherent discontent among the populace (Garraty, 1979; Innes, 1990). The (then titled) "great depression of the 1890s" and the large numbers of destitute families that resulted shook many people's complacency about the normalcy of social problems. At a public meeting called in Boston in 1893 leading citizens expressed the view that, "the problem was of a different sort from that which was normally dealt with by the charitable agencies of the city, for the existing distress was... due chiefly to non-employment, and not to the ordinary causes of poverty" (Garraty, 1979: 121). The same year a large body of jobless, "Coxey's army", marched to Washington petitioning for work. Seven American states instituted jobless surveys in 1893 and 1894.

The troubling metaphor of vague "restless armies" persisted over the next decades, though without any definite distinction of the unemployed from other needy groups. For instance, one magazine article in 1914 that alerted Americans to its "large standing army of the unemployed" conceded that, "there is no roll for the registration of the recruits", but "it is believed that the attendance at municipal lodging houses is a fair index of the extent of Unemployment" (Kingsbury, 1914: 433).[29] Severe unemployment problems in 1914-15 were followed by labor shortages as the war created great demand for labor. The Federal Employment Service, from its roots in the Bureau of Immigration, became a national organization administered into 13 regions. Labor offices in the US were first established in Ohio as a way to find and recruit more workers into the labor market during the war. After the war Congress cut support and reduced its services (Johnson, 1921).

A commitment to measuring unemployment in the US increased in 1921 when President Harding called a conference of business leaders to consider the problem. The purpose was to ascertain the amount and distribution of "needed employment" (Innes, 1990: 123). But both the president and chairman Hoover declared that the treasury should not be responsible for remedying unemployment and that any federally legislated aid was "paternalism that will undermine the whole system" (Innes, 1990: 123). The available data was clearly inadequate, since estimates of unemployment ranged from 3.5 to 5.7 million and the conference chose which measure to endorse by vote.

Interest for better data sharpened with the depression of the 1930s, but a standardized definition did not appear until national policy efforts were taken. During the Hoover years there was little idea of how many were unemployed and little public policy for combating unemployment.[30] At a national level the only working force data before the Depression were the decennial census questions about what gainful occupation people were in. This was useful only for long-term data and not for the short term redress of public policy. Unlike other industrialized countries where unemployment insurance or trade union records gave an indication of unemployment, the US had no recurring measure. In 1931 the US government conducted a special unemployment census in 18 cities. Over the 1930s numerous local censuses were conducted, but there was no national census until 1940 (U.S. National Commission, 1979).[31] At a national level the strategy was to encourage charity and wait for private initiatives to solve the problem. The "unemployment czar" had to telephone around to governors to get an idea of the numbers, and the estimates of official agencies at the time varied widely (Piven and Cloward, 1993: 49fn). Despite a year's worth of work of the American Statistical Association the statisticians were still unprepared to define unemployment and bypassed the difficult issue (Innes, 1990: 126-27).

A more definite framework for measuring unemployment was only decided once social policies began to distinguish between those who were regarded as genuine workers and others who were unemployable. The first major initiatives of the Roosevelt administration did not make this distinction. The Federal Employment Relief Administration (FERA), which existed from May 1934 until 1935, was aimed at providing general relief and reinvigorating the economy.[32] It was officially meant for "all needy unemployed persons and/or their dependents. Those whose employment or available resources are inadequate to provide the necessities of life for themselves and/or their dependents were included" (Piven and Cloward, 1993: 74). Thus, despite the prominent use of the word "unemployment", it made no real attempt to distinguish those who were in need due to lack of available work. This general relief was viewed as temporary and troubled many who viewed the handouts as undermining work ethics and morality. In 1935 FERA was dismantled and replaced with the Works Progress Administration (WPA) which provided public works to those who could work, while "unemployables" such as widows, orphans and the disabled were turned over to other local relief programs. It was the institutional solution of the WPA relief that first led to a concerted effort to define the concept of unemployment in America.

Statistics were developed through local efforts to count the number of jobs required to take care of the jobless and to establish the proportion in need of relief. "Accordingly a set of concepts that were oriented around the possession of a job at any given time was a logical one" (Bancroft, 1958: 45). The expressed goal was to give unemployment relief only to those who already had a "gainful occupation". The concept was well suited to an environment where a lack of social programs meant that virtually any able-bodied persons without employment faced immediate destitution, and government was concerned with the proper administration of a particular policy approach: to determine how many public works jobs to provide in each locality (Bancroft, 1958). Accordingly, the subsequent census attempted to measure unemployment according to a "gainful occupation" concept in which the unemployed were envisioned as any individuals over 10 years of age with a gainful occupation who were not currently engaged in work. The definition of unemployed as of 1936 was worded officially as: "Thus an unemployed person may be defined as one of working age who is able and willing to work and *who normally would be employed*, but is not currently engaged in a gainful occupation" (U.S. National Commission, 1979: 16). Individuals were asked if they had (ever) worked gainfully, and if they were working currently. Retired or seasonal workers were therefore included in the category of unemployment and new entrants to the labor market were excluded. The 1930 census instructed enumerators not to report occupations for those no longer following an occupation due to old age, permanent invalidity or who only occasionally worked or did so for a short time daily (Bancroft, 1958).

Defenders of the gainful work measure proclaimed that it was more objective than other local efforts which had tried to gauge individuals' willingness and ability to work. The apparently self-evident nature of such claims is evident, for instance, in one 1939 article by John Webb in the *Journal of the American Statistical Association.*

> When, for instance, does age become a handicap as real as the loss of an arm or a leg? Ask the unemployed miner of 55 years if he is able to work and the answer most likely will be: yes;" ask him why he lost his job and he is very likely to answer "too old". Ability to work, therefore, is not a fact that can be determined objectively in many important instances (Webb, 1939: 20-21).

He points out that people may be willing to work at one wage but not at another. "Moreover, 'willing to work' is not only relative as between an individual and a particular job, it is also relative as between the individual and economic conditions" (Webb, 1909: 21).

But the gainful work concept was displaced after the Second World War with the pronounced changed in the government's concerns and preferred "solutions". "The term "labor force" itself was originally used by the National Industrial Conference Board and other estimators of unemployment during the 1930s as synonymous with the total number of gainful workers. It was essentially the "working population" or some equivalent that did not change in size except as the population and its basic characteristics changed" (Bancroft, 1958: 45). The labor force was viewed as a reservoir of potential workers, thus not varying with business cycles. It was understood that employment and unemployment had to move in opposite directions because unemployment was the unused portion of the labor supply. This conception was initially reinforced by the war effort. "The need for more labor in war industry led to a change in the questionnaire to uncover potential workers" (Innes, 1990: 129). In 1945 a category of "inactive workers", regarded as in the labor force but not actively seeking work, was eradicated.

War-time mobilization of housewives, blacks and retirees disrupted previously held notions of who should be in the labor force. The war disrupted some delicate political compromises about whose work should count as employment. Under Southern pressure, New Deal social programs had often excluded Southern agricultural workers (Skocpol, 1995: 30, Weir, 1992). Agriculturalists in the south had been angered at New Deal programs whose minimum wage regulation undermined their ability to pay very low wages to black farm-workers. A FERA observer reported from Georgia in 1934 that "for blacks, to be getting $12 a week - at least twice as much as common labor has ever been paid down there before - is an awfully bitter pill for Savannah people to swallow" (Piven and Cloward, 1993: 76n). The Governor of Georgia forwarded an angry farmer's letter to President Roosevelt which said, "I wouldn't plow nobody's mule from sunrise to sunset for 40 to 50 cents per day when I could get $1.30 [per day] for pretending to work on a ditch". A Du Pont vice-president similarly complained how in South Carolina, "A cook on my houseboat at Fort Myer quit because the Government was paying him a dollar an hour as a painter" (Piven and Cloward, 1993: 82-3n). The political compromise was that, the kinds of employment that blacks served on the bottom of the racial caste ladder were not recognized as employment. As Skocpol explains,

> The core social insurance programs established by the New Deal—old age insurance and unemployment insurance—did not reach most American blacks. The agricultural and service occupations open to most blacks at that time were simply excluded from social insurance taxes and coverage. Had this not been done to propitiate politically powerful southern Democrats and representatives of commercial farmers, it is doubtful that the Social Security Act could have gotten through Congress (Skocpol, 1995: 218-219).

The terms of these compromises had to be renegotiated with the new commitments to full employment that were issued after the war.

Post war proclamations of government obligations to contain unemployment would have been unthinkable if not preceded by strong experiences of the effect government spending had on aggregate employment.[33] Keynes' ideas *per se* may have had little direct impact on the Roosevelt or even the Truman administration's thinking, as some have argued (Salant, 1989: 28-29, Stein, 1969: 131).[34] Regardless of the prevailing views about economic theory, new government commitments came directly after a sharp downturn in 1937-38 which was largely brought about by inadvertent fiscal tightening. Budget deficits were trimmed by three billion dollars from 1936 to 1937, a huge sum equivalent to 3.5 percent of GDP. One-time veterans' "bonuses" which had been paid in 1936 were not paid in 1937 and the new social security payroll taxes (that would not pay out substantial benefits until the next year) began in 1937. Over the five months following that September the Federal Reserve's index of industrial production fell by a staggering 29 percent. The budget deficits of Roosevelt's first term were due almost exclusively as a result of the Depression and it was only in the spring of 1938 during the so-called "second New Deal" that Roosevelt endorsed deliberate budgetary deficits as a way to stimulate the economy (Lee, 1989). It was only with the annual report for the 1939 fiscal year of the Secretary of Commerce that government responsibility was officially accepted for economic performance. Remaining doubts about the ability of fiscal policy to stimulate aggregate employment were largely erased by the dramatic employment effects of government spending in anticipation of the Second World War. Unemployment, later estimated to have been 25 percent of the civilian labor force in 1933 and 17 percent in 1937, was brought down to less than two percent in 1943-45 as a result of increases in the armed forces and government deficit spending (Salant, 1989: 45).

After the war there was widespread fear of post-war recession (Weir, 1992). In Roosevelt's 1944 State of the Union address he proposed an economic bill of rights which included the "right to a useful and remunerative job". Even the Republican opponent, Thomas Dewey proclaimed that, "if at any time there are not sufficient jobs in private employment to go around, the government can and must create job opportunities, because there must be jobs for all in this country" (cited in (Weir, 1989: 82). The Employment Act of 1946 was much less specific in its commitments and policy levers than the failed *Full* Employment Act of 1945 but it nonetheless institutionalized a new array of government commitments. It called on government to:

> [U]se all practical means ...to foster and promote free competitive enterprise and the general welfare, conditions under which there will be afforded useful employment opportunities, including self employment for those able, willing and seeking to work and to promote maximum employment, production and purchasing power. [35]

The act was the first employment policy targeted to unemployment other than relief programs. It required annual data on unemployment and created the executive CEA and Congressional Joint Economic Committee, which were eager consumers for a measure that would track the overall tightness of demand in the labor market (Innes, 1990). "It should be remembered that the employment and unemployment concepts were developed for use as current indicators in a setting where measurement of change was of prime importance" (Bancroft, 1958: 51).

The new policy "solution" of macroeconomic demand stimulus inspired new political commitments against unemployment, but the new Labor Force Model also reflected an attempt to defend the boundaries of the prevailing employment prototype. The previous method of defining the unemployed as those jobless who previously had a "gainful employment" was a good solution to the stop-gap public works programs of the 1930s but not necessarily for the late 1940s. New policy commitments had been made to balance the nation's supply of labor with sufficient macroeconomic demand, not towards meeting some inventory of the impoverished population through public works.

After World War II many people who had practiced a gainful occupation under exceptional war-time circumstances no longer sought employment and returning GIs were expected to take their positions. If the government had maintained the old "gainful employment" concept, then the housewives, retirees and share-croppers demobilized after the war would have represented a huge burden of the "unemployed" that the government would have been responsible for. The Democratic Party was split over support of the 1946 Full Employment Act between northern liberals and southern agrarians who were dominated by the political influence of landlords that thrived on sharecropping arrangements and did not want to loose their captive labor to new social programs (Skocpol, 1995: 30, Weir, 1992). The new concept of unemployment also had to meet the political need to reestablish employment norms that, as in any war, had been disrupted.[36]

Instead of measuring the potential labor supply "what was important was to distinguish the active, current, 'legitimate' job seekers from all other persons who, under different circumstances, might become job seekers or might have been jobseekers" (Bancroft, 1958: 45). The new concept of unemployment was to resolve the question of which individuals were in the labor force according to whether they had been "actively seeking work". The labor force framework emerged as a way to measure the immediate unmet macro-supply of labor under the prevailing conditions of the moment rather than some potential labor reserve. Surveys asked individuals who currently lacked a job not whether they had a gainful occupation but whether they were actively seeking for work. Thus "labor force" came to denote the employed plus the unemployed at a period of time that reflected overall business conditions. Surveys demonstrated that the labor force (in this new conception) was variable according to changing behaviors, not just demographics. The new concept ensured both that the government would only be measuring those jobless who would be best effected by macroeconomic stimuli, and that the commitment against unemployment extended only to the kind of workers who were regarded as most core to the economy.[37]

Notes

1   The very first workers' association fund against job loss was created by the British foundry workers union in 1831 (Heclo, 1974: 68).

2   The first public unemployment insurance was actually in small Swiss cantons a few
    years earlier. Bern attempted a voluntary fund for those who expected to be unemployed
    in the winter. The first compulsory scheme came nearby in St. Gallen after a 1894
    referendum. But the program was voted down two years later after unemployment was
    higher than expected and higher income workers resented paying for the mostly lower
    income beneficiaries (Heclo, 1974: 69). The experience of St. Gallen discouraged other
    municipalities. Referendum for initiating such programs were defeated in Zurich in
    1898 and Basle in 1890. Discouraged by the Swiss experience, Ghent began
    experimenting with subsidizing union insurance plans. For a discussion of the often
    complex bargaining between labor and business that led to different forms of
    unemployment assistance, see Mares, 2000.

3   Though Steinmetz shows how in the proliferation of Ghent-style programs into
    Germany the funds were most likely to be set up in somewhat more conciliatory
    conditions where there had not been very recent political violence and some social
    democrats sat in government.

4   Taking a job with sub-standard wages might be in the interest of individual workers but
    diminishes the wages of other workers. On collective action problems, see Olson, 1965.

5   It described unemployment as "a social question... over which the worker has no
    control" (Garraty, 1979: 11).

6   By 1899, after the unusually deep depression, B. Seebohm Rowntree's reproduction of
    Booth's study in his native town of York did distinguish between those completely
    without employment and those who suffered merely from "irregularity" of work. B.
    Seehohm Rowntree, *Poverty: A Study of Town Life* (London, 1902): xii-xx, 119-21 cited
    in (Garraty, 1979: 128).

7   In Britain Topalov argues, "Unemployment, before becoming a theoretical concept in
    the field of economics, was born as a tool for social action, or, better said, social
    surgery" (Topalov, 1998: 12).

8   The inventory function of unemployment was cited by some who opposed the Insurance
    Act of 1911 because it required roughly equal contributions from employers, workers
    and the state to funds for compensating certain trades; but neither the state nor the labor
    unions had a direct interest in maintaining the inevitable surplus and should not be
    charged with the upkeep of labor reserve any more than for the inventory of other
    productive units. "If Unemployment is in reality an indispensable function of modern
    industry, the question must be raised whether the cost of maintaining the function should
    not in justice fall upon those in whose interest it is discharged" (Hobson, 1917: 1).

9   The first labor exchange in England had been established in 1885, but was on a purely
    voluntary basis and served only a local area in Egham (Johnson, 1921: 182).

10 That the prototype of employment was the male breadwinner is evident as early as
    Beveridge's 1909 opus, "Society is built upon labor... its ideal unit is the household of
    man, wife and children maintained by the earnings of the first alone. ...The wife, so
    long at least as she is bearing and bringing up children, should have no other task—but
    how, if the husband's earnings fail and she has to go out to work? Everywhere the same
    difficulty recurs. Everywhere reasonable security of employment for the bread-winner
    is the basis of all private duties and all sound action" (Beveridge, 1909: 1).

11 As reported in the *British Fortnightly Review* in October 1913 and cited in (Johnson,
    1921: 238).

12 The British unions had demanded to manage any compulsory unemployment scheme.
    The Parliamentary Committee of the British Trade Unions Congress (TUC), when
    questioned by the president of the Board of Trade, argued that if non-union members

were also covered under the insurance program, "You will have men to support who never have been and never will be self-supporting. They are at present parasites on their more industrious fellows and will be the first to avail themselves of the funds the Bill provides" [quoted in (Harris, 1972: 317f and appearing in, Rothstein, 1992: 45). The Liberal government denied these demands and set up the first compulsory system in 1911.

13 Job changers in the Soviet Union were legally required to find a job in a specific amount of time, and anti-parasite laws persecuted those jobless without excuse (Porket, 1995: 34).

14 On Yugoslav unemployment see Porket, 1995; Primorac and Babic, 1989; Woodward, 1995.

15 Hungarian unemployment and formal unemployment benefits existed in the 1950s and 1980s. East German benefit schemes existed until 1977 and statistics which were kept up until 1958 show an average of ten to fifteen thousand yearly recipients. Bulgarian unemployment was reportedly very high in the mid-1950s and an entitlement scheme was established in 1958.

16 Wiley used a much smaller set of findings from the 1960s and estimated unemployment at 1.3 percent. Grannick, using a richer set of later data concluded a range of 1.5-3 percent. See also Lane, who extrapolating largely from the turnover data of a single region, estimates one to three percent (Lane, 1987: 66). Lower Soviet levels of turnover, as shown below, are primarily an artifact of the larger size of socialist firms and greater enterprise-based social benefits.

17 Comparisons between economic "systems" have reinforced the widely held assumption about state-run economies that they did not have unemployment (Kornai, 1992; Porket, 1995). Unlike capitalist economies where unemployment is thought to be the inevitable concomitant of free labor markets, socialist planning agencies are viewed as eliminating—or at least hiding—unemployment by directly allocating workers to jobs. This view treats unemployment as an inevitable byproduct of free labor markets that is bypassed or suppressed under "command" economies. The institutional logic of socialism is identified and contrasted in broad dualities against the workings of market economies. One prevalent view argues that those socialist workers who would not have been employed under capitalist conditions should be thought of as the "hidden unemployed". As proof this view characterizes the surge in post-communist unemployment after 1990 as exposing previously disguised forms of joblessness. Others argue that the fundamental mechanisms of socialist economies systematically militate against the existence of unemployment. Typical of the "hidden" unemployment view, Porket asserts that, "unemployment assumes two forms, that of open unemployment and that of hidden unemployment" (Porket, 1995: xv. See also Feiwel, 1974; Góra and Rutkowski, 1990). He extrapolates from the hypothetical situation of "pure command socialism" in which "labour is not free, a labour market does not exist, and open unemployment (whether frictional, voluntary, or involuntary) is absent" (Porket, 1995: 7). By this account unemployment did exist on a large scale under communism, but it was hidden or disguised behind the factory gates. Redundant workers who would have been laid off under capitalism were instead retained in order to placate the population and disguise enormous inefficiencies. Instances of open involuntary joblessness are thereby dismissed as "deviant" and unrepresentative cases. This interpretation has been popular with recent post-communist politicians in Eastern Europe and their Western advisors because this view excuses them from policies that might have caused unemployment by asserting that such policies merely reveal previously disguised forms of unemployment.

But "hidden unemployment" as an analytical category is both analytically problematic and not specific to communism. It relies on a counter-factual that is ultimately arbitrary as to when a job should be regarded as "true" employment, and conversely which jobs should count as disguised unemployment. Forms of unemployment are best understood as regulative fictions that are as real as the administrative categories they conform to. Regarding some forms of employment as real while others are considered illusory amounts to what one commentator has called an exercise in metaphysics. Two labor market categories may be causally related, but that does not justify treating them as function—much less analytical—equivalents. Would we treat a portion of German women utilize incentives to be housewives as "hidden employees"? Ultimately, the idea that communist unemployment is "hidden" hinges on the imputation that layoffs would have occurred if there had been labor markets in Soviet-style economies. This claim, that labor markets did not exist under socialism, is consistent with the Party's own official declarations that workers were not a commodity under their rule; but the claim is belied by a wide literature on socialist labor markets that has demonstrated how the relative scarcities of workers' skills, regions, and exit possibilities influenced their levels of wages and benefits. See, for example Adam, 1984; Atkinson, 1992; Berliner, 1952; Galasi, 1985; Milanovic, 1994; Sabel and Stark, 1982; Szelenyi, 1978; Winiecki, 1991. The regime also explicitly used higher wages as a price mechanism to induce labor into priority industries and regions.

18 This estimate is derived by simply calculating the total labor force by adding the first and last columns. A quick look shows the unemployed to be about a tenth of that sum from 1923 to 1929.

19 (Baykov, 1947: 146-47). Vacancy rates, 1918-21 data and 1928-1930 data are from Markus. Total 1923 employment data from Markus and represents the 1923-24 period. Yearly data after 1923 span two calendar years because the Soviet calendar began October first.

20 "In the early years of Soviet power, providing work (or reducing unemployment) was not a priority. …During the period of War Communism and the New Economic Policy, unemployment continued at levels comparable to those of Western European countries" (Lane, 1987: 25).

21 Gorbachev, in his 1987 book *Perestroika* similarly writes, "[U]nder socialism, work is the foundation for social justice. Only work determines a citizen's real place in society, his social status. And this precludes any manifestations of equalizing... On this point we want to be perfectly clear: socialism has nothing to do with equalizing" (1987: 100).

22 In the 1970s and early 1980s new rules increasingly discouraged quitting. By 1984 workers were required to give 2 months notice, while management was required only one month for a termination (Malle, 1987: 378-79).

23 The author points out that in Britain during the war, one could also be imprisoned for quitting one's job without permission.

24 Employment bureaus, closed with the "eradication" of unemployment in 1931, were reopened in the USSR in 1967. They provided information and advice about jobs and assisted state planning agencies with retraining and transferring labor as well as with formulating proposals for labor planning. There was increasing use of these bureaus but "A study in 1980 of 156 production units showed that only 31 percent of labour requirements were filled through administrative channels and of these 19 percent were school graduates" (Lane, 1987: 52). The bureaus were an intermediary instrument that workers and enterprise directors could use but neither were required to make an offer or accept a job.

25 In 1969 Job Placement Bureaus were introduced as information services on vacancies and skills. These were increasingly envisioned as helping to help organize the allocation of labor and having a monopoly of information so workers will not be hired at the gate. Their role was often been semi-passive and intermediary, but if we include placement through these offices the total organized allocation of labor as part of the total increase—though is still decidedly does not encompass the majority of new employment. The numbers present the percent of increases in employment that were allocated through all forms of organized allocation. In 1967, the *Orgnabor* portion of new employment allocation was 2.2 percent, and 12.3 percent of all organized labor allocation. In 1971 the numbers were 3.8 percent and 12.1 percent; but if one counted labor allocation through labor offices the *orgnabor* portion was 20.8 percent. In 1976 the three numbers were respectively, 5.3, 15.4, and 32.6 percent. And in 1981 the respective numbers were 5.6 percent, 15.3 percent, and 32.6 percent (Malle, 1987).

26 Enterprises in the West tend to have an average of 1.1-1.4 factories (each firm averages little more than a single production site) while in Hungary, for example, large state enterprises averaged 4-5 factories each. In advanced capitalist economies, between forty to seventy percent of workers are typically in small-scale industry. By comparison, in Hungary in the mid 1960s less than twenty percent of the labor force was employed in enterprises with less than 1,000 workers (Révész, 1990: 44).

27 To take an example from another communist economy, the Polish Labor Law of 1949 workers who left their jobs did not automatically loose their employment relationship at their old enterprises, even when they stopped drawing a salary. Workers could claim that they were taking leave for illness, harvesting or family reasons, or students could move back and forth between schooling, training and employment without ever technically loosing their employment status (Heynes, 1997).

28 Similarly, in post-Soviet Russia unemployment levels are understated in situations where firms cease paying wages and perhaps offer plant-level amenities, but refuse to lay-off workers because they do not have funds for severance payments.

29 "America is awakening to a realization of the fact that she has a large standing army of unemployed—an army probably many times larger than the regular army of which the President of the United States is commander-in-chief. ...The sane men of this country have at last sighted this army. They are beginning to realize that its presence in our midst, disorganized and uncommanded, constitutes one of the greatest social problems which confronts this country today" (Kingsbury, 1914: 433).

30 Before the Federal Emergency Relief Administration relief grants passed in 1933 had been targeted to unemployables such as orphans and widows (Piven and Cloward, 1993: 74).

31 There had been a failed attempt at a national census in 1937.

32 The animating spirit at the time was quoted from one official at the time as "to distribute as much money as possible, as fast as possible, to as many as possible" (Piven and Cloward, 1993: 75).

33 This paragraph draws heavily from (Salant, 1989).

34 Keynes' ideas were nonetheless influential in dispelling the prevailing theories that condemned deficit spending and government intervention and as part of a larger intellectual movement the ideas clearly affected economic doctrine and policy.

35 Public Law 304, 79th Congress, 15 U.S.C., 1021. It passed without opposition in the Senate and by a 320-84 majority in the House of Representatives.

36 In England after the First World War many trade unionists called for the "un-dilution" or "reconcentration" of labor that had been diluted by the exigencies of the war. "What elements existing actually in Labour at this moment would it be wise to draw off from

the Labour-market and to place in reserve?" (Hobson, 1917: 4). S.G. Hobson, for instance, argued in 1917 that it would be both humane and efficient to remove the comparatively aged by lowering pension age for men (from seventy to sixty) and that the age of entrance to the labor market be raised from fourteen to eighteen. The labor surplus that resulted after World War I was regarded as different from the normal workings of the economy. The massive redeployment of labor suggested the question of what kinds of labor should be part of the labor force and its reserves in the first place. "We should select from the inevitable surplus of Labour that will result from the war, the amount and kind of Labour to put back into our reserves. Not leaving the selection to chance, we ought deliberately to determine and define the classes and quantities of Labour which must be taken out of the Labour market and restored to its pre-war state of simple potentiality" (Hobson, 1917: 3).

37 Since its adoption at the International Conference of Labor Statisticians in 1947, the basic framework has become almost universal for international (and most domestic) labor statistics. On the connection between the export of Keynesian ideas and the hegemony of the United States' role as a super-power and its direct influences of other countries economic policies through direct-aid programs, see (Hirschman, 1989).

Chapter 8

Comparing the Political Importance of Unemployment Across the European Union

Unemployment seems to carry greater political weight in some countries than others, even when nations hold essentially the same concept of unemployment. The same unemployment rate can represent a much greater threat to those in power in some countries than others. But what accounts for these differences? How do we measure them? And can the approach developed in this book usefully inform an explanation of these differences?

Individual-level Eurobarometer polling data can provide a useful proxy for approximating the comparative importance of unemployment between European Union countries. A number of hypotheses are then tested to explain these differences. The most obvious hypothesis is that unemployment is more politically virulent when compensatory social protections are weak, or when the duration of jobless spells is longer. As we shall see, the evidence does not support these claims. Another set of hypotheses draw on the insight that unemployment is defined against particular norms of employment. To the extent that employment in a country does not guarantee a basic livelihood, or does not resemble the prototypical ideal of a full-time industrial breadwinner, then unemployment will be less politically salient. Although the data is limited, it supports this hypothesis. The data also suggests that the more that the unemployed use state employment exchanges to search for work, the more they will blame the government if they fail to find adequate employment. These findings support the notion that the political meaning of unemployment is constructed around institutionalized meanings of employment.

A Puzzle: Unemployment is more important in some countries than others

Europeans consistently identify unemployment as the political issue most important to them, but their concerns about unemployment do not correspond to the differences in national unemployment rates.[1] In 1990 Spanish unemployment stood at almost double the French rate (16.2 versus 8.9 percent) but significantly fewer Spaniards were likely to identify unemployment as their most pressing political issue (55 percent versus 89 percent). Simple regression analysis shows that a country's unemployment rate explains less than 2 percent of the variation in how highly citizens prioritize unemployment as a national political issue.[2] Recent changes over time in a country's unemployment rate also fail to show any discernible relationship with how highly people prioritize the unemployment problems.[3] *Clearly the quantitative rate of unemployment is an insufficient proxy for comparing its political salience* across Western Europe.[4]

It has been noted that the same unemployment rate in Britain may mean something very different from what it would in Italy where the unemployed typically take part in familial and informal economic activities.[5] In some countries like Germany and France a small increase in unemployment can famously bring large-scale protest and threaten to bring down governments. Spanish unemployment, by contrast, remained around twenty percent for over a decade without major electoral consequences for the ruling party.[6] Before explaining these kinds of differences, it is useful to construct some kind of proxy to measure what is being explained.

Measuring the Political Importance of Unemployment

There are no accepted measures of the political salience of unemployment.[7] The political importance of unemployment is not the same as merely the prominence of unemployment questions in national political debate or the intensity of disagreement over solutions. In a country where unemployment *is* a pressing political problem the issue might not appear as such in debates if, for example, the problem is regarded as inevitable or preferable to its alternatives. Moreover, it would be desirable to have an indicator of the political quality of unemployment that would not automatically increase or decrease along with the quantity of unemployment in a country.

One useful indicator of the political salience of unemployment can be derived from individual-level survey data. The standardization of Europe-wide polling and increased levels of European unemployment have made it possible to reliably compare the employed to the unemployed in their responses to general political questions. We can test the salience of unemployment with the help of a 1991-92 Eurobarometer data set.[8] I follow the methodological lead of Christopher Anderson who looks separately at the responses of the unemployed and the employed to a number of political questions. He finds a variety of ways that the political opinions of the unemployed differ from those with employment.[9] I focus on the only significant difference that holds across each and every country. There is considerable variation between countries in the total portion of respondents who claim to be satisfied or very satisfied with the way democracy works in their country. Regardless of the overall level of "democratic satisfaction" there is a consistent gap: the unemployed in each and every country are at least five percent less likely to be satisfied with democracy than are the country's employed respondents.[10]

It is possible to compare the size of each country's opinion gap between the employed and the unemployed in their support of the democratic system. This gap gives some indication of unemployment's political salience for that country. Although Anderson does not use the data for this purpose, we can infer that *the more different are the political views of the unemployed from those of the employed, the more politically salient is unemployment in that country.* The survey data is a blunt but useful tool as a first estimation. In fact it is difficult to imagine a hypothetical survey question that would be superior. Even if the Eurobarometer asked respondents to estimate for themselves "how much they blamed the government for unemployment", we could not rely on this kind of self-reporting. There are of course definite limits to using any individual opinion data since individual attitudes do not automatically aggregate into group or national politics and any survey will have problems abstracting across cultural and institutional differences. But the data is nonetheless useful as a reliable measure of the political *quality* of unemployment that is completely independent of the unemployment rate.

Table 8.1 Opinion gap in democratic support by country (1990)

Country	Percent of democratic support by the employed minus democratic support by the unemployed
Germany	24.6
Belgium	16.2
Portugal	15.6
Netherlands	13.1
Italy	11.7
France	11.7
Britain	11.3
Ireland	10.6
Denmark	7.5
Greece	5.6
Spain	5.0

Source: Anderson, 1997

A quick look at the data suggests that it is consistent with general impressions of the salience of unemployment in national politics. In the countries with the smallest attitudinal gaps, Spain and Greece, incumbent Socialist Parties have repeatedly won elections despite very high urban rates of unemployment.[11] The countries with the largest opinion gaps, Belgium and Germany, have been racked by massive protests against unemployment. The relatively high gap in democratic support in Portugal is echoed by data showing that the Portuguese unemployed are as almost twice as left-leaning (compared to the employed) than in any other surveyed country (Anderson, 1997) and have a particularly close relationship with the Portuguese Communist Party.[12] The exceptionally large opinion gap in

Germany is perhaps exaggerated by reunification, which has created disproportionate unemployment in the former German Democratic Republic where there is also disproportionate political disenchantment.

Data Analysis and Discussion: Four Hypotheses

Hypothesis #1: The greater the policy effort exerted on mitigating the effects of unemployment, the smaller will be the opinion gap between employed and unemployed.

This is a more precise version of a similar question in an earlier paper by Christopher Anderson (1997). Policy effort was measured by using social spending as a portion of GDP or, alternately, as total government spending as a portion of GDP. Surprisingly, greater social spending did not diminish the opinion gap in political support between employed and unemployed. But these global spending measures are imprecise indicators of support for the unemployed. Some countries which spend a high proportion of their GDP on total government expenditure or overall social spending might focus their energies on pensions, health or education instead of sheltering the effects of unemployment. I therefore substitute more specific measures of the state's effort to aid the unemployed. When greater portions of the unemployed receive benefits or their benefit levels replace a higher portion of their previous wages then the gap in democratic support should be correspondingly smaller. This hypothesis would be confirmed by a negative correlation coefficient between measures of unemployment aid and the gap in democratic support.

There are strong reasons to suggest this hypothesis. The more generously the unemployed are treated, then the less different they should be from the employed. Historically, unemployment programs have often been introduced by governments as a way to diffuse protest and buy off opposition (Esping-Andersen, 1990; Piven and Cloward, 1993; Steinmetz, 1993).

Table 8.2 Unemployment generosity and differences in democratic support

	Measure of generosity toward the unemployed	Correlation Coefficient	Regression (R-Square)
A.	Index of the wage-replacement rate of unemployment benefits[13]	+0.05	0.003
B.	Percent of unemployed who receive unemployment benefits	+0.31	0.098
C.	Ratio of unemployment benefit recipients to the number of those surveyed as unemployed[14]	+0.42	0.089

Source: OECD, 1995

Three measures of the generosity and scope of unemployment support for the unemployed are listed below with their correlation coefficients and regressed R-squared values. The results unexpectedly appear to disprove the hypothesis. It is not surprising that the relationship is very weak since we are asking much from so few observations. More surprising is that the coefficient is positive in each case. Countries where policy treats the unemployed more generously have a *greater* gap in democratic support between the employed and unemployed.

Hypothesis #2: The longer the average duration of unemployment spells, the more politically salient is unemployment.

Perhaps differences in the size of the gaps in democratic support can be explained by differences in the average duration of unemployment spells. In countries where spells of unemployment are shorter, the unemployed should have political views that are less different from the employed. Conversely, in countries where people circulate quickly in and out of jobs then unemployment should be of less political consequence. Akerlof (1990) and Feldstein (1973) have made the similar argument that American unemployment should not have been regarded as a serious problem because it mostly resulted from rapid churning between jobs rather than long spells without work. Considerable variation does exist in the extent of long-term unemployment between European countries. In countries such as Denmark, Portugal, and Britain about thirty percent of the unemployed had been jobless for over a year in 1990; this proportion doubles to about sixty percent in countries such as Belgium and Italy. The results of statistical analysis are demonstrated below. This hypothesis also clearly fails. Contrary to expectation the relationship is very weak and unexpectedly negative. Long-term unemployment does not correspond to greater political salience of unemployment.

The rejection of the first two hypotheses fits well with the theoretical claims of the first chapter. Unemployment is only politically damaging to those in power insofar as people attach as certain concept of unemployment whose causal and descriptive accounts lead them to blame the government. Indicators of the salience of unemployment would be more useful if they took into consideration the interpretive lens through which people understand its effects. Hypotheses three and four attempt to partially address these concerns.

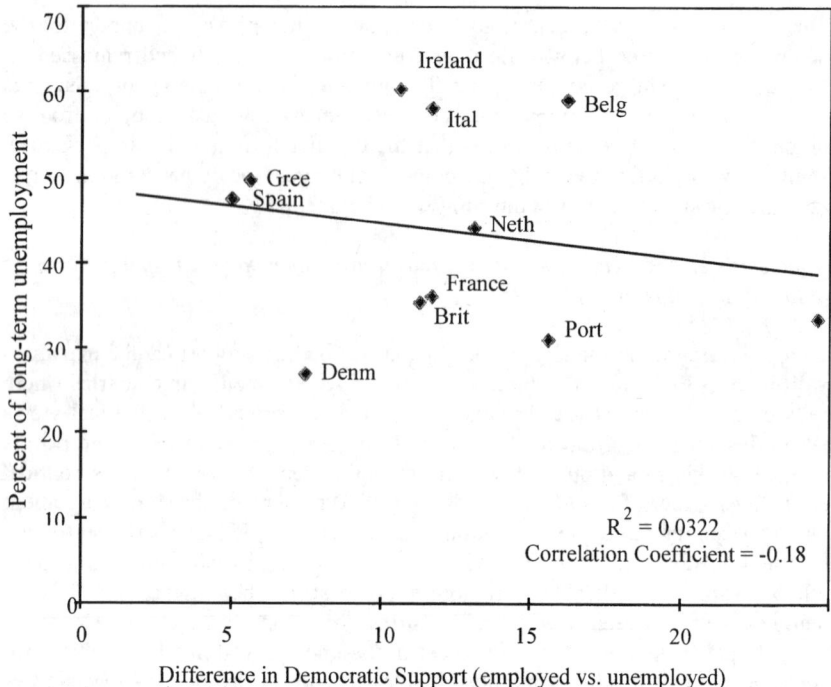

Figure 8.1 Differences in democratic support vs. percentage of long-term
unemployed

Hypothesis #3: The political salience of unemployment depends on the prevailing character of employment.

> *3A: The more that employment secures a minimum livelihood the greater will be the political salience of unemployment.*
> *3B: The more employment is in industry the greater will be the political salience of unemployment.*
> *3C: The more prevalent is self-employment, the less will be the political salience of unemployment.*

If a country has a more significant portion of working poor, then having a job does not imply income security and the distinction between having a job or being unemployed is blurred. Wage norms and labor regulations construct the meaning of unemployment through defining the content of employment. In the indices and scattergram below I measure the degree to which employment is generally a guarantee against poverty. The proportion of full-time workers who earn less than two-thirds of median earnings is taken as a proxy for the incidence of working poverty.[15] The larger the portion of workers earning such low pay the less significant is a lack of employment and, I hypothesize, the less politically salient will be unemployment in that country. The strong negative correlation coefficients and the scattergram below support this hypothesis. More low-paid employment correlates with less salience. These findings are even stronger if, due to the exaggerating effects of German reunification, we were to exclude Germany.[16]

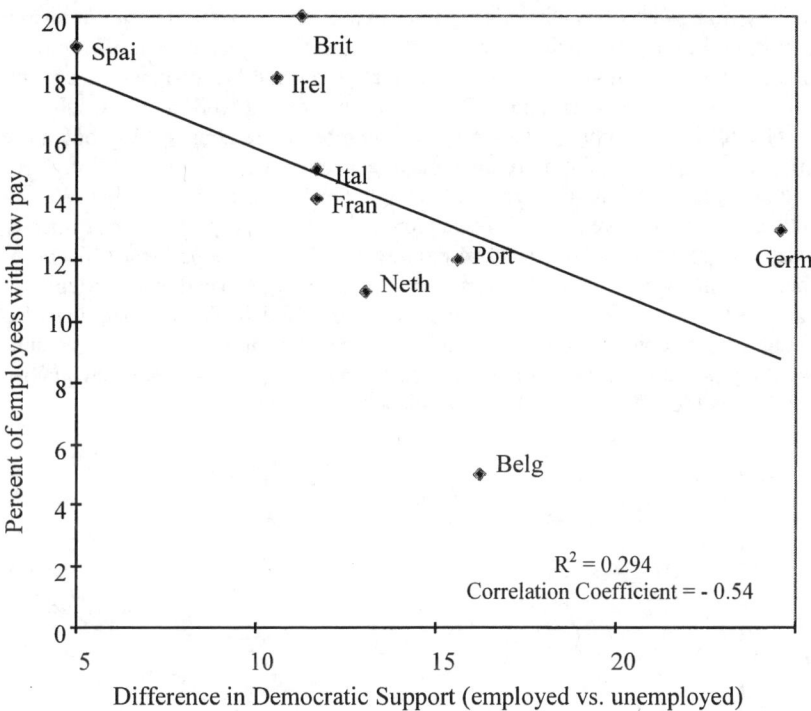

Figure 8.2 Differences in democratic support vs. percentage of employees with low pay (less than 66 percent of median earnings)

Table 8.3 Livelihood guaranteed by employment and gap in democratic support

	Percentage of full-time employees earning less than 66 percent of median earnings
Correlation coefficient	-0.54
excluding Germany	-0.78
Regression (R-Square)	0.29
excluding Germany	0.61

In order to understand how unemployment is politically *interpreted* I have suggested that it is important to understand its prototypes and cognitive architecture. Not all those without work are regarded as unemployed, and some kinds of unemployment are regarded as more salient than others. Unemployment is most meaningful when counterpoised against certain kinds of employment. The meaning and importance of unemployment has been historically linked to the emergence of industrial employment. In post-war industrial capitalist economies the prototypical unemployed person has been an able-bodied, prime-age male industrial breadwinner with plant-specific skills who has been laid off from full-time formal work as the result of a plant closing in a declining industry. For a number of reasons spelled out more clearly in Chapter Nine, the more unemployment resembles its industrial "core" (or prototypical) form, the more salient that unemployment is typically regarded. We can hypothesize that the more a country's employment is in industry, the more politically salient is unemployment. Agricultural employment dilutes the political salience of unemployment because family farmers always have work to do and other agricultural workers tend to be casually attached to their jobs and habitually drift between seasonal work. Services, "post-industrial" jobs, and "atypical" work such as sub-contracting, part-time work, home work, and temporary contracts make the category of employment less distinct, diluting the salience of unemployment.[17]

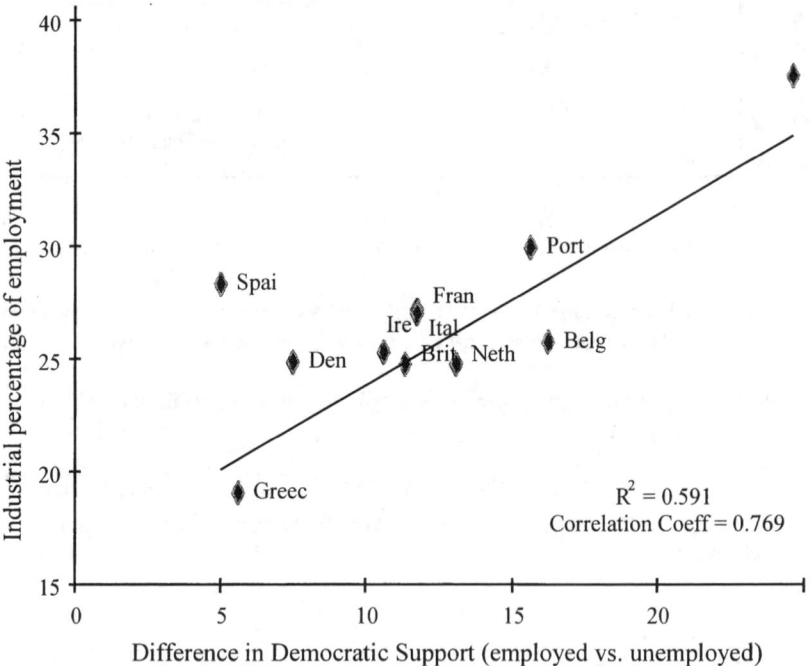

Figure 8.3 Industrial portion of employment vs. difference in democratic support

Figure 8.3 shows the observed relationship between the salience of unemployment and the portion of each country's labor force who are industrial employees. The strongly positive correlation coefficient indicates that more industrialized employment corresponds to a greater political salience of unemployment. The regression analysis suggests that the industrial portion of employment can explain almost 60 percent of the variation in unemployment's political salience.

Further evidence suggests that a blurring of the distinction between employment and non-employment corresponds to a diminishing of unemployment's political salience. Self-employment makes unemployment less politically salient by blurring the distinctions between labor force categories. In self-employment there is typically little spatial or temporal separation between work and non-work and it is highly arbitrary how to differentiate the normal business-seeking activity of the entrepreneur from the active job-search of the nominally unemployed. I hypothesize that greater prevalence of self-employment and unpaid family workers should, all else equal, correspond to less distinct differences between employment and unemployment—and therefore less political salience of unemployment evidenced by a negative correlation coefficient. As predicted, the relationship, though weak, is negative: more self-employment corresponds to less political salience.

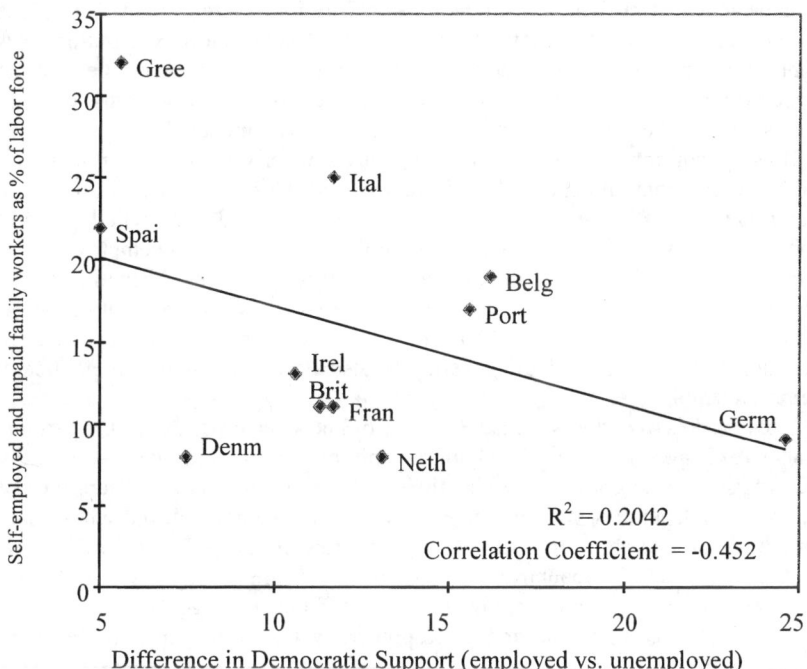

Figure 8.4 Self-employed and unpaid family workers as percent of labor force vs. difference in democratic support

Hypothesis #4: When the unemployed rely more on government labor exchanges to find jobs they are more likely to blame the government for their joblessness.

The unemployed use different ways to look for work in different European countries. In some countries the local governmental labor exchange offices serve as the primary channel for finding a job. Governments typically make registration at a labor exchange a prerequisite for obtaining unemployment benefits. In some places, such as France or Spain, individuals who register as unemployed gain eligibility for health care and can count working years towards a pension. In other places, such as Greece, few of the unemployed collect benefits and there is little other reason to register since few jobs are allocated through the exchanges. In Spain 60 percent of people looking for jobs find one through unofficial channels (Estivill, 1993: fn14). These differences may have political consequences for the salience of unemployment.

I hypothesize that to the extent that when more people rely on state institutions to provide them with jobs they are also more likely to blame the government when job opportunities are inadequate. Even when high rates of registration are an artifact of small governmental incentives (such as reduced-rate transportation passes for the unemployed) people may nonetheless be cognitively more oriented toward holding the government accountable. Conversely, low registration rates in a country may reflect tight restrictions on eligibility for benefits or few decent jobs allocated through the labor offices. Despite the fact that low registration rates might be the result of a lack of government resources for job-seekers, the fact that people do not look to the government in these circumstances might paradoxically diminish the political cost of unemployment to the government.

Thus the political costs of unemployment are smaller when the government has made lesser commitments. As discussed in Chapter One, institutional commitments create their own cognitive orientations. Governmental policies establish their own evaluative logics. We know that the rate of unemployment in an economy is sensitive to the duration and size of unemployment benefits as well as to the particular ways that benefits are monitored (Fleck and Sorrentino, 1994, Humphrey, 1994, Tsebelis and Stephen, 1994). We can hypothesize that such institutional commitments by the government also affect the way people politically interpret unemployment.

In testing this hypothesis we have no way of knowing to what extent registrants at labor exchanges are actually relying on this method to find work—especially when registration is combined with other methods of job search. Therefore we take as our independent variable only the portion of the unemployed whose *only* method of job search is registration (the top row in Table 8.4 below). It is hypothesized that in countries where more unemployed rely solely on governmental offices to find employment, they will blame the government more in their political interpretations, and correspondingly unemployment will be more politically salient.

Table 8.4 Methods of job search among the unemployed in labor force surveys
(Percent of job searchers who use indicated methods of search)

	Belg	Den	Fra	Germ	Gre	Ire	Ital	Neth	Port	Span	UK
Only registered at exchange	12.3	...	17.3	47.4	...	5.6	41.5	1.3	7.6	...	1.4
Both registered and other method	76.8	90.4	70.7	38.8	14.9	66.7	50.6	61.7	40.0	92.1	62.4
Private employment office	11.5	17.8	14.2	7.8	...	15.7	1.3	16.3	...	0.5	24.2
Direct employer contact	25.4	39.7	18.5	4.8	7.1	14.3	13.5	3.0	10.3	...	5.4
Through the press	27.7	30.5	26.4	22.7	3.7	26.3	1.0	30.6	2.8	17.0	24.8
Asked friends, relatives	7.0	1.8	7.4	1.8	2.5	10.2	6.3	2.1	12.9	32.8	6.5
Other methods	5.2	0.0	4.2	1.7	1.2	0.0	28.5	9.7	13.4	41.8	1.5
Only another method	10.9	9.6	11.9	13.8	84.7	27.7	7.9	38.0	52.4	7.8	36.2
Private employment office	1.3	...	1.5	3.8	...	4.4	...	5.6	...	...	8.1
Direct employer contact	3.2	4.1	3.9	1.7	33.5	5.3	3.2	4.1	11.4	...	3.1
Through the press	4.1	4.7	3.9	6.2	20.9	12.9	0.2	20.9	4.2	2.1	19.5
Asked friends, relatives	1.5	...	2.0	1.1	24.0	4.9	1.4	4.0	21.2	5.0	3.6
Other methods	...	...	0.7	1.1	6.2	....	2.9	2.4	15.4	0.7	1.8

The results indicate that some relationship appears to exist, as evidenced by the strongly positive correlation coefficient. Almost half of the observed variation in our proxy for the salience of unemployment can be explained by the different search habits among job seekers (as shown by the R-squared). The fit would be much closer if not for Italy. Here there is only an intermediate level in the political salience of unemployment but a very high level of unemployed who only seek work through registration. However, in Table 8.4 above we can see (by combining the top two rows) that *total* levels of registration are not particularly high in Italy. Similar or greater portions of the unemployed also register in Belgium, Denmark, France, Germany and Spain, but they tend to combine registration with other methods of job-search. Regardless of how we wish to treat Italy the findings suggest that it may be theoretically fruitful to consider the political impact of unemployment in terms of institutions which shape the cognitive maps by which people blame the government for joblessness.

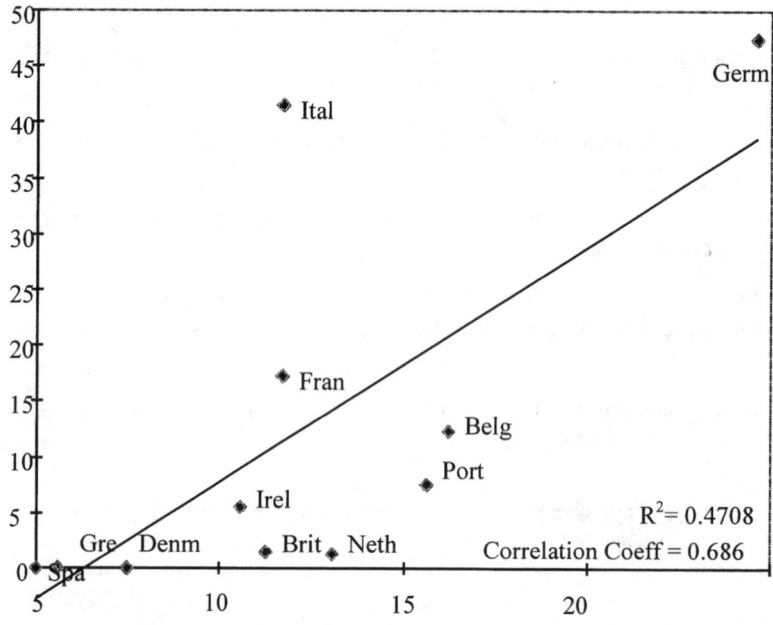

Difference in Democratic Support (employed vs. unemployed)

**Figure 8.5 Percent of registration-only job searchers and difference in
democratic support**

Conclusion

The data permit only a cursory indication of which theoretical relationships might be most promising. The measure of individual-level opinion gaps is an imperfect indicator for what must be accomplished by more country-specific case studies of the changing political valence of unemployment. It has been suggested that neither the generosity of unemployment compensation nor the duration of unemployment spells strongly influence the political salience of unemployment. Evidence instead indicates that national differences in the political importance of unemployment are better traced to differences in national patterns of employment and the form of state commitments to providing employment.

There may be complex contradictory causation at work here. Perhaps more generous programs for compensating joblessness and shorter unemployment spells actually *do* tend to diminish the salience of unemployment; but perhaps it is impossible to observe these effects because they are systematically overwhelmed by counter-effects related to the character of employment. Unions, labor parties and others concerned with protecting the quality of jobs are also particularly fearful of unemployment. Workers worry that they too may become unemployed and they fear the downward wage pressure exerted by desperate job-seekers willing to accept sub-standard jobs. Those countries that generously protect (and thereby prolong the status of) the unemployed are the very same countries which try to set high minimum standards for employment norms. Unemployment benefits (unlike early retirement) help job-seekers to hold out for jobs that make better use of their skills and maintain their accustomed income levels. Governments which give greater compensation to the unemployed therefore paradoxically increase the political salience of unemployment by increasing the relative significance of *not* having a job. The political results of caring for the unemployed and maintaining high employment standards might have opposite effects on the political salience of unemployment. The overall effect of either tendency is therefore relatively weak and uncertain. It is difficult to disentangle the two effects from one another.[18]

If nothing else, the foregoing discussion provides a useful thought experiment for operationalizing theoretically-informed intuitions about differences in the political meaning of unemployment. Before speculating on how such notions might inform predictions about the future, it is worth a more sustained theoretical discussion. This is the topic of the next chapter.

Notes

1   An early-1990s Eurobarometer survey shows that almost a quarter of Europeans recently placed unemployment atop a long list of the issues most important to them, ranking far higher than specific national issues, crime, immigration or the environment—none of which are top ranked by more than even nine percent of voters. See Eurobarometer 41.1 and 42 cited in Anderson, 1997.

2   The adjusted R-squared value is 0.0178 with a 95 percent confidence interval. The respective unemployment rates and percent of respondents who chose unemployment as the most important political issue are as follows: Belgium 6.7, 48.3; Denmark 7.7, 34.9; France 8.9, 69.0; Germany 4.8, 51.1; Greece 6.4, 37.2; Ireland 13.4; 56.0; Italy 9.1, 48.5; Netherlands 6.2, 32.7; Portugal 4.6, 50.0; United Kingdom 7.0, 44.9. Unemployment data from EUROSTAT, Short Term Indicators and is seasonally adjusted.

3   Using simple regression analysis we see only a very weak relationship that is in the opposite direction as expected. Regressing the percentage of respondents who place unemployment atop their issue agenda against changes in the unemployment over the last year (or two years, or three). Using seasonally-adjusted EUROSTAT unemployment data the adjusted R-squared does not exceed 0.11 and greater reductions in unemployment unexpectedly correspond to greater concern with unemployment (expressed in the issue agenda). Perhaps large reductions in unemployment should not be taken as an indication that concern over the issue has fallen but could, on the contrary, indicate that great concern over the issue has caused anti-unemployment policies.

4   Nor is the issue ranking of unemployment on surveys a dependable measure of the political importance of unemployment. Scholarship on American popular attitudes toward the economy shows that when citizens declare that some economic issue has become more pressing they are largely parroting media or government proclamations; but these statements about the economy do not necessarily translate into political judgments about the government (Haller and Norpoth, 1997; Hetherington, 1996; Wlezien, et al., 1997).

5   See E. Pugliese, 'Models of Unemployment in Europe', paper presented at the 10th Conference of the Europeanists,: Chicago, March 14-16, 1996.

6   The PSOE was reelected in 1986, 1989, and 1993 with unemployment at twenty-two, seventeen, and twenty-three percent respectively. They won reelection even when their absolute majority control of Parliament left little doubt about which party was accountability for policy performance. J.M. Maravall, *Surviving Accountability*, Florence: Robert Schuman Centre at the European University Institute, Jean Monnet Chair Papers, no. 46, pp.32-33.

7   By political salience I mean the political threat or political importance posed by unemployment. The perhaps overly general word "salience" is used here to capture general features of unemployment's political valence, including voting effects, protest effects, and the prominence with which people hold unemployment as an evaluative criteria when making political decisions. The English word derives from Latin "salire" which means "to stick out" or "leap". In future work and with more finely-tuned data it would be useful to further disaggregate these effects.

8   The Eurobarometer 41.1 and 42 from which this data is pooled has a sample size of approximately 1,500-2,000 persons from each country.

9   Evidence suggests that the differences in the political attitudes of the unemployed v*is à vis* the employed persist even when controlled for other socio-economic factors associated with unemployment (Schlozman, 1979).

10 I focus on the difference between the employed and unemployed's overall support of the political system for two reasons. First, unlike questions about voter participation or ideological leanings, the question about overall system support is sufficiently general that results will not reflect national peculiarities such as voting laws or partisan politics. Second, it is the only question in Anderson's data set for which the difference between employed and unemployed is large and in the same direction for all countries. Anderson

also finds that the unemployed generally vote less, are more left-leaning, and are less interested in politics; but these differences do not hold in all countries.

11 In the Spanish case, the Socialist party won four consecutive elections despite very high unemployment. They won reelection even when their absolute majority control of Parliament left little doubt about which party was accountability for policy performance. The PSOE was reelected in 1986, 1989, and 1993 with unemployment at 22, 17, and 23 percent respectively (Maravall, 1997: 32-33). Spanish tolerance of unemployment is especially surprising since public opinion studies indicate that Spanish public opinion is particularly sensitive to economic conditions and government is held responsible for economic conditions (McDonough, et al., 1986).

12 Personal communication with Miguel Glatzer. The Portuguese unemployed are moreover far more politically interested than the typical Portuguese employed person, a relationship that is the opposite in almost every other country. Belgium, by contrast, is the only country where the unemployed are more right-leaning than the employed (Anderson and Guillory, 1997).

13 The OECD combines a number of composite measures to derive this overall average (OECD, 1995: Table 8.1).

14 This measure (from OECD, 1995, Table 8.4.B) compares the availability of unemployment compensation across OECD countries. There is first an attempt to correct for some of the different ways that survey answers are treated in different countries. The number of unemployed people was then compared to the number who receive benefits to yield the "coverage rate" of the unemployed. At the top are many countries (such as Austria, Belgium, Canada, Denmark, Finland, Ireland, and the Netherlands) where the number of beneficiaries is actually higher than the number of unemployed. This is possible because the governments not only extend benefits to job seekers without any work but also to people working part-time or in public works programs, who don't count as officially unemployed but are not acceptably employed. In the middle are countries like France, Sweden and Germany where the number of beneficiaries is almost equal to the number of officially unemployed (98 percent, 89 percent, and 93 percent, respectively). On the other extreme side of the spectrum is the United States where only 34 percent of those who meet the definition of being unemployed actually receive benefits. Accompanying the U.S. was Greece at 30 percent and Portugal at 36 percent.

15 The findings also hold, though somewhat less strongly, if we take fifty or eighty percent of the median as our proxy.

16 A disproportionate amount of East Germans were unemployed. Their disillusionment with democracy might be more a function of disappointment with reunification than their employment situation *per se*.

17 Perhaps the first argument against the applicability of the standard labor force framework of unemployment to service sector work is Moore, 1958. Many have argued that in the new post-industrial, post-Fordist age unemployment is a less relevant distinction because income is ever more decoupled from employment (Aronowitz, 1994; Gorz, 1985; Jessop, 1993; Keane, 1988; Offe and Heinze, 1992; Rifkin and Heilbronner, 1996; Walters, 1996).

18 There are two reasons for this difficulty: firstly because the limited number of data points make it impractical to conduct multi-variant regression analysis; secondly because some countries which give less policy effort to income maintenance for the unemployed might give greater effort to moving the unemployed out of unemployment (through active labor market measures or programs such as early retirement).

PART IV
THEORY AND PREDICTIONS

Chapter 9

How the Meaning of Unemployment is Constructed

A prudent Prince neither can nor ought to keep his word when to keep it is hurtful to him and the causes which led him to pledge it are removed... No prince was ever at a loss for plausible reasons to cloak a breach of faith (Machiavelli 1992: 46).[1]

The social contract is unavoidably a relational contract, that is the behavior of the government in the case of unforeseen contingencies is not specified but there are stated goals and objectives that act as criteria for what should be done when unforeseen contingencies arise (Maravall 1997: 9).

These two quotes portray very different pictures of how rulers manage inconvenient commitments to the public. The first conveys the limber dexterity with which past promises can always be recast. But the second attests to the ways in which existing relationships set the terms by which such reinterpretation must take place. The tension between these two maxims also applies to how rulers confront unemployment. On the one hand, governments can always redefine their commitments against unemployment; but on the other hand, they will meet with public disapproval if they abandon established responsibilities.

It is a truism of politics that unemployment is politically damaging for those in power. Every month the unemployment rate is announced with great fanfare, a pulse not just of the economy but also of the likely course of political events. Unemployment is thought to be capable of bringing down governments. Fear of unemployment can motivate governments to take extraordinary measures such as to synchronize their spending to coincide with electoral cycles, to spend huge sums of money on social compensation that discourages work and stokes inflation, to arrange bargaining between employer groups and organized labor, or to lash themselves to the wheel of central planning. But why is unemployment such a threat to those in power? Why, moreover, does unemployment seem to be a greater political threat in certain places or times than it is in others? And finally, what can governments do to protect themselves by shaping the meaning of unemployment?

Unemployment as Institutionally Constructed

At the outset of the industrial revolution there was no "unemployment", despite the large number of victims from enclosure and other dislocations. Before the mid-1890s the term "unemployment" was virtually nonexistent in the European languages.[2] There was talk only of individuals being "without a job", "at leisure", or "idle".[3] Well into the industrial era the term "unemployed" had no special meaning apart from the more general notion of "unoccupied". It was against the prevailing tendency to view unemployment as a purely individual problem that Beveridge titled his 1909 book, *Unemployment as a Problem of Industry*. One reason that unemployment had not been viewed as a distinctive social problem was that in the early industrial mills when work was slack laborers could turn to farming and the household economy of their relatives.[4] Unemployment did not always exist as a social condition and could exist only under certain kinds of social arrangements. As Garraty argues,

> Unemployment connotes a certain kind of relationship to one's work. Slaves can not properly be called unemployed, nor can truly independent artisans, writers, shopkeepers or farmers. It is too hard to imagine that these groups want to work but can not connect with the means to do so. In order to be unemployed labor must be free, yet dependent. It is typified by the worker who absolutely must be under hire to have any means of livelihood. One must be free to quit work and also liable to be dismissed, but in doing so lost the means for livelihood (Garraty, 1979: 5).

The history of unemployment makes it clear that "unemployment" is not a timeless category with universal characteristics, but is instead a social invention that has been continually revised. Numerous historical studies recount how the emergence of unemployment as a distinct and important social problem emerged alongside industrialization.[5] Unemployment was only created as a conceptual and linguistic category with the emergence of certain kinds of industrial employment, and only when the state began to regard it as a *social* rather than a purely individual problem.

It may be disorienting to think of unemployment this way because we are used to treating unemployment as a consistent yardstick that makes labor market comparisons possible between different places or time periods. But other kinds of demographic and macro-economic barometers have also been revealed as changing political artifacts.[6] Even the political significance of population trends such as fertility and immigration rates have depended on the ways that politicians interpret them (Teitelbaum and Winter 1998). One retrospective study of the productivity index shows that the measure, largely ambiguous and subject to manipulation, has evolved to serve changing political ends.[7] Folbre similarly describes how over the course of Nineteenth Century America, as unionists demanded breadwinner wages women who took care of family and worked in the household were redefined in censuses from productive workers to "dependents" (1991). Likewise the category of "retirement" arose only with the institutionalized creation of pensioners and social security as a compromise between organized labor demands for a secure old age and business desires to remove elderly workers who were impeding rapid technological advance (Graebner 1980).[8]

Unemployment is not merely politically constructed in the more general sense that social constructivist philosophers treat all perceived reality as a construction (Berger and Luckmann 1966; Searl 1995). The concreteness of unemployment as a relevant category in political and economic life derives from standardized conventions about how to count it, and from state administrative rules about social policy eligibility and benefits.[9]

This chapter represents a first step in theoretically applying to political economy and policy studies the historical insight that unemployment is constructed. Past studies that have explored how unemployment is variably constructed have not done so because they have tended to be a mixture of ethnographic history that eschews generalizations and technological determinism that stresses the inevitable concomitants of industrialization. In neither case has there been an attempt to draw out the more general dimensions along which the construction of unemployment differ or how politics shape these differences.

Policies Reconstruct the Boundaries of Unemployment

Unemployment changes with the institutions that define its boundaries.[10] The range and meaning of a particular concept of unemployment depends on the specific ways that governments draw distinctions in their social indicators, their political rhetoric and—especially—their policies. All modern governments "propound rules governing the use of productive assets; they establish legal frameworks governing recurring relationships such as those between employers and employees" (Block 1994: 696). Regardless of how market-oriented or deregulatory a government may be, its policies at least implicitly designate what shall count as work, who should work, and who should not have to work.[11] As Deborah Stone's research on comparative national disability policies underscores, program eligibility and benefits rules demarcate the boundaries between needs-based and work-based distribution:

> Society must develop a set of rules to determine the boundaries of the two systems, rules that specify who is subject to each distributive principle and what is to be distributed within each system. ...the boundary is something that each society has to invent, to redesign in the face of changing social conditions, and to enforce (Stone 1985: 17).

The work/need boundaries set by social policies help to enforce work by distributing resources conditionally—thus designating those situations where people are expected to work and strongly encouraging them to do so (Piven and Cloward 1993). The category of unemployment shapes the boundary between: on one side, the expectation that citizens must work to sustain themselves, and on the other side, the government's commitments toward those who are legitimately without work.[12] "The unemployed" designate those who are expected to earn a livelihood through work-based distribution, yet recognized as legitimately in need of work. These particular boundaries of unemployment have important consequences in defining the lines of responsibility between worker, firm and state.

The architecture of the standard Labor Force Framework for population surveys exemplifies how the boundaries of labor market categories depend on the particularities of their underlying institutional arrangements. As illustrated in the figure below, the Labor Force Framework divides the entire population into three mutually exclusive categories: employed, unemployed, and those who are "out of the labor force". The unemployed are distinguished from those who are presumed to be unavailable for work because they are either already employed or are entirely out of the labor market.

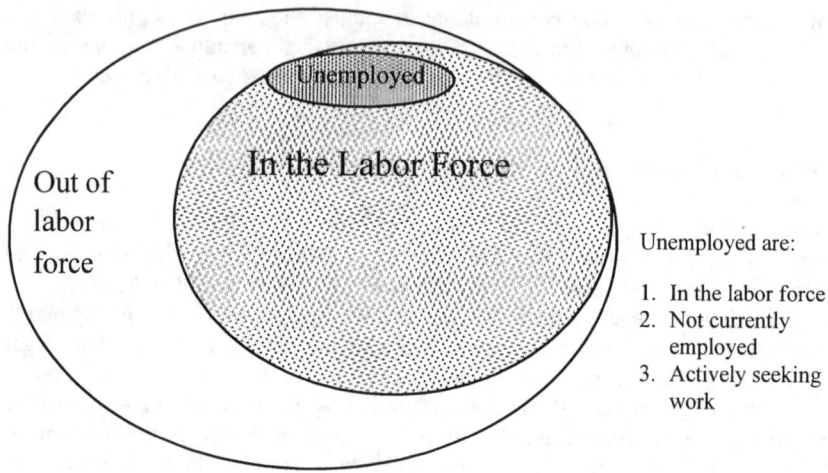

Figure 9.1 How the Labor Force Framework categorizes the population

In drawing such distinctions the modern notion of unemployment critically depends on the *involuntary* nature of its situation, as opposed to mere "idleness" or "leisure". People who choose not to work are distinguished from those who are genuinely unemployed. But, as any public caseworker or survey-taker can confirm, it is never entirely clear when the lack of employment is really an individual's active choice.[13] As economists Lindbeck and Snower reflect,

> Strange as it may seem to the layman, economists have found it difficult to agree on what should be meant by involuntary unemployment and to pose coherent arguments that show why people who are willing and able to work at the prevailing wages in market economies cannot find jobs when they seek them (1988: 19).[14]

It is a testament to the non-universal character of unemployment that in no country with standard International Labor Organization (ILO) methods for counting unemployment do the unemployed coincide even approximately with those who are eligible for unemployment benefits or even the registered unemployed. About a third of the registered unemployed typically would not count as such in standard labor force surveys; and about a third of those who are statistically unemployed are typically not registered. Benefit eligibility for the statistically unemployed varies far more widely (OECD 1995).

Economic models as well as the eligibility rules of unemployment relief recognize that unemployed individuals are only willing to accept work offers above a certain wage and within a range of locations, hours, and skills.[15] An individual who chooses employment under one set of rules and benefits might decide not to work under different institutional arrangements.[16] The rate of unemployment is highly sensitive to the exact definition of what counts as "active job search" (Rettore, Torelli et al., 1990; Tsebelis and Stephen, 1994). Choices about accepting work are also shaped by the availability and generosity of public aid and unemployment benefits. The extent of unemployment in an economy is sensitive to the duration and size of unemployment benefits as well as to the particular ways that benefits are monitored (Tsebelis and Stephen, 1994).

The important consequences of these different labor market boundaries are evident in the varying elasticity of labor supply and variations in the character of unemployment between countries. Swedish, American and Japanese retirement systems, for instance, induce workers to stay employed longer by giving older workers incentives to stay in their jobs. Continental European early retirement programs induce workers to retire earlier. Small restrictions in the eligibility of disability and sick leave programs greatly reduce sickness and disability.[17] As Richard Freeman's survey of labor market regulation wryly concludes, "Institutions which pay people not to work will in fact reduce work" (Freeman, 1998: 9).[18]

The present approach differs from most economic models of unemployment in its focus on the mobility of labor force categories. Conventional models examine how different incentives affect individual choices between work and leisure.[19] Different insights are apparent if we instead focus on how different institutional arrangements correspond to different types of employment and joblessness. Treating such policy and classification rules as *boundaries* is useful for two reasons. First of all the mobile quality of boundaries highlights how the contours of the category of unemployment are not universal and can be revised. Second, the spatial metaphor of boundaries captures the way that a change in one labor force category also transforms the other labor force categories that it is defined against. Changed unemployment policies, for example, can alter the character of employment. Extending unemployment insurance to new kinds of jobs will encourage more people to enter those jobs and to stay in those jobs long enough to obtain coverage, while discouraging people from taking other jobs.[20]

Institutions construct *qualitatively* different kinds of unemployment in the same manner. If the unemployed are distinguished from the larger set of non-employed according to whether they actively search for employment (as they are in the standard Labor Force Framework), then it is important to examine how such search activity is itself conditioned by labor-market and welfare institutions.[21] Long-term unemployment in Europe has made evident how artificial the distinction often is between the unemployed and those who have left the labor force. In some OECD countries in 1990 about half of the unemployed found employment within a year (Canada, US, Netherlands), while in many countries only a quarter to a third did (Spain, Australia, UK) (OECD 1995: 34).[22] As has long been pointed out, comparisons between unemployment rates across different time periods or countries are hindered—even with the same standard measurement techniques— because unemployment may be qualitatively different, especially with different levels of benefit generosity or policy different strategies for combating unemployment (National Commission, 1979; Fleck and Sorrentino, 1994; Humphrey, 1994).[23]

These relationships are evident in even the very earliest examples of social policies. When a basic right to subsistence was established under the English Speenhamland system (1795 to 1832), a battery of changing regulations officially defined the category of "paupers" and granted them basic social protection. Karl Polanyi's *The Great Transformation* describes how at different times paupers seeking relief had to meet local residency requirements, obtain written character references, survive waiting periods, and demonstrate a willingness to toil at public workhouses (Polanyi [1944] 1957). As poor people responded by changing their work and living habits to conform to the changing rules, the stipulations effectively reconstructed the life of pauperhood. In one period paupers constantly migrated in search of generous townships; in another period they strove to establish long-term residency. In one period paupers eschewed small amounts of paid work that might disqualify them from aid; at another period they were required to perform make-work to gain eligibility. The "least eligibility" principle stipulated that public relief should be more onerous and less profitable than common manual labor. In practice this meant two things: first that the bottom of the labor market effectively set the bounds for the wretchedness of public relief. Second, the relief system also reshaped the margins of the labor market. By granting payment up to a defined subsistence level the state largely eradicated the market for day laborers who might work below that wage. Wage rates fell as employers expected their pay to be supplemented by the dole. We can interpret Polanyi's account as describing how the treatment and requirements for those recognized as "paupers" set the boundaries between social protection and the imperatives of employment. It is the dynamics of this relationship between the regulation of employment and that of unemployment that we turn to in the next section.

All Work is not Employment: Defining against Employment Prototypes

The category of unemployment presupposes a distinction between work and employment. Some form of "work" is always possible for individuals, even if it is only begging, thieving, growing food in abandoned lots, searching through dumpsters, or shining shoes. "Unemployment" is fundamentally premised on the designation of a certain subset of more suitable work (here referred to as "employment") with its own institutional rules and policy supports.[24]

The meaning of unemployment therefore depends largely on the meaning of *employment*.[25] The meaning of unemployment depends chiefly on which forms of work government regards as exemplifying "employment", as against more general notions of "work".

Governmental protections, rights, and requirements pertain only to certain kinds of work. Not all productive effort counts as employment and many kinds of productive work, like taking care of relatives, are unrecognized by institutions regulating employment. Social protection and labor policies also inevitably designate which types of individual needs constitute legitimate claims on the state for support in lieu of this employment.

A few examples help to make clear how "employment" is selectively defined as against other forms of less-recognized work. Work that fails to qualify as official employment is often illegal, while officially recognized employment may be protected through business subsidies, tax breaks, social security, workers compensation, labor codes and other regulations. Immigrants typically must satisfy a battery of requirements in order to be recognized as employees. Children under certain ages may not be employed. Work performed in childcare or eldercare is typically recognized as a job only if money is exchanged and the provider satisfies certain licensing and social security requirements.

The question of whether or not an individual is "employed" often depends less on whether they are working than whether their activities count administratively or statistically as employment. Table 9.1 illustrates how not all work counts as employment. This is true both for registered unemployment as counted by registration at labor offices and for unemployment as counted by surveys (although each type has its distinct discrepancies between work and employment). Notice that of the 20 situations described in the chart, only in the three starred (*) examples does work status match employment status.

What counts as unemployment can be understood by how policies emphasize a distinction between "peripheral" and "core" employment.[26] Some workers are viewed as contingent and peripheral to the labor market, hired or laid-off according to fluctuations in demand or production. "Core" workers, meanwhile, are treated as essential to the firm, and their displacement would be regarded as unacceptable— both because their skills are considered difficult to replace and because their continuing employment is important for maintaining industrial peace (Berger and Piore 1980; Doeringer and Piore 1985; Saint-Paul 1996a).

Unemployment is thus defined not simply against employment in general, but against particular *prototypical* conceptions of employment. In other words, some kinds of jobless workers are generally considered more unemployed than others. As Walters explains, "unemployment will be devised... according to a model of normal employment and its social responsibilities. ...It is the tacit norm against which casual labour is pathologized" (1994: 269). For the purpose of explaining political outcomes, a "core" notion of unemployment does not refer to how much firms desire job continuity for certain types of workers. "Core" or "exemplary" unemployment instead refers to the greater political commitments that would be transgressed by these kinds of joblessness.

Table 9.1 Disjunction between work and employment

Work Status	Employment Status		
	Administratively Unemployed	Administratively Employed	Administratively Out of the Labor Force
Not working but would want job	*Unemployed*	• Long-term trainee • Extended maternity leave • Registered self-employed without business • Involuntary "leave" • "Zero-hours contract"[27]	• Early retiree because no available jobs • Disability because no available jobs • Discouraged workers
Engaged in remunerative activity	• Unemployment benefits supplemented by non-reported work • Workfare • Unemployed who receive state support for entrepreneurship.	*Employed and not seeking more work* • Employed but seeks more work, i.e. under-employed[28]	• Works after age limit • Combines pension and unreported work
Not active Labor Supply	• Very long-term unemployed unlikely to be reemployed	• On maternity leave without income from supplementary work • Military draftee	*Not working and out of the labor force*

Note: An individual's "work status" is reported on regular labor force surveys from which are derived the official unemployment rate. An individual's "employment status" determines his/her eligibility for unemployment benefits and social security.

Take the hypothetical example of two people at adjacent phone booths calling help-wanted listings. One is a middle-aged steel worker who has recently been laid off; the other is a 16-year old girl in a wheelchair who has never held a job. Whereas the statistician sees both as equally unemployed, the politician and most citizens do not. We should not understand the politics of unemployment only with the eyes of a statistician. Statisticians may tally the numbers, but it is the politicians who choose measures and instill them with meaning. And it is the populace who interprets whether the government is living up to expectations. The steel-worker is more exemplary of unemployment than the teenager because he represents a more prototypical view of employment.[29] In post-war industrial capitalist economies the prototypical unemployed person has been an *able-bodied, prime-age male industrial breadwinner with plant specific skills who has been laid off from full-time formal work as the result of a plant closing in a declining industry.*

Why have these kinds of joblessness typically been of greater concern to governments than other kinds? Piore explains that one factor is the especially clear distinction that has tended to exist between work life and non-work life for industrial workers.

> The modern concept of unemployment derives from one particular employment relationship, that of the large, permanent manufacturing establishment. Employment in such institutions involves a radical separation in time and in space from family and leisure time activity and was (and is) relatively permanent. When employment ties of this kind are severed, there is an empty space in the worker's life which is sharply defined and that space is what is meant by unemployment (Piore, 1987: 1836).

As a first approximation we might also conjecture that the political impact of unemployment is more significant where the economic impact is graver. Andrew Glyn makes a similar argument reflecting on why discussion of unemployment tends to focus on industry.

> So why should industrial jobs be singled out? The explanation is in the nature of industrial work. Traditionally in the OECD countries this has been relatively well paid, mainly carried out by men, working full-time with skills that are specific to industrial work and requiring only basic education as a prerequisite. Major declines in industrial employment result in large-scale, geographically concentrated redundancies which flood local labour markets with less-educated labour (Glyn, 1995: 3).

The fact that industrial workers are accustomed to being relatively well-paid means that it is difficult for them to find other high paid employment because they only have skills for a particular type of work which is unlikely to be available when plants are closing and an industry is in decline. Similarly, the interruption of work for prime-age workers is more problematic than for older workers because they can rely less on family, do not have significant social security, and cannot go into early retirement programs. As for the unemployed being prototypically male, a consequence of wage norms and presumptions about the male's role as bread-winner suggest that his whole family depends on his income and will be without income when he loses his job.[30]

But upon further consideration, employment prototypes are more political than they might first appear. There is no basis to conclude that handicapped girls or other peripheral workers need a job less than the steel workers, or that they suffer less from the lack of a job. On the contrary, industrial workers generally earn better-than-average wages and are thus more likely to have reserves to draw on and are more likely to find a low-paying job than, for instance, a handicapped girl, a migrant farm-worker, or a young mother. Yet it would not be unusual for the state to recognize only the steel worker as unemployed and even continue paying him jobless benefits when he turns down low-wage jobs that the more marginal workers would gladly take. Economic need alone cannot explain the centrality of the prime-age industrial bread-winner as the employment prototype for unemployment.

Unemployment indeed emerged as a political concept when governments were embracing large-scale industry as the cornerstone of progress and prosperity. Large-scale industry was regarded as critical for healthy government coffers, success in warfare, and general technological advance. Industrial workers in this context represent a particularly potent threat to public order. More skilled workers tend to have higher expectations, and working in large plants gives industrial workers relatively greater organizational capacity for large-scale political action.

Moreover, unemployment emerged and was cast as a political problem during a time when industrial breadwinners were particularly well-organized and mobilized by social-democratic and communist movements. It was not until many years later that it became apparent that the industrial workers would never become the majority in any country (Przeworski, 1985). The Great Depression, which established unemployment as the great yeast of revolutionary discontent, was also at the height of Fordism and the worship of large-scale industry.[31] The very policies that reinforced the Fordist industrial model also established industrial concepts of unemployment.

As discussed in Chapter Eight, the Labor Force Framework through which we today most commonly use to define unemployment is itself a byproduct of the particular employment solutions that emerged in America after the Second World War.[32]

Governments Face Constraints and Opportunities when Reconstructing Unemployment

Governments act to avoid the political costs of economic problems. For instance, governments may try to manipulate the timing of the business cycles so that upswings coincide with elections (Nordhaus 1975; Tufte 1978; Alesina 1989). Even non-democratic regimes have been shown to engage in investment cycles that spur the economy to head off discontent, and then slacken off until again induced by popular grumbling over the economy (Bauer 1981). In order to mitigate dissatisfaction and unrest, some governments have partially devolved macroeconomic policy-making to neo-corporatist peak bargaining associations

(Schmitter 1981; Cameron 1984). The literature on welfare state "retrenchment"[33] has shown that in the face of potential political costs, politicians seek to lower the visibility and hide responsibility for unpopular outcomes (Lipsky, 1984; Pierson, 1994; Pierson, 1996; Rothstein, 1998; Baxandall, 2001a).[34] Welfare state retrenchment theories suggest the possibility that governments, fearing political backlash, might manipulate the institutions through which policy commitments are perceived.

A wide body of scholarship has also demonstrated that, whether intended or not, social policy institutions create their own evaluative logics that both politically constrain government action and open up new possibilities.[35] For instance, more centralized political systems have greater capacity to design and implement obfuscatory methods of cutbacks but, as Hirschman argues, they also have more trouble shifting the blame (1981). Rothstein points to the greater political resilience of universal social programs as opposed to means-tested ones, and argues that some kinds of arrangements have an easier time appearing fair than others:

> The manner in which an existing policy is administered is causally linked to whether or not it will be politically possible for government to attack it. ...[D]epending on the institutions we select for furnishing citizens with these basic resources, we create different types of moral logic in the social policy discourse" (Rothstein, 1998: 18).[36]

Esping-Andersen similarly argues that it is more politically costly for governments to defect from the commitments of insurance-based social programs than universal programs because these programs are generally developed through a process of consensus and produce a strong sense of entitlement (Esping-Andersen 1995). Lipsky's earlier study of welfare programs concludes more generally that,

> Programs... are not simply government "outputs". Rather they structure the relationship of citizens to the state. To say that there is a relationship implies that there are sets of mutual expectations, not necessarily explicit, that establish the ways in which parties in the relationship behave and regard each other (Lipsky, 1984: 4).

The argument developed here similarly seeks to demonstrate how different institutionalized definitions of unemployment carry differing commitments and expectations on the government. It is technically quite arbitrary, but politically very important, what gets defined as unemployment. Governments have considerable leeway to redefine expectations and to portray their own economic leadership under more favorable conditions by reconstructing the meaning of unemployment.

Every institutional adjustment not only alters the obligations of the citizenry but also the commitments of the state. Categories such as "employed", "unemployed", "retired", or "disabled" are regulative fictions that construct expectations and commitments. Any time governments define who is obligated to work and what kind of work they should do (and all governments do this),[37] they simultaneously create political and financial obligations on themselves. Institutionalized definitions of unemployment represent cognitive commitments toward future action.[38] Economic pressures are interpreted and prioritized according to pre-existing commitments that frame the government's choice of policy responses. Each response alters labor force boundaries and thus reshapes the meaning of the category of unemployment by which citizens blame the government for joblessness. New constructions of unemployment reorient the way that government will subsequently be held politically accountable.

For example, governmental regulations define a certain degree of impaired sight as "blindness". Other laws provide financial support to blind people and recognize that they should not have to work. These rules help to define not only who need not work (blind people); they also help reinforce the expectation that other (sighted) people should work. If some epidemic or other tragedy were to create widespread blindness, the government would then be under prior obligation to expend great resources helping the large numbers of new blind people. Failure to do so would disappoint established expectations and make the government less popular. This example helps illustrate both how governments are compelled to follow past commitments, and why they often might like to change them.

Some employment institutions and social policy arrangements make unemployment more politically salient than others. One of the chief determinants of the salience of unemployment is the degree to which the status of "unemployment" is institutionally distinct from that of "employment", as well as from other forms of "non-employment".[39] The more that employment is a regulated status that carries certain minimum income and security, the greater will be the cost of losing employment.

Using New Policy Solutions to Redefine Policy Problems

The unemployment commitments that governments inherit also constrain subsequent policy-making. Governments have the capacity to reinvent the concept of unemployment; but they are also politically restrained by the need for sufficient consistency with past concepts such that new definitions will be viewed as legitimate.[40] They cannot credibly introduce at will wholly new and unfamiliar standards for their own evaluation.[41] They require what Jon Elster has called "upstream legitimacy" (1993).[42] Past commitments cannot be discarded without political costs, or at least not without new institutional investments.[43]

The political constraints and opportunities that governments face can be understood by analogy to the ways that public confidence lifts or lowers the fortunes of economies or governments.[44] Since Keynes, the importance of business confidence in the economy has been well appreciated (Keynes 1964 [1935]) Hirschman has observed how popular confidence depends on certain understandings about what kinds of state actions are proper and effective; and that these expectations themselves effectively bind governments because transgressing these norms will produce real economic effects.

At any one time there is a general understanding, an unwritten "social contract", about the rules which make an economy work and about the boundaries assigned to the state's economic role. The harm caused by breaching these rules and boundaries is likely to outweigh the benefits that are calculated to accrue from the purely "mechanical" effects of state action (Hirschman, 1989: 353).

Here Hirschman discusses the mechanisms by which individual decisions underlie larger economic outcomes such as multiplier effects or capital flight. Governments are similarly constrained in pursuing new economic policies by the need to foster *prior* public confidence about their labor and social policies. As scholars of public policy implementation have shown, policies that lack political support will tend to fail (Pressman and Wildavsky, 1984; Chisholm, 1989); but political support itself largely depends on a pre-existing belief in the government's ability to succeed. This is true even in authoritarian regimes because they rely on elite cohesion. Governments are therefore constrained by a kind of vicious circle that inhibits new policy approaches.

On the one hand, ...the newly proposed policy can work only provided people are already convinced that it will do so; on the other hand, it stands to reason that this conviction arises most typically among the economic operators once they have lived through a positive experience with that policy" (Hirschman, 1989: 353).

In Hirschman's account new economic concepts can only gain a foothold when disbelief is "suspended by some exogenous happening" such as well-timed wars and depressions that lead to positive experiences with new policy instruments. In order for a new policy approach to take root what is needed is "for actors to 'stumble' more or less accidentally on an action that will then give rise to the new attitude" (353).[45]

Governments need not be so naive or passive. Governments do not merely maneuver around their existing commitments. They also strategically rearrange these commitments.[46] They may escape the vicious circle Hirschman describes by addressing their new commitments to policy problems where they can *already* show some success from their "new" approach. They may reconstruct social policies and indicators around solutions where they can demonstrate progress and where they expect more. Governments reverse-engineer new definitions of the problem of unemployment to conform to newly embraced policy solutions. These redefinitions are politically self-serving, but they need not be deceitful or duplicitous. Purely as a matter of conserving their effort, governments tend not to bother measuring problems that they will not be trying to solve.[47] They define the problem of *un*employment according to how they intend to advance, regulate and legitimate a particular kind of employment and non-employment.[48]

The political impetus to advance and protect a certain kind of employment may inadvertently cause governments to increase the political costs of unemployment if other economic factors cause a decline in that type of work. The state may have conflicting commitments *for* a particular kind of employment as *against* its associated unemployment. This is what occurred in Hungary with state industrial employment. It may arguably be a problem of European social democratic governments closely associated with unions of declining industries. Regardless of whether or not social democratic labor policies increase unemployment, their commitments to protect employment standards and protect industrial employment through policies intended to protect labor from unemployment may ironically make unemployment more politically damaging (Baxandall, 2001).

The theoretical approach advanced here does not require that government officials thoroughly anticipate how new policies will recast political expectations through changes in the boundaries of unemployment. We need only ask how notions of prototypical employment guide government decision; how governments adjust labor force boundaries to foster employment goals; and how the resulting differences in employment correspond to differences in which kinds of joblessness count as unemployment.

There are conflicting incentives for government to define unemployment more inclusively or more narrowly in social policies. There are a number of reasons for government to prefer more restrictive, *narrower* definitions of unemployment. First of all, the less inclusive eligibility criteria are for unemployment relief, then the less difficulty government will have compelling people to work because the population will be less discerning about what jobs they find unacceptable.[49] Second, as a social indicator, narrower definitions make the problem appear smaller when people evaluate the competence of the state's economic rule. "To make an official count of some phenomenon is often to confer recognition that the phenomenon is real and to risk that its measurement will embarrass those in authority" (Starr 1987: 41). Moreover, because construction of social indicators are "cognitive commitments" toward future action (Starr, 1987: 53), the smaller the scope of the recognized unemployment problem, the less the government will be politically compelled to spend resources to alleviate the problem. Social programs that ease the pain of unemployment reinforce the notion that a problem exists and that the government is implicated in the problem. "A person who is not receiving, or who has ceased to receive benefits is less likely to be socially recognized as a 'genuine' unemployed person" (Gallie, 2000). In order to achieve a near-zero unemployment rate, governments need only eradicate all job-loss benefits, and recognize as officially unemployed only those job-losers who do have a previous work history but have performed no paid work for an extended duration while searching in vain for even the most lowly position.

But, on the other hand, there are a number of reasons for governments to promote a *broader* category of unemployment. Governments benefit politically when commitments to unemployment are perceived as fulfilled. Recognizing and remedying unemployment also ameliorates the potential erosion of popular support. An additional motivation for recognizing and subsidizing joblessness as unemployment is to increase labor mobility. Workers who have less fear of job loss will be less resistant to restructuring and will hold out for jobs that make better use of their skills (Katzenstein 1985).[50] Perhaps most importantly, unemployment policies are useful for regulating work and encouraging certain forms of employment. In this respect governments prefer wider definitions of unemployment because they give greater control over the shape of employment. The more people are (or in case of job loss would hope to be) registered as unemployed, the more they will be guided by rules about the proper way to exit their old jobs, search for new ones, etc. Lastly, governments who have championed a particular prototype of employment are likely to regard the exemplary sectors of the workforce, management and government as an important constituency. Once they have committed to broad definitions of unemployment, governments may continue to commit ever-greater resources to these politically costly labor force boundaries rather than risk tensions with crucial allies.

These factors are in a more general tension with one another. The status of unemployment is, on the one hand, a technology for returning workers to jobs and a useful threat to encourage disciplined work; but, on the other hand, unemployment expands entitlements to state resources and acts as a barometer against which the government is judged. The tension is broadly between defending a particular notion of employment and avoiding the political exposure from unemployment. The category of unemployment is a double-edged sword for governments. It exhibits their successes but also their failures.

Distinguishing Causal Mechanisms and Explaining "Path Dependence"

We may disaggregate the multiple ways that unemployment generates political effects and determine when these effects are likely to compound over time. The political effects of unemployment can be distinguished along two dimensions. First, political effects can be subdivided according to whether they are aggregated from accretion of changed individual behaviors or, alternately, if the causal mechanism is triggered through social representations. Secondly, we can distinguish political mechanisms according to whether they are triggered by the material losses from unemployment, or whether the insults of unemployment are more socially constructed. This yields four possible combinations which can be called: sociotropic effects, pocketbook effects, benchmark effects, and psychological effects. Each of these effects presents different mechanisms for the possibility of longer-term shifts in the politics of unemployment through self-reinforcing feedback mechanisms.

By distinguishing between these kinds of causal feedback mechanisms we can also distinguish the ways in which these effects may or may not build in political importance over time. Mechanisms that are self-reinforcing or provide positive feedback are especially important over time in generating lasting political legacies, or "path dependence" since they will tend to build over time (Pierson, 1993, 2000; Mahoney, 2000; Hacker, 1998). These are indicated as positive (+) in Figure 9.2. Other effects of unemployment have mechanisms which tend to dissipate their political effects and therefore do not generate lasting political legacies. These negative feedback mechanisms (–) are also indicated in Figure 9.2 below.

	Aggregation of individual effects	**Effects from social representations**
Socially-constructed insult	I. _Psychological_ – The unemployed tend to feel disgraced, disorientated and depressed, but they therefore participate less in politics. – The unemployed tend more often to be psychologically-alienated, but therefore often exit the labor force rather than remain unemployed.	IV. _Benchmark_ + Once economic competency is defined in a distinct concept of unemployment, it becomes a benchmark for future success. Subsequent blaming or credit-claiming utilizes this concept and reinforces its perceived importance. + Conceptual boundaries are reflected in government policies whose administrative criteria then reinforce the perceived importance of conceptual categories. – In pursuit of policy "success", government introduces new policies that erode the institutional importance of old benchmarks.
Materially defined insult	II. _Pocketbook_ + Job losers consume less, slowing the economy and may thereby create higher levels of unemployment. – Unemployment creates fear of job loss among the employed, but they therefore become more politically quiescent.	III. _Sociotropic_ + Public discussion of unemployment makes people more likely to use unemployment as a prime measure of economic health when evaluating the competency of government.

**Figure 9.2 Typology of mechanisms for the political salience of
unemployment and their potential returns to scale**

I. Psychological Effects[51]

For evidence of the psychological pain of unemployment, one can look as far back as Freud, who argued that a person's work is virtually central to their sense of identity and social place: "No other technique for the conduct of life attaches the individual so firmly to reality as laying emphasis on work; for his work at least gives him a secure place in a portion of reality, in the human community" (Freud 1961: 30fn). Other psychological studies have confirmed that because employment is a chief source of identity and organizational frame for daily life, unemployed individuals suffer intense emotional distress along with the more obvious interruption of income and loss of status (Jahoda, 1982; Clark and Oswald, 1994). Studies show unemployment to be arguably the strongest single economic predictor of the incidence of individual pathologies like homicide and heart disease.[52]

But the fact that the unemployed suffer psychologically poses little threat to those in government because those who suffer unemployment tend to blame themselves or to be disengaged and alienated from politics (Anderson, 1997). Moreover, the unemployed have difficulty mobilizing collective action because as a group they tend to be: disorganized, heterogeneous, focused on self-help strategies, represented poorly in political networks, meagerly endowed with material resources, and their most capable leaders tend to defect to the ranks of employment.[53] However much the anxiety of the unemployed deserves our compassion, the pain does not tend over time to force government action.

II. Pocketbook Effects

Unemployment leads to a loss of income. And to some extent, individual political attitudes follow their pocketbooks. All else being equal, it stands to reason that individuals are inclined to feel more favorably towards government when their pockets are full than when they are empty. In addition to the unemployed themselves, their families and support networks also suffer material deprivation from unemployment. By one estimate, in the United States the fraction of the population suffering from unemployment is two and a half to three times larger than the unemployment rate in any given year (Hibbs, 1987).

Pocketbook effects, however, tend to be of little political significance compared to more socially-constructed effects. One factor may be that pocketbook effects lack strong self-reinforcing mechanisms of political feedback. Economically, reduced income among the unemployed may lowers consumption, further slowing the economy and causing more unemployment. Growing unemployment may also make the deprivation of unemployment increasingly severe as it becomes more difficult to find a job. But these effects may be outweighed by the fact that greater fear of job loss makes the more-politically-significant ranks of the employed more politically quiescent.

III. Sociotropic Effects

The more general problem with equating material deprivation from unemployment with political discontent is that a large body of research on political opinion, voting and protest suggests that individual economic circumstances do not directly determine political sentiment.[54] As Lewis-Beck concludes, "[T]he strength of pocket-book voting depends on the development of a particular pattern of causal reasoning about the responsibility for personal economic conditions" (Lewis-Beck, 1988: 36). People tend to view the state of the economy based on "sociotropic" or collective evaluations, rather than "pocketbook" or personal ones (Fiorina, 1981; Kinder and Kiewiet, 1981; Lau and Sears, 1981; Abramowitz, 1988). Although ordinary citizens may not fully understand the details or causality of economic policy, they hold their leaders politically accountable based on their broad perceptions of the material situation.[55] Evidence suggests that unemployment is a particularly prominent criterion for popular evaluation of the economy. Indeed, public opinion reacts more quickly to unemployment than to inflation (Conover, Feldman et al. 1986). The unemployment rate is a strong predictor of the survival of West European parliamentary systems (Warwick, 1992).[56]

Indicators of *perceived* business conditions are a consistently better predictor of how people vote than surveys of personal financial well-being (Kinder and Mebane 1983).[57] Schlozman and Verba found that those who lose their jobs generally "did not see themselves as victims of broad social forces or governmental ineptitude but of specific events connected with their particular employment circumstances" (Schlozman and Verba, 1979: 194).[58] Research on protest and collective violence moreover finds no correlation with economic indicators of relative deprivation. Economic deprivation leads to resistance only when injustice is perceived, when those who are deprived are mobilized, and when they see opportunities for change (Snyder and Tilly, 1972; Eisinger, 1973; Tilly, 1978; McAdam 1982; Tarrow, 1998; McAdam, Tarrow and Tilly, 2001).[59]

Sociotropic effects may become self-reinforcing. The more people express discontent toward the government because of unemployment, the more people notice unemployment and base their evaluations of the government in terms of unemployment.

IV. Benchmark Effects

Both benchmark and sociotropic effects capture how economic misfortune consistently translates into blaming the government only when interpreted through understandings of social conditions and their causal relation to the state. But whereas sociotropic effects measure the ways that individuals consider the objective material trends within the larger economy, the benchmark effect further describes how such criteria are themselves ongoing social constructions.[60] The language of "benchmarks" as distinct from sociotropic effects is introduced here because it captures both the way that broad social indicators are used to evaluate the competency of economic rule and the ways in which these criteria are social artifacts that can be redefined. Benchmark effects differ from sociotropic-type effects because the triggering categories are themselves socio-institutionally constructed.

Benchmark effects can be self-reinforcing and thus create lasting political legacies. Politicians reinforce the notion that they should be blamed or credited for high or low levels of unemployment by themselves taking credit (or accusing others) for particular unemployment levels (Graziano, 1989). Mindful of past experiences of political damage from unemployment, governments are likely to construct institutions that protect established conceptions of employment and provide aid for the unemployed according to established labor market boundaries. In this case, government policies will further a self-reinforcing feedback loop in which policies re-inscribe the conceptual boundaries that makes unemployment politically salient, thereby prompting more such policies.

We have seen that governments may redefine employment to take advantage of anticipated future events or because outside events induce governments to institutionally redefine a new prototype. In this case, the new labor market policies make unemployment less politically salient and less binding on future policy.

Concluding Remarks

Two final points of qualification are presented by way of conclusion. Government has been portrayed here as the primary, almost lonesome actor in the construction of the political meaning of unemployment. It steers the economic ship with the commitments it has inherited and navigates the treacherous currents of popular legitimacy. Other kinds of politics have been regarded here as important, but they may seem curiously distant—such as in determining the compromises over which kind of employment is held to be exemplary. This book has been an initial foray into relatively unexplored questions. The research would certainly be enriched by more sustained attention to other political agents such as sectoral coalitions, unions, particular bureaucratic bodies, employers, and political entrepreneurs.[61] The focus on government and governed does not preclude future attention on other actors. On the contrary, it is a necessary first step for understanding how others bring power to bear on policy-making.

The construction of unemployment takes place, however, in the technocratic details of eligibility and measurement procedures. The government remains the ultimate authority for recognizing what constitutes at least official "unemployment" (Tant, 1995: 254). The very fact that economic categories like unemployment are not normally regarded as "constructed" makes it all the more important to study them as they are crafted, in the hands of the authorities.

Another potential objection to the theoretical is its two-way causality. Governments are constrained by popular evaluations in the way they make policy; and at the same time government policies shape popular evaluations. Analysis of how the meaning of unemployment is constructed, therefore lacks cleanly separated dependent and independent variables. This is true, however, of any analysis of socially-constructed effects: changes in the world alter the way the world operates and is perceived. Attention to these feedback loops has the benefit of highlighting the ways that self-reinforcing effects can over time generate persistent, "path dependent" outcomes. In sorting out the sequencing of events, the use of comparative quantitative data may be limited by the fact that measures mean different things within the different contexts they measure. Social-constructivist views—even institutionally grounded ones—may be constrained in their quantitative sophistication. Electoral studies of sociotropic assessment by voters sacrifice sociological richness for cleaner data. This data indicates that not only do voters form political judgements based on the economy, but their assessment of the economy depend in some dynamic way to their prior political judgments (Harrington, 1993; Converse, 1969; Maravall, 2001) In other words, mutual causation seems to be not just a feature of sociologically-informed methodology, but inherent to the relationship between politics and economy.[62]

Notes

1   Cited in Maravall, 1997: 8.
2   The German word for without work *arbeitlosigkeit* was rarely used before 1890. Karl Marx discussed not *arbeitlosigkeit* but *unbeschäftigen* (the idle or not busy). French *chômage* existed through the middle ages, but its source is telling. It derives from *kauma* (burning heat) in Greek via medieval Latin *caumare*, which means to take one's ease during the heat of the day. Again, the word derives from the concept of being at leisure (Garraty, 1979).
3   Alfred Marshall's *Principles of Economics*, published in 1890 and often thought of as the founding statement of neoclassical economics, treats full employment as given and uses only the expression "inconsistency of employment" (Garraty, 1979: 121). American dictionaries, beginning with that edited by Webster in 1828, applied the term mainly to inanimate resources: "unemployed land, capital, or money" (Topalov, 1998: 7).
4   In agriculture and various family enterprises family and market activities were so intermingled "that the line between them was difficult to draw and adjustments to variations in economic conditions were made through changes in the distribution of time between various tasks. These changes were not registered by measures of unemployment at all" (Piore, 1987: 1836).
5   See Polanyi (1944) 1957: 224; Thompson, 1967; Garraty, 1979; Keyssar, 1986; Salais, Baverez et al., 1986; Kumar, 1988; Whiteside and Gillespie, 1991; Grantham, 1994; Walters, 1994.
6   "Statistical entities are simultaneously real and constructed, invented and discovered" (Daston, 2000). "Unemployment, inflation, growth, poverty, fertility: these objective phenomena, and the statistics that measure them, support descriptions of economic situations, denunciations of social injustices, and justifications for political actions. They are inscribed in routinized practices that, by providing a stable and widely accepted language to give voice to the debate, help to establish the reality of the picture described" (Desrosieres, 1998: 1). For an early history of how the notion of objectivity came to be associated with economic statistics see Poovey, 1998.

7   Productivity measures were developed during post-war boom years by neo-Marxists who wanted to show that capitalism was still undergoing crisis. After the economy slowed in the 1970s, productivity numbers then became an ideological tool against militant labor demands by showing that higher wages were not justified by labor's contributions to production (Block, 1986).

8   Even a seemingly objective public problem such as drinking-while-driving involves the imputation of causality in ways that foreclose other kinds of solutions and responsibilities. Gusfield shows how a particular view emphasizing the motorist as "cause" of alcohol-related auto fatalities has prevented solutions from attributing responsibility to the alcohol industry or the lack of alternative transportation (Gusfield, 1981).

9   Unlike many other politically relevant but less concrete categories and cultural dispositions (such as patriotism or ethnic community) the boundaries of the category of unemployment are determined by particular authorities and are codified in definite ways. Unemployment may have definite boundaries, but such definitions are not therefore fixed. As Nietzsche quips, "Only that which has no history is definable" (Nietzsche, 1998: 53).

10   "Categories contribute to shape social reality through the agency of institutions" (Topalov, 1998: 2).

11   Even the most minimalist government that is limited to the protection of private property rights will still have to designate the boundaries of employment. Such a government, for instance, would have to define who is an employee in order to resolve basic disputes over liability.

12   As Moon has argued, social policy steps into the moral breach between societal expectations for individual self-sufficiency and the undeniable fact that individuals in industrial society can sometimes be deprived of the possibility for livelihood, well-being, and dignity for no fault of their own (Moon, 1988).

13   For example, at the unemployment office a laid-off steel worker might not qualify for benefits if he were to only apply for jobs as a movie actor or corporate C.E.O.; but should he still qualify if he rejects job offers to sell fast-food or door-to-door encyclopaedias?

14   One argument points to surveys and psychological studies that show the unemployed tend to be less contented than the employed. It concludes that the unemployed therefore do not choose joblessness. The relative unhappiness of the unemployed is a constant across gender, age, and education groups (Clark and Oswald, 1994). The problem with this argument is that, while the unemployed may be less happy as a group, we do not know what their alternative employment options were. Their available job prospects were presumably less conducive to happiness than average forms of employment. There is a more basic tension between the practice in economics of treating preferences as "revealed" in behavior, and on the other hand treating unemployment as purely involuntary. Rational calculating individuals should understand when they must relocate or accept lower wages in order to find work. Presuming that economic actors are capable of rationally readjusting their expectations, it is unclear how anything but the most fleeting lack of employment is not a voluntary and revisable preference, at least in the sense that it is based upon a person's standards of dignity and entitlement. "In a choice-theoretic paradigm there can be no room for a concept such as involuntary unemployment" (De Vroey, 1994: 19).

15   Economists, for instance, regard individuals as having "reservation wages" below which they are unwilling to work.

16 Posing the matter this way avoids unproductive disagreements between Left and Right over whether unemployment is a choice. The Right, equating choice with individual responsibility, claim that because unemployment is chosen it is therefore best prevented by policies which reduce the attractiveness of this choice. The Left, claiming that the unemployed have no choice, argue therefore that more jobs must be created.

17 For an extensive review of this literature, see Freeman, 1998.

18 Similarly, a 12-nation micro simulation study finds that social security incentives dramatically affect retirement decisions (Gruber and Wise, 2002).

19 See, for instance, Danziger, Haverman et al., 1981; Aaron, 1984.

20 Policies also regulate the boundaries of different forms of *non*-employment by selectively supporting different exemptions from work. Governments determine, for example: what age is a worthy retirement, how infirm one must be to justify not working, and whether parenthood or training should be supported in lieu of employment. Przeworski argues that norms of non-employment best explain why work-time reduction schemes are not more widely embraced as a solution to unemployment. When leisure is viewed as an activity that requires spending money then people are unwilling to forego income gains for leisure (Przeworski, 1995).

21 More recent American research underscores that the labor-force attachment of the unemployed is not so different from other non-employed persons who merely respond to surveys that they "want jobs". Judging by the chance that an individual is actively in the labor force the following year, the unemployed are only half again as "attached" to the labor force as other non-employed job-wanters whose insufficient search activity does not qualify them as unemployed (Castillo, 1998).

22 The unemployed constituted only one-eighth of the larger set of non-employed (OECD, 1995: 186). Even among 25-54 year old men, unemployment accounted for only as much as half of non-employment (OECD, 1995: 191).

23 "In countries without an all-embracing social security system, unemployed people cannot rely on social security benefits during spells of unemployment. They have to find some way of support, which is usually found in the informal sector. If workers are thus occupied they would not be regarded as unemployed, even though if social security benefits were available, the same workers would probably not be in the informal sector and would be counted as unemployed. A comparison of unemployment data between countries with and those without proper social security systems is therefore difficult" (Barker, 1992). Esping-Andersen also urges that employment comparisons must be viewed alongside differences in social policy (Esping-Andersen, 1990).

24 Unemployment is sometimes concentrated in a particular area where there are virtually no jobs (such as when the mines close in a coal town); but if conditions are bad enough then workers will move or will otherwise endeavor to scrape out their own meager subsistence. When there are many workers who have skills in industries that are in decline the unemployment is typically described as "structural" or due to a "skills-mismatch"; but this still does not prevent workers who are willing to take a large pay-loss from moving into unskilled work. Pointing out these possible choices does not mean that unemployed workers are lazy or that the government has no moral responsibility to help them. It simply highlights the contrast between strong theoretical presumptions that unemployment is not voluntary and the fact that there is almost always *some* available work, albeit poorly paid, dangerous, or worse than begging.

25 On deep historical sources of different national conceptions of employment, see (Biernacki, 2001).

26 "An analytic distinction is needed, therefore, between the relatively stable and rigid part of a policy and its more changing and flexible components. Using a visual metaphor, the

stable part may be called the *core* of the policy, the flexible part, its *periphery*. To say that the core represents the rigid part of the policy is not to suggest that it is immutable, but only that it changes more gradually and continuously than the elements of the periphery that are its transitory end-products. A radical transformation or abandonment of the core signifies a major change in policy—revolution rather than evolution, so to speak" (Majone, 1989: 190). For other attempts to incorporate how thinking is done through catagories to economic analysis, see Fryer and Jackson, 2003.

27 Big retailers in the U.K. sometimes place would-be employees on permanent stand-by. Without any minimum hours stipulated in the contract the worker is nonetheless administratively and statistically treated as employed. For a discussion see (Walters, 1996: 201).

28 As the ILO explains, "The limitation of the concepts of unemployment and visible underemployment as social indicators becomes evident, for example in the situation of persons who, though fully employed in terms of hours, have low earnings and seek extra work" (ILO, 1990: 147).

29 The notion of employment prototypes is consistent with what Furstenberg and Thrall identify as a "job rationing ideology" which sets priorities as to who has the greatest obligation to work and the greatest right to a job, acting as a prior queuing mechanism for entrance to the active labor market (Furstenberg, 1975). They cite as evidence a pilot study showing that individuals believe different categories of people should work and should be entitled to a job at rates that correspond to the categories of people who do participate at the highest rate, ie: core workers.

30 The male prototype is clear in Beveridge's 1909 *Unemployment: A Problem of Industry*, "Society is built upon labor... its ideal unit is the household of man, wife and children maintained by the earnings of the first alone. The household should have at all times sufficient room and air according to its size—but how, if the income is too irregular always to pay the rent? The children, till they themselves can work, should be supported by the parents—but how, unless the father has employment? The wife, so long at least as she is bearing and bringing up children, should have no other task—but how, if the husband's earnings fail and she has to go out to work? Everywhere the same difficulty recurs. Everywhere reasonable security of employment for the bread-winner is the basis of all private duties and all sound action" (Beveridge, 1909 1; Walters, 1994). As our earlier discussion of dependency makes clear, the traditional male bread-winner role was largely created by the institutionalization of these presumptions rather than the presumptions simply reflecting existing roles.

31 See for example, Walker and Guest, 1952; Fridenson, 1978; Sabel and Piore, 1984; Stinchcomb, 1990: 62-66; Sabel and Zeitlin, 1997. Keyssar criticizes the singular focus among western historical studies of unemployment on the Great Depression. He states, "Most modern scholarship dealing with the problem of the unemployment possesses the peculiar distinction of being both ahistorical and haunted by memories of a single historical period" (Keyssar, 1987: 201).

32 Since its adoption at the 1947 International Conference of Labor Statisticians the Labor Force Framework has become almost universal for international (and most domestic) labor statistics. See Hirschman, 1989 on the connection between the export of Keynesian ideas and the U.S. role as a hegemonic super-power that influenced other countries' economic policies through direct aid programs. For a fuller exposition, see (Baxandall, 2001b).

33 The notion of retrenchment is inseparable from an analysis of government's social commitments. The language of "retrenchment" has been favored over terms such as "cutbacks" or "spending reductions" precisely for this reason. It captures the fact that

governments may be pulling back from social commitments even while they increase total welfare state spending (Clayton and Pontusson, 1998; Baxandall, 2001a).

34 Pierson claims that, "[T]he success of retrenchment advocates will vary with the chances for lowering the visibility of reforms. Those seeking retrenchment will try to avoid political outcries by diminishing the visibility of their cutbacks or by trying to hide their own responsibility for unpopular outcomes" (Pierson, 1996: 177). One way that this prediction has been borne out in recent years is that the United States government has reduced spending commitments by changing the way that inflation is tabulated rather than openly cutting inflation-indexed entitlement spending. On other ways that governments dodge accountability, chiefly through inter-party maneuvering see (Maravall, 1997).

35 For a similar kind of argument about the institutional influences on popular evaluation of military conscription and tax-compliance, see respectively Levi, 1988; Levi, 1998.

36 See also Korpi, 1980; Taylor-Gooby, 1985; Korpi and Palme, 1998.

37 This is true even in "deregulatory" environments such as the US. For example, in articulating a commitment that poor single mothers should work for their child benefits (workfare) the government creates new obligations for training, child care, public works and job counseling. By articulating a new measure of success (out of poverty through employment) the government makes itself politically vulnerable if people get kicked off welfare and do not manage to find jobs or get out of poverty, or when economic downturns make it harder to find work.

38 Desrosieres similarly discusses the "investment" in particular labor force boundaries, "The amplitude of *the investment in forms* realized in the past is what conditions the solidity, durability, the space of validity of [social] objects thus constructed. ...This alchemy is the bread and butter of any institute of statistics when it publishes unemployment figures or price indexes. The idea of investment is interesting in that it draws attention to the *cost* of stepping through the mirror, of passing from one world of realities to another—a cost of which the budget of the statistical institution is only a part" (Desrosieres, 1998: 11, 111).

39 The more general point here is that the category of unemployment is more salient when it is more institutionally distinct from the other categories against which it is defined. The discussion above presumes a standard ILO/OECD Labor Force Framework, but unemployment has historically also been defined against such categories as non-union workers, social parasites, work-shirkers, and men of leisure (Baxandall, 2001b).

40 This is consistent with Visser and Hemerijck's general hypothesis "that, rather than confronting the extremely uncertain event of a complete institutional overhaul, policy actors will choose to patch up institutions with new structures or transpose them to new functions as long as possible, because these two strategies of institutional change are less costly, less risky, and less politically divisive" (Visser and Hemerijck, 1997: 57).

41 On the ways in which continuity with the past is necessary to produce consensus, see Burke, 1987 (1790); Shils, 1981.

42 Downs similarly argues that in party competition, "Ideological *immobility* is characteristic of every responsible party, because it cannot repudiate its past actions unless some radical change in conditions justifies this" (Downs, 1957: 110).

43 Commitments to legitimacy provide definite mechanisms for what is sometimes called path-dependence (Pierson, 2000). They represent "barriers to exit" because once claims are made transgressing them is a benchmark of betrayal that is politically unpopular. There are also "returns to scale" because once legitimacy has been established along particular benchmarks there is both an incentive to credit claim along the same lines for

those achievements and it becomes already established that such accomplishments yield political gain.

44 See also the notion of "bootstrapping" in Sabel, 1995.

45 Similar kinds of Catch-22 situations have been identified in the problem of tax collection (Levi, 1988). Rothstein characterizes the difficulty of effectively implementing tax policy when citizens and officials have antagonistic expectations, "If …[a] Russian tax official could make Russians believe that his tax bureaucrats would be honest and that they would have means to make sure that (almost) all other citizens paid their taxes, most Russians would pay their taxes" (Rothstein, 2000).

46 Scholars have long realized that inherited traditions, beliefs, and concepts are reinvented and manipulated to accommodate new needs and interests. Such a view need not imply, as Downs does, "that social groups use ideologies as smoke screens or tools; their real end is whatever benefits them most" (Downs, 1957: 112fn. See also Roemer, 1994). The strict separation between true subjectively-held beliefs and communication on one hand, and ends-oriented strategic action on the other is a central feature in, for instance, the work of Jurgen Habermas (1985, 1987). But a per person can both use a set of beliefs instrumentally and have those same beliefs influence their own understanding of the world. As Hay asserts, ideas can be "both strategic and reflexive" (2001: 199). For applied examples, see Halbwachs, (1950) 1980; Hobsbawm and Ranger, 1983; Przeworski, 1985; Schwartz, 1991; Bates, Figueriredo et al., 1998: 634; McNamara, 1998; Rothstein, 2000.

47 Like all organizations, governments adapt their institutions around the kinds of information they are concerned with (Stinchcombe, 1990). For instance, local authorities in New England no longer keep track of witches or blasphemers because they no longer try to do anything about them.

48 Politicians also choose among alternatives to the unemployment measure that puts them in the best light, highlighting employment levels, focusing on particular sub-groups or regions, or comparing to similar countries, for instance, when the unemployment figures are gloomy. In this way there may be both government-initiated changes in the meaning of unemployment and also substitution between unemployment and other economic problems. According to Visser and Wijnhoven, in the 1980s, in countries where unemployment levels were not highlighted and governments instead focused other metrics, unemployment was in fact perceived as a less important national problem, even when the unemployment rate did not decline (Visser and Wijnhoven, 1990).

49 All other things being equal, governments would generally prefer more people actively working in order to expand state power and available slack (Levi, 1988). As Maier also points out, "time is a scarce collective as well as individual resource. If a society needs its citizens' time, it must purchase or commandeer it against alternative claims" (Maier, 1987: 153).

50 Many economists, especially those prescribing to "efficiency wage" theory of unemployment, also regard moderate levels of unemployment as increasing efficiency by helping to solve management's problems with monitoring their labor force. Employers pay premium wages as an inducement to workers not to shirk from work and the worker has an additional incentive because, in the absence of full employment, the worker can expect some trouble finding another job (Shapiro and Stiglitz, 1984; Bulow and Summers, 1986; Akerlof and Yellen, 1990).

51 Strictly speaking, psychological effects need not be purely individual-based, as evidenced by the field of social psychology. I use the term here to describe the combination of methodological individualism and a subjective universe constructed out of individual experience.

52 Powerful evidence for the preeminent importance of unemployment can be found in a 1976 study *Estimating the Social Costs of National Economic Policy*, which linked American data on economic distress—measured by unemployment, inflation, and real income per capita—to social pathologies as measured by age- and sex- specific rates of mortality, cardiovascular-renal disease, homicide, mental hospital admission, and imprisonment. Regardless of age, sex or race, unemployment showed the most significant correlation to the various pathologies. See Brenner, 1976, cited in Schlozman 1979: 54.

53 Survey data shows that the unemployed vote less and tend to be politically apathetic (Anderson, 1997). For studies of the psychology of the unemployed and their tendency to blame themselves, see Jahoda, 1982. On the impediments of disorganized groups for collective action see Olson, 1965.

54 Surveying the international literature Blount concludes, "Unemployment has always been a particularly problematic predictor of the vote in the economic voting model". And that, "Unemployment may be a poor predictor of rational economic voting because, contrary to the assumptions of previous researchers, its meaning is neither unambiguous nor well understood" (Blount, 2002: 92,94).

55 There is controversy over whether voting is retrospective or based on expected future performance and whether personal or national well-being tends to be more important. For a review, see Kiewit, 1983.

56 Robinson likewise finds that among numerous economic factors unemployment is the most effective predictor of cabinet administration durability in the eight European democracies between 1958 and 1982 that were studied (Robertson, 1984). Schmidt however finds no negative correlation between higher unemployment and incumbent electoral success (Schmidt, 1984).

57 "Only very few citizens are motivated to vote against the incumbent simply because they see their financial situation has deteriorated. In election surveys from these six nations, retrospective personal economic circumstance (no matter how it is measured) virtually always fails to register statistically significant main effects on legislative vote" (Lewis-Beck, 1988: 155). The exception is U.S. Presidential elections, where there is a mild but significant effect (Kiewit, 1983: 49; Markus, 1988). Evidence from post-communist countries shows that individuals who suffer greater economic hardship are less likely to express support for the political system but sociotropic interpretations still dominate these effects (McIntosh and MacIver, 1992; McIntosh, 1994; Mishler and Rose, 1996).

58 Research on American presidential voters in 1984 confirms this finding. It also suggests that those whose economic condition has improved disproportionately tend to ascribe their success to personal causes, while those who are worse off tend more often to blame external causes. Only 40 percent of respondents perceived any effect of government economic policies on their own personal economic conditions, and less than 60 percent perceived government policies as even effecting national economic conditions (Feldman and Conley, 1991).

59 Tocqueville concluded from the French Revolution that it was not squalor and hardship that caused people to rebel but the frustration of rising expectations during the latter days of the *ancien regime* (Tocqueville 1983 [1856]).

60 This is not a distinction that is typically made within the literature on sociotropic voting.

61 Another area of future research would be to disaggregate what has here been called political "salience" into the different dimensions along which unemployment is politically important. For instance, we might ask whether voting behavior, issue prominence, and protest trends all move in similar directions. It would be interesting to

know whether some aspects of political salience react differently than others to changes in the definition of unemployment. Finally, another future project would extend the present research strategy to examine the political construction of other indicators such as: inflation, productivity, pauperism, disability, the Freedom House Index, the UN quality of life index. It would be interesting to see the similarities and differences in how such politically-charged indicators have been invented and reconstructed over time.

62 This does not mean that sociotropic methods are equivalent to socio-institutional analysis of benchmarking. Where the latter approach sees the meaning of economic categories as shifting, the former approach sees voters as shifting the criteria by which they draw political evaluations from a cognitively static world—such as shifting between retrospective and prospective voting, or between intertemporal, exonerative, antidotal, distributional and oppositionist postures (Stokes, 2001).

Nor should the above discussion be interpreted as saying that methodologically-individualist approaches do not have unique contributions to make to understanding the politics of unemployment. Rational choice analysis suggests that the number of jobs at a workplace is a collective good and that individual workers expecting possible job-loss will free ride on its provision rather than making sacrifices to ensure greater total employment for the group. It has been argued that whether organized labor will respond to lay-offs with work disruptions or strikes depends on information asymmetries, rules permitting employers to target union militants for dismissal, and the strategies by which unions defend strictly organizational interests (Golden, 1997).

Chapter 10

The Future of Unemployment

If the preceding pages have conveyed one central idea it is that questions about differences in the meaning of unemployment should be framed in terms of the variable political meanings of *employment*. The previous chapters show how this approach illuminates a number of questions: the origins of political commitments against unemployment, the reasons commitments change over time, why unemployment is more politically important in some places and times than others. Though most closely applied to Hungary, the theory has helped explain changes in the meaning of unemployment in America, Britain, the Soviet Union, and municipalities around Geneva. Different distinctions between work and employment also help explain differences in the political salience of unemployment across the European Union and among post-communist countries.

This is a peculiar moment in history to be writing about differences in the meaning of unemployment. In some respects, changes in the meaning of unemployment have reached their own "end of history". With the fall of the Soviet Empire and the growing importance of global economic organizations (such as the IMF, EU and WTO), there has been a convergence around the Labor Force Framework method as the standard conceptual architecture for understanding and measuring unemployment. Although different institutional boundaries in policy still foster differences in the degree to which unemployment is politically important; the basic definition of unemployment has been almost completely standardized world-wide.

But the standard Labor Force Framework may have triumphed only to become obsolete and irrelevant.[1] The basic assumptions underlying the Labor Force Framework are rapidly eroding and new kinds of social policies have emerged with radically different conceptual premises.[2] The theoretical approach developed here helps us speculate about unemployment's future political importance and conceptual evolution.

The Obsolescence of Unemployment

The Labor Force Framework was built around the prototype of the full-time industrial bread-winning wage-earner who worked fixed hours with an indefinite contract at the premises of his employer. This sort of employment is increasingly rare in advanced economies.[3] In recent years employment has become more contingent, fixed-term, temporary and part-time. It is characterized by subcontracting, consultancies, multiple job-holding, youth internships, and working out of the home, as well as more multiple wage-earning families and early retirees (Rogers and Rogers, 1989). Workers with these kinds of employment relations are not readily classified into the Labor Force categories of the employed, unemployed, or those out of the labor force.[4] Unlike a coal miner or steel worker, a self-employed consultant is always actively seeking work but never unambiguously unemployed.

A burgeoning literature on the re-invention of work and the putative end of employment-as-we-know-it suggests that industrial-era meanings of unemployment are obsolete. In reaction to rising long-term joblessness, new technologies, and "atypical employment", these studies herald a new post-industrial, post-Fordist age in which unemployment is a less relevant distinction because income is ever more decoupled from traditional employment relationships.[5] Walters points to the diminished political importance of unemployment and argues that its very relevance is fading the way "pauperism" did during the nineteenth century.[6] As new kinds of labor markets do not fit the old categories, political interests no longer crystalize around joblessness and lack an intuitive experience of "unemployment".[7]

Consider the following characterization of the new model of employment made during a downsizing at AT&T, a company where employment once typified long-term industrial bread-winner careers. The vice-president for human resources at AT&T, James Meadows explained as far back as 1996 that,

> People need to look at themselves as self-employed, as vendors who come to this company to sell their skills. ...In AT&T, we have to promote the whole concept of the work force being contingent, though most of our contingent workers are inside our walls. ...'Jobs' are being replaced by 'projects' and 'fields of work', [people are] jobless but not workless (*The New York Times*, Feb. 13, 1996).[8]

The dominant ideas about contemporary business paint a portrait of "virtual corporations" without long-time career attachments or even a definite staff or headquarters and of workers who see themselves their own brands or the CEO of their own skill sets.[9]

Many of these claims are, of course, overdrawn. Employees on average do report lower perceptions of job security and believe that employers are less loyal than they used to be. But the growth of "atypical employment" has been uneven in different places over the last decades and there are convincing arguments that industry is still the critical keystone to national economies.[10] In America, a supposed vanguard of the New Economy, job stability has declined for prime-age men, but average tenure in firms overall has barely declined in recent decades.[11] A number of prominent firms that once embodied the old-style social contract, such as Kodak and IBM, have diluted their commitments to long-term employment; but this commitment never covered more than a small percentage of the workforce in the first place (Charness and Levine, 2000).

Politically, the opinions of the business press and the fate of a few flagship firms may be more important than the statistical average. The previous chapters have shown that the meaning of unemployment is politically constructed precisely because it is a product of changes in the *prototype* of employment, not purely secular trends in the labor market. Despite convergence on standard procedures for measuring the labor force, unemployment will continue to be a political construction. Post-industrialism will not impose technological imperatives on some superstructure of unemployment politics. Future concepts of unemployment are open to divergent possibilities that will depend on the institutionalization of particular policy approaches.

Unemployment may have become less politically salient in recent decades because governments claim less competence to affect the macro-economy. Governments that believe they have more control over the economy are willing to promise more or to assert their own yardstick of success, which they will then be held accountable for. Governments who believe they have little control make fewer commitments. Governments asserted strong responsibility for the level of joblessness when they believed Keynesian demand management could master unemployment. By contrast, contemporary governments see themselves as inexorably pulled between the competing pressures of job creation, social inequality, and public debt (Esping-Andersen, 1995; Iversen and Wren, 1998).

Governmental retreat from competency over employment helps explain the persistence the Labor Force Framework. Governmental leaders will not commit themselves to new ways of defining and measuring success over joblessness until they discover new ways where that they anticipate achieving that success.

New Prototypes of Unemployment?

To understand what happens without new policy commitments, we can look at the history of the concept of "*under*-employment". The idea of under-employment emerged largely from frustration with the inadequacy of the Labor Force Framework to capture the dynamics of Third World labor markets. Under-employment was put forward to describe the widespread situations where people perform paying work but need more paid work to meet their needs. Like unemployment, the concept was officially embraced by the International Labor Organization. But lacking attachment to any specific policy solutions, it remains merely an esoteric indicator among a few economists (ILO, 1990). Under-employment is a problem addressed by general policies to mitigate poverty and increase productivity. Lacking specific policy instruments, under-employment is not distinct from economic deprivation more generally and is unable to mobilize or orient politics.

What kinds of new employment prototypes might be attached to emergent policies to forge a new concept of unemployment? A few are considered in the pages below.

E-ployment?

Scholars have long argued that new technologies are changing the nature of work (Bell, 1973; Braverman, 1974; Zuboff, 1988). While claims about the virtual nature of New-Economy employment are often overstated,[12] new communication technologies have the potential to change the character of unemployment through the role they play in changing the prototype of employment. The industrial prototype of employment presupposes a radical separation in place and time between, on the one hand, work at the job and, on the other hand, leisure at home (Piore, 1987). This separation can be undermined by work that involves cell phones, pagers, lap top computers that are brought home, and workers who log-on or receive email away from the office.[13]

Information technology also can make less heterogeneous the prototypes of job search, on one hand, and that of employment, on the other. These activities become less distinct when people can more easily search and apply for jobs from their desks or home computers, posting their resumes and conducting virtual initial interviews. The notion that one is either at a job *or* hitting the pavement looking for work is simply no longer true. Employers often post job openings on their home pages. And independent web sites have become major mechanisms for job search and matching.[14] The site Monster.com, for instance, receives two million hits per day and 30,000 new résumés.[15]

We might imagine the ways in which unemployment would be transformed if government aggressively institutionalized a digital "New Economy" prototype of employment. Early last century, governments embraced industrial employment as the key to progress, power and prosperity. So too we might imagine twenty-first century governments organizing their economies around the idea that the most important productive activity was electronic commerce. If "e-commerce" was to become the emergent prototype of employment, one consequence might be a further retreat by governments from responsibility for insuring unemployment because of the difficulty distinguishing which electronic work is conducted within the boundaries of the nation-state. Internet transactions are effectively already subsidized through exemptions on sales taxes. Many politicians defend this privileged status because of what is claimed to be the special importance of this part of the economy.

On the other hand, the Web might provide new definitions of productive participation for future policy initiatives. Perhaps unemployment insurance regulations will some day only regard individuals as "actively seeking work" if they have recently logged onto electronic job-search sites and completed on-line training courses. Perhaps employment will be institutionally defined by having a web-site in the dot-com domain and receiving a minimum number of monthly "hits". A pre-requisite for a politically important prototype of digitally-defined unemployment would be policies that used such indicators as benchmarks of some policy's success or triggers for aid.

Hours Deficits?

It is easier to imagine how the meaning of unemployment might be transformed from a variety of other redefinitions of employment that already have advocates and small-scale experiments. For example France and Germany have experimented with using reductions in the length of the working week as a major instrument against unemployment.[16] This strategy, sometimes called work-sharing, can sometimes gain the support of business if it is combined with wage moderation and increased labor flexibility about working hours. Work-sharing policies are particularly attractive to Continental European polities with Christian-Democratic or Green values against work-dominated lifestyle, policy capabilities for regulating work time, and budgetary problems.[17]

If work-sharing ever became the dominant instrument for combating unemployment, then we would expect unemployment to become a different kind of benchmark for labor utilization. The unemployment rate might become an indicator for whether the workday needed to be further shortened or could be allowed to expand. As a measure of labor utilization, perhaps current methods for measuring unemployment would be replaced by indexes of the amount of over-time opportunities that went unfilled. Any such policies would require a whole new institutional apparatus for measuring and regulating work time, perhaps something along the lines of the systems that lawyers and many consultants have constructed around the concept of "billable hours".

Basic-income Insufficiency?

One alternative approach that has received considerable attention is a basic citizen's income. Alternately called a "guaranteed income minimum" or "basic income guarantee", the idea is to ensure all citizens some basic income floor, which would allow government to eliminate minimum wages and all social policies that attempt to determine who really wants to work.[18] Such a strategy differs fundamentally from unemployment and social-security approaches because it takes the insufficiency of incomes rather than the interruption of incomes as the fundamental problem it addresses (Walters, 1996: 205). In addition to its simplicity, the appeal of this approach is that it intrudes far less on businesses and workers' lives. The idea has received lukewarm support from Milton Friedman and a mild version was almost passed in the United States under the Nixon administration.[19]

A citizen's-income approach would collapse all practical distinctions between unemployment and being out of the labor force. It would not distinguish between what kinds of work count as employment because individuals would be left to pursue whatever kinds of work they could find in pursuit of their creative and consumer aspirations. A basic income would not so much eliminate unemployment as make it meaningless (Walters, 1996: 206).

Without any institutionalized pretense to distinguish the voluntary from the involuntary jobless, the number of job-seekers without employment would no longer reflect socio-economic hardship or macroeconomic imbalances. Unemployment would loose political salience.

Community Participation?

Another set of alternative strategies would continue to distinguish employment from work, but would expand the institutional definition of employment to include forms of socially-productive work that are not remunerated by the market. These might include things as: child-rearing, caring for the elderly and disabled, training and continuing education, and volunteer community work.[20]

Some European countries already give pension credit for years spent child-rearing or caring for the elderly and disabled (Compston, 1997).[21] The German government subsidizes companies who hire unemployed persons for certain environmental work or public-interest projects such as cleaning monuments. Denmark has tried numerous strategies to free up employment spots through publicly-funded leave policies that allow the unemployed to temporarily withdraw from the labor market on leave for child-minding or education. The Danish government has found that they can save money on the leave system because the payment is less than unemployment benefits. Child-care leave also reduces demand for publicly provided child care (Compston, 1997). Any wide-scale initiative to expand the boundaries of employment to child-care would greatly reduce unemployment among women and would require contentious new administrative rules defining a parent and what activities count as care.

Arguments to expand employment to include training could be seen as furthering competitiveness.[22] To the extent that training emerges as a central policy instrument for regulating the labor market, we might expect unemployment defined increasingly in terms of skill mismatches. We could expect development of complex administrative systems for skill classification to determine when unemployed persons had rejected a suitable job for their skill set.

How would expanding the concept of employment to include other forms of socially-beneficial work affect government accountability for unemployment? Unemployed might come to represent the government's failure to motivate individuals without sufficient paid work to engage in other socially-productive endeavors. One could imagine that such a concept of unemployment would become a kind of benchmark for the lack of social capital.

One could also imagine that defining which activities qualify as beneficial to the community would be important and politically divisive. Could work credit for community organizing be obtained, for instance, if an individual was organizing against the government or its policies? The eligibility criteria would give the government institutionalized leverage to decide what life activities are deemed socially valuable.

Population Dependency?

A final example of future paths for redefining unemployment is embodied by the "Dutch Miracle" and, to a lesser extent, Blair's "Third Way" in Britain.[23] An under-appreciated aspect of these much-studied reorientations of social policy is how they essentially reverse the Beveridge employment prototype. They encourage temporary and part-time work, while eradicating the privileged recognition of full-time breadwinner jobs.

They involve a fundamental redefinition of labor market problems as problems of *inactivity* rather than unemployment. Cox, who observes a similar tendency in Danish policies, notes how such policies reject the basic goal of earlier social security principles that, "that those outside the workforce would not live in poverty. The new reforms, by contrast, strive to increase participation in the work force and use sanctions to punish those who fail to move quickly into paid work" (Cox, 1999: 2).[24] In the Netherlands a key institutional change was a change from corporatist bargaining over unemployment to bargaining over dependency ratios (that is, the ratio between the employed and inactive portions of the working age population). Whereas earlier tripartite agreements set parameters for wages and social spending according to potential shifts in the unemployment rate, the latter agreements stipulated what should take place under different shifts in the dependency ratio.[25]

Notes

1   "Some twenty years ago almost everybody supposed that enduring mass unemployment would lead to political instability. Governments would not survive mass unemployment. Even the stability of Western democracies would be at stake. These predictions were false" (Visser, 1990:71).

2   For a definition of such "radical" policy and a review of their inroads in Europe see Compston (1997).

3   Esping-Andersen similarly asserts that, "Contemporary welfare states and labour market regulations have their origins in, and mirror, a society that no longer obtains: an economy dominated by industrial production with strong demand for low-skilled workers; a relatively homogenous and undifferentiated, predominantly male, labour force (the standard production worker); stable families with high fertility; and a female population primarily devoted to housewifery" (Esping-Andersen, 1999: 5).

4   In a response to difficulties applying the standard labor force model to may less developed countries ILO conferences in 1982 and 1988 suggested a "relaxation" of certain criteria about "active search" in the definition of unemployment and recommended that business registration might be a workable, if somewhat arbitrary, way of designating which self-employed persons are really employed. See Chernyshev, 1994: 97-98.

5   See, for instance, Aronowitz and DiFazio, 1994; Beck, 1992; Gersuny, 2001; Gorz, 1985; Jessop, 1993; Keane, 1988; Offe, 1992; Reich 2001; Rifkin and Heilbronner, 1996; Walters, 1996. Perhaps the first argument against the applicability of the labor force framework of unemployment to service sector work is Moore, 1958. For a

criticism of the purported inevitability and utopian possibilities of post-industrial decoupling of income from employment, see Pixley (1993).

6   We can speak of the demise of unemployment if we interrogate unemployment from a discursive and governmental perspective. Unemployment is losing much of its salience and centrality within modes of government. ...For the years of postwar "settlement", the assumption was that any government that presided over a return to mass unemployment would be ejected from office. ...More recently, numerous governments have demonstrated that some association with mass unemployment is by no means a serious obstacle to success at the polls (Walters, 1996: 198).

7   Changing employment relations have also made other alternative methods to measuring unemployment even more obsolete. Measures such as the job-seeker vacancy ratio or indexes of "help wanted" advertisements in the newspapers rely on some kind of organized registration system at exactly the time that labor markets are become more less organized around central mechanisms.

8   Castells argues that "the actual operational unit in our economies is the business project, operated by ad hoc business networks" (Castells, 2001:168). A similar statement appears, for instance in a special 1996 issue of the Academy of Management's magazine, *Executive*, describing terms of the new employment contract: "Your employability will be high, although perhaps not at this employer. We work on great projects, but as each project ends, it is up to you to find a new place for yourself within the company—otherwise, you must find a new place for yourself outside the company" (quoted in Charness, 2000: 382).

9   A large literature makes these kinds of assertions. See, for instance, Capelli, 1999; Davidow and Malone, 1992; Hyde, 1998; Locke, 1995; Castells, 2000: 216-302; Pescovitz, 2000.

10 On industry, see Cohen and Zysman, 1987. The OECD, *1998 Employment Outlook* shows an increase in the share of temporary arrangements in total employment since the early 1980s in Australia, France, the Netherlands, and Spain; little change in Denmark, Finland, Germany, Ireland, Italy, Japan, Sweden, and the UK; and drops in Belgium, Greece, and Portugal (OECD, 1998).

11 See review of the literature in Charness and Levine, 2000.

12 As Freeman points out, studies of job tenure show only limited decline for men and increased tenure for women (Freeman, 2002: 14). And those American states that rate high on "new economy" indexes, show no greater extent of job churning compared with lower-rated states (Freeman, 2002: 13). High tech industries show no greater use of contingent workers or atypical employment than other industries. They do find greater use of these workers among fast-growing industries, but largely as a result of these jobs in the fast-growing construction and personal supply services industries (Neumark and Reed, 2002).

13 On the ways in which new technologies undermine the previous radical separation between work and non-work through off-site work and telecommuting see (Autor, 2000). An estimated 25 million Americans and 9 million EU residents telecommute, that is, spend at least one day a week working at home while maintaining contact to the office through computer technology (Freeman, 2002: 11).

14 In the United States the Current Population Survey reported that 16 percent of Americans—and especially younger workers—searched for a job on line in 2001. Half unemployed Americans with home Internet access reported on-line job search. In the UK studies show that three-quarters of British workers who were looking for a new job and had Internet access reported that they searched over the Web. All but one of the top

20 Fortune 1000 companies post vacancies and accept applications online (Freeman, 2002: 15, 35).

15 Jon Gertner, "The History of American Capitalism in a Single Industrial Complex", *The New York Times Magazine*, June 8, 2003, p. 46.

16 On the mixed results of these efforts, see Freedman and Gottschalk, 1998, and Hunt, 1999. On their promise, see Przeworski, 1995.

17 The reason polities with strong Christian Democracy leanings tend to reduce work time are not directly related to religious values, but instead to the welfare-regime characteristics of these economies and the partisan power of the strong parties who promote a less-commodified family life without the deep concern (found in Social Democracies) for inadvertently creating bifurcated labor markets from part-time work (Burgoon and Baxandall, 2004).

18 This policy approach has received a large amount of attention from academic circles and Continental European politicians. For a history, description and bibliography, see http://basicincome.org last viewed July 1, 2003. Also see, Moyniham, 1973, and Parijs and Standing, 1986.

19 Alaska residents effectively receive some form of citizens' income from oil pipeline revenue. Although the amounts are small the simplicity and universality of this arrangement is sometimes cited as a precedent by advocates of a basic income approach.

20 Pixley argues that embrace of any post-industrial options to move away from wage-labor based views of participation will be executed in ways that further marginalize the unemployed and disempower the jobless. She claims that there is no alternative to full employment that does not seriously weaken the citizenship of whole categories of the population (Pixley, 1993).

21 On recognizing care as employment see, Harrington, 1999; Metcalf, 1992; Stone, 2000. In so far as citizens who lose their jobs use the years credited to their pensions to retire early this change is already underway. On the other hand, the American shift in 1996 from Assistance for Dependent Children to workfare-based programs has been a movement away from supporting child-rearing as its own form of participation.

22 Training is also an attractive solution because it reduces unemployment without creating inflationary wage pressures.

23 In Britain such moves have been restricted to tentative experiments with "participation allowances".

24 See also Clasen, 2000; Cox, 1998.

25 As Visser and Hemerijck describe, "The ratio of active to inactive workers became institutionalized as the more relevant policy indicator. If the I/A ratio exceeds predetermined reference levels then the unions know that the government suspends the linking mechanisms that increases social benefits in line with average contractual wage rises... . Higher levels of participation thus became the core policy concern of the Lubbers-Kok cabinet" (Visser and Hemerijck, 1997: 141). Visser and Hemerijck locate the articulation of the new problem definition as from 1987 to 1991 (Visser and Hemerijck, 1997: 157). But a look at the data on inactivity/activity ratios shows that the most dramatic changes occurred *before* the problem was redefined. The long-term uninterrupted increase in inactivity had already reversed in 1985. As predicted by the theory, the new problem definition was framed in terms of a solution where progress could be readily demonstrated.

Bibliography

Aaron, H. and G. Burltess, ed. *Retirement and Economic Behavior*. Washington, DC: Brookings Institute, 1984.

Abramowitz, A., D.J. Lanoue, and S. Ramesh. "Economic Conditions, Causal Attributions, and Political Evaluations in the 1984 Presidential Election." *Journal of Politics* 50 (1988):839-862.

Adam, Jan, ed. *Economic Reforms and Welfare Systems in the USSR, Poland and Hungary*. London: Macmillian, 1991.

Adam, Jan. *Employment and Wage Policies in Poland, Czechoslovakia and Hungary Since 1950*. London: Macmillan, 1984.

Adam, Jan. *Planning and Market in Soviet and East European Thought, 1960s-1992*. NY: St. Martin's Press, 1993.

Adirim, Itzchak. "A Note on the Current Level, Patterns and Trends of Unemployment in the USSR." *Soviet Studies* 41, no. 3 (1989): 449-61.

Akerlof, George, and Janet L. Yellen. "The fair-wage effort hypothesis and unemployment." *Quarterly Journal of Economics* 105 (1990): 255-83.

Alesina, Alberto. "Politics and Business Cycles in Industrial Democracies." *Economic Policy* 8 (1989): 58-98.

Állami Bér- és Munkaügyi Hivatal (ABMH). "Az Aktív Foglalkoztatáspolitika és a Munkanélküliség Kezelése [Active labor market policies and the handling of unemployment]." Budapest, 1988.

Amsden, Alice H., Kochaniwica Jacek, and Lance Taylor. *The Market Meets its Match*. Cambridge, MA: Harvard University Press, 1994.

Anderson, Christopher J. "Desperate Times Call for Desperate Measures? Unemployment and Voter Behavior in Comparative Perspective." Unemployment's Effects: The Southern European Experience in Comparative Perspective: Princeton University, Nov 14-15, 1997.

Anderson, Christopher J. *Blaming the Government: Citizens and the Economy in Five European Democracies*. Edited by Gregory S. Mahler, *Comparative Politics Series*. Armonk, NY: M.E. Sharpe, 1995.

Anderson, Christopher, and Christine Guillory. "Political Institutions and Satisfaction with Democracy: A Cross-National Analysis of Consensus and Majoritarian Systems." *American Political Science Review* 91, no. 1 (1997): 66-81.

Andorka, Rudolf. "The Importance and the Role of the Second Economy for Hungarian Economy and Society." *AULA* 2 (1990): 95-113.

Andorka, Rudolf. *A Magyar Községek Társadalmának Átalakulása (Transformation of Hungarian Village Society)*. Budapest: Magvető, 1979.

Angelusz, Robért, Lajos Nagy, and Robért Tardos. "Unemployment as Reflecteed in Hungarian Public Opinion." *Acta Oeconomica* 41 (1989): 212-220.

Antal, Laszlo. "It Must Not Happen Again: Contributions to the evaluation of the anti-reform iof the early 1970s." *Acta Oeconomica* 40, no. 1-2 (1989): 139-49.

Aronowitz, Stanley and Willaim DiFazio.*The Jobless Future*, Minneapolist: University of Minnesota Press, 1994.

Árvay, Janos, and Andras Vértes. *The Share of the Private Sector and the Hidden Economy in Hungary*. Budapest: GKI Economic Research, 1995.

Atkinson, Anthony B. *Economic Transformation in Eastern Europe and the Distribution of Income*. Cambridge, UK: Cambridge University Press, 1992.

Bagguley, Paul. "Protest, Acquiescence and the Unemployed: Acomparative anaysis of the 1930s and the 1980s in Britain." *British Journal of Sociology* 43, no. 3 (1992): 443-61.

Bajka, Gábor, Imre Kormos, and János Kutas. "Ózd és környéke forglalkoztatási gondjainkak enyhítési lehetőségi [Ózd and its environs' posibilities for alleviating employment struggles]." *Munkaügyi Szemle* 40, no. 11 (1996): 29-34.

Baker, Dean. "The NAIRU: Is it a Real Constraint?" In *Globalization and Progressive Economic Policy*, edited by Gerald Epstein and Robert Pollin Dean Baker, 369-90. Cambridge: Cambridge University Press, 1998.

Baksay, Zoltán. *A Munkaerőhelzet Alakulása és a Munkanélküliség Felszámolasa Margyarországon (1945-49)*. Vol. 99, *Értekezeesek a Történeti Tudományok Köréből*. Budapest, 1983.

Balázs, István. "The Transformation of Hungarian Public Administration." *Public Administration* 71, no. 1/2 (1993): 75-88.

Ball, Terence, James Farr, and Russell Hanson, eds. *Political Innovation and Conceptual Change*. Cambridge, UK: Cambridge UP, 1989.

Bancroft, Gertrude. "Some Problems of Concepts and Measurement." In *The American Labor Force: Its Growth and changing composition*. NY: John Wiley & Sons, 1958.

Barber, John. "The Development of Soviet Employment and Labour Policy, 1930-41." In *Labour and Employment in the USSR*, edited by David Lane, 50-65. Sussex: Wheatsheaf Books, 1986.

Barker, F.S. *The South African Labour Market: Critical Issues for Transition*. Pretoria: J.L. van Schaik, 1992.

Barta, Barnabás and András Klinger, Károly Miltényi and György Vukovich. "Hungary." In *Working Women in Socialist Countries: The Fertility Connection*, edited by Valentina Bodrova and Richard Anker. Geneva: ILO, 1985.

Bartlett, David. *The Political Economy of Dual Transformations: Market Reform and Democratization in Hungary*. Ann Arbor: University of Michigan Press, 1997.

Bartlett, David. "Losing the Political Initiative: The Impact of Financial Liberalization in Hungary." In *The Waning of the Communist State: Economic Origins of Political Decline in China and Hungary*, edited by Andrew Walder. Berkeley: University of California Press, 1995.

Bartók, Jáanos, and Tamás Terestyéni. "A Telezíviós Tájékoztatás és a Közönség a Válaszást Követő Időszakban [The TV-News and the Public After the Elections]." *Jel-Kép*, no. 2 (1995): 13-20.

Bauer, Tamás. *Tervgazdaság, Beruházas, Ciklusok (Planned economy, investments, cycles)*. Budapest: Közgazdasági és Jogi, 1981.

Baxandall, Phineas. "When is Unemployment Politically Important?: Explaining Differences in Political Salience Across European Countries." *West European Politics*, 24, 1 (January, 2001): 75-98.

Baxandall, Phineas. "Hungary: Retrenchment Amidst Radical Restructuring." In *Diminishing Welfare: A Cross-National Study of Social Provision*, edited by G.S. Goldberg and M. Rosenthal. New York: Greenwood Publishing Group, 2000.

Baxandall, Phineas. "Jobs versus wages: not so simple a trade-off." *Dollars & Sense* 206 (July-August, 1997): 8-11, 41.

Baxandall, Phineas. "Social Rights under State Socialism? Pensions and Housing in Hungarian Welfare State Development." Program on Central and Eastern Europe Working Paper Series, no. 34. Minda de Gunzburg Center for European Studies (1994).

Baykov, Alexander. *The Development of the Soviet Economic System.* London: Cambridge U.P., 1947.

Beck, Ulrich. *Risk Society: Towards a New Modernity.* London: Sage Publications, 1992.

Bell, Daniel 1973. The Coming Post-Industrial Society: A Venture in Social Forecasting (NY Basic Books).

Bell, Janice. "Unemployment Matters: Voting Patterns During the Economic Transition in Poland, 1990-1995." *Europe-Asia Studies* 49, no. 7 (1997): 1263-1291.

Berecz, Frigyes. "Mik a Lehetőségi és feltéttelei Vállalati Szinten a Hatékony Foglalkoztatésnak? Lehet-e ennek Reális Eszköze a Vállalaton Belüli Munkaerő Átcsoportositás, Vagy a Hatékonyan Nem Fogalkoztatható Létszám Tás, Vagy a Hatékonyan Nem Foglalkoztatható Létsám Leépitése? [What are the possibities and conditions at the enterprise level for full and efficient employment? Is there really a marriage of internal switching groups or is it not possible to efficiently employ reduced staff levels.]." Budapest, 1983.

Berend, Iván. *The Hungarian Economic Reforms 1953-1988.* Cambridge, UK: Cambridge UP, 1990.

Berend, Iván. *Capital Intensity and Development Policy.* Budapest: Adadémiai Kiadó, 1985.

Berend, Iván. *A szocialista gazdaág fejlődése Magyarországon, 1945-1975 [The development of the economy in Hungary, 1945-1975].* Budapest: Akadémia Kiadó, 1979.

Berend, Ivan, and Ránki György. *The Hungarian Economy in the Twentieth Century.* London: Croom Helm, 1985.

Berend, Iván T. "The Crisis of the Hungarian Reform in the 1970s." *Acta Oeconomica* 40, no. 1-2 (1989): 105-38.

Berényi, J. *Foglalkoztatottság és életszínvonal" (Employment and living standards).* Budapest: Kossuth, 1967.

Berger, Peter, and Thomas Luckmann. *The Social Construction of Reality: A Treatise in the Sociology of Knowledge.* New York: Doubleday, 1966.

Berger, Suzanne, and Ronald Dore, eds. *National Diversity and Global Capitalism.* Ithaca: Cornell University Press, 1996.

Berger, Suzanne, and Michael J. Piore. *Dualism and Discontinuity in Industrial Societies.* Cambridge: Cambridge University Press, 1980.

Bergson, Abram. "Technological Progress." In *The Soviet Economy: Twards the Year 2000,* edited by Abram Bergson and Herbert S. Levine. London: Allen and Unwin, 1983.

Berliner, Joseph S. "The Informal Organization of the Soviet Firm." *The Quarterly Journal of Economics* 66, no. 3 (1952): 342-365.

Bernhard, Michael. "Legitimation and Instability: The Fatal Link." Program on Central and Eastern Europe Working Paper Series, no. 2. Cambridge, MA: Minda de Guzburg, Center for European Studies, 1990.

Bertola, Giuseppe. "Cross sectional efficiency and labor hoarding in a matching model of unemployment." Cambridge, MA: National Bureau of Economic Research, 1993.

Betlen, Anna. "Érdekvédelem, Vállalkozás, Nagypolitika: Önsegítő Egyesületek a Munkanélküliség Ellen (Interest Protection, Enterprise, and Large Politics: Self-help Organizations Against Unemployment)." *Esely,* no. 4 (1993): 48-63.

Beveridge, William. *Unemployment: A Problem of Industry.* (London: Longman's Green, 1909.

Bielasiak, Jack. "Workers and Mass Participation in 'Socialist Democracy'." In *Blue-Collar Workers in Eastern Europe*, edited by Jan F. Triska and Charles Gati, 88-107. London: George Allen & Unwin, 1981.

Bihari, Péter. "A (strukturális) munanélküliségről [About (structural) unemployment]." *Közgazdasági Szemle* 28, no. 10 (1981): 1164-79.

Blank, Rebecca, and David Card. "Recent Trends in Insured and Uninsured Unemployment: Is there an Explanation?" *Quarterly Journal of Economics* 106, no. 4 (1991): 1157-90.

Block, Fred. "The Roles of the State in the Economy." In *The Handbook of Economic Sociology*, edited by Neil J. Smelser and Richard Swedberg, 691-706. Princeton, NJ: Princeton University Press, 1994.

Block, Fred and Burns, Gene A. "Productivity as a Social Problem: The Uses and Misuses of Social Indicators." *American Sociological Review* 51 (1986): 767-780.

Blount, Simon. 2002. Unemployment and Economic Voting. *Electoral Studies* 2 (1):91-100.

Blue Ribbon Commission. "Hungary in Transformation to Freedom and Prosperity." Indianapolis, IN: Hudson Institute, 1990.

Blyth, Mark. "Any More Bright Ideas? The Ideational Turn in Comparative Political Economy." *Comparative Politics* 29, no. 2 (1997): 229-250.

Bonin, John P., Derek C Jones, and Louis Putterman. "Theoretical and Empirical Studies of Producer Cooperatives: Will Ever the Twain Meet?" *Journal of Economic Literature* 31, no. 3 (1993): 1290-320.

Booth, William James. "A Note on the Idea of the Moral Economy." *American Political Science Review* 87, no. 4 (1993): 949-54.

Borsányi, György. "The Great Depression and the Organized Working Class in Hungary (1929-33)." In *Studies on the History of the Hungarian Trade-Union Movement*, edited by E. and A. Zsilák Kabos, 153-81. Budapest: Akadémiai Kiadó, 1977.

Bowers, John, David Deaton, and Jeremy Turk. *Labour Hoarding in British Industry*. Oxford: Basil Blackwell, 1982.

Braun, Judit, Károly Kendra, and Anna Matoricz. "A munknélküli járadék folyósitás anomáliái, valamint az ujrakezdök-pályakezdök vállalkozói kölcsöne müködésének értékelése [Ongoing anomolies of unemployment, evaluation of the operation of entreprenuerial loans for new workers]." Budapest, 1993.

Braverman, Harry 1974. *Monopoly Capital: The Degradation of Work in the Twentieth Century*, (NY, Monthly Review Press)

Brenner, Harvey. "Estimating the Social Costs of National Economic Policy." Washington, D.C.: Government Printing Office: Study prepared for the use of the Joint Economic Committee, Congress of the United States, 1976.

Breslauer, George. "Soviet Economic Reforms Since Stalin: Ideology, Politics, and Learning." *Soviet Economy* 6, no. 3 (1990): 252-80.

Breslauer, George. "On the Adaptability of Soviet Welfare-State Authoritarianism." In *The Soviet Polity in the Modern Era*, edited by Erik Hoffman and Robbin Laird. New York: Adeline Publishing Company, 1984.

Brittan, Samuel. "The Economic Consequences of Democracy." *British Journal of Political Science* 5, no. 2 (1975): 129-59.

Bruszt, Laszlo. "'Without Us but For Us'? Political Orientation in Hungary in the Period of late Paternalism." *Social Research* 55, no. 1-2 (1988): 43-76.

Budget and Social Policy Project. "Unemployment and unemployment related expenditures." background paper, Budapest: Blue Ribbon Commission, 1990.

Bulow, J., and Lawrence Summers. "A theory of dual labor markets with application to industrial policy, discrimination and Keynesian unemployment." *Journal of Labor Economics* 4, no. 1 (1986): 376-414.

Bunce, Valerie and Maria Csanádi. "Uncertainty and the Transition: Postcommunism in Hungary." *East European Politics & Society*, 13 (1993): 32-50.

Burnside, Craig. "Labor hoarding and the business cycle." Cambridge, MA: National Bureau of Economic Research, 1990.

Burgoon, Brian and Phineas Baxandall, "Three Worlds of Work Time: Policy and Politics in the Work Time of Industrialized Countries" *Politics & Societies*, 32, 4 (2004).

Buroway, Michael. *The Politics of Production: Factory Regimes Under Capitalism and Socialism.* London: Verso, 1985.

Cameron, David. "Social Democracy, Corporatism, Labour Quiescence and the Representation of Economic Interest in Advanced Capitalist Society." In *Order and Conflict in Contemporary Capitalism*, edited by John Goldthorpe. Oxford: Oxford University Press, 1984.

Campbell, John L. "The Fiscal Crisis of Post-Communist States." *Telos* 92 (1992): 89-99.

Canache, D., et al. "Meaning and measurement in cross-national research on satisfaction with democracy." *Public Opinion Quarterly*, 65 (2001): 506-528.

Capelli, Peter. *The New Deal at Work: Managing the Market-Driven Workforce.* Cambridge, Mass: Harvard Business School Press, 1999.

Carey, John M. "Parchment, Equilibria, and Institutions," *Comparative Political Studies*, 6-7 (2000): 735-761.

Castillo, Monica D. "Persons outside the labor force who want a job." *Monthly Labor Review*, July (1998): 34-42.

Charness, Gary, and David I. Levine. "When are Layoffs Acceptable? Evidence from a Quasi-Experiment." *Industrial and Labor Relations Review* 53, no. 3 (2000): 381-400.

Chernyshev, Igor, ed. *Labour Statistics for a Market Economy: Chalenges and Solutions in the Transition Countries of Central and Eastern Europe and the Former Soviet Union.* Budapest/NY: Central European University Press, 1994.

Chisholm, Donald. *Coordination without Hierarchy: Informal Structures in Multiorganizational Systems.* Berkeley: University of California Press, 1989.

Christian, David. "Labour in a non-capitalist economy: the Soviet counter-example." In *Unemployment: are there lessons from history*, edited by Jill Roe, 85-104. Sydney, Australia: Hale & Iremonger, 1985.

Clark, Andrew E., and Andrew J. Oswald. "Unhappiness and Unemployment." *The Economic Journal* 104, no. May (1994): 648-59.

Clasen, Jochen. "Motives, means and opportunities—reforming unemployment compensation in the 1990s." *West European Politics* 23, no. 2 (2000): 89-112.

Cohen, Stephen S., and John Zysman. *Manufacturing matters: the myth of the post-industrial economy.* New York: Basic Books, 1987.

Comisso, Ellen, and Paul Marer. "The Economics and Politics of Reform in Hungary." In *Power, Purpose, and Copllective Choice: Economic Strategy in Socialist States*, edited by Ellen Comisso and Laura D'Andrea Tyson, 245-78. Ithaca: Cornell University Press, 1986.

Commander, Simon, János Köllő, Ceciolia Ugaz, and Balacs Vilagi. "Hungary." In *Unemployment, Restructuring, and the Labor Market in Eastern Europe*, edited by Simon Commander and Fabrizio Coricelli, 1-38. Washington D.C.: The World Bank, 1995.

Compston, Hugh, ed. *The New Politics of Unemployment: Radical Policy Initiatives in Western Europe.* Edited by Hans Keman for European Consortium for Political Research, *European Political Science Series*. NY and London: Routledge, 1997.

Connor, Walter D. "Workers, Politics, and Class Consciousness." In *Socialism's Dilemmas: State and Society in the Soviet Bloc*, edited by Walter D. Connor. NY: Columbia University Press, 1988.

Conover, Pamela Johnston, Stanley Feldman, and Kathleen Knight. "Judging Inflation and Unemployment: The Origins of Retrospective Evaluations." *Journal of Politics* 48, no. 3 (1986).

Cook, Linda J. *The Soviet Social Contract and Why it Failed: Welfare Policy and Workers' Politics from Brezhnev to Yeltsin*. Cambridge: Harvard UP, 1993.

Cox, Robert Henry. "The Social Construction of an Imperative: Why Welfare Reform Happened in Denmark and the Netherlands, but not in Germany." Annual Meeting of the APSA: Atlanta, Sept. 2-5, 1999.

Cox, Robert Henry. "From Safety Net to Trampoline: Labor Market Activation in the Netherlands and Denmark." *Governance* 11, no. 4 (1998): 397-414.

Cox, Robert Henry. "Creating welfare states in Czechoslovakia and Hungary: why policymakers borrow ideas from the west." *Government and Policy* 11 (1993): 349-64.

Csepeli, György, I. Kolosi, M. Nemény, and A. Örkény. "Our Futureless Values: The Forms of Justice and Injustice Perception in Hungary in 1991." *Social Research* 60, no. 4 (1994): 865-92.

Csepeli, György, and A. Örkény. "Cognitive Walls in Europe." Budapest University of Economic Sciences, Department of Sciology (mimeo). Budapest, 1994.

Csoba, Judit. "A Munkanélküliek Kapcsolatainkak Alakulása A Munkanélküliség Ideje Alatt (The Relationship of Connections Among the Unemployed and Variation in the Duration of Unemployment)." *Esely*, no. 4 (1993): 64-73.

Cui, Zhuiyan. *Wrestling with the Invisible Hand*. Cambridge, MA, Harvard University Press (forthcoming).

Danziger, S., R. Haverman, and R. Plotnick. "How income transfers affect work, savings and income distribution." *Journal of Economic Literature* 19 (1981).

Daston, Lorrain. "Why statistics tend not only to describe the world but to change it." *London Review of Books*, 13 April 2000.

Davidow, William and Michael Malone. *The Virtual Corporation:Structuring and Revitalizing the Corporation for the 21st Century*. NY, Harper Business Publishers, 1992.

Davies, R.W. "The ending of mass unemplolyment in the USSR." In *Labour and Employment in the USSR*, edited by David Lane, 19-35. Sussex: Wheatsheaf Books, 1986.

De Vroey, Michel. "Involuntary Unemployment: Unravelling the Conceptual Muddles." Discussion Paper, 9425. Louvain, Belgium: Dept. of Economics, Catholic University of Louvain, 1994.

Deacon, Bob and Michelle Hulse. "The Making of Post-communist Social Policy: The Role of International Agencies." *Journal of Social Policy*, 26, 1 (1997): 43-62.

Desrosieres, Alain. *The Politics of Large Numbers: A History of Statistical Reasoning*. Cambridge, MA: Harvard University Press, 1998.

Diamond, Larry. "Economic Development and Democracy Reconsidred." *American Behavioral Scientist* 35, no. 4 (1992): 450-99.

Doeringer, Peter B., and Michael J. Piore. *Internal Labor Markets and Manpower Analysis*. 2nd ed. Armonk, NY: M.E. Sharpe, 1985.

Duch, Raymond. "Tolerating Economic Reform: Popular Support for Transition to a Free Market in the Former Soviet Union." *American Political Science Review* 87, no. 3 (1993): 590-608.

Eisinger, Peter. "The Conditions of Protest Behavior in American Cities." *American Political Science Review* 67 (1973): 11-28.

Eith, Ulrich. "Political Behavior in Eastern Germany Since 1989." The German Road from Socialism to Capitalism: Eastern Germany ten years after the collapse of the GDR: Harvard University, 1999.

Ekiert, Grzegorz. "Democratization Processes in East Central Europe: A Theoretical Reconsideration." *British Journal of Political Science*, 21 (1991): 285-313.

Elster, Jon. "Constitution-Making in Eastern Europe: Rebuilding the Boat in the Open Sea." *Public Administration* 71, no. 1/2 (1993): 169-217.

Esping-Andersen, Gosta. "After the Golden Age: The Future of the Welfare State in the New Global Order." Geneva: United Nations Research Institute for Social Development, Occassional paper, no. 7. March 1995.

Esping-Andersen, Gosta. *The Three Worlds of Welfare Capitalism*. Princeton, NJ: Princeton University Press, 1990.

Esti, Béla, Ilona S. Balog, and Tibor Szánto. *A Magyar Munásmozgalom Képeskönyve [Illustrated book of the Hungarian Workers Movement]*. Budapest: Kossuth Könyvkiadó, 1984.

Evans, Geoffrey, and Stephen Whitefield. "The Politics and Economics of Democratic Committmentment: Support for Democracy in Transition Socieities." *British Journal of Political Science* 25, no. 4 (1995): 485-514.

Evans, Geoffrey, and Stephan Whitfield. "Identifying the Bases of Party Competition in Eastern Europe." *British Journal of Political Science* 23 (1993): 521-48.

Fair, Ray C. "Excess Labor and the Business Cycle." *The American Economic Review* 75, 1 (1985): 239-46.

Fajth, Gaspar. "Measuring Unemployment in Central and Eastern European Countries." In *Employment and Unemployment in Economies in Transition: Conceptual and Measurement Issues*, edited by OECD, 87-99. Paris: OECD, Centre for Co-operation with the European Economies in Transition, 1993.

Falus-Szikra, Katalin. *Munkabér, Ösztönés, Elosztás*. Budapest: Kossuth Könyvkiadó, 1979.

Fazekas, Károly, and János Köllő. *Munkaerőpiac Tőkepiac Nélkül [Labor market without capital market]*. Budapest: Közgazdági és Jogi Könyvkiadó, 1990.

Fazekas, Károly and János Köllő. "Fluctuations of Labour Shortage and State Intervention after 1968." In *Labour Market and Second Economy in Hungary*, edited by P. Galasi and G. Sziráczki, 42-69. Freankfurt: Campus Verlag, 1985.

Feher, Ferenc, and Agnes Heller. *Hungary 1956 Revisited*. London: Allen and Unwin, 1983.

Feiwel, George R. "Causes and Consequences of Disguised Industrial Unemployment in a Socialist Economy Soviet Studies." *Soviet Studies* 26, no. 3 (1974): 344-62.

Fekete, György, and György Varga. "Household Plot Farming of Cooperative Peasants." *Acta Oeconomica* 2 (1967): 354-61.

Feldman, Stanley, and Patricia Conley. "Explaining Explanations of Changing Economic Conditions." In *Economics and Politics: The Calculus of Support*, edited by Helmut Norpoth, Michael S. Lewis-Beck and Jean-Dominique Lafay, 185-205. Ann Arbor: University of Michigan Press, 1991.

Feldstein, Martin. "The Economics of New Unemployment." *The Public Interest* 33, no. Fall (1973): 3-42.

Feldstein, Martin S. *Lowering the Permanent Rate of Unemployment, Joint Economic Committee, 93 Congress 1 Session*. Washington D.C.: Government Printing Office, 1973.

Ferge, Zsuzsa. "Unemployment in Hungary: The Need for a New Ideology." In *Social Policy, Social Justice, and Citizenship in Eastern Europe*, edited by Bob Deacon, 158-75. Aldershot: Averbury, 1992.

Ferge, Zsuzsa. *A Society in the Making*. White Plains, NY: M.E. Sharpe, 1979.

Figyelő. "A nagy halkra kell vászni! [The big fish should be hunted!]." March 11 1993, 28.

Figyelő. "A foglalkoztatáspolitika válságos helyzetben (Ózdi tanulságok) [Employment policy in a critical region (lessons of Ózd)]." Mar. 23, 1989: 23.

Finkel, Steven E., Edward N. Muller, and Mitchell A. Seligson. "Economic Crisis Incumbent Performance and Regime Support: A Comparison of Longitudinal Data from West German and Costa Rica." *British Journal of Political Science* 19, July (1989): 329-51.

Fiorina, Morris P. "Short Term and Long-Term Effects of Economic Conditions on Individual Voting Decisions." In *Contemporary Political Economy*, edited by D. A. Hibbs and H. Fassbender. Amsterdam: North-Holland, 1981.

Fleck, Susan, and Constance Sorrentino. "Employment and unemployment in Mexico's labor force." *Monthly Labor Review* November (1994): 3-22.

Fligstein, Neil. *The Transformation of Corporate Control*. Cambridge: Harvard University Press, 1990.

Folbre, Nancy. "The Unproductive Housewife: An Evolution in Nineteenth Century Economic Thought." *Signs* 16, no. 3 (1991): 463-84.

Fraser, Nancy, and Linda Gordon. "A Genealogy of 'Dependency': Tracing a Keyword of the U.S. Welfare State." In *Justice Interuptus*, edited by Nancy Fraser, 121-44. New York: Routledge, 1997.

Freeman, Richard B. "The Labour Market in the New Information Economy" National Bureau of Economic Research, Working Paper 9254 (October 2002).

Freeman, Richard B. "War of the Models: Which Labour Market Institutions for the 21st Century?" *Labour Economics* 5, no. 1 (1998): 1-24.

Freeman, Richard B. "The Limits of Flexible Labour Markets." *Oxford Review of Economic Policy* 11, no. 1 (1995).

Freeman, Richard B. and Peter Gottschalk., eds. *Generating Jobs: How to Increase Demand for Less-SkilledWorkers*. NY: Russel Sage Foundation, 1998.

Freud, Sigmund. *Civilization and Its Discontents*. Translated by James Strachey. New York: W.W. Norton & Company, 1961.

Frey, Mária. "New Job Creating Intitaives Outside the Mainstream Labour Market in Hungary." Budapest, Labor Research Institute, National Report for the Council of Europe Study Group of Co-ordinated Research in the Employment Field. Nov. (1995).

Frey, Mária. "Formerly Unemployed as Entrepreneurs." Budapest: ILO/Japan Project, ILO/Japan Project on Employment Policies working papers, no. 16. Employment Policies for Transition in Hungary, 1994.

Frey, Mária. "The Role of the State in Employment Policy and Labour Market Programmes: The Hungarian Case in International Comparison." ILO/Japan Project, Employment Policies for Transition in Hungary, no. 3. Budapest: ILO, 1994.

Fridenson, Patrick. "The Coming of the Assembly Line in Europe." In *The Dynamics of Science and Technology*, edited by Edwin T. Layton Wolfgang Krohn, Jr., and Pereter Weingard, 160-75. Dordrecht: D. Reidel Publishing Co., 1978.

Friedman, Milton. "The Role of Monetary Policy" *American Economics Review* LVIII, no. 1 (1968): 1-17.

Fryer, Roland G. Jr., and Matthew O. Jackson "Categorical Cognition: A Psychological Model of Categories and Identification in Decision Making," National Bureau of Economic Research Working Paper No. 9579 (March 2003).

Furstenberg, Frank F., and Charles A. Thrall. 1975.Counting the Jobless: The Impact of Job Rationing on the Measurement of Unemployment. The Annals of The American Academy of Political and Social Science 418:45-59.

Gábor, István. "The Major Domains of the Second Economy." In *Labour Market and Second Economy in Hungary*, edited by Peter and György Szirácaki Galasi, 133-78. NY: Frankfurt: Campus Verlag, 1985.

Gábor, István. "Modernity or a New Kind of Duality? Second Thoughts about the 'Second Economy'." In *Transition to Capitalism? The Communist Legacy in Eastern Europe*, edited by János Mátyás Kovács, 3-19. New Brunswick, USA: Transaction Publishers, 1994.

Gábor, István and Galasi, Peter. "Labour Market." In *Labour Market and Second Economy in Hungary*, edited by Peter and György Szirácaki Galasi, 26-41. NY: Frankfurt: Campus Verlag, 1985.

Gábor, István R. "Lépéskényszerek és Kényszerlépések: Jegyzetek Két Évtized Kormányzati Munkaerő- és Bérpolitikáiról [Steps of Compulsion and Forced Steps: Taking Stock of Two Decades of Manpower and Wage Politics]." *Közgzdasági Szemle* 35, no. 7-8 (1988): 803-817.

Gábor, István R. "Prospects and Limits to the Second Economy." *Acta Oeconomica* 43, no. 3-4 (1991): 349-352.

Gábor, István R. "Too Many, too Small: Small Entrepreneurship in Hungary—Ailing or Prospering?" In *Restructuring Networks in Post-Socialism: Legacies, Linkages, and Localities*, edited by Gernot Grabher and David Stark, 158-75. Oxford, UK: Oxford University Press, 1997.

Galasi, Péter. "Szegények és Gazdagok [Wealthy and Poor]." Paper presented at the Paper for the 'Project on the Impact of the Reform of the State Budget on the Distribution of Income', TÁRKI, Budapest 1995.

Galasi, Péter and György Szirácak, ed. *Labour Market and Second Economy in Hungary*. Vol. 10, *Socio-Economic Labour Market Research*. NY.Frankfurt: Campus Verlag, 1985.

Garraty, John A. *Unemployment in History: Economic Thought and Public Policy*. NY: Harper and Row, 1979.

Gershenkron, Alexander. *Economic Backwardness in Historical Perspective*. Cambridge: Harvard University Press, 1962.

Gershuny, Jonathan. *Changing Times: Work and Leisure in Post-industrial Societies* (Oxford: Oxford University Press, 2000).

Glyn, Andrew. "The Assessment: Unemployment and Inequality." *Oxford Review of Economic Policy* 11, no. 1 (1995).

Golden, Miriam A. *Heroice Defeats: The Politics of Job Loss*. Edited by Peter Lange, *Cambridge Studies in Comparative Politics*. Cambridge: Cambridge University Press, 1997.

Goldstein, Judith. *Ideas, Interests and American Trade Policy*. Ithaca: Cornell University Press, 1993.

Goldstein, Judith, and Robert Keohane, eds. *Ideas and Foreign Policy*. Ithaca: Cornell Univesity Press, 1993.

Góra, Marek, and Michal Rutkowski. "The Demand for Labour and the Disguised Unemployment in Poland in the 1980s." *Communist Economies* 2, no. 3 (1990): 325-34.

Gorz, Andre. *Paths to Paradise: On the Liberation from Work*. London: Pluto Press, 1985.

Goven, Joanna. "The Gendered Foundations of Hungarian Socialism: State, Society, and the Anti-Politics of Anti-Feminism." Ph.D. dissertation, 1993.

Graebner, William. *A History of Retirement: The Meaning and Function of An American Institution, 1885-1978.* New Haven: Yale UP, 1980.

Grantham, George. "Economic History and the History of Labour markets." In *Labour Market Evolution: The Economic History of Market Integration, Wage Flxibility and the Employment Relation,* edited by George Grantham and Mary MacKinnon. NY: Routledge, 1994.

Graziano, Loretta. 1989. Unemployment: The Voter's Conception of Reality. Political Psychology 10, 1:155-168.

Gregory, Paul R., and Irwin Collier. "Unemployment in the Soviet Union: Evidence from the Soviet Interview Project." *American Economic Review* 78, no. 4 (1988): 613-32.

Gruber, Jonathan and David A. Wise. "Social Security Programs and Retirement Around the World: Micro Estimation" NBER Working Paper No. w9407 (December 2002).

Gsovski, Vladimir. *Church and State Behind the Iron Curtain.* second edition ed. Westport, CT: Greenwood Press, 1973.

Gusfield, Joseph R. *The Culture of Public Problems: Drinking-Driving and the Symbolic Order.* Chicago: University of Chicago Press, 1981.

Guzzardi, Walter. "How to Deal with the New Unemployment." *Fortune,* October 1976, 132-34.

Gyorgyné, Papp. "Az ötnapos munkahét és a megnővekedett szabadidő [the five-day week and the growth of leisure time]." *Budapesti Népmüvelő,* no. 1-2 (1984).

Gyurkó, L. "Introductory Biography." In *János Kádár, Selected Speeches and Interviews.* Budapest: Akadémai Kiadó, 1985.

Habermas, Jürgen. *Theory of Communicative Action,.* Vol. 1. Boston: Beacon Press, 1987.

Habermas, Jürgen. 1985. Remarks on the Concept of Communicative Action. In *Social Action,* edited by G. Seebass and R. Tuomela. Boston: D. Reidel.

Haggard, Stephan, and Robert R. Kaufman. *The Political Economy of Democratic Transitions.* Princeton, NJ: Princeton UP, 1995.

Hall, Peter A. "The Role of Interests, Institutions, and Ideas in the Comparative Political Economy of the Industrialized Nations." In *Comparative Politics: Rationality, Culture, and Structure,* edited by Mark Irving Lichbach and Alan S. Zuckerman, 174-207. Cambridge, UK: Cambridge University Press, 1997.

Hall, Peter A. "Policy Paradigms, Social Learning and the State." *Comparative Politics* 23 (1993): 275-96.

Hall, Peter A. *The Political Power of Economic Ideas: Keynesianism Across nations.* Princeton: Princeton University Press, 1986.

Haller, H. Brandon, and Helmut Norpoth. "Reality Bites: News Exposure and Economic Opinion." *Public Opinion Quarterly* 61 (1997): 555-575.

Halmos, Csaba. "Political and Economic Reform and Labour Policy in Hungary." *International Labour Review* 129, no. 1 (1990): 41-57.

Hankiss, Elemér. *East European Alternatives:* Oxford UP, 1990.

Hanson, Brian. "Which Came First: New Coalitions or New Policies? The Politics of Trade Policy Liberalization in Europe." European Political Economy Workshop: Interests and Coalitions: Center for European Studies, Harvard University, Cambridge, MA, 1999.

Haney, Lynne "Familial welfare: building the Hungarian welfare society, 1948-1968", *Social Politics* 7, 1 (2000): 101-122.

Harrington, Mona. *Care and Equality: Inventing a New Family Politics.* New York: Alfred A. Knopf, 1999.

Harris, John. *Unemployment and Politics.* Oxford: Clarendon Press, 1972.

Hay, Colin. 2001. "The 'Crisis' of Keynesianism and the Rise of Neoloibealism in Britain: An Ideational Institutionalist Approach." In *The Rise of Neoliberalism and Institutional*

Analysis, edited by J. L. Campbell and O. K. Pedersen. Princeton, NJ: Princeton University Press.

Heclo, Hugh. *Modern Social Politics in Britain and Sweden: From Relief to Income Maintenance*. New Haven: Yale UP, 1974.

Hellman, Joel. "Winners Take All: The Politics of Partial Reform in Post-Communist Transitions." *World Politics* 50, no. 1 (1998): 203-34.

Hetherington, Marc J. "The Media's Role in Forming Voters' National Economic Evaluations in 1992." *American Journal of Political Science* 40, no. 2 (1996): 372-395.

Hethy, Lajos, and Csabo Mako. "Worker participation and the socialist enterprise: a Hungarian case study." In *The Quality of Working Life in Western and Eastern Europe*, edited by C. Cooper and E. Mumford, 296-326. Westport, CT: Greenwood, 1979.

Hewett, Ed A. *Reforming the Soviet Economy: Equality versus Efficiency*. Washington D.C.: Brookings Institutions, 1988.

Heynes, Barbara. "Meaning and Measurement in the Postcommunist Labor Market: Employment and Unemployment in Poland, 1992-1996." *Social Research* (forthcoming) (1997).

Hibbs, Douglas A. "Political Parties and Macroeconomic Policy." *American Political Science Review* 71, no. 4 (1977): 1467-87.

Hipple, Steven and Kosanovich, Karen. "Computer and Internet use at work in 2001." *Monthly Labor Review* (Feb) 2003: 26-35.

Hirschman, Albert O. "How the Keynesain Revolution was Exported from the United States, and Other Comments." In *The Political Power of Economic Ideas: Keynesianism Across Nations*, edited by Peter Hall, 347-59. Princeton: Princeton University Press, 1989.

Hirschman, Albert O. "The Changing Tolerance for Income Inequality in the Course of Economic Development." In *Essays in Trespassing: Economics to Politics and Beyond*, 39-58. Cambridge, UK: Cambridge University Press, 1981.

Hobson, S. G. *Guild principles in war and peace*. London: G. Bell & Sons Ltd., 1917.

Holmlund, Bertel, and Per Lundborg. "Wage Bargaining, Union Membership, and the Organization of Unemployment Insurance." *Labour Economics* 6 (1999): 379- 415.

Holzman, Franklyn. *International Trade Under Communism, Politics and Economics*. NY: Basic Books, 1976.

Horning, Bruce C. "Labor hoarding and the business cycle." *International Economic Review* 35, 1 (1994): 87-111.

Horvath, Erika. *A gyestöl a gyedig (from gyes to gyed)*. Budapest: MNOT/Kossuth Kiadó, 1986.

Humphrey, John. "Are the Unemployed Part of the Urban Poverty Problem in Latin America?" *Journal of Latin American Studies* 26, no. 3 (1994): 713.

Hunt, Jennifer. "Has Work-Sharing Worked in Germany?" National Bureau of Economic Research, NBER working paper series, no. 6878. Cambridge, MA, 1999.

Huszár, I., O. Gadó, R. Hoch, J. Kovács, and J. Timár. "Fundamental Problems in the Long-Range Manpower Planning and Living Standards Policies." *Acta Oeconomica* 9, no. 2 (1972): 137-51.

ILO. *Surveys of economically active population, employment, unemployment and underemployment*. Geneva: ILO, 1990.

Innes, Judith Eleanor. *Knowledge and Public Policy: The Search for Meaningful Indicators*. Second, expanded ed. New Brunswick, NJ: Transaction Publishers, 1990.

International Monetary Fund. "Hungary: Economic Policies for Sustainable Growth." Occasional Paper, no. 159. Washington, D.C.: IMF, 1998.

Iván, P., and Zs. Mausecz. "Population and Employment Policy—Forecast for 1985." *Acta Oeconomica* 9, no. 1 (1972): 27-45.

Iversen, Torben, and Ann Wren. "Equality, Employment, and Budgetary Restraint: The Trilemma of the Service Economy." *World Politics* 50, no. 4 (1998): 507-46.

Jacobsen, John Kurt. "Much Ado About Ideas: The Cognitive Factor in Economic Policy." *World Politics* 47, no. 1 (1995): 283-310.

Jacoby, Wade. *Imitation and Politics: Redesigning Modern Germany.* Ithaca: Cornell University Press, 2000.

Jacoby, Wade. "Tutors and Pupils: International Organizations, CEE Elites, and Western Models." 1998 Annual Meeting of the APSA: Boston, Sept. 3, 1998.

Jahoda, Miarie. *Employment and Unemployment.* Cambridge: Cambridge University Press, 1982.

Jessop, Bob. "Towards a Schumpterian Workfare State? Preliminary Remarks on Post-Fordist Political Economy." *Studies in Political Economy* 40, no. Spring (1993): 7-39.

Johnson, Julia E., ed. *Selected Articles on Unemployment.* second and enlarged ed, *Debaters handbook series.* New York: H.W. Wilson Company, 1921.

Juhász, Gábor. "Kitétel erősíti a szabályt? [Strengthening the dismissal law?]." *Héti Világgazdaság (HVG)*, June 20 1987, 52-53.

Juhász, William, ed. *Hungarian Social Science Reader (1945-65).* New York: Aurora Editions, 1965.

Kalecki, Michal. *The Last Phase in the Development of Capitalism.* New York: Monthly Review Press, 1972 (1943).

Káposztás, Ferenc. "A foglalkoztatás távlati tervezésének módszertani továbbfejlesztésére [Towards a further methodological improvement of long-range planning of employment]" proposal. Budapest: ABMH [State Wage and Labor force Office, Labor and living standard division], June 30, 1979.

Karajánnisz, Manolisz. "5x5 Kérdés a gazdaságról: A pártok gazdasági elképzelései a választások előtt [5 times 5 questions about the economy: The parties' economic thinking in the run-up to elections]." In *Magyarország politikai évkönyve [Hungarian political yearbook]*, edited by Sándor Péter Sándor Kurtán, Vass László, 688-97. Budapest: Demokrácia Kutatások Magyar Központja Alapítvány, 1994.

Kaser, M., and E. Radice. *The Economic History of Eastern Europe 1919-75.* Vol. 2. Oxford: Clarendon Press, 1986.

Katzenstein, Peter J. *Small States in World Markets.* Ithaca: Cornell University Press, 1985.

KB Gazdaságpolitikai Osztály. "A foglalkoztatEaspolitika és a munkaerőgazdaálkodás elvi, politikai értékeléséhez, az uj tennivalók meghatározásához [Employment policy and the principles of laborforce management: towards policy appraisal and the specification of new tasks]." confidential internal report. Budapest, April 5, 1976.

Keane, John. *Democracy and Civil Society: On the Predicaments of European Socialism, the Prospects for Democracy, and the Problem of Controlling Social and Political Power.* London: Verso, 1988.

Kennan, John. "The Economics of Strikes." In *Handbook of Labor Economics*, edited by Orley AShenfelter and Richard Layard, 1091-1137. Amsterdam: Elsevier Science Publishers, 1986.

Kertesi, Gábor and György Sziráczki. "Worker Behavior in the Labour Market." In *Labour Market and Second Economy in Hungary*, edited by Péter Galasi and György Sziráczki, 216-246. NY, Frankfurt: Campus Verlag, 1985.

Keszthelyiné, R.M. "Az indirekt adók újrelosztó hatásai [The Redistributional Effects of Indirect Taxes]." Paper presented at the Paper for the 'Project on the Impact of the Reform of the State Budget on the Distribution of Income', TÁRKI, Budapest 1995.

Keynes, John Maynard. *The General Theory of Employment, Interest, and Money*. New York: Harvest/ HBJ, 1964 (1935).

Keyssar, Alexander. "History and the Problem of Unemployment." *Socialist Review* 19, no. 4 (1989): 15-34.

Keyssar, Alexander. *Out of Work: The First Century of Unemployment in Massachusetts*. London: Cambridge University Press, 1986.

Kiewit, Roderick. *Macroeconomics and Micropolitics*. Chicago: Chicago University Press, 1983.

Kinder, Donald R., and Roderick D. Kiewiet. "Sociotropic Politics." *British Journal of Political Science* 11, no. April (1981): 129-41.

Kinder, Donald R., and Walter R. Jr. Mebane. "Politics and Economics in Everyday Life." In *The Political Process and Economic Change*, edited by Kisten Monroe, 141-80. New York: Agathon Press, 1983.

Kingsbury, John A. "Our Army of Unemployed." *Review of Reviews*, April 1914, 433-39.

Kis, János. "Once More on Mandatory Labor." In *Politics in Hungary: For a Democratic Alternative*, edited by Béla Király, 221-29. Boulder, CO: Social Science Monographs, 1985 [1989].

Kiss, Á., and J. Timár. "The Supply of Qualified Manpower—Labour Force Structure—Education." *Acta Oeconomica* 6, no. 3 (1971): 201-218.

Kőhegyi, Kálmán. "Small Ventures in the 1990s." *Acta Oeconomica* 49, no. 3-4 (1998): 397-414.

Kolberg, Jon Evind, ed. *Between Work and Social Citizenship*. NY: ME Sharp, 1992.

Köllő, János, and Károly Fazekas. "Patterns of Unemployment in Hungary—A Case Study." *Structural Change and Economic Dynamics* 1, no. 1 (1990): 103-118.

Köllő, János. "Unemployment and the Prospects for employment policy in Hungary." In *Unemployment and Evolving Labor Markets in Central and Eastern Europe*, edited by Jenö Koltay, 183-227. Aldershot: Avebury, 1995.

Koltay, Jenö. "Unemployment and employment policy in Central and Eastern Europe: similarities and differences." In *Unemployment and Evolving Labor Markets in Central and Eastern Europe*, edited by Jenö Koltay, 1-30. Aldershot: Avebury, 1995.

Könczei, György. "The Story of the Poor Soldier: Disabled People in Hungarian Society." *Economy and Society (BKE, Budapest)* 2 (1995): 188-224.

Kónya, L. "Conditions of Setting up Simple Forms of Cooperatives in the Hungarian Industry." *Acta Oeconomica* 27, no. 1-2 (1981): 77-92.

Kopstein, Jeffrey. "Chipping away at the state: Workers' resistance and the demise of East Germany." *World Politics* 48, no. 3 (1996): 391-423.

Kormos, Imre, and Ference Munkácsy. *Foglalkotatáspolitika válságos helyzetben (Ózdi tanulságok) [Employment Politics in Critical Areas (lessons from Ozd)]*. Budapest: Közgazdasági és Jogi Könyvkiadó, 1989.

Kornai, János. "Lasting Growth as the top Priority: Macroeconomic Tensions and Government Economic Policy in Hungary." European Bank for Reconstruction and Development, Working Paper no. 15, December (1994).

Kornai, János. "The Post-Socialist Transition and the State: Reflections in the Light of Hungarian Fiscal Policy." *American Economic Review* 82, no. 2 (1992): 1-21.

Kornai, János. *The Socialist System: The Political Economy Of Socialism*. Princeton: Princeton University Press, 1992.

Kornai, János. *Economics of Shortage*. Amsterdam: North Holland, 1980.

Korpi, Walter. "Eurosclerosis and the sclerosis of Objectivity: on the role of values among economic policy experts." *The Economic Journal* 106, no. 439 (1996): 1727-46.

Korpi, Walter. "Social Policy and Distributional Conflict in the Capitalist Democracies." *West European Politics* 3 (1980).

Korpi, Walter, and Joakim Palme. "The Paradox of Redistribution and Strategies of Equality: Welfare State Institutions, Inequality, and Poverty in the Western Countries." *American Sociological Review* 63, no. October (1998): 661-687.

Kovács, Imre. "Did We Indeed Consume Too Much?" *Acta Oeconomica* 46, no. 1-2 (1994): 143-62.

Kovács, János Mátyás. "Compassionate Doubts About Reform Economics (Economic Science, Ideology, Politics)." In *Reform and Transformation in Eastern Europe*, edited by János Mátyás Kovács and Márton Tardos, 299-334. NY: Routledge, 1992.

Központi Statisztikai Hivatal (Central Statistical Office). "Magyar Statisticai Évkönyv (Statistical Yearbook of Hungary), 1990." Budapest, 1990.

Kumar, Krishan. "From Work to Employment and Unemployment: the English Experience." In *On Work*, edited by R. Pahl. Oxford: Basil Blackwood, 1988.

Lackó, M. "The Extent of the Illegal Economy in Hungary Between 1970 and 1989—a Monetary Model." *Acta Oeconomica* 44, no. 1-2 (1992): 161-190.

Lafay, Jean-Dominique. "Empirical Analysis of Politco-economic Interaction in the East European Countries." *Soviet Studies* 23, no. 3 (1981): 386-400.

Laki, Mária. "Central Economic Management and the Enterprise Crisis in Hungary." *Acta Oeconomica* 35, no. 1-2 (1985): 195-211.

Laki, Mária. "Liquidation and Merger in the Hungarian Industry." *Acta Oeconomica* 28, no. 1-2 (1982): 87-108.

Lampert, Nick. "Job Security and the Law in the USSR." In *Labour and Employment in the USSR*, edited by David Lane, 256-77. Sussex: Wheatsheaf Books, 1986.

Lampland, Martha. *The Object of Labor: Commodification in Socialist Hungary*. Chicago: University of Chicago Press, 1995.

Lane, David. *Soviet labour and the Ethic of Communism*. Boulder, CO: Westview Press, 1987.

Lane, Robert. *Political Ideology*. New York: The Free Press, 1962.

Láng, Zsanna, and Donát Bonifert. "A Vállalkozások, Válamint a Rugalmas Foglalkoztatási Formák Szerpe a Munkanélküliég Csökkentésésben (The role played by enterprises in forms of flexible employment for reducing unemployment)." Budapest: Piacgazdaság Alapítvány, 1994.

Lange, Peter, and Lyle Scruggs. "Where Have All the Memeber Gone." annual meeting of the American Political Science Association: Washington, DC, Sept. 1997.

Lau, Richard R. and Sears, David O. "Cognitive Links Between Economic Grievances and Political Responses." *Political Behavior* 4 (1981): 92-111.

Lavigne, Marie. *The Economics of Transition: From Socialist Economy to Market Economy*. 2nd ed. NY: St. Martin's Press, 1999.

Layard, R., S.J. Nickell, S.J. and Jackman, R. *Macroeconomic Performance and the Labour Market*. Oxford: Oxford University Press, 1991.

Lee, Bradford. "The Miscarriage of Necessity and Invention: Proto-Keynesianism and Democratic States in the 1930s." In *The Political Power of Economic Ideas: Keynesianism Across Nations*, edited by Peter Hall, 129-171. Princeton: Princeton University Press, 1989.

Lehmann, Hartmut, Jonathan Wadsworth, and Alessandro Acquisti. "Grime and Punishment: Job Insecurity and Wage Arrears in the Russian Federation." *Journal of Comparative Economics* 27, no. 4 (1999): 595-617.

Lengyel, György, and István Tóth. "A vállalkozói hajlandóság terjedése (A growing willingness to venture)." *Szociólogiai Szemle* 97, no. 1 (1993).

Lenin, Vladimir I. "Karl Marx." In *Collected Works*, 43-91. Moscow: Progress Press, 1971 [1914].

Levi, Margaret. *Consent, Dissent, and Patriotism*. Cambridge: Cambridge University Press, 1998.

Levi, Margaret. *Of Rule and Revenue*. Berkeley, CA: University of California Press, 1988.

Lewis, Paul, ed. *Eastern Europe: Political Crisis and Legitimacy*. New York: St. Martin's Press, 1984.

Lewis-Beck, Michael. *Economics & Elections: The Major European Democracies*. Ann Arbor: University of Michigan Press, 1988.

Lindbeck, Assar, and Dennis J. Snower. *The Insider-Outsider Theory of Employment and Unemployment*. Cambridge, MA: MIT Press, 1988.

Lipset, Seymour MartinL. *Political Man*. expanded edition ed. Baltimore: John Hopkins University Press, 1981.

Lipsky, Michael. "Bureaucratic Disentitlement in Social Welfare Programs." *Social Service Review*, no. March (1984): 3-27.

Locke, Richard M., and Wade Jacoby. "The Dilemmas of Diffusion: Social Embeddedness and the Problems of Institutional Change in Eastern Germany." *Politics & Society* 25, no. 1 (1997): 34-65.

Locke, Richard M., and Kathleen Thelen. "Apples and Oranges Revisited: Contextualized Comparisons and the Study of Comparative labor Politics." *Politics & Society* 23, no. 3 (1995): 337-67.

Lomax, Bill. *Magyarország 1956 [Hungary 1956]*. Budapest: Aura Kiadó, 1989.

Lomax, Bill. "Hungary—The Quest for Legitimacy." In *Eastern Europe: Political Crisis and Legitimation*, edited by Paul G. Lewis. NY: St. Martin's Press, 1984.

Lukács, János. "Organizational Flexibility, Internal Labour Market and Internal Sub-Contracting—Hungarian Style." In *Economy and Society in Hungary*, edited by Rudolf Andorka and László Bertalan, 15-33. Budapest: Karl Marx University Department of Sociology, 1986.

Machiavelli, Niccoló. *The Prince*. NY: Dover Publishers, 1992.

Magyar, Lajosné. *A munkaidő-csökkentés: elvi és gyakorlati problémai (The worktime reduction: problems of principle and practice)*. Budapest: Közgazdasági Jogi Könyvkiadó, 1969.

Magyar Szocialista Munkáspárt. *A Magyar Szocialista Munkáspárt határozatai és dokumentumai 1975-1980*. Budapest: Kossuth Könyvkadó, 19.

Maier, Charles S. *Dissolution: The Crisis of Communism and the End of East Germany*. Princeton: Princeton University Press, 1997.

Maier, Charles. "Why did Communism Collapse in 1989?" *Center for European Studies Central and Eastern Europe Working Paper Series*, 7. Cambridge, MA: Harvard University, 1991.

Maier, Charles. "The Politics of Time: changing paradigms of collective time and private time in the modern era." In *Changing Boundaries of the Political*, edited by Charles Maier: Cambridge University Press, 1987.

Majone, Giandomenico. *Evidence, Argument and Persuasion in the Policy Process*. New Haven: Yale UP, 1989.

Malle, Silvana. "Planned and Unplanned Mobility in the Soviet Union Under the Threat of Labour Shortage." *Soviet Studies* 39, no. 3 (1987): 357-87.

Manchin, Robert. "Individual Economic Strategies and Social Consciousness." *Social Research* 65, no. 1-2 (1988): 77-95.

Maravall, José María. "Surviving Accountability." Florence: Robert Schuman Centre at the European University Institute, 1997.

Maravall, José María, Luiz Carlos Pereira, and Adam Przeworski, eds. *In Economic Reforms in New Democracies: A Social-Democratic Approach*. Cambridge: Cambridge University Press, 1993.

March, James G. "Bounded Rationality, Ambiguity, and the Engineering of Choice." In *Decisions and Organizations*, edited by James March, 266-93. Oxford: Blackwell, 1989.

Mares, Isabela. "Strategic Alliances and Social Policy Reform: Unemployment Insurance in Comparative Perspective." *Politics & Society* 28, no. 2 (2000): 223-244.

Markus, Boris. "The Abolition of Unemployment in the U.S.S.R." *International Labour Review* 33, no. 3 (1936): 356-90.

Markus, Gregory. "The Impact of personal and national economic conditions on the presidential vote: a pooled cross-sectional analysis." *American Journal of Political Science* 32 (1988): 137-54.

Márkus, M., and A. Hegedüs. "Leisure Time and Division of Labour." *Acta Oeconomica* 8, no. 2-3 (1972).

Marx, Karl. *Capital: A Critique of Political Economy*. New York: International Publishers 1978 [1873].

Marx, Karl. "The Communist Manifesto." In *The Marx-Engels Reader*, edited by Robert C. Tucker, 469-500. New York: W.W. Norton, 1978 [1848].

McAdam, Doug. *The Political Process and the Development of Black Insurgency*. Chicago: Chicago University Press, 1982.

McDonald, Jason Lee. "Elite Economists and Political Change in Hungary Since World War II." Ph.D. dissertation, University of California, Berkeley., 1992.

McDonough, Peter, Samuel H. Barnes, and Antonio Lopez Pina. "Economic Policy and Public Opinion in Spain." *American Journal of Political Science* 30, no. 2 (1986): 446-479.

McIntosh, Mary, Martha Abele MacIver, Daniel G. Abele, and Kina Smeltz. "Publics Meet Market Democracy in Central and East Europe, 1991-1993." *Slavic Review* 53, no. 2 (1994): 483-512.

McIntosh, Mary, and Martha Abele MacIver. "Coping with Freedon and Uncertainty: Public Opionion in Hungary, Poland and Czechoslovakia 1989-1992." *International Journal of Public Opinion Research* 4, no. 4 (1992): 375-91.

Metcalf, Hilary. "Hidden Unemployment and the Labor Market." In *Understanding Unemployment*, edited by Eithne McLaughlin. London: Full Employment UK, 1992.

Mieczkowski, B. "The relationship between changes in consumption and politics in Poland." *Soviet Studies* 30, no. 2 (1978): 262-69.

Milanovic, Branco. "Cash Social Transfers, Direct Taxes, and Income Distribution in Late Socialism." *Journal of Comparative Economics* 18, 175-97 (1994): 175-97.

Milanovic, Branko. "Income Distribution in Late Socialism: Poland, Hungary, Czeckoslavakia, Yugoslavia and Bulgaria Compared, Second Draft." Socialist Economies Unit, The World Bank, 1992.

Miller, William L., Stephen White, and Paul M. Heywood. *Values and Political Change in PostCommunist Europe*. New York: St. Martin's Press, 1998.

Mishler, William, and Richard Rose. "Trajectoies of Fear and Hope: Support for Democracy in Post-Communist Europe." *Comparative Political Studies* 28, no. 4 (1996): 553-81.

Modigliani, Franco, Jean-Paul Fioussi, Beeniamino Moro, Dennis Snower, Robert Solow, Alfred Steinherr, and Paolo Sylos Labini. "An Econmists Manifesto on Unemployment in the European Union." *BNL Quarterly Review*, no. 206 (1998).

Molnar, L., F. Nemes, and S. Belane. *Ipari munkasok politai aktivitasa [Political activities of industrial workers]*. Budapest: Kossuth Kiado, 1970.

Moon, Donald. "The Moral Basis of the Democratic Welfare State." In *Democracy and the Welfare State*, edited by Amy Gutman, 27-53. Princeton, NJ: Princeton University Press, 1988.

Moore, Barrington. *Soviet Politics—The Dilemma of Power: The Role of Ideas in Social Change*. Cambridge, MA: Harvard University Press, 1951.

Moore, Wilbert E. "The exportability of the "Labor Force" Concept." *American Sociological Review* 68 (1958).

Móro, Mária. "Az Állami Vállalatok (Ál)privatizációja (State Enterprise (Pseudo) Privatization)." *Közgazdasági Szemle*, 38, 6 (1991): 565-84.

Morris, Micheal. "Are Poverty and Unemployment Social Problems? The Dynamics of Public Definitions." *Sociology and Social Research* 69, no. 3 (1985): 396-411.

Moyniham, Daniel. *The Politics of a Guaranteed Income*. NY: Vintage, 1973.

MSZMP. *Az MSZMP IX. kongresszusának jegyzőkönyve. 1966 nov. 28-dec 3-ig (9th Congress of the Hungarian Socialist Workers Party)*. Budapest: Kossuth Könyvkiadó, 1967.

MSZMP. *Az MSZMP VIII. kongresszusának jegyzőkönyve. 1962 nov. 20-24-ig (8th Congress of the Hungarian Socialist Workers Party)*. Budapest: Kossuth Könyvkiadó, 1963.

Munkaügyi Ministérium, Foglalkoztatási Főosztály [Labor Ministry, employment division]. "Hódmezővásárhely foglalkoztatási helyzetének vizsgálatáról és az azóta eltelt időszakban történtekről [Examination and of history of this past period of the market place of hódmező]." Budapest, Munkaügyi Ministérium. December (1990a).

Munkaügyi Ministérium [Labor Ministry], "Az újrakezdési kölcsön jogszerütlen kammattámogatása visszavonásának felhasználásáról [On the abolishment of unlawful use of interest on the start-up loans]." Budapest, Interest Reconciliation Council (ÉT) Labor Market Board, government draft memorandum. Mar. 26, 1991.

Nagy, Gyula. "A kettészakadt társadalom [A Society torn in half]." *Jelkép* 10, no. 4 (1989).

Natl Com. (National Commission on Employment and Unemployment Statistics). "Unemployment Statistics in the United States and The Republic of Germany: Problems of International Comparison,." Background paper, no. 30. Washington, D.C.: Carol Jusenius and Bukhard von Rabenau, 1979.

Népszabadság. "Pontos-e a Munkanélküliség-Mérce (Is the Unemployment measure Accurate?)." August 11, 1993: 14.

Népszabadság. "munkanélküliség és kisvállalkozás [Unemployment and small business]." Sep. 22 1988, 3.

Népszabadság. "A Munkaerő- és Bérhelyzetről [About Manpower and Wages]." Sept. 8 1984, 5.

Népszabadság. "A teljes foglalkoztatásról [About full employment]." Jan. 22 1983, 5.

Nesporová, Alena. "Measuring Employment in Central and Eastern Europe." In *Employment and Unemployment in Economies in Transition: Conceptual and Measurement Issues*, edited by OECD, 33-46. Paris: OECD, Centre for Co-operation with the European Economies in Transition, 1993.

Neumark David and Deborah Reed, 2002 "Employment Relationships in the New Economy" NBER working paper 8910, April.

Neumann, László. "Circumventing Trade Unions in Hungary: Old and New Channels of Wage Bargaining." *European Journal of Industrial Relations, 3*, 2 (1997): 183-202.

Neumann, László. "Labor Conflicts of Privatization." *Acta Oeconomica* 43, no. 1-2 (1990): 213-230.

Nielsen, Klaus. "Flexible Adjustment and Political Stability: The Terms of the Debate." *Scandinavian Political Studies* 12, no. 4 (1986).

Nietzsche, Friedrich 1998 [1887] *On the Geneology of Morality.* Indianapolis, Hackett.

Nordhaus, William D. "The Political Business Cycle." *Review of Economic Studies* 42 (1975): 133-67.

Noti, Stephan. "The Shifting Position of Hungarian Trade Unions Amidst Social and Economic Reforms." *Soviet Studies* 39, no. 1 (1987): 63-87.

Nove, Alec. *The Economics of Feasible Socialism.* London: Feorge Allen and Unwin, 1982.

Nyers, Reszó. "National Economic Objectives and the Reform Process in Hungary in the Eighties." *Acta Oeconomica 35* 1-2, no. 1-16 (1982).

Nyers, Reszó. "Our Road, Our Objectives and Principles—As Reflected in the Events of 25 Years." *Acta Oeconomica 5*, no. 1-2 (1970): 3-18.

OECD. *1998 Employment Outlook.* Paris: OECD, 1998.

OECD. *OECD Economic Surveys: Hungary.* Paris: OECD, 1997.

OECD. *The OECD Jobs Study: Evidence and Explanations.* Paris: OECD, 1995.

Offe, Claus. "Capitalism by Democratic Design? Democratic Theory Facing the Triple Transition in East-Central Europe." Sociological Working Papers, no. 18. 1992.

Offe, Claus, and Rolf G. Heinze. *Beyond Employment: Time, Work and the Informal Economy.* Cambridge, UK: Polity Press, 1992.

Ollman, Bertell. "Market Mystification in Capitalist and Market Socialist Societies." *Socialism and Democracy* 11, no. 2 (1997): 35-45.

Olson, Mancur. *The Logic of Collective Action.* Cambridge: Harvard University Press, 1965.

Örkeny, Antal and Csepeli, György. "Perceptions of Social Inequality in Hungarian Society." *Comparative Social Research* 14 (1994): 173-92.

Országos Munkaerőpiaci Központ. "Állásnélküliek Jogai, Lehetőségei 1990-ben [The Laws and Opportunities for those without Jobs in 1990]." Budapest: OMK, 1990.

Országos Orvossakértői Intézet. *Statistikai Beszámoló* [Statistical Report]. Budapest: Országos Egészségbiztosítási Pénztár [National Health Administration], jelentés (Draft Statistical Report), 1995.

Oxenfeldt, A. and E. van den Haag. "Unemployment in Planned and Capitalist Economies."*Quarterly Journal of Economics* 68 (1954): 43-60.

Pacek, Alexandaer C. "Macroeconoic Conditions and Electoral Politics in Eastern Europe." *American Journal of Political Science* 38, no. 3 (1994): 723-44.

Pahl, Raymond E. "Does Jobless Mean Workless? Unemployment and Informal Work." *Annals, AAPSS, 493,* (Sept. 1987): 36-46.

Pakulski, Jan. "Legitimacy and Mass Compliance: Reflections on Max Weber and Soviet-Type Societies." *British Journal of Political Science* 16, no. 1 (1991): 35-65.

Parijs, Van, ed. *Arguing for Basic Income.*

Pescovitz, David. "The Company Where Everybody's a Temp." *New York Times Magazine,* June 11 2000, 94-96.

Pierson, Paul. "Increasing Returns, Path Dependence, and the Study of Politics." *American Political Science Review* 94, no. 2 (2000): 251-267.

Pierson, Paul. "The New Politics of the Welfare State." *World Politics* 48, no. 1 (1996): 143-79.

Pierson, Paul. *Dismantling the Welfare State? Reagan, Thatcher and the Politics of Retrenchment.* Cambridge: Cambridge University Press, 1994.

Piirainen, Timo. *Towards a new Social Order in Russia: Transforming Structures and Everyday Life.* Aldershot: Dartmouth, 1997.

Piore, Micheal J. "Historical Perspectives and the Interpretation of Unemployment." *Journal of Economic Literature* 25, no. 4 (1987): 1834-1850.

Piven, Francis Fox, and Richard Cloward. *Regulating the Poor: The Function of Public Welfare.* NY: Vintage Books, 1993.

Pixley, Jocelyn. *Citizenship and Employment: Investigating Post-Industrial Options.* Cambridge: Cambridge University Press, 1993.

Pohl, Rüdiger. "The Macroeconomics of Transformation: The Case of East Germany." presented at the conference, The German Road from Socialism to Capitalism: Eastern Germany ten years after the collapse of the GDR: Center for European Studies, Harvard University, June 18-20, 1999.

Pokol, Béla. "Changes in the System of Political Representation in Hungary." In *Economy and Society in Hungary,* edited by Rudolf Andorka and László Bertalan, 267-86. Budapest: Karl Marx University Department of Sociology, 1986.

Polanyi, Karl. *The Great Transformation.* Boston: Beacon Press, 1946.

Pollin, Robert. "Can Marx, Kalecki, Friedman, and Wall Street All Be Wrong?" *Review of Radical Political Economics,* Fall (1998).

Poovey, Mary. *A History of the Modern Fact: Problems of Knowledge in the Sciences of Wealth and Society.* Chicago: University of Chicago, 1998.

Porket, J.L. *Unemployment in Capitalist, Communist and Post-Communist Economies.* New York: St. Martin's Press, 1995.

Posusney, Marsha Pripstein. "Irrational workers. The moral economy of labor protests in Egypt." *World Politics,* 46, no. 1 (1993): 83-120.

Pravda, Alex. "Political Attitudes and Activity." In *Blue-Collar Workers in Eastern Europe,* edited by Jan F. Triska and Charles Gati, 43-69. London: George Allen & Unwin, 1981.

Pressman, Jeffrey, and Aron Wildavsky. *Implementation.* 3rd. ed. Berkeley: University of California Press, 1984.

Primorac, Emil, and Mate Babic. "Systemic changes and unemployment in Yugoslavia, 1965-84." *Slavic Review* 48, no. 2 (1989): 195-213.

Pryor, Frederic L. *A Guidebook to the Comparative Study of Economic Systems.* Englewood Cliffs, NJ: Prentice-Hall, 1985.

Przeworski, Adam. "Less is More: The Future of Unemployment Lies in Leisure.*Dollars & Sense* Jul/Aug (1995): 12-15+.

Przeworski, Adam. "Economic Reforms, Public Opinion, and Political Institution: Poland in the Eastern European Perspective." In *Economic Reforms in New Democracies: A Social-Democratic Approach,* edited by José María Maravall, Luiz Carlos Pereira and Adam Przeworski. Cambridge: Cambridge UP, 1993.

Przeworski, Adam. *Democracy and the Market.* Cambridge, UK: Cambridge University Press, 1991.

Przeworski, Adam. *Capitalism and Social Democracy.* Cambridge: Cambridge University Press, 1985.

Radnay, József. "Négy évtized a magyar munkajogban" (Four decades in Hungarian labor law)." *Munkaügyi Szemle* 29, April (1985): 16-23.

Rattinger, Hans. "Unemployment and Elections in West Germany." In *Economics and Politics: The Calculus of Support,* edited by Helmut Norpoth, Michael S. Lewis-Beck and Jean-Dominique Lafay, 49-62. Ann Arbor: University of Michigan Press, 1991.

Reich, Robert. *The Future of Success* (NY: Alfred A. Knopf, 2000).

Remmer, Karen L. "The Political Impact of Economic Crisis in Latin America in the 1980s." *American Political Science Review* 85, no. 3 (1991): 777-800.

Rettore, E., N. Torelli, and U. Trivellato. "Unemployment and Search for Work: Exploratory Analysis of Labour Market Attchment Using CPS-Type Data." *Labour* 4, no. 3 (1990): 161-90.

Révész, Gábor. *Perestroika in Eastern Europe: Hungary's Economic Transformation, 1945-1988.* Boulder: Westview, 1990.

Révész, Gábor. "Enterprise and Plant Size Structure of the Hungarian Industry." *Acta Oeconomica* 22, no. 1-2 (1979).

Révész, Sándor. *Aczél és Korunk (Aczél and Our Age)*. Budapest: Sík Kiadó, 1997.

Radio Free Europe. "Hungary 1957-1961: Background and Current Situation." Munich, Germany: Radio Free Europe Evaluation and Analysis Department, Special Report, unpublished "E" distribution—700. May 16, 1961.

Rice, M. "Public Administration in Post-Socialist Eastern Europe." *Public Administration Review* 52, no. 2 (1992): 116-25.

Rifkin, Jeremy, and Robert Heilbronner. *The End of Work: The Decline of the Global Labor Force and the Dawn of the Post-Market Era*. New York: Putnam, 1996.

Rigby, T.H. "A Conceptual Approach to Authority, Power and Policy in the Soviet Union." In *Authority, Power and Policy in the USSR*, edited by Archie Brown and Peter Reddaway T.H. Rigby. London: Macmillan, 1980.

Rigby, T.H., and Ferenc Feher. *Political Legitimation in Commusist States*. London: Macmillan, 1982.

Rimlinger, Gaston. *Welfare Policy and Industrialization in Europe, America and Russia*. NY: Wiley, 1971.

Robertson, John D. "Toward a Political-Economic Accounting of the Endurance of Cabinet Administrations: An Empirical Assessment of Eight European Democracies." *American Journal of Political Science* 28, no. 4 (1984): 693-709.

Rogers, Gerry, and Janine Rogers, eds. *Precarious Jobs in Labour Market Regulation: The Growth of Atypical Employment in Western Europe*. Brussels/Geneva: ILO/International Institute for Labour Studies, 1989.

Róna-Tas, Ákos. *The Great Surprise of the Small Transformation: The Demise of Communism and the Rise of the Private Sector in Hungary*. Ann Arbor: University of Michigan Press, 1997.

Róna-Tas, Ákos. "The first shall be last? Entrepreneurship and communist cadres in the transition from socialism." *American Journal of Sociology*, no. 100 (1994): 40-69.

Rose, Richard. "What is the Demand for Price Stability in Post-Communist Countries?" *Studies in Public Policy*, 282. Glasgow, Scotland: Center for the Study of Public Policy, University of Strathclyde, 1997.

Rose, Richard. "Comparing Workers in Russian Enterprises." *Studies in Public Policy*, 258. Glasgow, Scotland: Center for the Study of Public Policy, University of Strathclyde, 1996.

Rose, Richard, and Christian Haerpfer. "Adapting to Transformation in Eastern Europe." *Studies in Public Policy*, 212. University of Strathclide: University of Strathclyde, Glasgow, 1993.

Rose, Richard and Makkai, Toni. "Consensus or Dissensus in Welfare Values in Post-Communist Societies?" *Studies in Public Policy*, 219. Glasgow: University of Strathclyde Center for the Study of Public Policy, 1993.

Rosser, J. Barkley, Jr., Marian V. Rosser, and Ehsan Ahmed. "Income Inequality and the Informal Economy in Transition Economies." *Journal of Comparative Politics* 28, no. 1 (2000): 156-71.

Rothschild, Joseph. *Return to Diversity: The Political History of East Central Europe Since World War II*. Oxford: Oxford UP, 1989.

Rothschild, Joseph. "Political Legitimacy in Contempporary Europe." In *Legitimation of Regimes*, edited by B. Denitch. Beverly Hills: Sage, 1979.

Rothstein, Bo. *Just Institutions Matter*. Edited by Robert E. Goodin, *Theories of Institutional Design*. Cambridge: Cambridge, UK, 1998.

Rothstein, Bo. "Administration and Legitimacy: A Comparative Perspective." Annual meeting of the American Political Science Association: Boston, Sept. 1996.

Rothstein, Bo. "Labor Market Institutions and Working Class Strength." In *Structuring Politics: Historical Institutionalism in Comparative Analysis*, edited by Kathleen Thelen and Frank Longstreth Sven Steinmo, 33-56. Cambridge: Cambridge University Press, 1992.

Roxburgh, Ian, and Judith Shapiro. "Russian Unemployment and the Excess Wages Tax." *Communist Economics & Economic Transformation* 8, no. 1 (1996): 5-27.

Rózsa, József. "A Teljes és Hatékony Foglalkoztatás feltételrendzere [The system of providing full and efficient employment]." Budapest: Állami Bér- és Munkaügyi Hivatal (ABMH), Területi Főostály [State Wage and Labor force Office, regional department], 4427/1982. IV/30. Jan. 31, 1983.

Rutkowski, Michal. "Labour hoarding and future open unemployment in Eastern Europe: the case of Polish industry," 1990.

Sabel, Charles F., *Learning by Monitoring*. Cambridge, MA: Harvard University Press, 2000.

Sabel, Charles F., "Bootstrapping Reform: Rebuilding Firms, the Welfare State and Unions." *Politics and Society*, Winter, (1994): 5-48

Sabel, Charles F., and Jonathan Zeitlin, eds. *Worlds of Possibility: Flexibility and Mass Production in Western Industrialization*. Cambridge: Cambridge University Press, 1997.

Sabel, Charles, and Michael Piore. *The Second Industrial Divide*. NY: Basic Books, 1984.

Sabel, Charles F, and David Stark. "Planning, Politics, and Shop-Floor Power: Hidden Forms of Bargaining in Soviet-Imposed State-Socialist Societies." *Politics & Society* 4 (1982): 439-75.

Saint-Paul, Gilles. *Dual Labor Markets: A Macroeconomic Perspective*. Cambridge: MIT Press, 1996.

Saint-Paul, Gilles. "Exploring the political economy of labour market institutions." *Economic Policy* 23, no. Oct. (1996): 263-306.

Salais, Robert. "Why was Unemployment so Low in France During the 1930s?" In *Interwar Unemployment in International Perspective*, edited by B. Eichengreen and T.J. Hatton, 247-88. Boston: Kluwer, 1988.

Salais, Robert, N. Baverez, and B. Reynaud. *L'invention du chomage: historie et transformations d'une catégorie en France des années 1890 aux annés 1980*. Paris: Presses Universitaires de France, 1986.

Salant, Walter S. "The Spread of Keynesian Doctrines and Practices in the United States." In *The Political Power of Economic Ideas: Keynesianism Across Nations*, edited by Peter Hall, 27-51. Princeton: Princeton University Press, 1989.

Schlozman, Kay and Sidney Verba. *Injury to Insult: Unemployment, Class, and Political Response*. Cambridge: Harvard UP, 1979.

Schmidt, Á. "Some Problems Concerning the Calculation of Socialist National Income." *Acta Oeconomica* 1, no. 3 (1968): 221-28.

Schmidt, Manfred G. "The Politics of Unemployment: Rates of Unemployment and Labour market Policy." *West European Politics* 7, no. 3 (1984): 5-24.

Schmitter, Phillipe. "Interest Intermediation and Regime Governability in Contemporary Western Europe and North America." In *Organizing Interests in Western Europe*, edited by Suzanne Berger. Cambridge: Cambridge University Press, 1981.

Schneider, Friedrich, and Bruno S. Frey. "Politco-economic Models of Macroeconomic Policy: A Review of the Empriical Evidence." In *Political Business Cycles*, edited by Thomas D. Willett, 239-75. Durham: Duke University Press, 1988.

Schwartz, Solomon M. *Labour in the Soviet Union*. London: Cresset Press, 1951.

Schweber, Libby. "Progressive Reformers, Unemployment, and the Transformation of Social Inquiry in Britain and the United States, 1880s-1920s." In *States, Social Knowledge, and the Origins of Modern Social Policies*, edited by Dietrich Rueschmeyer and Theda Skocpol. Princeton, NJ: Princeton University Press, 1996.

Schweitzer, Iván. "Will the Industrial Pyramid Be Set Afoot?" *Acta Oeconomica* 39, no. 1-2 (1988): 111-122.

Schweitzer, Iván. "Some Interrelations Between Enterprise Organization and the Economic Mechanism." *Acta Oeconomica* 27, no. 3-4 (1981): 289-300.

Scott, James C. *Seeing Like a State: How Certain Schemes to Improve the Human Condition Have Failed*. New Haven: Yale University Press, 1998.

Scott, James C. *The Moral Economy of the Peasant*. New Haven: Yale University Press, 1976.

Searl, John R. *The Construction of Social Reality*. New York: Free Press, 1995.

Seleny, Anna. "Constructing the Discourse of Transformation: Hungary 1979-82." *East European Politics and Society* 8, no. 3 (1994): 439-66.

Seleny, Anna. "Hidden Enterprise, Property Rights Reform and Political Transformation in Hungary." Program on Central and Eastern Europe Working Paper Series, no. 11. Cambridge: Harvard University, 1991.

Semjén, András and István János Tóth, "Unofficial Economic Activities and Fiscal Discipline in Hungary as Mirrored in Consecutive Enterprise Surveys on Tax Behaviour," Institute of Economics, Hungarian Academy of Sciences, KTK/IE Discussion Papers 2002/11 (Budapest, November 2002).

Shapiro, Carl, and Joseph E. Stiglitz. "Equilibrium Unemployment as a Worker Discipline Device." *American Econoomic Review* 74, no. 3 (1984): 433-44.

Sik, Endre. "The Social Consequences of Unemployment in Hungary—A household Perspective." *Innovation* 9, no. 3 (1996): 355-69.

Sík, Endre. "Egy ló-öszvér a lovakról és a szmarakról; Adalék a második gazdaság hazai eszmetörténetéhez [About a horse-mule and horses: A contribution to the theoretical history of the second economy]." *Közgzdasági Szemle* 48, no. 7-8 (1996): 704-725.

Sikkink, Kathryn. *Ideas and Institutions: Developmentalism in Brazil and Argentina*. Ithaca: Cornell University Press, 1991.

Simon, Herbert. *Administrative Behavior*. New York: Macmillian Company, 1947.

Simon, János. "The Culture of Unemployment in Hungary." Working Papers of Political Science, no. 17. Budapest: Institute for Political Science of the Hungarian Academy of Sciences, 1997.

Simon, János. "Politika alulnézetből: avagy hogan politizálnak a munkanélküliek? [The view from below: or how the unemployed see politics]." In *Magyarország politikai évkönyve [Hungarian political yearbook]*, edited by Sándor Péter Sándor Kurtán, Vass László, 653-64. Budapest: Demokrácia Kutatások Magyar Központja, 1994.

Skocpol, Theda. *Social Policy in the United States: Future Possibilities and Historical Perspective*. Princeton: Princeton University Press, 1995.

Smith, Kenwyn K. *Paradoxes of group life: understanding conflict, paralysis, and movement in group dynamics, Jossey-Bass social and behavioral science series*. San Francisco: Jossey-Bass, 1987.

Smith, Steven Rathgeb and Michael Lipsky. *Non-Profits for Hire: The Welfare State in the Age of Contracting*. Cambridge, MA: Harvard University Press, 1993.

Snyder, David, and Charles Tilly. "Hardship and Collective Violence in France: 1830-1960." *American Sociological Review* 37 (1972): 520-32.

Sochor, Zenovia A. "Soviet Taylorism Revisited." *Soviet Studies* 33, no. 2 (1981): 246-64.

Soós, Attila Károly. *Terv, Kampány, Pénz (Plan, campaign, money)*. Budapest: Jogi és Közgazdasági Kiadó, 1986.

Soós, Károly. "Wage Bargaining and the 'Policy of Grievances': A contribution to the Explanation of the First Halt in the Reform of the Hungarian New Economic Mechanism in 1969." *Soviet Studies* 39, no. 3 (1987).

Soskice, David. "Strike Waves and Wage Explosions, 1968-1970." In *The Resurgence of Class Conflict in Western Europe*, edited by Colin Crouch and Alessandro Pizzorno, 221-46. London: Macmillan, 1978.

Standing, Guy. "Labour Market Governance in Eastern Europe." *European Journal of Industrial Relations* 3, no. 2 (1997): 133-59.

Standing, Guy. "Toward Economic Democracy and Labour Flexibility? An Era of Experimentation." In *In Search of Flexibility: The New Soviet Labour Market*, edited by Guy Standing, 363-400. Geneva: ILO, 1991.

Standing, Guy. "Meshing Labour Flexibility with Security: An Answer to British Unemployment?" *International Labour Review* 125, no. 1 (1986): 87-106.

Standing, Guy and Guy Vaughan-Whitehead, Guy, eds. *Minimum Wages in Central and Eastern Europe: from protection to destitution*. NY, Budapest, London: Central European University Press, 1995.

Stark, David. "Recombinant Property in East European Capitalism" (mimeo). Dept. of Sociology, Cornell University, Ithaca, NY, 1995.

Stark, David. "Recombinant Property in East European Capitalism." *American Journal of Sociology*, 101, 4 (1996): 993-1027.

Stark, David. "Privatization Strategies in East Central Europe." Working Papers On Transitions From State Socialism, Cornell Project on Comparative Societal Analysis, Ithaca, NY, no. 91-6 (1991).

Stark, David. "Privatization in Hungary: From Plan to Market or Plan to Clan." *East European Politics and Society*, 4, 3 (1990).

Starr, Paul. "The Sociology of Official Statistics." In *The Politics of Numbers*, edited by William Alonso and Paul Starr, 7-57. New York: Russell Sage Foundation, 1987.

Stein, Herbert. *Fiscal Revolution in America*. Chicago: University of Chicago Press, 1969.

Steinmetz, George. *Regulating the Social: the welfare state and local politics in imperial Germany*. Edited by Nicholas B. Dirks Sherry B. Ortner, Geoff Eley, *Princeton Studies in Culture/Power/History*. Princeton, New Jersey: Princeton University Press, 1993.

Stewart, Michael. "Gypsies, Work and Civil Society." In *Market Economy and Civil Society in Hungary*, edited by C.M. Hann, 140-62. London: Frank Cass, 1990.

Stinchcombe, Arthur. *Information and Organizations*. Berkeley, CA: University of California Press, 1990.

Stokes, Susan C., ed. 2001. *Public Support for Market Reforms in New Democracies*. Cambridge: Cambridge University Press.

Stone, Deborah. "Why We Need a Care Movement." *The Nation*, March 13, 2000, 13-15.

Stone, Deborah A. *The Disabled State*: Temple University Press, 1985.

Summers, Lawrence H. *Understanding Unemployment*. Cambridge, MA: MIT Press, 1990.

Swianiewicz, S. *Forced Labour and Economic Development: An Enquiry into the Experience of Soviet Industrialization*. London: Oxford University Press, 1965.

Szabó, Gábor. "Administrative Transition in a Post-Communist Society: The Case of Hungary." *Public Administration* 71, no. 1/2 (1993): 89-103.

Szabó-Medgyesi, Éva. "Non-Agricultural Activities of Agricultural Enterprises in Hungary." *Acta Oeconomica* 34, no. 3-4 (1985): 361-81.

Szakszervezeti Tanács, (Information Bulletin of the Hungarian Trade Unions). "Budapest, Hungarian Trade Union Council, International Section." 1948-51.

Szalai, Erzébet. "Rendszerváltás és a hatalom konvertálasa (Regime change and the conversion of power)." *Szociológiai Szemle*, no. 2 (1997): 77-99.

Szalai, Erzébet. "The New Stage of the Reform Process in Hungary and the Large Enterprises." *Acta Oeconomica* 29, no. 1-2 (1982): 25-46.

Szalai, Erzébet. *Kiemelt vállalat—beruházási érdek (Preferred company—investment interests).* Budapest: Adadémiai Kiadó, 1981.

Szalai, Julia. "Why the Poor are Poor." *New Hungarian Quarterly* XXXVII, no. 144 (1996): 70-78.

Szamuely, László. "Establishment and Erosion of the Soviet Model of CPE as Reflected in Economic Science in Hungary 1945-1980." Discussion Papers 1/96. Frankfurt: Institute for Transformation Studies, 1996.

Szatmári, Miklós. "A reform propagaájának helyzete és feladatai [The position and tasks of propaganda for the reform]." *Társadalmi Szemle* 10 (1967).

Szelenyi, Ivan. "Social Inequalitites under State Socialist Redistributive Economies." *International Journal of Comparative Sociology* 61 (1978): 87-.

Szirácki, György. "Employment Policy and Labour market in Transition: From Labour Shortage to Unemployment." *Soviet Studies* 42, no. 4 (1990): 701-722.

Szirácki, György. "Redundancy and Regional Unemployment: A Case Study in Ozd." In *Market economy and civil society in Hungary*, edited by C.M. Hann, 125-139. London: Frank Cass, 1990.

SZOT. "A Munkaerőhelyzet változása és a foglalkoztatáspolitika [Workplace transformation and employment policy]." working paper (mimeo). Budapest: Közgazdasági és Életszinvonalpolitikai Osztály [Economic and Living Standard Policy Group], Sept. 1, 1988.

SZOT Társadalombiztositási Főigazgatóság, [SZOT Social Security Administration]. "Foglalkoztatott nyudijasok és ösztönző nyugdijpótlékban részesültek adatai [Data on employed pensioners and the incentrives of pension allowances." Budapest, 1981.

Szőke, Gy. "A Chapter of Recent Economic History—Mergers of Agricutlural Cooperatives Over Two Decades." *Acta Oeconomica* 39, no. 3-4 (1988): 357-67.

Tant, A.P. "The Politics of Official Statisitics." *Government and Opposition* 30, no. 2 (1995): 254-66.

Tarrow, Sidney. *Power in Movement: Social Movements, Collective Action, and Politics.* Cambridge: Cambridge University Press, 1994.

Teitelbaum, Michael S., and Jay Winter. *A Question of Numbers: High Miration, Low Fertility and the Politics of National Identity.* New York: Hill & Wang, 1998.

Thompson, E.P. "The Moral Economy of the English Crowd in the Eighteenth Century." *Past and Present* 42, no. 1 (1971): 56-97.

Thompson, E.P. "Time, Work Discipline and Industrial Capitalism." *Past and Present* 38 (1967): 56-97.

Tilly, Charles. *From Mobilization to Revolution.* Wellesley: Adison, 1978.

Timár, János. "Particular Features of Employment and Unemployment in the Present Stage of Transformation of the Post-Socialist Countries." draft submitted for OECD country report. Budapest, June 1998.

Timár, János. "Idő és munkaidő (A munkaidő és a társadalmi újratermelés időalapjának néhány problémája Magyarországon) [Time and Work Time (Work time and some problems with the social reproduction of social reproduction of established time]." *Közgazdasági Szemle* 32, no. 11 (1985): 1299-1313.

Timár, János. "Strategies and Realities for Employees and Management." In *Labour Market and Second Economy in Hungary*, edited by Péter Galasi and György Sziráczki, 247-63. NY, Frankfurt: Campus Verlag, 1985.

Timár, János. "The Level of Employment and its Equilibrium in Socialism." *Acta Oeconomica* 4, no. 2 (1969): 169-179.

Timár, János. *Planning the Labor Force in Hungary.* White Plains, NY: International Arts and Sciences, 1966.

Timár, Mátyás. *Reflections on the economic development of Hungary 1967-1973.* Budapest: Adadémiai Kiadó, 1975.

Tocqueville, Alexis De. *The Old Regime and the French Revolution.* New York: Anchor Books, 1983 (1856).

Toonen, Theo. "Analyzing Institutional Change and Administrative Transformation: A Comparative View." *Public Administration* 71, no. 1-2 (1993): 151-168.

Topalov, Christian. "Inventing the language of unemployment, 1880-1910: A case study in the sociology of the construction of categories" (mimeo). Ecole des Hautes Etudes en Sciences Sociales, Paris, 1998.

Treml, Vladimir G. "Interaction of Economic Thought and Economic Policy in the Soviet Union." *History of Political Economy* 1, no. 1 (1969): 187-216.

Tsebelis, George, and Roland Stephen. "Monitoring Unemployment Benefits in Comparative Perspective." *Political Research Quarterly* 47, no. 4 (1994): 793-820.

Tucker, Joshua A. "Its the Economy, Comrade! Economic Conditions and Election Results in the Czech Republic, Hungary, Poland, Russia, And Slovakia, 1990-1996." Doctoral dissertation, Harvard University, 2000.

Tufte, Edward R. *Political Control of the Economy.* Princeton: Princeton University Press, 1978.

Turner, Lowell. *Fighting for Partnership: Labor and Politics in United Germany.* Ithaca: Cornell University Press, 1998.

U.S. Bureau of the Census. "The Labor Force of Hungary." edited by Samuel Baum. International Population Statistics Reports, Series P-90, No. 18. Washington D.C.: U.S. Government Printing Office, 1962.

U.S. National Commission. "Counting the Labor Force: Readings in Labor Force Statistics." Washington, D.C.: United States Commission on Employment and Unemployment Statistics, Dec. 1979.

Új Magyar Lexicon. "munkanélküliség." Budapest: Akademeai Kiado, 1962: 64.

Valkó, György, and György Sáfrán. "A szigorított javitó-nevelő munka végrehajtásának tapasztalatairól [The experiences of applying enforced educative labor]." *Ugyészégi Értesitő,* no. 1 (1988).

Van Apeldoorn, Bastiaan. "Transnationalization and the Restructuring of Europe's Socioeconomic Order." *International Journal of Political Economy* 28, no. 1 (1998): 12-53.

Verbélyi, Imre. "Options for Administrative Reform in Hungary." *Public Administration* 71, no. 1/2 (1993): 105-20.

Visser, Wessel, and Reien Wijnhoven. 1990. Politics do matter, but does unemployment? Party Strategies, ideological discourse and enduring mass employment. *European Journal of Political Research* 18 (1):71-96.

Visser, Jelle, and Anton Hemerijck. *'A Dutch Miracle': Job Growth, Welfare Reform and Corporatism in the Netherlands.* Amsterdam: Amsterdam University Press, 1997.

Völgyes, Iván. "Hungary: the lumpenproletarianization of the Working Class." In *Blue-Collar Workers in Eastern Europe,* edited by Jan F. Triska and Charles Gati, 224-35. London: George Allen & Unwin, 1981.

Voska, Éva. "Rope Walking: Ganz Danubius Ship and Crane Factory Transformed into a Company." *Acta Oeconomica* 43, no. 1-2 (1990): 285-302.

Voska, Éva. "Company Liquidation Without a Legal Successor." *Acta Oeconomica* 37, no. 1-2 (1986): 59-71.

Walker, Charles R. and Robert H. Guest. *The Man in the Assembly Line*. Cambridge: Harvard University Press, 1952.

Walters, William. "The Demise of Unemployment." *Politics & Society* 24, no. 3 (1996): 197-219.

Walters, William. "Discovering 'Unemployment': New Forms for the Government of Poverty." *Economy and Society* 23, no. 3 (1994): 265-90.

Warwick, Paul. "Economic Trends and Government Survival in West European Parliamentary Democracies." *American Political Science Review* 86, no. 4 (1992): 875-87.

Weatherford, Stephen M. "Economic 'Stagflation' and Public Support for the Political System." *British Journal of Political Science* 14, no. (April) (1984): 187-205.

Weaver, Kent. "The Politics of Blame Avoidance." *Journal of Public Policy* 6, no. Oct-Dec (1986): 371-98.

Webb, John N. "Concepts used in Unemployment Surveys." *Journal of the American Statistical Association* 34, no. March (1939): 49-56.

Webb, Sidney. "The Problem of Unemployment in the United Kingdom; with a Remedy by Organization and Training." *Annals of the American Academy* 33, no. March (1909): 420-39.

Weber, Max. "'Social Psychology of World Religions'." In *From Max Weber*, edited by H.H. Gerth and C. Wright Mills. New York: Oxford University Press, 1946.

Weir, Margaret. *Politics and Jobs*. Princeton: Princeton University Press, 1992.

Weir, Margaret. "Ideas and Politics: The Acceptance of Keynesianism in Britain and the United States." In *The Political Power of Economic Ideas: Keynesianism Across Nations*, edited by Peter Hall, 53-86. Princeton: Princeton University Press, 1989.

Westerm, Bruce, and Katherine Beckett. "How Unregulated Is the U.S. Labor market? The Penal System as a Labor Market Institution." *American Journal of Sociology* 104, no. 4 (1999): 1030-60.

White, Ann. *Destalinization and the House of Culture*. NY: Routledge, 1990.

White, Stephen. "Economic Performance and Communist Legitimacy." *World Politics* 38, April (1986): 462-82.

Whiteside, Noel, and James A. Gillespie. "Deconstructing Unemployment: Developments in Britain in the Interwar Years." *Economic History Review* 44, no. 4 (1991): 665-82.

Wiles, Perer. "A Note on Soviet Unemployment in U.S. Definitions." *Soviet Studies* 23, April (1972): 619-28.

Winiecki, Jan. "Large Industrial Enterprises in Soviet-type Economies: The Ruling Stratum's Main Rent-seeking Area." *Communist Economies* 1, no. 4 (1991): 363-83.

Wlezien, Christopher, Mark Franklin, and Daniel Twiggs. "Economic Perceptions and Vote Choice: Disentangling the Endogeneity." *Political Behavior* 19, no. 1 (1997): 7-17.

Woodward, Susan L. *Socialist Unemployment: The Political Economiy of Yugoslavia, 1945-1990*. Princeton, NJ: Princeton University Press, 1995.

Yee, Albert S. "The Causal Effects of ideas on Policies." *International Organization* 50, no. 1 (1996): 69-108.

Zaslavsky, Victor. *The Neo-Stalinist State*. NY: M.E. Sharpe, 1982.

Zimmermann, Susan. "A Szabad Munkaerő Nyomában: 'Utolérő' Fejlődés és női munka Magyarországon [On the Track of a Free Labor Market: "Catch-up" Growth and Womens' Work in Hungary]." *Eszmélet* 25, no. Spring (1995): 166-83.

Zsolnay, Piroska. "Ózd Város 1995-1998. közötti időszakra vonatkozó szpciálpoliticai cselekvési programjára." Government draft proposal, Ózd, Hungary, 1995.

Zuboff, Shoshana 1988. *In the Age of the Smart Machine: The Future of Work and Power* (NY Basic Books).

Index